Diane di Prima

Diane di Prima

Visionary Poetics and the Hidden Religions

David Stephen Calonne

BLOOMSBURY ACADEMIC
NEW YORK · LONDON · OXFORD · NEW DELHI · SYDNEY

BLOOMSBURY ACADEMIC
Bloomsbury Publishing Inc
1385 Broadway, New York, NY 10018, USA
50 Bedford Square, London, WC1B 3DP, UK

BLOOMSBURY, BLOOMSBURY ACADEMIC and the Diana
logo are trademarks of Bloomsbury Publishing Plc

First published in the United States of America 2019
Paperback edition published 2020

Cover design by Eleanor Rose
Cover photograph © Damon Agapiou

Library of Congress Cataloging-in-Publication Data
Names: Calonne, David Stephen, 1953- author.
Title: Diane di Prima: visionary poetics and the hidden religions / David
Stephen Calonne.
Description: New York, NY: Bloomsbury Academic, 2019. |
Includes bibliographical references and index.
Identifiers: LCCN 2018058906 | ISBN 9781501342905 (hardback: alk. paper) |
ISBN 9781501342929 (epdf) | ISBN 9781501342936 (xml-platform)
Subjects: LCSH: Di Prima, Diane. | Poets, American—20th century—Biography. |
Beats (Persons)
Classification: LCC PS3507.I68 Z57 2019 | DDC 811/.54 [B]—dc23
LC record available at https://lccn.loc.gov/2018058906

ISBN: HB: 978-1-5013-4290-5
PB: 978-1-5013-6657-4
ePDF: 978-1-5013-4292-9
eBook: 978-1-5013-4291-2

Typeset by Deanta Global Publishing Services, Chennai, India

CONTENTS

ACKNOWLEDGMENTS

Because I teach University courses on Beat literature, it perhaps would seem inevitable that I would become increasingly fascinated by Diane di Prima. My students have been equally intrigued. They responded powerfully to her ecstatic and lyrical poetry, to the wild imagination and humor exhibited in *Memoirs of a Beatnik*, and to her autobiographical reflections concerning her spiritual experiences in *Recollections of My Life as a Woman*. I became puzzled by the lack of scholarship devoted to an artist I believed possessed genius. After completing *The Spiritual Imagination of the Beats*, which contains a chapter devoted to her, I continued studying Di Prima's complete oeuvre as well as conducting a compulsive Internet search through used and rare book dealers to locate several difficult-to-find works. My teaching, lecturing, and research led ultimately to the composition of *Diane di Prima: Visionary Poetics and the Hidden Religions*. As a native Californian who came of age during the heady countercultural revolution of the 1960s, I retrospectively now see an undeniable pattern in my scholarship. I have returned constantly to this Dionysian period of American literary history to attempt to fathom its deeper meaning and significance. I realized recently that all my books in one way or another have concerned authors who were either born in California or who spent much of their lives there: William Saroyan, Henry Miller, Charles Bukowski, and now—Diane di Prima.

Many people have been essential to the long task of shepherding this book to completion. I thank Haaris Naqvi at Bloomsbury for his strong interest in my project from the outset. Katherine De Chant and Amy Martin assisted me with professional aplomb during the early preparation of my manuscript. I thank both Project Manager Leeladevi Ulaganathan and Copy Editor M.S. Sowmya for their superb work in the final stages of producing this book: they were both always extremely helpful. I also thank the two anonymous reviewers from Bloomsbury whose comments contributed greatly to the revision of my manuscript. I am also grateful for the wise counsel of Nancy M. Grace, whose scholarship on Di Prima and Beat literature was of inestimable value to me during the genesis of this monograph. The Interlibrary Loan staffs at Eastern Michigan University and the University of Michigan have been unfailingly useful to me in obtaining essential books and articles. Working on an author such as Di Prima has posed unique challenges since many of her important diaries, notebooks, recordings, teaching materials, lectures, and fictional works remain unpublished and are housed in a variety of University archives and collections across the United States. Thus I have been particularly dependent on the good offices of a number of people whom I would like to heartily thank here: Elspeth Healey, Special Collections Librarian at the Kenneth Spencer Research Library, University of Kansas; Tim Hogdon and Aaron N. Smithers, Research and Instructional Services Department, Lois Round Wilson Special Collections Library, University of North Carolina, Chapel Hill; Delinda Stephens Buie, Curator of Rare Books, Archives and Special Collections, University of Louisville; and Kate Hutchens, Reader and Reference Services Librarian, Special Collections Library, University of Michigan, Ann Arbor. Each of these kind individuals went far beyond the call of duty in patiently fielding my questions and supplying much needed materials in a timely fashion.

My thanks also to Oliver Harris and the organizers of the European Beat Studies Network conference "Paris Interzone: The Transcultural Beat Generation (Collaboration, Publication, Translation)" held at the University of Chicago Center in Paris where I presented an excerpt from the draft manuscript in September 2017. Thanks as always to Maria Beye as well as to William Byrd (1538–1623). Music has always been an essential and sustaining part of my life and over the last several years one of my most intense pleasures has been playing on my piano Volumes XXVII and XXVIII of the *Musica Britannica* edition of William Byrd's *Keyboard Music*. It strikes me now that perhaps there was an unconscious connection in my mind while I wrote *Diane di Prima: Visionary Poetics and the Hidden Religions* between this great Renaissance composer whose splendid music sometimes leads me to euphoric states and the subject of this book who herself was so often inspired by the great minds of the Renaissance and who sought in her own, very gifted way a rebirth of our capacity to feel wonder and joy.

LIST OF FIGURES

Introduction

Diane di Prima (1934–) has been subjected to a curious critical reception. As the major female author often associated with a male-dominated Beat movement, one might expect Di Prima would have elicited particular fascination and scholarly investigation, yet her writings have often been either misconstrued or unceremoniously ignored. Anthony Lioi speculated concerning Di Prima's exclusion from the canon: "One is tempted to blame it on *brutta figura*, a failure to keep up appearances for the sake of community standards. A woman poet who did not destroy herself in the 1950s, an intellectual Italian, esoteric and syncretistic among Catholics and Neopagans, a pan-sexual in the feminist wars of orientation, di Prima does not genuflect in the right direction. The resulting obscurity of her work is a critical disaster of the first order."[1] Di Prima herself echoed these sentiments, declaring, "I would encounter the same barriers time and again; they would rise up in response to my politics, my mode of dress, my deliberately cultivated Italian/American manner, New York accent, the concerns of the characters in my short stories, the street slang in my poems . . . if we chose to write the language and speech of the blue-collar family or street folks we had grown up around, we were automatically invisible to a large part of the literary world."[2] Independent of the academic establishment, Di Prima did not play the careerist literary game and also was extremely generous toward fellow artists, giving unstintingly of her time and energy. Recently William Marling in *Gatekeepers: The Emergence of World Literature and the 1960s* (2016) has suggested that "by doing so much for others, she may have sacrificed a strong position in the field."[3] In addition to her early poems which indeed are composed in the speech of "street folks," Di Prima developed an original, dense, idiosyncratic style rooted in visionary traditions unfamiliar to many readers which sometimes demanded substantial philosophical background to interpret. While several of her works—such as the popular *Memoirs of a Beatnik*—are accessible to a wide audience, *The Calculus of Variation* and several of her poems are highly allusive. Indeed, Di Prima acknowledged this when describing the composition of *Revolutionary Letters* (1971; 2007), created during her intense political activity of the late 1960s: "Most of my poetry was too intellectual when I tried to read it on the street. So I wrote the *Revolutionary Letters* almost as theatre, as street theatre."[4]

Placing Di Prima within a single category has indeed proved challenging, since her work shares characteristics with a variety of artistic "schools." She was at the center of the 1950s New York avant-garde when Willem de Kooning, Franz Kline, Jasper Johns, John Cage, Merce Cunningham, Zen Buddhism, Miles Davis, and bebop jazz burst on the scene; she was also involved with experimental theatre, composing plays employing random techniques derived from the *I Ching* which could be performed differently each time, with no stage directions. Her career spans the Beat movement's inception and its transition into 1960s hippie counterculture and crosses geographical lines: a native New Yorker, in California she became close to poets Robert Duncan, Michael McClure, and Kirby Doyle, as well as artists such as George Herms, Wallace Berman, and Marjorie Cameron. In addition, in her own poetic practice Di Prima linked a diversity of poetic traditions: her immersion in the imagism and esoteric poetics of Ezra Pound; her close association with Robert Duncan and Charles Olson; her friendship with Frank O'Hara of the so-called New York School—she would also publish with her Poets Press John Ashbery's *Three Madrigals*—and of course her Beat connections with Allen Ginsberg, Jack Kerouac, Gregory Corso, William S. Burroughs, and employment of "hipster" language in early books such as *This Bird Flies Backward*, and *Dinners and Nightmares*.

Di Prima, like Picasso and Stravinsky, believed that a creative person must be in a constant state of transformation. She affirmed Jean Cocteau's belief that "the artist has to be like an acrobat. Whenever 'they've' figured out what your 'shtick' is (what you're doing)—the critics, the public, whatever—you've had to have already pole-vaulted into a whole other area of art." While some aspects of Di Prima's approach derived from the Beat movement, she objected to being labeled as a member of the group, although it is the case that Herbert Huncke, John Clellon Holmes, and Jack Kerouac had employed the term: "Yeah, I don't like being called Beat. Not because I didn't have work that would definitely be called Beat, but because it's such a small percentage of all my work. It's like being frozen in one moment—someone takes a photo of you in 1958 and that's what you're supposed to be for the rest of your life. That's silly."[5] In a late poem, "Keep the Beat" (2010), she asserts the Beats are "not a 'Generation'/dig–/*it's a state of mind.*" She goes on to declare "'Beat' poetry's older/than the *grove of academe*/older than/Apollo/or Pythagoras/it's one of the ways/that Dionysios plays/*tongues of ecstasy*." There is "nowhere to go/nowhere to fall but/into the arms/of the Father/Mother/the *yabyum*/Dionysios! *Evoe!*" "Evoe" is the cry of the Bacchantes—the female followers of Dionysus—which they shouted in moments of orgiastic ecstasy, while *yabyum*—as we shall see in later chapters—is a Tantric sexual practice.[6] Indeed this excerpt vividly illustrates Di Prima's tendency to combine a variety of cultural traditions—here ancient Greek and Tibetan—into her poetics, while also declaring that Beat authors represent a subset of a much larger historical movement in which she situates her own work.

When one constructs a genealogy of nineteenth- and twentieth-century American women poets—from Emily Dickinson to Sylvia Plath—one may readily observe that Di Prima does not fit neatly into their ranks. Rather, it was Hilda Dolittle (H.D.) (1886–1961)—a theme to which shall return in Chapter 5—who represented the tradition Di Prima considered herself to be continuing:

> I feel very close to H.D. . . . is definitely a gut connection, almost like a mother figure for me. There's a way in which Gertrude Stein is a teacher. . . . But I belong to a tradition that maybe is more a hermetic order within the writing thing or something . . . amongst the alchemists . . . the tradition of the possibility of transmutation. A hermetic tradition where magic and art come together, in some vision of what the possibility is for the human creature. . . . I see that part of my tradition is Pound and Keats, part H.D. . . . . Paracelsus, moves from there to Dante, Cavalcanti, that I feel certain visionary concepts of the Sufi tradition. . . . Maybe it's a visionary tradition. I see it as hermetic in the sense that it's never really emerged as a single school. . . . And that one of the main moving things for it is love, Eros is a changer, not only connecter, but changer of the human possibility, perhaps. It's hard to explain. But it jumps the lines from one discipline to another a lot.[7]

In *The Mysteries of Vision: Some Notes on H.D.*, Di Prima describes H.D.'s encounter with Azrael, the angel of death, in her poetry: humanity is

> on the verge of our own death as a species, the creation (not so conscious) of our own Azrael. The invitation to us as artists is to enter more planes, move in more dimensions than we humans had ever dreamed existed— and so of course we limit ourselves in new ways, hauling our white picket fences off into the warpings of relativist space: materialism, romanticism, feminism, historicity.[8]

For Di Prima, these are reductive academic categories which limit the expressive possibilities of a radically new conception of human selfhood and spiritual potential.

Di Prima thus situated herself within a specific literary tradition she has named "hermetic." Ancient writings known as the *Corpus Hermeticum* and attributed to Hermes Trismegistus or "Thrice-Great Hermes," which were concerned with *gnosis* or self-knowledge, became central to a tradition of esoteric wisdom. John Milton in one of his early masterworks "Il Penseroso" memorably paid homage to the inspiration these mystical texts evoke in the poetic imagination: "Or let my lamp at midnight hour,/Be seen in some high lonely tower,/Where I may oft outwatch the Bear,/With thrice great Hermes, or unsphere/The spirit of Plato to unfold/What worlds, or what vast regions hold/The immortal mind that hath forsook/Her mansion in this fleshly nook." Hermetic philosophy emerged out of a syncretism which developed between ancient Greek and Egyptian thought and Sir Isaac Newton (1643–1727) both translated and composed a commentary upon the *Tabula Smaragdina*, the "Emerald Tablet"—an alchemical section of the *Corpus Hermeticum*. Newton immersed himself in countless alchemical texts, copied out passages and conducted alchemical experiments: he would persist for several days without eating or sleeping during these obsessive bouts with his secret studies. Newton would ultimately compose approximately a million words on the subject of alchemy. The *Tabula Smaragdina* contains the famous saying "as above, so below," the macrocosm mirrors the microcosm. This is the concept of "correspondence" between the earthly and cosmic realms which will become a key theme in Di Prima's work. As Brian P. Copenhaver has pointed out in *Hermetica: The Greek Corpus Hermeticum and the Latin Asclepius*, when the classical and Egyptian worlds began to encounter one another, "Greeks and Romans responded by finding Hellenic matches for the Egyptian deities—Thoth and Hermes, Imhotep and Asclepius, Zeus and Amon, and so on" When Di Prima employs the word "hermetic," she means to signify this tradition and as we shall see, she would compose poems inspired by Thoth, also known as Tahuti. The texts of Trismegistus merge with a number of other historical currents would which Di Prima will later name "the hidden religions" including not only ancient Egyptian and Greek wisdom, Paracelsus and Sufism—as she adumbrated above— but also alchemy, magic, Gnosticism, Kabbalah, "paganism," "witchcraft," Eastern spiritual traditions such as Vajrayana Tibetan Buddhism and Native American shamanism. These "religions"—or better *spiritualities* or *inner modes of knowledge*—are "hidden" because the monotheistic, orthodox faiths—Christianity, Judaism, and Islam—have regarded them as antinomian or "heretical." In *R.D.'s H.D.*—her essay on Robert Duncan's *The H.D. Book*—Di Prima reveals that "another aspect is that when we talk of Poetics of Influence we are speaking of lineage: the 'mouth to ear' tradition they speak of in the Kabbalah, and in Tibet . . . . In our European/American poetry there is a precision of lineage, and it is often told, addressed by the poets themselves. It can be traced as accurately as the Soto and Rinzai masters of Zen. Only, we have not paid it that attention."[9] In addition to H.D., Di Prima has also acknowledged the significance in her poetic practice of the great African American female blues singers, including Bessie Smith, Billie Holiday, Sara Martin, Trixie Smith, and Ida Cox; jazz greats Thelonious Monk, Miles Davis, and her friend Cecil Taylor; and singers of the 1960s such as Joan Baez and Janis Joplin.[10]

Di Prima's affinity for African American culture, her mystical sensibility, her radical politics, as well as refusal to limit herself regarding gender/

sex roles as dictated by the repressive, Cold War United States in which she came of age make her a unique figure in American literary history. Gloria Anzaldua in *Bordlerlands/La Frontera* provided a framework for understanding Di Prima's "crossing of borders" in which Beat/not-Beat, linguistic conventions, gender, as well as psychological identity are fluid rather than strict categories. Anzaldua analyzes the ways as a "Mexican-American" she straddled different languages—Spanish and English, various "dialects" or "lower-class" Spanish—just as Di Prima moves between Beat "hip" lingo and "groovy" hippy speech to lofty alchemical, esoteric symbolic language. And as we shall see in Chapter 1, Di Prima's sufferings at the hands of her parents as a child contributed to her preternatural sensitivity as well as her status as an "outsider" to the "norms" of American society: she thus developed what Anzaldua calls *la facultad*:

> *La facultad* is the capacity to see in surface phenomena the meaning of deeper realities. . . . Those who are pushed out of the tribe for being different are likely to become more sensitized (when not brutalized into insensitivity). Those who do not feel psychologically or physically safe in the world are more apt to develop this sense. Those who are pounced on the most have it the strongest—the females, the homosexuals of all races, the darkskinned, the outcast, the persecuted, the marginalized, the foreign.

Anzaldua thus draws the connection between *la facultad*, the mystical temperament and the liminal personality which precisely describes Di Prima.

Thus Di Prima's bisexuality is another way she was "pushed out of the tribe" for being "different." As we shall see, she was an important and early example of a woman who would challenge conventional gender roles during the repressive 1950s and fought for sexual freedom throughout her life. Anzaldua's employment of the word "tribe" here is significant for Di Prima evinced a deep interest in Native American culture and shamanism. Indeed, the gift of possessing *la facultad* shares many characteristics in common with shamanism. The shaman often encounters his/her mystical vocation during adolescence and goes on a vision quest to experience their individual encounter with the sacred: Di Prima underwent a rite of passage when she discovered her role as poet which mirrors that of the Native American shaman. Robert Duncan—who as we shall see became a significant influence on Di Prima—in the summer of 1949 met the distinguished scholar of Native American culture Jaime de Angulo through correspondence with Ezra Pound who had suggested he contact him. The historian of California Kevin Starr has remarked: "de Angulo's English-language redactions of Native American stories and myths, which he read over Berkeley radio station KPFA-FM with great success in 1949–50 just before his death from cancer, made of him a quasi-cult figure to the Beat generation of the 1950s, beginning with poet Robert Duncan." Henry Miller would pay tribute to de Angulo and Beat poets Philip Lamantia and Gary Snyder also learned from his vast store of knowledge about Native American cultures.

One may set Di Prima's relationship to shamanism within the context of questions concerning gender and sexuality. Duncan believed that

> in Jaime's generation's writings on the American Indian they had noticed immediately the homosexual shaman, and Jaime's transvestite was a male lesbian, which means that you cross sex lines. I think that the crossing of sex lines meant to the Indian that you could also cross between the living and the dead. . . . And of course the central idea in shamanism is going across.

The French term *berdache* formerly employed to refer to "feminine" Native American men has been replaced with "two-spirits" and there has been extensive recent scholarship exploring the links between shamanism and sexuality: we remember that the prophet Teiresias in Sophocles's *Oedipus Tyrannos* is bisexual and T. S. Eliot's unforgettable portrait in *The Wasteland* is of a being whose prophetic powers derive from the fact that he/she is "liminal" in precisely the ways Duncan described, having "crossed every line entirely": "I Tiresias, though blind, throbbing between two lives,/Old man with wrinkled female breasts, can see/At the violet hour, the evening hour that/strives Homeward, and brings the sailor home from sea."[11] As we shall see, Di Prima's own "going across" the conventional borders of sexuality and marriage—as well as her challenging traditional notions of what is considered in our culture as "religious"—will define both her poetics and her liminal, mystical psychology.

Di Prima was at the vanguard of the movement to explore and delineate a new consciousness, and her work is a reflection of her inquiries over a period of six decades. She is at once an "autobiographical" writer for the subject matter of her poems and prose often derives directly from her personal experience, yet her work also chronicles the striking changes in American life in an almost documentary fashion. Di Prima's friend Allen Ginsberg defined the shift in awareness following the Second World War, arguing in an interview that the threat of atomic apocalypse fostered a need in intelligent young people to search for answers to their psychological quandaries in ancient spiritual traditions:

> Then from the 50s on there was the introduction of literal Himalayan wisdom with Zen Buddhist roshis, teachers. Zen Masters coming to America, adding an element of wisdom that had been amateur before the Theosophists. The 60s—the introduction of the Tibetan lamas, the *Tibetan Book of the Dead* and techniques of mind training that are really radical and interesting that were just guessed at in the West

once the continuity of the old Gnostics had been broken back during the Dark Ages. The East didn't go through the Dark Ages, through the destruction of the wisdom transmission principles and the West did have a breakdown. . . . There was no breakdown of the transmission of the wisdom practices in the East. There is still some direct lineage back to Buddha and Chinese Buddhism in China and Zen Buddhism back to Japan. There is a direct lineage of teacher to teacher, from generation to generation, from Buddha's time to the present Zen Masters. Same with the Tibetan lamas. There is a direct lineage of unbroken transmission of mind training with the Tibetan Vajrayana Buddhists.

Whereas in the West, the old Gnostic schools that came from the same sources during the Dark Ages there was an inquisition. There was a breakdown of the transmission of Gnostic contemplative practices. In India there is the direct transmission of the ancient pronunciation and chanting in Sanskrit from generation to generation, unbroken. There is nobody who knows how ancient Greek was sung and chanted. There was a breakdown in that transmission both in the field of contemplative practice and in the field of poetic practice. So nobody knows how Homer was sung. Or how Sappho was sung. Whereas in the East there was no breakdown in the chanting of Sanskrit.

That's a really important thing. The accumulated wisdom, the tie-binding wisdom so characteristic of high civilization broke down in the West. So we got cut off from our roots, so to speak.

Thus during the 1950s and 1960s, a new American religious sensibility was being born which was extremely receptive to reestablishing a direct connection to these spiritual traditions which had been ignored or forcibly erased from the historical record. As Robert N. Bellah has noted in "The New Consciousness and the Crisis in Modernity," "the churches were even less well prepared to cope with the new spirituality of the sixties. The demand for immediate, powerful, and deep religious experience, which was part of the turn away from future-oriented instrumentalism toward present meaning and fulfillment, could on the whole not be met by the religious bodies."

In response to this felt need for a deeper understanding of what Georges Bataille has called *l'expérience intérieure*—inner experience—over a period of several decades Di Prima began to map out a theory of history beginning with Paleolithic times and moving through the Medieval, Renaissance, and Modern periods.[12] She studied texts such as G. Rachel Levy's *The Gate of Horn: Religious Conceptions of the Stone Age and Their Influence on European Thought* and Margaret Murray's works on witchcraft, developing a new historical narrative grounded in the archaic sources of goddess mythology. She also read Giorgio de Santillana's (1902–74) *Hamlet's Mill: An Essay on Myth and the Frame of Time* (recommended by Paul Feyerabend in *Against Method*), John Michell's books on Atlantis, Robert Graves's *The White Goddess*, and Martin L. Nilsson's *Primitive Time Reckoning*. Di Prima would celebrate "pagan" rituals to mark the solstice and equinox, the turnings of the earth in relation to stars rather than by the calendar. In creating a new interpretation of the meaning of human history, she sought to fathom and understand from these esoteric traditions what might be relevant for modern humanity's needs.

Although she spent just a year and half at Swarthmore, Di Prima became an autodidact with a fierce appetite for knowledge. She amassed a library of some 4,000 volumes and preferred to own her own books rather than borrow from a library since she was fond of copiously annotating her texts. Di Prima possesses one of the most impressive, wide-ranging, and intellectually curious sensibilities among contemporary American writers. She feels equally at home with Robert Fludd, the Buddhist mystic Tsogyal, Thelonious Monk, Isaac Newton, and Giordano Bruno. She has a restless and probing intelligence, delving into intellectual provender from an impressive array of sources. On her reading list for her course in the "Hidden Religions in the Literature of Europe" which she offered at the New College of California from 1980 to 1987, we find cheek by jowl with academic classics such as Northrop Frye's *Fearful Symmetry: A Study of William Blake* and essays on Isaac Newton, several other texts by authors some would consider outré such as J. Norman Lockyer's *The Dawn of Astronomy: A Study of Temple Worship and Mythology of the Ancient Egyptians*; Dion Fortune's *The Mystical Qabbalah*, and John Michell's *The View Over Atlantis*. In *Diane di Prima: Visionary Poetics and the Hidden Religions*, I shall pursue the influence of key texts on her intellectual development and trace out connections between her own trajectory and other countercultural figures. For example, Di Prima would have extensive conversations with William S. Burroughs concerning magic and the occult, and Burroughs also read and praised texts by John Michell as well as Dion Fortune's *Psychic Self-Defense*. I also discuss the *I Ching*, John Dee's *Monas Hieroglyphica*, Heinrich Cornelius Agrippa's *De Occulta Philosophia*, Johannes Trithemius *Steganographia*, Milarepa, Gnostic texts, the Kabbalah, Tarot, Paracelsus, *The Tibetan Book of the Dead*, as well as Di Prima's studies with a succession of gurus including Shunryu Suzuki, Chogyam Trungpa, and Tarchin Rinpoche.

In Chapter 1, The Blood of the Poet, 1934–52, I explore Di Prima's childhood, her difficult relationship with her parents, and the compensatory fulfilling connection to her grandfather Domenico as well as her discovery of John Keats at the age of fourteen and dedication to the life of the poet. In Chapter 2, Return to New York: From Ezra Pound to the *I Ching*, 1953–60, I turn to her brief career at Swarthmore College, her meetings with Allen Ginsberg and Ezra Pound and early experiments with the *I Ching*. In Chapter 3, Tell all the gods we're returning back to find them: From *Dinners and Nightmares* to Paracelsus, Alchemy, and Tarot, 1961–67 I study *The Freddie*

Poems, her immersion in Tarot, Agrippa, John Dee, alchemy, Kabbalah, and her journey to the West Coast. In Chapter 4, The Age of Aquarius and the Wolf: *Revolutionary Letters, Monas Hieroglyphica, Loba*, 1968–79, I trace Di Prima's permanent move to California and analyze the ways the new energies of the hippy era influenced her work. This was an extraordinarily prolific period during which *Memoirs of a Beatnik* was published as well as one of her masterworks, *Loba*. Di Prima also commenced in-depth studies of the British scholar of Renaissance philosophy Frances Yates as well as the Italian thinker Giordano Bruno. The *Revolutionary Letters* appeared in 1971, and her friendship with Robert Duncan blossomed. She began teaching in 1974 at the Naropa Institute in Boulder, Colorado, where Chogyam Trungpa established a center for Tibetan Buddhism. In Chapter 5, The Hidden Religions, H.D., Angels, and Tibetan Buddhism, 1980–92, I explore her course on the Hidden Religions in the Literature of Europe which she conducted at the New College of California, her studies of H.D.'s "angel magic," as well as her increasing interest in Vajrayana which we see in poems such as "Tsogyal." In Chapter 6, Speech of the Heart: Poet Laureate of San Francisco, 1993 to the present, I study *Recollections of My Life as a Woman* as well as *Time Bomb* (2006). In addition, Di Prima was made Poet Laureate of San Francisco in 2009. During her later period, she created some of her strongest works such as *The Poetry Deal* (2015). I also seek to show that in addition to her achievements as poet, she has been also a provocative prose writer, producing several important essays as well as fiction, including her unpublished novella *Not Quite Buffalo Stew*. Di Prima is prolific and there is not yet a complete bibliography of her oeuvre. She also published many limited print editions with small presses, thus obtaining copies of some of her works can sometimes be challenging. Her papers and a large quantity of unpublished manuscripts are housed at the University of North Carolina, the University of Louisville, and several other universities.

I shall argue in *Diane di Prima: Visionary Poetics and the Hidden Religions* that her work taken as a whole constitutes a kind of new scripture for the Beat/hippie generation. She has made intensive studies of Renaissance Magic, Gnosticism, alchemy, Buddhism, Tantra, "paganism," and esoteric philosophy, shaping this knowledge into writings in a wide variety of styles. Di Prima continued to evolve over a sixty-year career and to experiment with a variety of poetic forms—from the sestina to *haibun* and *pantoum*. She shared the Beat fascination with occult, mystical, and Eastern philosophies, and emerged as the most learned among them in her investigations of these subjects. Di Prima resembles a writer such as Henry Miller in her straddling of "street language" and the languages of high culture. She can move effortlessly from the hip lingo of "cool," "pad," "chick," and "groovy" of her early poems and stories to learned disquisitions on Giordano Bruno, John Keats, or the Tibetan *dakini* Tsogyal, to the urgent, incendiary, political declarations of the *Revolutionary*

Letters, just as Miller was the author of explicit texts such as *Tropic of Cancer*, *Tropic of Capricorn* and *Sexus* as well as letters and essays on Ramakrishna, Vivekananda, Buddha, and St. Francis. Thomas J. Ferraro has rightly asserted that "feminist scrutinizing of literary history reveals Diane di Prima as the strongest of the female Beats, arguably the strongest and certainly the most salient female Italian American creative writer to date."[13] I shall demonstrate Di Prima's centrality in the history of modern American literature through a close study of the ways her visionary poetics are rooted in the history of the hidden religions.

1

The Blood of the Poet:

1934–52

Born in Brooklyn, New York, on August 6, 1934, Diane di Prima's childhood was suffused with the language and culture of Italy. She retained only vague memories of her paternal grandparents, Rosa di Prima, who died when Diane was two years old, and her husband; however, maternal grandparents Antoinette Rossi and Domenico Mallozzi were significant influences. Most Italians arrived in the United States between 1880 and 1920 and during peak years there were more than a quarter of a million immigrants. Out of the total of 2,300,000 Italians who arrived between 1899 and 1910, only 400,000 came from the northern regions: the vast majority were from the provinces of Southern Italy—Calabria, Basilicata (Lucania), Apulia, Campania, Abruzzi—and the island of Sicily. Di Prima's maternal grandparents were Sicilian, and grandfather Domenico—a striking man with blue eyes (uncommon among Italians Di Prima tells us in her poem "April Fool Birthday Poem for Grandpa") and white hair—often took his granddaughter to the opera. Di Prima recalled that Domenico "wasn't allowed to listen to operas because he got so emotional about them, so he and I would sneak off and listen to operas, and he would tell me the stories of them." This is likely one source of the often-soaring *bel canto* lyricism of Di Prima's poetry: she recalled hearing celebrated baritone Tito Gobbi (1913–84) as well as the renowned tenors Enrico Caruso (1873–1921), Mario Lanza (1921–59), and Beniamino Gigli (1890–1957) frequently played on phonograph records during her childhood.[1] Domenico read Dante to his granddaughter and introduced her to the great "heretical" philosopher, mathematician, and theorist of the infinite universe Giordano Bruno (1548–1600): Bruno's rejection of orthodox Christianity and his attraction to the "hermetic" wisdom of Hermes Trismegistus—"Thrice-Great Hermes"—would shape Di Prima's own intellectual trajectory.

The texts of Trismegistus were thought to have been written at the time of Moses, but later research by Isaac Casaubon (1559–1614) determined that they originated between second and third century CE. Antoine Faivre has remarked that "Bruno did not desire a reformed Christian church but rather a return to the cults or beliefs of ancient Egypt as described in the *Corpus Hermeticum* and particularly in the *Asclepius*." Bruno would undergo eight years of imprisonment and interrogation by the church authorities before being declared a heretic by Pope Clement VIII and condemned to death. On February 17, 1600, Bruno was led on a mule into the Campo de' Fiori in Rome, hung upside down, naked, and gagged.

Some accounts claim a metal spike was driven through his cheeks to pin his tongue and a second spike vertically through his lips—due to his record of supposedly impious words—before being burned at the stake: his ashes were cast into the Tiber river. Bruno's persecution, death by fire, and martyrdom became, for Di Prima, symbols of the ways unwelcome

FIGURE 1.1 *Bronze statue of Giordano Bruno by Ettore Ferrari (1845–1929), Campo de' Fiori, Rome. Wikimedia Commons.*

antinomian ideas may be crushed by those in political or religious power. Bruno represented the heroic example of dying for a cause which would also mark the idealistic, revolutionary fervor of the 1960s when members of the counterculture challenged the orthodoxies of what was then named "The Establishment" of the American government, reactionary religious institutions, and monolithic, ecologically destructive corporations. As we shall see in Chapter 4, Di Prima would devote one of her greatest poems to Joan of Arc whom she also depicts as sacrificing herself for a greater cause which emphasizes Joan's roots in heterodox beliefs. Martyrdom and self-sacrifice could take extreme forms during the 1960s, as when Buddhist nuns immolated themselves in protest of the war in Vietnam—an event which Di Prima would memorialize in a moving poem.

Di Prima was deeply influenced by her grandfather's participation in the robust tradition of Italian American radicalism: Domenico, an atheist, was friends with Emma Goldman—also a great influence on the young Henry Miller—and would name Di Prima's mother Emma after her. He also counted among his comrades the famous anarchist Carlo Tresca who was assassinated in 1943. Domenico wrote for *Il Martello, The Hammer*— an anarchist newspaper located on the Lower East Side—and brought the young Diane with him to revolutionary rallies.[2] Philip Lamantia (1927– 2005)—the great surrealist poet who like Di Prima had Sicilian roots and whom she would later meet in California—became involved in the Italian anarchist movement in San Francisco during the 1940s: Lamantia distributed leaflets, attended rallies, and corresponded with fellow anarchists in America and abroad. Dana Gioia in "What Is Italian American Poetry?" has emphasized the fact that the status of Italians "as economic and social outsiders in America also colors their political views. It often makes them suspicious or critical of established power. Anarchy appeals to the southern Italian worldview. Revolution and resistance also exercise a mythic charm. Early Italian American poets were usually political radicals, though rarely loyal and obedient members of any party." Domenico memorably told his granddaughter that if you are hungry, have a piece of bread and then proceed to eat it, you will still remain hungry. However, if you sit with a friend, break it in half and eat together, your hunger as well as your friend's shall be assuaged: Domenico considered this communitarian motto a "law of nature." This philosophy of life is of course diametrically opposed to the greed, selfishness, and materialism characteristic of American capitalism with its relentless emphasis on individual "success" and rampant consumerism. Di Prima's familial background accounts for the coalescence in her sensibility of practical political theory and high idealism, a communal radical politics linked to esoteric philosophical traditions. Her grandfather's search for the significance of life, he once told her, had ended in "nothing." But Diane vowed she "would make meaning in the world. Make meaning for him, for myself. The dark was luminous, of that I was certain. That much I *knew*."[3]

Di Prima's allusion to the luminous dark recalls the conceptions of Pseudo-Dionysius the Areopagite (fifth to sixth century CE), an important figure for Kenneth Rexroth, Robert Duncan, Alan Watts, and several Beat writers including Michael McClure and Philip Lamantia. His *via negativa* or "negative theology" held that the divine cannot be described in words and this concept would greatly influence the evolution of Christian mysticism. The opening of Chapter One of Pseudo-Dionysius's *The Mystical Theology* asks: "What is the divine darkness? . . . Lead us up beyond unknowing and light,/ up to the farthest, highest peak/of mystic scripture,/where the mysteries of God's Word/lie simple, absolute and unchangeable/in the *brilliant darkness* of a hidden silence."[4] In her autobiographical *Recollections of My Life as a Woman* (2001), imagery of "light" is pervasive and in the section about her grandfather "light" and "stars" recur, suggesting Domenico's studies of Giordano Bruno and Di Prima's own engagement with mathematics, astronomy, and cosmology was inspired by Bruno's life and work. At age six, she wrote her first, brief rhyming poem in order to "remember forever" the stars over an apartment from which her grandparents were relocating: the poem sprang from "an impulse to try to hang on to moments of time."[5] Domenico—who died when Di Prima was eleven—worked in the pharmacy of his nephew and Diane felt at home when she spent time with him there: "Is it we have been alchemists together? We are so still. High windows in the back, with stained glass on the borders. We meet each other, timeless, in this light."[6] Larissa Bendel in *The Requirements of Our Life Is the Form of Our Art: Autobiographik von Frauen der Beat Generation* has noted that Domenico's world for Di Prima "represents safety, security, but also initiation, conspiracy." The imagery here also suggests a kind of sacred space—note the "high windows" and "stained glass"—a cathedral of love where grandfather and granddaughter, both secret magicians "conspire" together, share an eternal, illuminated sanctuary away from the modern world's uncertainty, anxiety, chaos, and faithlessness where they pursue the alchemical quest for the Philosopher's Stone. As we shall see in Chapter 3, alchemy would also become a central fascination for Di Prima later in her career when she discovered the writings of Paracelsus.

Her grandmother Antoinette would hide her rosary beads whenever her atheist husband Domenico appeared, and her "pagan" Italian Catholicism and reverence for St. Lucy made an indelible impression upon Di Prima. In the section entitled "The Southwest" from *The Calculus of Variation* (1972; written 1960–63), she recalls her grandmother's relationship with the saint: "Was it St. Lucy carries her eyes in a dish. And you do not eat bread on her day, or wash. And the one where you bless the salt, which one was that? Fingering my grandmother's rosary, what I thought was my grandmother's rosary."[7] As a Sicilian, St. Lucy—Lucia of Syracuse (283–304 CE)—would of course have special importance to Di Prima's grandmother: "her eyes in a dish" alludes to the legend that when Lucia was tortured her eyes were gouged out, or in another version she removed her own eyes in order to discourage an admiring suitor. This "pagan" honoring of *light*—the name Lucy is derived from Latin *lux*, *light*—and the changing of the seasons become a dominant theme in Di Prima's thought: she would later read Martin P. Nilsson's *Primitive Time-Reckoning* (1920), devoting several poems to recording and celebrating the equinox and the summer solstice. In addition, due to this powerful matriarchal environment represented by her grandmother, young Diane began to see men as "peripheral" to the lives of independent and self-sufficient women: they were a kind of exciting luxury, but essentially "fragile." The strength of these powerful Italian women is memorably evoked by Lawrence Ferlinghetti in his poem "The Old Italians Dying" in which he recalls elderly anarchists who had been devoted to Sacco and Vanzetti as they peruse *L'Umanita Nova* newspaper and who are now dying. Ferlinghetti then turns to the death of these venerable patriarchs and their widows who wear black, long veils. They will live longer than their husbands and they are both *madre di terra* and *madre di mare*.[8] The powerful matriarchs are mothers of the earth and mothers of the sea. It is from her strong Italian grandmother that Di Prima perhaps first encountered the notion of the Goddess, the Earth Mother, the fecundating and eternal cycle of life as incarnated in the creative and sexual power of woman which would become a central theme in her poetry and prose.

It would be an understatement to suggest that Di Prima's parents proved more problematic than her maternal grandparents. To punish her daughter for supposed misbehavior, mother Emma would instruct Diane to "pull up your skirt and pull down your pants," command her to go retrieve a hairbrush, and proceed to beat her. Dressing Diane and performing the morning ablutions were often accomplished with fierce anger: she scrubbed her daughter's flesh during baths until it reddened. Di Prima's father Francis would strike her with a belt, slapping her face until her nose bled, and during these merciless thrashings became sexually aroused: he "would sit me on his lap with a hard-on to 'comfort' me—or worse, I don't remember, only sense." In her poem "To My Father," Di Prima remembered:

> You are still the fierce wind, the intolerable force
> that almost broke me.
> Who forced my young body into awkward and proper clothes
> Who spoke of his standing in the community.
> And men's touch is still a little absurd to me
> because you trembled when you touched me.[9]

Following these vicious attacks, Di Prima confessed to sometimes hitting herself to assure herself she was "real," that she in fact existed: a typical maneuver of those traumatized by childhood sexual abuse. There is sometimes a connection between such victimization, the resulting psychological dissociation, and a mystical temperament, a yearning to escape to a better, more just world where such transgressions would not be tolerated as well as an affinity for a profound inner life. As Di Prima declared:

> The secret gnosticism of Dante, of my grandfather, who so claimed the here and now in his politics, passed through the hysteria and grief of my mother, and arrived as the message "this world is intolerable." Translated by me, age two or three, to "This world is not real. Does not take precedence." Skill at astral travel, at "seeing" other worlds, not separate from the inability to see my own face.[10]

In esoteric thought, the "astral body" is capable of voyaging outside the physical self throughout the universe. In an essay she would compose late in her career on poet Hilda Dolittle—*The Mysteries of Vision: Some Notes on H.D.* (1988)—this conception of discovering a kind of fissure in reality returns:

> In my own imaginings of the world as a child, I saw time as running in a straight line in which there were infinitesimal openings, or pockets. If you should "slip into" one of these, it led into a pocket of infinite dimension, a kind of detour, which however could not be seen from "above" and did not in any way break the continuity of the time line. In these pockets I included daydreams, some music, sudden realizations, imaginary friends, dreams, etc.[11]

Sight and *vision* have very different connotations: one can *see* the world, but not possess a deeper, wider, or more encompassing insight into its deeper nature, meaning, and purpose. We call poets such as William Blake, Arthur Rimbaud, Hart Crane, or H.D. "*visionary*" because their work is inextricably bound to a complex manner of imaginative perception which seeks precisely this more profound knowledge of the universe. Furthermore, chronological time measured by the clock is only one kind of time: the imagination, music, art, love, and intense experiences in nature can allow us momentary glimpses of another mode of temporality in which the divisions between self and cosmos seem to dissolve. These sometimes ecstatic experiences would become an inextricable aspect of Di Prima's visionary poetics which would be tied to the "hidden religions"—Gnosticism, Kabbalah, astrology, alchemy, shamanism, and Eastern thought—which began to command intense interest on the part of the nascent counterculture. The hidden religions would in fact become "alternative spiritualities" which were explored and practiced due to the prevailing dissatisfaction with "orthodox" monotheism in the forms of Christianity, Islam, and Judaism.

Di Prima's relationship to her Italian heritage is complex. At age seven, she was given a copy of *The Prince* and told by her father that to understand history she must read Machiavelli. Thus Bruno, Dante, and Machiavelli were a triumvirate of great Italian thinkers and poets to whom she was exposed at a very early age. Yet this "high culture" was set against the prejudice and hatred often reserved in America for "non-white" people. The execution of the Italian anarchists Sacco and Vanzetti in the electric chair in 1927—the judge referred to them as "Dagos" during the trial—was an event indelibly imprinted upon the Di Prima family and Italian Americans throughout the country: Diane would refer to their unjust trial and murder several times in her writings. In a lively late poem, "Whose Day Is It Anyway? The Poet Mulls Over Some of the Choices" (1988), Di Prima contributed to an anthology devoted to the controversy over the meaning of Columbus Day and the desire of Italian American writers to challenge the traditional narrative of the heroic "discovery" of America by the Italian Cristoforo Colombo (1451–1506)—the repeated refrain of the poem suggests that Columbus Day be renamed "Sacco and Vanzetti Day!"

In addition to suffering discrimination, being Italian American was an experience especially fraught with fear and anxiety during the years leading up to the Second World War when the sympathies of her father lay with a nation which had become an enemy of the United States. Di Prima was forbidden to speak Italian, yet she understood her parents (although they did not realize it) when they spoke to one another in their native tongue. Italian language and culture remained central to Di Prima's literary imagination: in high school she studied Latin, read Virgil and Ovid during her early twenties. Later she would create a translation, *Seven Love Poems from the Middle Latin* (1967). Her brief "Dream Poem" composed of five verses—"there is a fire above the ramparts of the world/shaped like battlements, or like the hair/of Orcagna's women/there is a fire beyond the skin of the world/a fire burns behind the skin of the world"— alludes to Andrea di Cione di Arcangelo (ca. 1308–68), the Italian artist known as Orcagna whose fresco painting *Dream of Life* depicts women with fiery red hair.[12] And when she published the first volume of her autobiography *Recollections of My Life as a Woman* (2002)—to preserve the flavor of her Italian/English "dialect"—Di Prima purposely included fragmentary sentences and later fought with her editor at Viking to keep this stylistic feature in her text intact. She also contributed an "Introduction" in 2001 to the Italian poet Giuseppe Conte's (1945–) *The Seasons—I Stagioni*. Finally, at least some of the affinity Di Prima would develop for Ezra Pound was likely due to his lifelong love affair with Italy and its culture. Pound would translate Guido Cavalcanti, lived for much of his life in Italy—his home base was Rapallo— and was partially responsible for the rediscovery and performance of the music of the great baroque composer Antonio Vivaldi (1678–1741).Thus as we shall see in the following chapters, Di Prima's connection to Italian culture remained pervasive throughout her career.

The tensions of Di Prima's young life gradually led to a climax: a key moment was the bombing of Hiroshima which occurred on her eleventh birthday: August 6, 1945. Although this was presumably a day of "victory" for the United States, the prevailing sentiment of the Di Prima clan was "we lost the war."[13] Psychological distance from "membership" in American society had of course already existed for Di Prima: this dramatic event was merely another form of the alienation she had experienced from childhood. In addition, the transgenerational struggles which are a common feature of "ethnic" groups in America in adjusting to the ways of their new land— the divisions which spring up between parents and children, the so-called generation gap—were experienced with great intensity among immigrant families. Indeed, this tormented dysfunction is often the subject of Italian American fiction, for example, in John Fante's *Wait until Spring, Bandini* (1938) and Helen Barolini's first novel *Umbertina* (1979) which dramatizes the "assimilation process" of three Italian American women. Thus her tumultuous family history and sexual abuse she had suffered caused Di Prima at age twelve to experience a psychological "breakdown": later she revealed possessing virtually no memories of her life from age seven to twelve. She threatened murdering her father with a knife: she was hurried to a doctor for an evaluation but her father never assaulted her again following this confrontation. Di Prima confessed to wanting to become a boy, an outcast, a bandit, or a pirate, and a few years later would identify with Jean Cocteau's "urchins in the snow." In the touching poem, "Backyard," Di Prima combined the theme of an angelic inner self—a concept as we shall see to which she would later return—and her psychologically wrenching familial drama in Brooklyn: "when angels turned into honeysuckle & poured nectar into my mouth/where I french-kissed the roses in the rain/ where demons tossed me a knife to kill my father in the stark/simplicity of the sky/where I never cried/where all the roofs were black/where no one opened the venetian blinds/O Brooklyn! Brooklyn!"[14] Di Prima employs three primary modes in her poetry: the lyrical autobiographical mode; the esoteric/mystical mode; and the overtly rhetorical-political mode intended to implement social change. "Backyard" is an example of the singing, lyrical mode in which she excelled and the lines contain condensed within their intricate, finely tuned music the announcement of her poetic vocation. The angels, honey and honeysuckle, nectar, mouth, french-kissing, roses: here is a kind of network of associated images of spiritual, erotic sweetness and the inspired poetic voice counterpointed against a set of darker, claustrophic, negative realities—rain, demons, killing, black roofs, venetian blinds which hide painful secrets. She has become a poet in order to transform anguish into song.

The psychological crucible Di Prima underwent during her childhood and adolescence mirrors the visionary crisis of the shaman in indigenous societies who in early adolescence often experiences a dissociation which announces his/her sacramental vocation. Di Prima now discovered philosophy and literature, reading Plato, Arthur Schopenhauer, Friedrich Nietzsche's *Also*

Sprach Zarathustra and *Jane Eyre*—during one year she read Charlotte Bronte's novel a dozen times.[15] While perusing Somerset Maugham's novels, she chanced upon a fascinating quotation from John Keats, leading her to read all the poet's letters as well as Percy Bysshe Shelley and Lord Byron. As we have seen, Di Prima had already composed poetry, and at age eight her older cousin Liz recited to her Rudyard Kipling's "If," which Di Prima soon memorized. This adoration of Keats thus was another key moment in her precocious poetic development and compelled Di Prima to make the decision to be a writer: she would now dedicate herself to the sacred task of art. She wept, realizing that a "normal" life would be impossible due to the dedication being an artist would require, vowing *Nulla dies sine linea*—"no day without writing a line"—which she inscribed on the covers of her composition notebooks.[16] As with the shaman, her crisis precipitated her vocation and devotion to the role of visionary poet. The act of writing about one's inner life, conflicts, joys, and friendships of course possesses therapeutic properties. By expressing hidden emotions, one to some extent exorcizes them and finds a way to deal with and ultimately transform them. This is often the function of a journal or diary. The task of then transforming this raw material into the form of the poem, story, essay, or novel demands a further discipline which is precisely what Di Prima now set herself to undergo.

She now matriculated at the intellectually elite Hunter High School in the winter of 1948 and became close friends with Audre Lorde (1934–92) who would become a distinguished writer: Di Prima later published Lorde's work in her Poets Press. As a black lesbian, Lorde would—like Di Prima— have several "identities" and in her work delineated the complexities of selfhood which would match Di Prima's as well as Gloria Anzaldua's multiple orientations. In her "biomythography" *Zami: A New Spelling of My Name* (1982), Lorde declared:

> Being women together was not enough. We were different. Being gay-girls together was not enough. We were different. Being Black together was not enough. We were different. Being Black women together was not enough. We were different. Being Black dykes together was not enough. We were different. . . . It was a while before we came to realize that our place was the very house of difference rather than the security of any one particular difference.

Robert Reid-Pharr has correctly observed that what is striking about reading Lorde's work "is not so much that she ignores questions of identity and origin, but instead that she is always careful to never be overwhelmed by them." Zora Neale Hurston in "How It Feels to Be Colored Me" also announced "I belong to no race nor time. I am the eternal feminine with its string of beads. I have no separate feeling about being an American citizen and colored. I am merely a fragment of the Great Soul that surges within the boundaries." Hurston conceived of her essential selfhood to be beyond the categories of "race" or "ethnicity." bell hooks—a serious student of Buddhism—has made similar declarations concerning the fraught question of "identity": "Asked to define myself, I wouldn't start with race; I wouldn't start from blackness; I wouldn't start with gender, with feminism. I would start by stripping down to what fundamentally informs my life, being a seeker on the path. Feminist and antiracist struggles are part of this journey. I stand spiritually, steadfastly, on a path of love— that's the ground of my being." It is precisely here that Di Prima—like Lorde, Hurston and hooks—breaks from the "essentialist" argument that women—as members of the gender "women"—have an intrinsic, shared "identity." Di Prima today might be considered to be espousing a gender queer position in which she seeks to avoid categorizing herself into one "identity." One may see here the connection with Buddhism as well since a central aspect of Buddhist thought is denying that such a thing as the "self" exists. Like hooks, Di Prima had from the beginning been "a seeker on the path," and for her the path led beyond various forms of category-making and reductionism.

One area of "particular difference" which Di Prima shared with Audre Lorde was an interest in the occult: the two belonged to a writing group composed of eight women calling themselves "The Branded" who met periodically to practice telepathy, magic trance, and seances to communicate with the dead—Keats and Shelley were among the favorite figures they attempted to contact.[17] While a flirtation with the paranormal marks many youths' adolescent phase—for example, experimenting with Ouija boards was a common experience among young people in America during the 1950s and 1960s—in Di Prima's case this fascination with occult studies was of central importance in her intellectual development: it would ultimately become an abiding preoccupation throughout her career and provided a seemingly inexhaustible fund of symbolic imagery for her writings. Indeed, as Ann Braude has documented in *Radical Spirits: Spiritualism and Women's Rights in Nineteenth-Century America*, the involvement two centuries ago of women in spiritualism was tied to their commitments to the Abolitionist movement and the struggle for sexual and political freedom. Thus Di Prima in the late 1940s in her emphasis on the personal rather than on fitting into institutions and orthodoxies, on inner experience and mystical explorations tied to political and social liberation was carrying on a venerable American tradition and was already anticipating—as did the Beats—the efflorescence of philosophical seeking which would mark the 1960s and the hippie movement. As we shall see in Chapter 3, this esoteric dimension of her thought reappeared in 1965 when she began in New Mexico studying Tarot cards which led to episodes of lucid dreaming and eventually to a quest for the hidden

FIGURE 1.2 *Audre Lorde. © Dagmar Schulz.*

roots of European spiritual traditions.[18] She also took four years of Latin courses, which would prove useful in both her translations of medieval Latin love poetry and studies of Renaissance figures such as Robert Fludd who composed their texts in Latin. A final important aspect of Di Prima's high-school career was her editing of the school publication *Scribimus*. This signaled what was to become a lifetime involvement in the practical aspects of the literary life: working in bookstores, mimeographing, buying and operating a printing press, starting her own publishing ventures The Poets Press and Eidolon Editions and her celebrated editing—with LeRoi Jones/Amiri Baraka for a period—of *The Floating Bear*.[19]

Although her years at Hunter were intellectually stimulating and replete with new discoveries and friendships, it was a time when Di Prima began to be starkly confronted with prejudice. She recalled that

> the most painful demonstration of my Otherness came in high school where I least understood it. It was in no way overt bigotry, but for that reason was even more difficult to identify and deal with. It took me many years to see it for what it was, but in the intellectual climate of the high school I went to, my love of "romantic" classical music, of opera, of *emotion* in art, in general was viewed simply as bad taste. Something I needed to be trained out of, or get over. Some kind of error in my perceptions which should be corrected, and, as they told me, I was very smart and it therefore could be corrected.
>
> It was years before I understood that my aesthetics is cultural: it comes from a world view that includes feeling, and does not see it as suspect. A world view in which feeling is at least as important as intellect, and where intuition the "I-feel-it-in-my-gut" level of information is respected.

Di Prima's Italian, Mediterranean culture was the polar opposite of the
Anglo-Saxon sensibility. We remember that in Nikos Kazantzakis's *Zorba
the Greek*, the uptight Englishman must be taught by Zorba how to dance
on the beach, how to flow with his passions and body and to leave behind—
at least for the time being—his fears and inhibitions. One is reminded of
another famous Englishman who was at war with the repressed sensibility
of his homeland—D. H. Lawrence—who counseled in his famous letter:
"My great religion is a belief in the blood, the flesh, as being wiser than
the intellect. We can go wrong in our minds. But what our blood feels and
believes and says, is always true. The intellect is only a bit and a bridle."[19]
In a sense, Di Prima strove to *balance* thought and feeling in her work, for
although she often "wears her heart on her sleeve," she was rigorous in her
unrelenting intellectual curiosity and in her approach to the art and craft
of poetry.

Two other important discoveries for the young Di Prima were dance and
the films of Jean Cocteau. Her intense fascination with dancing began at
age fifteen in 1949 when she began attending the New Dance Group on
East 59th Street and nourishing ambitions of entering the profession.[20] She
learned about the three "schools" of modern dance, practiced by Martha
Graham, Hanya Holm, and Jose Limon. Later in life she would compare
the difficult, challenging work of the classes she attended to her experiences
with Zen Buddhism at the *zendo*: dance concerts also became for her a
kind of "ritual religion."[21] She found in the balance, symmetry, and freedom
of bodies in expressive motion a way to release pent-up tensions which
had accumulated within her psyche and body from a traumatic family life
and the anxieties of postatomic America. Wilhelm Reich (1897–1957)—a
significant figure for Di Prima and the Beats (William S. Burroughs, for
example, famously constructed an orgone box to stimulate sexual energy)—
had theorized about the "armored personality" and how neurosis builds
itself up in the very structure of our physical bodies and may be released
through full genital orgasm. In dance, Di Prima declared that she had found
an intimacy with her own body greater than that which she had achieved
from any lover and felt a sublime sense of oneness with her own flesh.[22]
Experimenting with the form and content of contemporary "abstract" dance
also became connected in Di Prima's aesthetics with the composition of her
plays and poetry, for she would employ similar spontaneous and chance
techniques in her literary work. She would contribute a significant essay to
The Carolina Quarterly demonstrating how seriously she was devoted to
the art both as practitioner and theorist.

Her parents were ambitious for their daughter to complete high
school swiftly—earlier in her academic studies they had pushed her to
skip a grade—thus she spent two summers taking classes at Washington
Irving High School: she now viewed her first film by Jean Cocteau—
The Blood of the Poet.[23] She admired several Cocteau movies, including

Les Enfants Terribles, The Eagle with Two Heads, Les Parents Terribles, and *Eternal Return*. As with dance, the French poet and filmmaker's work was immediately compelling as if he was speaking to her directly and personally. Cocteau had a sense of "Magick," the gift to connect light and time in a miraculous fashion. He could transform reality through bending it to his will and made space and time appear to be relative concepts.[24] Cocteau's films are one of the ways that Di Prima began to explore the "metaphysics of light" which was confirmed with her reading of medieval philosopher Robert Grosseteste in 1959. Di Prima studied physics at Swarthmore and considered becoming a theoretical physicist, thus questions regarding light, space, and time were of particular interest, and she suggests that as in Einstein's theory, they were relative concepts. And we also note the spelling of magic as "Magick" in the manner of British occultist Aleister Crowley (1875–1947)—the word appeared first in his *Magick in Theory and Practice* (1929)—whose work Di Prima included in her syllabus for her course on "Hidden Religions in the Literature of Europe." Crowley's philosophy of *Thelema*—derived from ancient Greek *thelein* or "to will"— was encapsulated in the formula "The Science and Art of causing Change to occur in conformity with Will." Thus for Di Prima, one aspect of the art of film is that it allows one to shape reality: it is thus—like all art—a kind of *Magick*, the ultimate purpose of which is to discover one's true self. William S. Burroughs—echoing Crowley whom he had studied closely—in his essay "On Coincidence" declared: "I will speak now for magical truth, to which I myself subscribe. Magic is the assertion of *will*, the assumption that nothing happens in this universe (that is to say the minute fraction of the universe that we are able to contact) unless some entity *wills* it to happen." Di Prima would come to conceive of the poet as a kind of Magus, a "co-creator with God," a notion which she derived from Giordano Bruno and to which she will return in her essay "Role of the Hermetic in Poetry" (1982). It is clear that for her the "peak experiences" which we achieve through music, dance, literature, painting, and film suggest that the purposes of art and spiritual life may be said to be connected. Art, magic, and religion: the categories seem to fuse in such a way that their essential goals are difficult to clearly distinguish from one another. All seek to empower the self in such a way that the hidden mysteries of existence are revealed to it through the operation of will which causes something transformative to *happen*. Art, magic and religion are all performances that humans *do*, created through the agency of imagination and brought into being through ritualized action.

When it came time to select a college, her parents set three criteria for their daughter to meet: she needed to obtain a scholarship; it should be a small institution; and it must not be more than three hundred miles away from Brooklyn so Di Prima might return home on weekends. She was accepted at Swarthmore College in Pennsylvania, receiving the second highest amount of scholarship money—$300—and was informed that the highest sum of $1,000 was awarded only to those with English surnames. Before she left home, her father warned: "Now, don't expect too much. I want you to always remember that you are Italian"—thus implying that the bigotry she would encounter would of necessity limit her ability to be successful.[25] Thus Di Prima matriculated in 1951 and she swiftly found college life uncongenial: she felt the environment inhibited her ability to write. In the book of stories *Dinners and Nightmares* (1961), she declared that

> it was impossible to work at school. Which was true enough, in that place if you locked your door when you opened it there were four people sitting outside wondering whether or not you had killed yourself. I mean to say you had no privacy. Somebody went home from that place, thanksgiving that year and walked through the dining room where her folks were sitting and to the big french window and on out. Four flights up. It was that kind of school.[26]

She was appalled by "the pretentious, awkward intellectual life, clipped speech, stiff bodies, unimaginative clothes, poor food, frequent alcohol, and deathly mores by which I find myself surrounded. This is much worse than preferring Buxtehude to Bach. I cannot imagine four years in this place; I feel I've been buried alive."[27] It is also likely that "class differences" played a role in Di Prima's reactions. She identified—as she would throughout her life— not with the white Anglo-Saxon Protestant ruling Establishment of America and the class-based separations which the Ivy League and "competitive" private colleges perpetuated, but rather with the "ethnic minorities" of which she was a member. It is likely that she felt that by remaining at such a "pretentious" institution she was betraying her loyalty to a set of aesthetic and ethical principles which by necessity required her to be an "outsider" to the America of the 1950s, rather than preparing herself for a "career" by remaining in college. Finally, her main goal was to become a writer: everything else which got in the way of this goal she would jettison.

While at Swarthmore, Di Prima kept a diary—as she would throughout her life—in which she would confide not only her personal experiences but also record excerpts from her reading as well as ideas for her own projects. For example, in one diary entry she described a student party during which "Dabney and I rotated round each other like one of Van der Kamp's double stars, and Gorky brooded silently on the edge of things"—Peter Van de Kamp (1901–95) was a renowned Swarthmore astronomer.[28] Ultimately, the one aspect of college life she found most useful was the bookstore: there she discovered Ezra Pound and charged to her account—a bill she confessed she only finally paid off in the late 1980s—*The Cantos*, *The Spirit of Romance*, *Make It New*, as well as volumes by e. e. cummings and T. S. Eliot.[29] By Christmas of 1952, she had made the final choice to leave, helped in her decision by a girl named Lori by whom she was smitten. Lori was in love with Di Prima's best friend Joan O'Malley who appears in *Spring and Autumn Annals: A Celebration of the Seasons for Freddie* as well as *Memoirs of a Beatnik* where she is named O'Reilly.[30] When she informed her parents that she was leaving college, her father began screaming, picked Di Prima up, and flung her at the feet of her mother. She had just turned eighteen a few months previously and would now confront the world as a struggling writer.[31]

2

Return to New York:

From Ezra Pound to the *I Ching*, 1953–60

Following Christmas vacation, Di Prima spent three more weeks at Swarthmore and—knowing she would not return—did not study for final exams: February 2, 1953, was her last day in residence.[1] Now, at the age of eighteen she was back in New York and found a small apartment—521 East Fifth Street between Avenues A and B—at forty-five dollars a month in the Lower East Side's Polish neighborhood.[2] Although she had left college, Di Prima had not entirely abandoned academia: she now in a sense set about reconstructing her own private university. She attended the New School for Social Research, enrolled in a class in integral calculus at Brooklyn College where she earned a perfect score on her midterm examination, and also studied the theory of equations at Columbia. This mathematical and scientific talent—she had studied physics at Swarthmore—will appear later in her studies of the Renaissance magus John Dee (1527–1608/9). She also devoted herself to texts recommended by Ezra Pound (1885–1972) in *The ABC of Reading* (1934). Di Prima obtained a grammar of Homeric Greek—she also took a course in Greek at Hunter College—sounded out passages from the *Iliad*, read Dante in Italian, and continued to compose poetry.[3] Throughout her life, as we have seen, Di Prima would keep extensive diaries and notebooks, perhaps inspired by the example of Mary Shelley's journals:

> Insofar as I knew/acknowledged Womanhood, it was as Mary Shelley I saw myself. Her journals had been models for me of what could be done. And how to accomplish it. Terse and unimpassioned, they recorded even death in a monotone, and then went on in the same entry to say who had visited, what she was reading. Some might call the journals cold.

In her diary entry for May 11, 1953, she reflected on the decision to leave
Swarthmore:

> And what I am doing, I know is right, because only when I have made
> something by myself, without all the people will I be able to give myself
> without guilt to their lives and to the cycles that drive me, first to them
> and then into myself. Only when I have proven myself will the cycles
> become beautiful and right and then I shall live in them without self-
> questioning, and without fear. . . . And by September this round will be
> over, and I shall have gotten the first "creating" done, and will allow
> myself the first people spree.[4]

She would work at a variety of jobs including as an editor at a Columbia
University electronics lab; a file clerk in an office on Wall Street; and also
at Larry Wallrich's celebrated Phoenix Bookstore—later to be owned by
Robert Wilson—located at 18 Cornelia Street. Di Prima plunged into the
city's cultural life—dance, painting, poetry, and music and film would all be
of central significance. During the 1940s and 1950s in New York, all of these
fields of endeavor were interconnected: poets were friends with painters;
choreographers spent time with composers—one thinks here obviously of
Merce Cunningham and John Cage; filmmakers knew people in the literary
world; Willem and Elaine de Kooning attended a recital of John Cage and
Merce Cunningham; Robert Rauschenberg designed sets for the Judson
Dance Group; the Beat poets spent time with the Abstract Expressionists
and went to jazz concerts by Thelonious Monk. Di Prima spent days at the
Metropolitan Museum of Art, MOMA, and the Whitney, listened to Miles
Davis at Café Bohemia, and attended dance concerts and films. She also
saw Dylan Thomas (1914–53) several times when he was drinking at the
White Horse Tavern. She responded to his ecstatic lyricism and resonant
voice, listening often to his famous recordings: upon his early death on
November 9, 1953, at the age of thirty-nine, she felt time momentarily stood
still, later confessing in her prose work *The Calculus of Variation*—subtly
echoing the phrasing of John Milton's great elegy "Lycidas"—"I even once
sat on the lawn at Brooklyn College and wept for Dylan Thomas, he was
dead."[5] Of course a young and now Nobel Prize–winning musician and
poet greatly influenced by the Beats to whom Di Prima would dedicate her
Revolutionary Letters—born Bob Zimmerman in Hibbing, Minnesota—
would take Dylan's name for his own.

One of the most significant events of this first year back in New York
was her meeting with Freddie Herko, whom she encountered at Washington
Square Park one day while he was sitting alone in the rain on a bench.
She invited him to Rienzi's—a coffeehouse where Di Prima was "tolerated"
even though they were not particularly fond of "beatniks" on their premises
because she knew some Italian—and spent several hours conversing.

Herko had been studying at Juilliard with the intention of becoming a pianist, but dropped out to pursue a career in dance: he became one of Di Prima's closest friends over the next twelve years. He too had suffered from abusive parents and Di Prima would later publish *Poems for Freddie* (1966) chronicling their relationship. Di Prima had been born with spinal stenosis and developed a swayed back, thus her mobility had been hampered: she confessed in her diary that although she had studied dance with great pleasure for several years, she realized she "did not become a great dancer. This was the last thing that happened before I went home, and perhaps it has something to do with my strategic withdrawal."[6] Thus Herko reenergized Di Prima's already intense fascination with dance and would become in a sense a symbolic second self for her. In an essay published in 1955 in *The Carolina Quarterly* entitled "Movement and Tableau in the Dance," she argued that "dance shares with acting and musical interpretation a degree of transience that is unknown in other arts. It is an art embodied in the human body of an artist, an art without inanimate material expression outside the world of humans. This is its charm and its failing. It is what gives all 'show business' its strange and terrible urgency."[7] Di Prima connects dance with both performing a piece of music and with an actor performing a play: these three arts all take place in time and are by nature evanescent and of the moment. She goes on to suggest that Ezra Pound's categories of logopoeia, melopoeia, and phanopoeia—which are introduced in Chapter Four of *ABC of Reading*—might usefully be applied to the dance as well, arguing that

> the significance of these divisions lies in the fact that they classify a work of art according to the means by which a reaction is produced in a spectator, rather than by the type or degree of the reaction itself. The advantage of this type of criticism is that it concerns itself with relatively knowable qualities: qualities inherent in the object itself, and not buried deep in the psyche of the spectator.

Di Prima discusses Jose Limon's "The Moor's Pavanne" and also singles out for praise Jerome Robbins's "Age of Anxiety": "You are dragged forward, protesting all the way, until, assailed by Mr. Bernstein's overpowering score, ingenious staging, and the fine dancing of Nora Kaye, you succumb to the very powerful spell of the piece, which is the spell of its message."[8] One of her earliest published writings, "Movement and Tableau in the Dance" demonstrates the precocious sensibility of its young author who is already attempting to elaborate practical aesthetic criteria for evaluating works of art.

Beginning in 1954 and over the next few years, Di Prima earned money by modeling for painters Raphael Soyer and Nicolai Ckovsky as well as a number of artists who from 1955 to 1957 had studios in the Lincoln Arcade: she describes this period in *The Calculus of Variation*. Soyer would paint a portrait of Allen Ginsberg and Gregory Corso and depicted Di Prima along with Ginsberg in his "Village East Street Scene" (1965–66). Several European artists were deeply involved with esoteric traditions such as Wassily Kandinsky, author of *Concerning the Spiritual in Art* (1912), and Piet Mondrian, who was influenced by Madame Helena Blavatsky, becoming a member of the Dutch Theosophical Society in May 1909. As Catherine Spretnak has demonstrated, several American painters such as Jackson Pollock, Mark Rothko, and Robert Motherwell were also influenced by occult as well as Eastern spiritual traditions. Di Prima met several of the important Abstract Expressionists including Franz Kline (1910–62), Mike Goldberg (1924–2007), Willem de Kooning (1904–97)—as we shall see in Chapter 5, she devoted several poems in *L. A. Odyssey* (1969) to de Kooning's paintings—as well as pop artists Larry Rivers (1923–2002), Andy Warhol (1928–87), Jim Dine (1935–), and Jasper Johns (1930–). Di Prima dedicated her poem "Magick in Theory & Practice"—the title comes from a book by Aleister Crowley—to Mike Goldberg and addresses herself "to all you with gaunt cheeks who sit/glamourized by the sounds of art in the/last remaining lofts, shining like gold in ore in the/sleek grime of NYC under the shadow/of MOMA."

Jim Dine's "Job #1" included objects such as pieces of wood, a screwdriver, paint brushes, and paint cans attached to the canvas. Dine employed chance techniques in his work and also participated in one of the many New York "Happenings" of the period. In *The Smiling Workman* (1960) performed at the Judson Church, he appeared in a red smock, his head as well as hands had been painted red and mouth black. He proceeded to drink from paint jars while simultaneously painting "I love what I'm . . ." on a canvas behind him. He then poured paint over his head and leaped through the canvas. Di Prima's poem "The House"—dedicated to Dine—includes Dadaesque and surreal images featured in his work: "a bird cawed across great distances/ another icicle grew out of the ceiling"; "the house was waiting, quite a number of bats/eating bananas/floated too close to the ceiling/& had their brains dashed out by icicles/the floor was slimy with them/those who pushed unicycles, mostly angels/followed the signs w/out waving to anyone." Di Prima here exhibits a sinuous sensitivity, calling up vividly the absurdist and comic aspects of Dine's art, juxtaposing as in surrealism unicycles and angels, and yet suggesting a possibly hidden meaning encoded in her seemingly random images. Dine would later make a gift to Di Prima of one of his assemblages. Another Di Prima's poem, "Folly Beach," is dedicated to Jasper Johns who would become a subscriber to *The Floating Bear*. Johns grew up in South Carolina, and Folly Beach is located on Folly Island, south of Charleston. The poem describes Di Prima attending one of his exhibitions and the final stanza contains a catty allusion to a well-known dancer with the Merce Cunningham Dance Company: "Keen eyes of mosaic figures. Elegance/haughty & fat, like Valda Setterfield."

Di Prima now also made important contacts in the poetry world. She met Ted Joans (1928–2003) and they exchanged work in progress. Joans had discovered surrealism as a child when his mother gave him copies of *Minotaure* and he corresponded with Andre Breton to whom he declared: "The white poets of the Beat Generation have borrowed the hipster attitude from black Americans. They have adopted their argot, comportment, and jazz music—all of which embody a surrealist point of view. The Beat Generation owes practically everything to surrealism. I have discussed this subject with Kerouac, Corso, and Ginsberg." Di Prima would spend time with Joans in the Rienzi Café, and just as the cafes of Paris would provide thinking and writing spaces for Jean-Paul Sartre, Simone di Beauvoir, and Henry Miller, so too the cafes and bars of the East Village—such as the Tenth Street Coffee House on E. 7th Street and Le Metro Café on Second Avenue near 9th Street—became locales to both socialize and perform poetry readings for Di Prima, as well as authors such as Jackson Mac Low, Jerome Rothenberg, and Paul Blackburn.[9] However, as a woman, fitting into the emerging Beat scene proved challenging. W. J. Rorabaugh has observed that among the Beats—to put it mildly—women were often unfairly treated:

> To the Beat writers, women were sex objects; even in that role, women sometimes had to compete with men. While parents rarely minded a son moving to the Village to try out the Beat lifestyle, they vehemently opposed a daughter taking the same course of action. During the Fifties respectable middle-class young men could do things that young women could not do without being considered sluts or prostitutes. Parents might even try to commit a sexually promiscuous daughter to a mental institution. Beat gatherings had a big gender gap. Only a handful of Beat women, including the poet Diane di Prima, achieved fame. Talented women found it difficult to be accepted in a subculture ruled by highly competitive male poets, some of whom degraded or denigrated women. Public performances of poetry before largely male Beat audiences also inhibited women. Women like di Prima, the poet Denise Levertov, or the painter Joan Brown were rare.

However, Di Prima was able over the next decade—through strength of will, a fiercely independent spirit, discipline, and sheer hard work—to overcome many of the obstacles in her path. By opposing the typical gender stereotypes of the period, she was able to remake herself in such a fashion that she was not beholden to any vested interests of the Establishment and the literary world as then constituted.

In 1955, she began to correspond with Ezra Pound, sent him samples of her work and in spring, 1956, visited him with Pound's mistress Sheri Martinelli for two weeks at St. Elizabeth's in Washington, DC, where he had been incarcerated for "insanity/treason." During his almost thirteen years at St. Elizabeth's, Pound would be visited by virtually every significant American poet including T. S. Eliot, John Berryman, Elizabeth Bishop, Robert Lowell, Marianne Moore, William Carlos Williams, and Charles Olson. His passionate curiosity—Di Prima found Pound coherent, engaging, and voluble—as well as generosity made a deep impression on her. Late in her career, she composed an elegy for her maestro—"November 2, 1972 (for Ezra Pound)"—recalling: "remember I visited you/at 'St. Liz'/yr civil talk; the ravings of madmen around you/you handed me stolen food as I left/saying 'line those stomachs'/saying 'poets have to eat'/and walked me courteously to yr door/and waited for the warden to unlock it."[10] Di Prima contrasts Pound's "civil talk"—she likely meant this to suggest the double meaning of Pound's politeness and culture as well as his obsession in *The Cantos* and throughout his work with the idea of "civilization"—to the babble of the "madmen around you" and we also observe how Di Prima imitated Pound's telegraphic—as did Robert Creeley—idiosyncratic abbreviations as in her employment of "yr" in place of "your" or "sd" for "said." Pound would be a major influence on virtually all the Beats: John Clellon Holmes contributed an essay to a volume entitled *"What Thou Lovest Well Remains": 100 Years of Ezra Pound*; Gary Snyder learned from his precise, Chinese imagism; Allen Ginsberg made a pilgrimage to visit him in Venice; Ferlinghetti composed a poem in his homage.

As we shall see in later chapters, there were four key areas of Poundian influence on Di Prima's emerging aesthetics. First, Pound was well versed in heterodox thought as demonstrated in the chapter "Neo-Platonicks Etc." in *Guide to Kulchur* where he discusses the translator of Plotinus's *Enneads* Gemistos Plethon (ca. 1355–1452/1454), Marsilio Ficino (1433–99), Porphyry, Iamblichus, and Hermes Trismegistus: these sources would ultimately form the basis for Di Prima's own poetics. These works may be said to be esoteric in nature and the term derives from ancient Greek, *esoterikos*—belonging to an inner circle. Aristotle's works have been divided by some scholars into two categories: esoteric treatises intended to be used with advanced students within Aristotle's school; and exoteric works intended for the general public. Pound had also been the secretary of W. B. Yeats (1865–1939) who was a devotee of the Theosophy of Madame Helena Blavatsky (1831–91) and became a member of the Hermetic Order of the Golden Dawn, a secret society with which Aleister Crowley was associated. Pound also knew several significant figures in literary London such as the renowned scholar of Hermetic traditions, G. R. S. Mead as well as A. R. Orage, editor of *The New Age*. In *Guide to Kulchur*, Pound invoked the ancient mysteries, declaring "that prose is NOT education but the outer courts of the same. Beyond its doors are the mysteries. Eleusis. Things not to be spoken save in secret. The mysteries self-defended, the mysteries that cannot be revealed. Fools can only profane them. The dull can neither penetrate the secretum nor divulge it to others."[11] Robert Duncan—who would become an important figure in Di Prima's career—concisely summarized Pound's spiritual significance for his own work as well as for the Beats. Duncan declared that Pound in "*The Cantos* returns again and again to speak with sublime and ecstatic voice. In his affinity for Plotinus, Proclus, Iamblichus, or the ninth-century Erigenia, in his poetic cult of the sublime Aphrodite ('crystal body of air') and of Helios, not without Hellenistic hermetic overtones, in his fascination with form in nature ('germinal') having signature, Pound, as does H.D. in her later work, revives in poetry a tradition or kabbalah that would unite Eleusis and the Spirit of Romance." Duncan alludes here to the literal meaning of the Hebrew word *kabbalah* which means "tradition" or "something received."

Secondly, Di Prima would consistently employ the techniques of imagism in many of her poems. Pound defined the image as

that which presents an intellectual and emotional complex in an instant of time. . . . It is the presentation of such a "complex" instantaneously which gives that sense of sudden liberation; that sense of freedom from time limits and space limits; that sense of sudden growth, which we experience in the presence of the greatest works of art.

This definition for Di Prima also bears a philosophical meaning, for Pound's poetics is centered in a mode of sudden perception of enlightenment, or *gnosis*. The image must be presented concisely and Di Prima later acknowledged a fundamental lesson that she took from Pound: "the precise word, precise description, eliminating the extra word." Thirdly, this Gnostic philosophy had one source in Provencal culture—a subject of intense scholarly interest for Pound—and would later furnish Di Prima with the idea for *Loba* which she derived from Pound's allusion to the Old Occitan troubadour Peire Vidal. *Loba* also contains references to the great Cathar stronghold of Montsegur which Di Prima celebrates as a locus of Gnostic rebellion against church authority. And finally, in several poems throughout her career, Di Prima conducted an ongoing dialogue with Pound: with his philosophical ideas, his sometimes eccentric political and economic notions, and with his poetics. She would often allude to particular Pound poems or adapt his formal experiments to her own ends. For example, her poem "Apparuit" takes its title from Pound's eponymous poem composed in sapphics from *Personae* (1909) which refers to Dante's description of first seeing Beatrice in his *Vita Nuova*: she is a marvelous apparition, a wondrous beauty. Di Prima's "Apparuit" transforms the "message" of Pound's poem from an idealization of womanhood into a stark declaration of accepting woman in all her complex powers and roles: "she is serene/with grace & gentleness of the warrior/the spear/the harp the book the butterfly/are equal/in her hands."[12] This is a woman who is poised, kind, and fully competent to fight, hunt, play a musical instrument, study and appreciate nature:

a Renaissance Woman equal to a Renaissance Man. Di Prima would also allude to several verses from Pound's "Sestina: Altaforte" in one of her greatest poems, "Canticle to St. Joan" and also compose an homage to Pound in the rigorously strict sestina form.

Pound's orientation toward esoteric philosophical sources as well as his immersion in Chinese classics appealed to Di Prima as she began to develop as a writer. Her intellectual and artistic quest during the 1950s of course evolved against the backdrop of several crises which marked the Cold War period. Joseph McCarthy began his anti-Communist witch-hunting, and Julius and Ethel Rosenberg were executed in 1953. Di Prima when recalling this time often emphasized the prevailing sense of fear and foreboding. In an American culture which seemed bent on self-destruction and totally devoted to materialistic values, she began to see her position as essentially that of the religious outsider. She had already conceived her role as artist as devoted to a sacred mission, describing her task as that of a renunciant, a wandering saint, a sadhu (in Hinduism or Jainism a religious ascetic), or a bhikshuni (in Buddhism a fully ordained female monastic). She inscribed on the walls of her apartment to *kalon, kalon aiei*: in Greek, "the beautiful, the beautiful forever." Like John Keats and his "Ode to a Grecian Urn," she sought Truth as Beauty, Beauty as Truth, and the role of the artist was to be a rebel and explorer of unknown realms of consciousness. Thus Di Prima had independently already embarked on an intellectual path which the predominantly male Beat authors had also begun to discover and also notably emphasizes that it is a quest which she is undertaking as a female. This is significant for Di Prima's declaration that woman's spiritual unfoldment is of equal importance to that of men. The female bhikshuni, priestess, shaman has the right to equal respect as her male counterparts. One notes as well the ways Di Prima integrates the British romantic tradition of John Keats's poetry with Buddhist sacred practice: this is also a significant aspect of Beat poetics in the continual emphasis upon a rapprochement between Western and Eastern traditions.

Upon reading *Howl*, she realized Allen Ginsberg had now opened up American poetry to a new consciousness, recognizing him as a kindred spirit. In *Memoirs of a Beatnik* (1969) Di Prima recalled:

> I knew that this Allen Ginsberg, whoever he was, had broken ground for all of us—all few hundreds of us—simply by getting this published. I had no idea yet what that meant, how far it would take us. . . . We had come of age. I was frightened and a little sad. I already clung instinctively to the easy, unself-conscious Bohemianism we had maintained at the pad, our unspoken sense that we were alone in a strange world, a sense that kept us proud and bound to each other. But for the moment regret for what we might be losing was buried under a sweeping sense of exhilaration, of glee; somebody was speaking for all of us, and the poem was good. I was

high and delighted. I made my way back to the house and to supper, and we read *Howl* together, I read it aloud to everyone. A new era had begun.

Ginsberg was also employing the same type of colloquial, hip, "street language" as Di Prima in her own early poetry and he shared her mystical and visionary gifts. His poetry was dense with allusions to esoteric traditions: for example, in *Howl* he had packed into one line: "who studied Plotinus Poe St. John of the Cross and bop Kabbalah"—in an earlier draft the list included "Gurdjieff Reich Fludd and Vico." Ginsberg acknowledged that the "overt intention of this mystical name-dropping was to connect to younger readers, Whitman's children already familiar with Poe and Bop, to older Gnostic tradition. Whitman dropped such hints to his fancied readers." We note also the innovative Beat spiritual syncretism in "bop Kabbalah" which combines avant-garde jazz with the great Jewish mystical tradition. So too as we saw above, Di Prima could easily synthesize her love of John Keats and the search for beauty and truth with the interior quest in Buddhist tradition. Furthermore, this "older Gnostic tradition" invoked by Ginsberg also nourished the poetry and prose of Di Prima. Over the following four decades, the two poets became close friends and beginning in 1974, Di Prima taught at the Naropa Institute in Boulder, Colorado, where Chogyam Trungpa, Gregory Corso, Anne Waldman, William S. Burroughs, and Ginsberg all lectured.

She now corresponded with Lawrence Ferlinghetti, sent Kenneth Patchen a letter on January 28, 1956, and met Kerouac, Ginsberg, and Corso during the winter of 1957 in New York when they were en route to visit William Burroughs in Morocco. Di Prima shared with the Beats not only their philosophical orientation, but also a devotion to jazz and solidarity with the African American experience. One of the great moments for her during this period was hearing Billie Holiday's concert at Carnegie Hall on November 10, 1956, declaring that Holiday "was already for many of us the supreme artist, the one with no equal."[13] Later in her career, other singers such as Janis Joplin would also speak to her of the suffering and heartbreak of women's experience, but also joy in unfettered creative expression. Di Prima would become close with several African American writers including Audre Lorde, A. B. Spellman, Amiri Baraka, and Ted Joans and would be active during the 1960s and 1970s in the struggle for justice for African Americans as demonstrated in the *Revolutionary Letters* which celebrates the courage of the Black Panthers.

Finally, another significant influence of the mid-1950s was choreographer James Waring whom Di Prima met in 1956: he became an important mentor over the next two decades.[14] She had already begun reading D. T. Suzuki's books on Zen and now explored both Buddhism and "meditative composition" with Waring. Di Prima had long felt estranged from orthodox religion. She and her generation were suspicious of religion for people would inquire whether one was Catholic, Protestant, or Jewish—Americans only accepted Judeo-Christianity which she and her compatriots found limiting.[15] Waring was close friends with avant-garde composer John Cage who was a serious student of Zen as well as dancer Merce Cunningham and Di Prima learned from these artists an appreciation for spontaneity and randomness. Instead of struggling to fashion her poetry and prose through the dominating control of a mastering ego, she began experimenting with Cage's aleatoric techniques and improvisatory dance style of Cunningham.[16] Furthermore, Zen counseled allowing the mind to achieve what Martin Heidegger called—after Meister Eckhart—*Gelassenheit*, or "letting things be." Learning to "let go" is an often difficult task for those trained in Western educational systems for there is a great emphasis on "getting things done," "setting goals," and "achieving 'success'" in modern, technological culture and on the power and prestige of the "ego" as controlling master of reality. As Di Prima asserted in an essay on Buddhism's influence on her work composed later in her career, she first learned about Zen in the mid-1950s from the essays of D. T. Suzuki:

> What then appeared to us to be a Zen point of view was soon taken for granted as the natural—one might say axiomatic—mind-set of the artist. A kind of clear seeing, combined with a very light touch, and a faith in what one came up with in the work: a sense, as Robert Duncan phrased it years later, that "consciousness itself is shapely." A kind of disattachment goes with this aesthetic: "you"—that is your conscious controlling self—didn't "make" the work, you may or may not understand it, and in a curious way you have nothing to lose: you don't have to make it into your definition of "good art." A vast relief.[17]

Buddhism in its several varying traditions—Zen, Vajrayana, Tibetan—would remain of central significance for Di Prima throughout her life, and as we shall see in later chapters a shaping influence on her developing aesthetics and poetics.

In addition, Hermann Hesse's novella about the life of Buddha, *Siddhartha* was published in English translation (1951)—interestingly thorough the advocacy of a great American admirer of Hesse, Henry Miller—and became a bestseller among the 1960s flower children. Aldous Huxley's *The Doors of Perception* also appeared three years later in 1954, chronicling his profound experiences with mescaline. These texts indicated a major groundswell, the beginnings of a seismic shift in consciousness among thoughtful young people. As J. J. Clarke has argued in *Oriental Enlightenment: The Encounter between Asian and Western Thought*, it was during the Beat movement that the interest in Eastern philosophy emerged in American cultural life. But this was not the first time American writers and intellectuals had turned toward Asia for inner sustenance. A century previously, Henry David Thoreau,

Ralph Waldo Emerson, and Walt Whitman read the *Bhagavad Gita*, Buddhist texts, and studied the culture of the Native Americans and sought what the disciple of Whitman Richard M. Bucke called "cosmic consciousness": an epiphanic encounter with the deepest mysteries of the universe. In addition, the existentialist movement in France put great emphasis on authenticity and on actualizing one's own potential in responsible commitment to a cause which reflected one's own deepest values and aspirations. All of these cultural currents of course influenced Di Prima as she began to invent her own, personal syncretic form of belief to replace orthodox systems of faith which young people began to feel did not meet their deeper needs.

If Di Prima was rebelling against conventional notions of what one's "proper" religion should be, she was also breaking new ground in her personal relationships. Her first child Jeanne was born out of wedlock in 1957—she informed her partner matter-of-factly after her birth that he might want to come to visit his daughter—and Jeanne immediately became the center of Di Prima's life. Although the women's movement, sexual liberation, and the challenges to the nuclear family of the 1960s had not yet arrived, Di Prima was a pathbreaker. As Blossom S. Kirschenbaum would argue: "It was di Prima's stance, though, to live as though the revolution had already been accomplished—to separate sex from marriage and marriage from childrearing, and to improvise a quasi-familial supportive network." Jeanne was born in Gouverneur's, a hospital for the poor, and later Di Prima would recall in her autobiography *Recollections of My Life as a Woman* the oppression and terror she experienced there. This experience would appear also in *Loba*, where Di Prima describes her experiences in the poem "Nativity," the fourth poem in "Part 6: The Seven Joys of the Virgin." Although being a single mother was difficult, Di Prima began to establish herself as an independent and original force in the New York arts scene. Her work during the 1950s would absorb and reflect many of the influences we have sketched out previously and she met jazz musicians such as Cecil Taylor and writers Kenneth Rexroth, Edward Dahlberg, Paul Blackburn, Joel Oppenheimer, LeRoi Jones, Fielding Dawson, and Hubert Selby, Jr. (1928–2004). She frequently attended films with poet A. B. Spellman and Selby—author of the cult classic *The Last Train to Brooklyn* (1964), known to his friends as "Cubby." Dawson left her books by Robert Creeley and Charles Olson from the renowned experimental Black Mountain College in North Carolina which he had attended: Di Prima carefully studied and copied out their poems on her electric typewriter. She also discovered a book of line drawings by Henri Matisse published in the early 1950s. Impressed by his minimalist style and how much might be expressed through such a deft approach, she strove in her own work "to find the cleanest line that retained a lyric sense." This new, hip, "Beat" and succinct style was the essence of "cool" which according to Di Prima meant that "you had a lot of feeling but you just didn't state it, and nobody stated theirs.

Thus you built up this tension of all the unstated. It wasn't anger, but a web of interplay; things that you would say full out now, would then be stated in a small gesture—a little phrase or act would say the whole thing." The spare drawings of Picasso and Matisse, the newly discovered startlingly "modern" ancient Greek Cycladic sculptures with their striking angularity, the bare, non-vibrato style of Miles Davis's trumpet, the existential bravery of the antiheroes of Camus and Sartre, the unflinching taciturnity of film noir detectives: these were all "cool." One may see here a reaction against the "romantic" schmaltz of Hollywood and much contemporary culture: one may also posit that the threat of nuclear Armageddon compelled American youth into becoming "tough," into hiding their feelings out of fear of being pulverized and obliterated. Yet Di Prima did not endorse this new emotionally inhibited aspect of "cool." Indeed, she celebrated the warmth, joie de vivre and extroverted kindness of the Mediterranean sensibility.

This new cool aesthetic may be seen in the poems in Di Prima's first book—*This Kind of Bird Flies Backward*—which includes work composed as early as 1953. She began assembling the manuscript to be published by two young men who owned a print shop. Di Prima was enlisted to help by providing camera-ready copy which she typed out employing an IBM electric typewriter on a special coated stock paper. Ultimately the deal fell through, but in the meantime she had learned a great deal about the craft of printing in the process: over the next half-century she would be involved in a number of publishing ventures including her own Poets Press and Eidolon Editions. *This Kind of Bird Flies Backward* ultimately appeared as the first of thirteen pamphlets which LeRoi Jones—whom she met in 1958 and with whom she would have her second child, Dominique—printed on a small offset press under the Totem Press imprint, an offshoot of his important magazine *Yugen*.[18] Lawrence Ferlinghetti contributed "A Non-Introduction by Way of Introduction": "I don't know her, never saw her, never heard her. In the middle of the street is a manhole with a portable iron fence around it. And a sign: Poet At Work . . . . Here's a sound not heard before. The voice is gutty. The eye turns. The heart is in it."

Morris Dickstein has commented upon the Beats' intimate relationship with jazz, "which was undergoing a revolution in the 1940s, turning from large swing bands playing dance music to the amazing virtuosity of bop artists like Charlie Parker, Dizzy Gillespie, and Thelonious Monk. It was their improvisational freshness, complexity, and spontaneity that the Beats would try to recreate in their prose and poetry." In "Hymn," Di Prima paid tribute to John Coltrane as a sainted, spiritual figure "who brought us the flute and the bow/unchain in us the tears of longing and terror, of love/unleash us that we may speed again to thy side." Amiri Baraka described Coltrane's genius as "taking the music apart before our ears, splintering the chords and sounding each note, resounding it, playing it backward and upside down trying to get to something else." Di Prima would also dedicate her brief poem "Notes on

The Art of Memory" to Thelonious Monk: "The stars are a memory system/
for thru them/we remember our origin/Our home is behind the sun/or a
divine wind/that fills us/makes us think so."[19] This poem serves as homage
to Frances Yates's treatise *The Art of Memory* which traces the history of
mnemonic devices from antiquity through the Renaissance occultists as well
as to the inspired genius of Monk's music. As we shall see, several of Yates's
books became central in Di Prima's elaboration of her conception of the
"hidden religions" and she also required them as texts in her teaching. The
"divine wind that fills us" is *enthousiasmos*—in Greek the god within; or
inspiration, in Latin literally "to breathe into." When we look up at the night
sky covered with countless stars we sometimes feel a mysterious nostalgia,
as if our real "home" is not only planet Earth but that there is something
within us that corresponds to the matter out of which stars are also created.
The beauty of the stars reminds us that our destiny is cosmic. "Notes on
The Art of Memory" is a typical example of the ways Di Prima is able to
condense in a brief space a rich and complex pattern of imagery. For Di
Prima, the crystalline, syncopated, jagged, and Webern-like dissonant style
of Monk's inspired piano-playing is to be understood as seeking the same
unity of self and cosmos as the sages of antiquity and the occult magicians
of the Renaissance.

This Kind of Bird Flies Backward is replete with a new, jazz-inflected
language: "I don't forget things/fast enough, I sing/last summer's ballads/
winter long/like that's uncool"; or "August 1955": "I thought we'd dig a
coupla sets in hell"; "while you play square/games never out of bounds./Like
man don't flip, I'm hip you cooled/this scene. But you can hock the jazz/guitar,
in limbo they play ballads"; or in the poem "Riffs": SO BABE/WHO SEZ/
IT'S COOL/TO CUT/JUST CAUSE/THE HOUSE BURNED DOWN? walk
easy/hang loose/stay cool/just once/I dare you."[20] Yet this language—while
superficially "cool" in its seeming toughness, actually skewers the attitudes
of the bohemians in Di Prima's world, especially as related to male/female
relationships. For Di Prima, there is nothing wrong with being a "romantic"
who enjoys singing "last summer's ballads" during the winter, even though
it is considered "uncool." As Steven Belletto has pointed out, *This Kind of
Bird Flies Backward* "represents a female critique of Beat gender norms." If
to be "cool" means to lack sensitivity and awareness of others' feelings, it
is better to remain "uncool." As we shall see later, Di Prima's critique of the
ways the new generation has condemned the practices of their parents, but
not yet promulgated a truly liberatory philosophy, continues in *Dinners and
Nightmares* as well.

Along with these "Beat" poems, some of the lyrics are infused with
Christian religious imagery as in "January 17, 1955": "I wonder what
madness/has held me for a year, that I have not cracked/your sanctum
sanctorum, or dredged the Dead/Sea with my fingernails. . . ." The sanctum
sanctorum is of course the "Holy of Holies," while the *Dead Sea Scrolls* had

been discovered in a cave at Qumram in 1946–47. Other poems such as "Three Laments" are Zen-like koans illustrating Di Prima's characteristic comedic flair: (1) "alas/I believe/I might have become/a great writer/but/the chairs/in the library/were too hard" (2) "I have/the upper hand/but if I keep it/I'll lose the circulation/in one arm" (3) "So here I am the coolest in New York/what don't swing I don't push./In some Elysian field/by a big tree/I chew my pride/like cud."[21] Throughout her career, Di Prima never loses her sense of often boisterous and affirmative humor. While Jesus, it is reported, never laughed, one of the attractions of Zen for her was that it insisted on making self-mockery an essential part of the journey toward enlightenment. Zen was a positive form of "cool" for it aimed at disciplining the emotions in a way which allowed for deep feeling as well. The Zen monks of a thousand years ago were the original "cool cats" for they aimed at an affirmative rapport with the mysteries of life through being in tune with the ways of nature and through an often very modern sense of the paradoxies and absurdities of the human experience. If the Beats and hippies wanted to "be here now," then they were fulfilling an essential Zen precept.

Hip stylistic features recur in a sequence of poems entitled *Earthsong*, which while written from 1957 to 1959, were not published until 1968. Di Prima's characteristic wit appears in "The Passionate Hipster to His Chick," her homage to Christopher Marlowe's (1564–93) classic "The Passionate Shepherd to His Love":

Come live with me and be my love
And we will all the pleasures prove
That railroad flat or hot-rod wheel
Or tea-pads 3 AM conceal[22]

"Tea" was slang for marijuana and of course the pervasive "pad" one's domicile. Automobiles had become "hot-rods" for some adventurous youth while hitching a ride—as for Jack Kerouac and Neal Cassady—on railroad cars was a way to travel for free. In another poem, "Little Song for Later" occurs the verses: "so now.i know/I dig you/babe." Some of these terms from the 1940s and 1950s would continue to be employed by the hippie generation during the 1960s when it was not uncommon for someone to "dig"—or to greatly enjoy—some person or thing.

There is also a cycle of poems beginning with "Deathwatch—1" containing allusions to Di Prima's readings in Homer and classical literature for we find references to Hector, "Troy in the mud," "old Atlas," and "narcissus." In *Earthsong*, Achilles, Heracles, Ulysses, and Apollo appear, while in "Alba"—"the dawn/is rosy-fingered from fucking the mother of god"—an early example of the "obscenity" which will mark much Beat literature in tandem with Homer's famous epithet describing the lovely transition from night to day, "rosy-fingered dawn"—*rhododactylos Eos*.

Ezra Pound's first Canto of course is a magnificent, energetic translation in the style of the Seafarer of Book XI of Homer's Odyssey: "And then went down to the ship,/ Set keel to breakers, forth on the godly sea, and/We set up mast and sail on that swart ship." Both Pound and T. S. Eliot had formulated a modernist poetics which constantly counterpointed ancient literature and philosophy—both Western and Eastern—with contemporary concerns and this is a model which Di Prima and other Beat poets would follow. Her friend Philip Whalen ends his poem "Sourdough Mountain Lookout" with a phrase from the most celebrated Mahayana Buddhist sutra, the *Prajnaparamita,* the *Heart Sutra—Gate Gate Paragate Parasamgate Bodhi Svaha!* which he translates and modernizes into inimitable hipster lingo: "Gone/Gone/REALLY gone/Into the cool. O MAMA!" So too, while Di Prima is faultlessly "hip" and modern, her work is in constant dialogue with the past and with learned traditions. This is not an appropriation of "foreign" cultures—a criticism sometimes made of the counterculture's gravitation toward Native American or Asian or shamanic traditions—but rather an act of homage to those ideas and practices which nourished them in their quest for wisdom.

Earthsong contains one of Di Prima's best-known poems: here it is given no name but later was entitled "The Practice of Magical Evocation" when it appeared in *Selected Poems 1956-1975.* The poem is a response to Gary Snyder's "Praise for Sick Women" (1954) and in the later version, an epigraph—which is not in the original—appears from the Snyder work: "The female is fertile, and discipline (contra naturam) only confuses her." Di Prima opens with a declarative riposte: "i am a woman and my poems/are woman's: easy to say/this. The female is ductile/and/(stroke after stroke)/built for masochistic calm." Di Prima's "ductile" obviously responds to Snyder's "fertile"—"ductile" can mean both flexible and submissive and "stroke after stroke" in parentheses answers Snyder's parenthetical "contra naturam," against nature. Stroke may be both sexual intercourse and physical violence since the phrase is followed by "built for masochistic calm." In the second stanza, the speaker mockingly asserts "pelvic architecture functional," and "the cunt gets wide/and relatively sloppy/bring forth men children only." The unprecedented employment of the term "cunt" for "vagina" by a female poet illustrates the boldness which characterized Di Prima's poetics. The final stanza concludes:

woman, a veil thru which the fingering Will
twice torn
twice torn
          inside & out
the flow
what rhythm add to stillness
what applause?

The "veil" behind which woman's true identity is occluded and through which the "fingering Will"—a double metaphor of male sexual power—penetrates. Michael Davidson in *San Francisco Renaissance: Poetics and Community at Mid-Century* sees in the poem's ending an echo of W. B. Yeats's "Leda and the Swan" where "the raped Leda is 'so mastered by the brute blood of the air' that she assumes Zeus's 'knowledge with his power.' And after the rape, after the childbirth ('twice torn'), what does the woman receive from all this: 'what rhythm add to stillness/what applause?'"[23] In addition, Yeats's "A shudder in the loins engenders there/ The broken wall" may be interpreted as the violated female's hymen, as in Di Prima's "twice torn" chanted two times suggests repeated sexual aggression. Thus "The Practice of Magical Evocation" attempts to create through the lyrical and assertive "magic" of poetry a counter-practice to traditions of male patriarchy and entitlement.

Earthsong also contains poems illustrating Di Prima's ongoing cosmological thought. For example, in "Track" she reflects: "but there are holes in space . . ./all this about breaking gravity, what a farce!/You can't break time & distance: we revolve./Not around the sun, but around the space that/ Holds us from a thing . . ./How much time & what distance locks this orbit in place/No asteroid laughs at the sun: we revolve around/Silence."[24] From the beginning of her career, Di Prima explored the links between scientific and metaphysical questioning and we discover a pattern of posing philosophical quandaries and responses in poetic form. The concept of light—as both a central question for physicists and its meaning in terms of human spiritual evolution—becomes for Di Prima a primary trope. For example, in the poem "After Cavalcanti" we find the verses: "she lending light by looking/ makes Mozart/from day's dampness/she is the source/the sun/green springs where she bends her eyes/as soul/outstrips flesh/she surpasses soul." This is an adaptation of the Florentine Guido Cavalcanti (1255–1300) who was a major focus of Ezra Pound's scholarship—Pound includes a chapter on the Italian poet in *The Spirit of Romance* (1910)—and illustrates how for Cavalcanti, love and light are interweaving concepts. For Pound—as for Di Prima—Cavalcanti's works incarnated a tradition stretching back to the ancient Eleusinian mystery cults which continued through the Neoplatonic philosophers such as Plotinus and resurfaced in troubadour poets of the Middle Ages. As Pound lyrically announced in his "Credo": "I believe that a light from Eleusis persisted throughout the middle ages and set beauty in the song of Provence and of Italy." "A light from Eleusis" refers to the famous Eleusinian ceremonies of autumn—the Mysteria—which were conducted in the town of Eleusis near Athens to honor the goddess of grain Demeter and her daughter Persephone.[25] Indeed, Di Prima believed that "in certain ways Pound had a lot of hermetic knowledge of Europe" in his *Cantos* and she was rare among American poets in her appreciation of this central and generally unknown aspect of his work.

Pound had also admired the medieval philosopher Robert Grosseteste (1175–1253) who according to historian of astronomy John North "was one of the greatest of medieval scientists." Grosseteste produced a commentary on Aristotle's *Posterior Analytics*—probably composed in the 1220s—which was one of the first attempts to understand Aristotle's scientific method. Pound found Grosseteste's essay "De Luce" relevant to his own investigations of Cavalcanti's metaphysics of light and alluded to the philosopher in several of his *Cantos*, including numbers 55, 83, and 100. Peter Liebregts in *Ezra Pound and Neoplatonism* points out:

> This image of light is one of the dominant images in *The Cantos* and later prose works, and it is used by Pound in a Neoplatonic sense as an image to depict man's awareness of the permanent, a literal flash of insight. The image also links the various Neoplatonists in *The Cantos*, such as Robert Grosseteste, who hold that the essence of all bodies is light, through which each body, high or low, retains a link to its vital source. Johannes Scotus Eriugena's adage omnia quae sunt lumina sunt, "everything which is, is light" is a leitmotif of the poem, while light is also the central image in Canto XXXVI, Pound's translation of Guido Cavalcanti's "Donna mi prega," which describes Love as a form of Enlightenment.

Furthermore, in *Guide to Kulchur*, Pound declared:

> Grosseteste was a serious character . . . Grosseteste on Light may or may not be scientific but at least his mind gives us a structure. He throws onto our spectrum a beauty comparable to a work by Max Ernst. The mind making forms can verbally transmit them when the mental voltage is high enough. It is not absolutely necessary that the imagination be registered by sound or on painted canvas.

According to Grosseteste, light is the prime form of the cosmos and all substances are made up of light radiating at various intensities. David D. Lindberg has observed that Grosseteste's theory of the origin of the cosmos is

> an attempt to reconcile Neoplatonic emanationism—the idea that the created universe is an emanation from God, as light is an emanation from the sun—with the biblical account of creation ex nihilo . . . the cosmos came into existence when God created a dimensionless point of matter and its form, a dimensionless point of light. The point of light instantaneously diffused itself into a great sphere, drawing matter with it and giving rise to the corporeal cosmos.

One may see in Pound's elaboration of Grosseteste's cosmology a desire to correlate his conceptions of romantic love, the metaphysics of light, and his own poetics which turns on the centrality of the image as providing the momentary flash of *gnosis* or knowledge of the true self. We recall Dante's final beatific vision at the close of *Paradiso* XXXIII: "Nel suo profundo vidi che s'interna/legato con amore in un volume,/chi che per l'universo si squaderna/sustanze e accidenti e lor costume/quasi conflati insieme, per tal modo/che cio ch'I dico e un semplice lume"; (In that abyss I saw how love held bound/into one volume all the leaves whose flight/Is scattered through the universe around;/How substance, accident, and mode unite/Fused, so to speak, together, in such wise/That this I tell is one simple light.)[26] And we remember that Di Prima spoke of "the secret gnosticism of Dante" which she imbibed from her grandfather Domenico.

Di Prima also would read Grosseteste and we shall see in her essay "Light/and Keats" (1974) and in poems such as *Loba* the various ways she elaborates the meaning of light. In an unpublished letter of August 17, 1959, addressed to Freddie Herko, she revealed: "been reading medieval writers on light and motion. Grosseteste, who believed in rays of force emanating from objects, and said that light was the first corporeal form of matter. Which is, after all, what Einstein said too."[27] As she pondered medieval history and philosophy, Di Prima was also struck by parallels between former times and our contemporary world:

> And then, somebody in the 13th century said that motion was relative, and somebody in the 15th that knowledge & communication were impossible. And the whole thing they did, we're doing again. Right down to finally the universal feeling of doom, which parallels the one that hit with the black death in 1350. So maybe 50 yrs. will bring us to another renaissance. It's anyway a thought. It's fantastic how the whole thing repeats—existentialism, relativity . . . earlier, they had a form of utilitarianism worked out (roger bacon).[28]

Di Prima was prescient in predicting "another renaissance" which in some ways arrived earlier than "50 yrs." because the revolutions of the 1960s arrived less than a decade in the future—as we shall see in the following chapter—and brought about a radical change in American culture: prior modes of knowledge were now being rediscovered and both transcendental and apocalyptic themes emerged in literature, popular music, and film. Medieval and Renaissance history and culture became increasingly prominent influences among the young as books which reformulated Nordic and Germanic mythology such as J. R. R. Tolkien's *The Fellowship of the Ring* became bestsellers and the hippies began to dress in florid shirts and dresses reminiscent of Shakespearean times. Di Prima would include an excerpt from Grosseteste's *On Light or the Beginning of Forms* in Issue Number 29 of her literary magazine *The Floating Bear* in 1964, thus further demonstrating the continuity between Grosseteste's concerns and the emerging hippie orientation toward spiritual enlightenment.[29] The beauty of Grosseteste's prose—one line is variously translated from the Latin as "In the beginning of time, light drew out matter along with itself into a mass as great as the fabric of the world," or, slightly differently: "In this way it proceeded in the beginning of time to extend matter which it could not leave behind, by drawing it out along with itself into a mass the size of the material universe"—indicates one reason why Di Prima found this text so seductive. Like Paracelsus, whom she would discover in the mid-1960s, Grosseteste's "scientific" prose appears to be straining after a meaning which can only be fully communicated through the medium of poetic and lyrical metaphor.

The drive toward deeper levels of mystical experience which defined Beat culture also may be seen in Di Prima's experimentation with Jamaican marijuana sampled with James Waring and Freddie Herko which induced her first memories of a past life.[30] In the fall of 1958, she composed "Early Pot Notes" which includes the marvelous lines: "Dionysus dismembered comes together again in my own body rises from my flesh like from the earth=spring giving birth to yes." This is a splendid phenomenological description, illustrating how Di Prima sought to document directly her experiences with entheogens. Marijuana may give the user a timeless sense of eternal becoming in which one descends into an unknown place and dwells there, experiencing sights, sounds, smells, and colors which orient one to a hidden inner spiritual cosmos which exists alongside the "real" outside world from which one then emerges with new insight. As Michael McClure memorably phrased it in his "Peyote Poem," she seeks to "hear/the music of myself and write it down." It also indicates Di Prima's familiarity with James George Frazer's theory in *The Golden Bough* concerning the "dying and rising god" and of the Orphic mystery recounting the dismemberment of Dionysus Zagreus, god of ecstasy and wine. This is one of the earliest soundings of a theme which will recur throughout her mature work. Di Prima's body comes alive again from struggle, moves from winter to "spring" and thus recounts the theme of rebirth through dissolution. Caitlin and John Matthews argue that all of the mystery religions—Eleusinian, Orphic, Mithraic, and Celtic—involved this concept:

Above all it is the Orphic mysteries that we first come to terms with this perilous descent into darkness and re-emergence again into primal light. The suffering of Orpheus, who loses Eurydice (through fear, first pitfall of all mystery knowledge) and is then dismembered by the Maenads, is a paradigm of the suffering and rebirth of the sleeping soul. As a descendent of Dionysus, Orpheus is the intellectual image of a demi-god raised to deity by his sufferings in the underworld: a perfect symbol for all who follow the path of the Mysteries.

In Di Prima, Dionysus is "dismembered," yet is born again within her "own body." Persephone, goddess of spring, is the daughter of Demeter—both central figures in the Eleusinian Mysteries. Persephone is abducted by Hades but as in Di Prima's poem will eternally "rise" from winter and the land of the dead to give birth to another spring. In *Loba*, Di Prima will turn to the Sumerian myth of Inanna who enacts—like Persephone—a similar descent into the underworld.

In 1959, Di Prima also ingested peyote and had a vision of a "Newtonian" universe which was a life-changing event. Di Prima would claim that after her peyote visions, her poetry began to break out into freer, longer lines which as we shall see in the following chapter mark her volume *New Handbook of Heaven* (1963). Di Prima was experimenting with a variety of entheogens including marijuana, dexamyl, Dexedrine, peyote, and LSD. Like William Burroughs and Allen Ginsberg, she also sought to reflect upon and write about these experiences and their relationship to her inner, spiritual life. Far from seeking a frivolous "high," she sought—like indigenous peoples throughout the world—to incorporate these entheogens into her ritual sacred life: as we shall see, she would participate in Timothy Leary's experimental LSD commune at Milbrook in 1966. As Raymond H. Prince has argued in his essay "Cocoon Work: An Interpretation of the Concern of Contemporary Youth with the Mystical," young people became increasingly concerned during the 1960s with mystical states which he defines as "alterations of consciousness characterized by a radical change in the everyday sense of self and experience of time and space; a feeling of heightened significance attaches to the episode or its content; the mood is one of ecstasy; invariably, the subject is left dissatisfied with the adequacy of ordinary language to describe his experience." Several of the Beats began to theorize concerning the meaning of these euphoric experiences. For example, in October 1959 during his visit to Greece, Corso—a favorite poet of Di Prima's—reported in a letter to Allen Ginsberg that "on the lovely isle of Hydra I actually saw Death, yes, it was the morning after the big night . . . I saw there at that moment a skinless light, a naked brilliance and felt like I never felt before in my life; I had done a great thing, I stepped out of the circle and did not die, and outside the circle, dear friend, death holds its warrant; a summoning to something wonderful and beautiful I'm sure; I was scared and stepped back into the circle. . . . The scene was lovely, pure Greek isle of Homer, early morning, bright sun."

This engagement with the phenomenology of light is a continuing theme in Beat spirituality, and Corso's numinous encounter with a skinless light precisely describes what Philip Lamantia and Michael McClure defined— from Anglo-Saxon—as the *aelf-scin* or *weir* experience: "the solid spectral reality of light on particular objects in special moments of vision." These epiphanic moments may be experienced with entheogens, but also during intense reveries in which one enters—like the mystic—a timeless imaginative realm. In his poem "Greece" from *Long Live Man*, Corso again employs the same phrase to describe what he encountered on the island of Hydra: "skinless light." Like other Beats such as Michael McClure with whom she would establish a lasting friendship—he came to visit her in New York in 1960 and she would meet him again in California the following year—Di Prima also sought to redefine the poet's role in terms of indigenous traditions of spiritual seeking in which peyote was regularly employed in ritual ceremonies. In particular, during the late 1950s one may perceive the initial stages of Di Prima's explorations of shamanic wisdom. Indeed, the Native American scholar Barbara Tedlock in *The Woman in The Shaman's Body: Reclaiming the Feminine in Religion and Medicine* researched the "female shaman": not only males were visionaries in indigenous cultures, but women also occupied the role of religious seer and healer.[31]

Other female authors in the Beat circle also explored aspects of their mystical experiences in their writings. For example, Bonnie Bremser in *Troia*—her account of earning a living as a prostitute in Mexico to support her husband Ray Bremser—describes ingesting peyote and writing on the ceiling "THERE IS SALVATION. . . . That is what is known as seeing the light, and it is probably corny to talk about it as a great comprehension, probably telling too much of the truth when I say that this was one of my life's great religious manifestations" (capitals in original). Kay Johnson—who would become known as "Kaja" and who mysteriously disappeared from sight—composed a lyrical prose piece entitled "the white room" published in *The Outsider* in Spring, 1963, in which she describes the spiritual solitude of the dark night of the soul, declaring

this is what all our constructions of identity are protecting us from. This is why we build these constructions to protect us from our need of each other, to protect us from our own emptiness, our desperations, our hunger for each other. . . . Some of the saints know this. Some of the insane know it. The insane, when all constructions have broken, know it. Some of them know that their souls are not small, like uncracked nuts inside of them. . . . Yet some of the saints were not yet sainted enough to know it. They equipped themselves with devils and angels and visions, so as not to be lonely in their most extreme separation.

Carolyn Cassady—the wife of Neal Cassady—in her "Foreword" to *Grace Beats Karma* analyzes the importance of the idea of karma in interpreting the meaning of her life and reveals that she and Neal read Madame Blavatsky, Jakob Boehme, Meister Eckhart, Teilhard de Chardin "and many many other Western and Eastern thinkers. Along with the foundation texts of the Hindu, Buddhist, Taoist, and other world religions, the Christian Bible was illuminated and experienced in a more understandable and personal way." And as Maria Damon has argued, Janine Pommy Vega's "Poems to Fernando" are yet another striking example of the ways female Beat writers explored the concepts of suffering and spiritual transformation.

Thus several themes in Di Prima's developing philosophy began to emerge during the 1950s. Experimentation with altered states of consciousness, erotic ecstasy, Native American traditions, the existentialism of Jean-Paul Sartre and Albert Camus, and the intense pleasures of music and art were all now sources of inspiration. Willem de Kooning acknowledged that "existentialism . . . was in the air, and we felt it without knowing too much about it." The existentialists sought freedom; freedom from religious orthodoxy, freedom from the conditioning of family, culture, and nation through a fierce commitment to the quest toward individual selfhood and responsibility. Di Prima acknowledged that the new generation felt itself to be in a box, a maze from which they sought egress and the way out of the labyrinth might be existentialism, peyote, shamanism, the philosophy of Alfred North Whitehead: this was a time of sometimes euphoric experimentation and discovery.

In addition to her poetry, Di Prima also became entranced by the theatre, seeing plays by Ionesco, Beckett, and Jean Genet. She learned that anything could happen on the stage and reveled in the possibilities of a spontaneous imagination set free. She began to compose plays, inspired by James Waring whom as we have seen earlier was a significant influence, as well as by her studies of the *I Ching*: it was John Cage's *Music of Changes* (1951)—the revolutionary work of "indeterminate" or "chance" music for solo piano in which tempo, duration, and dynamics were determined through consulting the *I Ching*—which led Di Prima to purchase a two-volume, boxed set of the Chinese divinatory classic. At Black Mountain College in the early 1950s, Cage had asked Charles Olson to read his poetry, Robert Rauschenberg to exhibit his paintings and to play whatever music he desired, the pianist David Tudor to perform compositions of his choice, and Merce Cunningham to dance: all were free to do what they wished within a strict time interval. Cage sought a "purposeless purposefulness: it was purposeful in that we knew what we were going to do, but it was purposeless in that we didn't know what was going to happen in the total." This came to be known as "the first Happening." Influenced by John Cage as well as the choreography of Merce Cunningham, poets such as Jackson Mac Low would also study the Kabbalah, Zen, and the *I Ching* and employed chance technique in the composition of his poetry. In 1959, Di Prima attended Waring's composition class at the Living Theatre and sought to incorporate his chance techniques—which included playing with dice and employing cut-ups (juxtaposing sections of text randomly)—into her own playwriting, and she would stage manage Waring's Monday Night Series at the Living

Theatre as well. An early effort—*The Discontent of the Russian Prince*—was performed by Di Prima and Freddie Herko in October 1961. According to Di Prima, "It wasn't about anything, it was about getting up in the morning. It's the only play of mine that had a plot and the plot was getting up in the morning."[32]

Her play *Murder Cake* was composed during a single afternoon employing the *I Ching*, and she described her method as follows: "First I picked at random 6 characters (ones I liked, or symbolic) Then I picked 6 books by women writers. Then with dice I determined in what order the characters would speak. . . . It put me into some kind of thing where I had control but didn't have control." Published in the Spring, 1963, issue of *Kulchur*, *Murder Cake* was premiered at the Judson Memorial Church in 1963 and performed again in February 1964 along with Frank O'Hara's *Love's Labor* at the New York Poet's Theater. The six characters are Childe Harold, Emma, Mr. Knightley, Olimpia, Richard Lovelace, and Dante. Its title surrealistically places two things—"murder" and "cake"—together which the mind finds difficult to reconcile: what does a cake have to do with murder? The play is a concise six pages with no stage directions featuring clever Dadaesque lines such as Childe Harold's "Fate is an overturned tree. Who polishes the cosmos? A once-a-week maid, grumbling about her job," or Mr. Knightley's "A moth flew through the ginger ale. It was lovely." The dialogue is non-sequitur, absurdist, and illustrates Di Prima's enthusiasms of the time such as Bessie Smith, Dante, and Lord Byron. Emma's final speech—her name is taken from Jane Austen's eponymous novel—seems to encode a cryptic message:

> Whom nothing has loved, in the blue sea or in heaven, I stand before you, a girl with the mouth of a seagull and spidery-eyed. My long limbs are dripping water. Hell, what do you know about it. . . . Do not imagine I am giving birth . . . I was almighty, but funny, pretty funny. What a blemish, I was put to pasture at an early age, when eventually I found it necessary to go up the river to spawn.

The text eerily seems to escape meaning while at the same time one may make out the contours of a voice vaguely attempting to say something intelligible. Nancy M. Grace in her essay "Diane di Prima as Playwright: The Early Years" argues that "by speaking such feminist truths through the constellation of surrealistic images and language, Di Prima aims straight at the heart of oppression, daring to strike out against its very life—a premeditated killing, in other words, a Murder."[33] She is also "funny, pretty funny," suggesting again that meaning and non-meaning, order and chaos, control and loss of control—that is, the human condition itself—may be interpreted as a cosmic joke.

Thus *Murder Cake* emerged from the aleatoric process of random dice-throwing and as Di Prima noted above, what she sought while employing the *I Ching* in her composition was precisely this sense of "having control and not having control." Stephen J. Bottoms has observed that

> both pieces were composed almost entirely of lengthy, seemingly unrelated speeches, from seemingly unrelated characters. . . . The potential with such texts was that—in the absence of coherent narrative or characterization—a kind of pure theater could be constructed by juxtaposing the words with a similarly alogical use of movement and imagery. Indeed, di Prima describes *Murder Cake* as a "word score" rather than a play, "for a director to do with as s/he will." James Waring, who directed it, seems to have been particularly adept at this approach. As a choreographer, he was celebrated for his creation of "exquisitely lyric" visual forms through the collagelike assemblage of abstract movement and everyday materials: dance critic Jill Johnston once described his work as "a happening with dance as the protagonist . . . any token from life as we see it or know it is acceptable at any time in this illogical scheme of things." With *Murder Cake*, Waring simply treated di Prima's language as a kind of found object, as abstract sounds forming another layer of the collage.

While *Murder Cake* emerged from studying and experimenting with the *I Ching*, it is clear that during the early 1960s Di Prima began consulting the *I Ching* not only to stimulate her creative process, but also for advice as we see in a *Diary* entry from December 1960 in which she drew four hexagrams with inquiries concerning her personal life. Furthermore, as we shall see in the following chapter, the *I Ching* would inspire several of her works including the play *Poet's Vaudeville* (1962) and the prose work *The Calculus of Variation*.

Another intriguing play from this period—*The Discovery of America* (August 1960; revised August 1972)—is a brief, eleven-page work in three acts containing some hilarious reconsiderations of the shape of American history. We again have a wonderful cast of characters including several bats, Don Quixote, Mayan and Toltec Priests, Don Juan, a Princess, a Milkmaid, Puritans, George Washington, John Paul Jones, Pocahontas, Aaron Burr, Cortez, Henry David Thoreau. The three acts span the "discovery" of America by the Puritans and the dialogue is marked by total lunacy. In Act One, Scene 4, the Milkmaid declares "Squatters rights" and begins to sing "This land is my land, This land is your land, This land was made for you and me." This of course is from Woody Guthrie's famous song which became an anthem of the antiwar movement of the 1960s which had its origin in the labor movement. Here it is invoked as a means of asserting that "this land"— the land of America which had belonged to the Native Americans—now belongs to the "squatters" who are the recently arrived Puritans. Act Two, Scene I, opens:

> First Puritan: Iced cherries in vodka! Why am I so preoccupied with food?
> Second Puritan: It's as domestic as a creaking bed. Should I wait for an answer?
> Third Puritan: Just say The Wainscot.
> First Bat: Have you read The Marble Faun? It's better than the letters of Nijinsky.
> Phantom: oooooooog.
> Second Puritan: I'll bet anything old Al Hamilton wins. Hooray for our side!
> Fourth Bat: Yeah.
> Aztec Priest: (with hatchet) Blood. Blood
>   Blood. Blood. Blood
>   My dear you're exquisite.
> Princess: Go way, this is my big scene.
> Thoreau: And the last cocaine turned out to be Epsom salts. I sneezed.
> Don Quixote: Of course you did.

As in her earlier plays, Di Prima introduces actual literary works and artists—Thoreau, Nathanael Hawthorne's novel *The Marble Faun*, Nijinsky—into juxtaposition with a fantastical theatrical scene: the "real" author Henry David Thoreau carries on a conversation with the "fictional character" Don Quixote and every historical place and person is wrenched from its accustomed place in chronological time. The effect is to fracture and lampoon our ability to construct any coherent narrative of American history, and indeed to challenge the version we were given as children of the pure Puritans confronting the savage Native Americans, bringing Christian sweetness and light. Howard Zinn's *People's History* continued in this tradition and Di Prima is clearly marshaling all the weapons of absurd humor to bring our attention to the ways history is an ideological construct. Hayden White in his *Metahistory* revealed the extent to which history is ruled by narrative and fictional structures and told from a particular point of view and ideological perspective.[34] But Di Prima achieves all this with a very light and funny touch.

Di Prima worked for a period in the early 1960s at the Phoenix Bookstore, becoming friends with its new owner Robert Wilson and thus kept in close contact with the literary avant-garde. She recalled that during this period "you couldn't get books—the obscenity laws were very strong. We would receive packages of Olympia Press books by Jean Genet, Henry Miller, and William Burroughs wrapped in brown paper, sent from Paris to Turkey, and from Turkey to us, with the return address of a Turkish

Christian funeral home." As we have seen, Di Prima during this phase of her career had made contact with poets who would remain significant figures throughout her life, including Ezra Pound, Allen Ginsberg, and LeRoi Jones/Amiri Baraka would achieve fame with his play *Dutchman* (1964) which won an Obie award and recounts the dramatic encounter fraught with sexual tension between Lula—a white woman—and a black man named Clay on a subway in New York City: the play ends violently with Lula murdering Clay. Frank O'Hara wrote to Larry Rivers on April 18, 1964: "Roi has also had a resounding triumph at the Cherry Lane . . . with a one-act play called Dutchman. It's a thrilling play . . . Roi also had an almost full page on him in Newsweek. Isn't that heaven?" Baraka's own work would also mirror several of the themes which marked Di Prima's spiritual journey. For example, after leaving the army he immersed himself in Zen Buddhism and his poem "Black Dada Nihilismus" invokes Hermes Trismegistus. In an interview, Baraka declared: "The Black man is getting ready to come up with some later doctrines of how man, the Black man, will evolve into a higher state. The Black man's getting ready to go off into what they call the sixth race, another step in evolving, higher than what exists now." The notion of "root races" derives from the Theosophist Helena Blavatsky and it is clear that Baraka and Di Prima's relationship was based on a shared spiritual quest.

Di Prima would begin a love affair with Jones and aborted their first child in the late spring of 1960, inspiring one of her best-known poems, "Brass Furnace Going Out: Song, after an Abortion" in which she voices her anguish following this traumatic loss. Divided into twelve sections, the poem openly confesses the whirlwind of ambivalent feelings occasioned by the decision to terminate a pregnancy, as we see in section two in addressing her child: "I want you in a bottle to send to your father/with a long bitter note. I want him to know/I'll not forgive you, or him for not being born/ for drying up, quitting at the first harsh treatment." Section three opens, "who forged this night, what steel/clamps down?" echoing William Blake's "The Tyger," "What the hammer? What the chain,/In what furnace was thy brain?" Blake's creation whose fires also symbolize alchemical shaping forces—perhaps the verse which supplied the poem's title, brass furnace (the furnace in alchemy is the athanor in which the alembic is heated)—is now the womb of birth. Mircea Eliade has emphasized in *The Forge and the Crucible: The Origins and Structures of Alchemy* the sacred qualities ascribed to the furnaces, for they are "a new matrix, an artificial uterus where the ore completes its gestation. Hence the infinite number of precautions, taboos, and ritual acts which accompany the smelting." Furthermore, in alchemical thought, an "abortion" is the term applied to the alchemical opus or "work" when it fails to be completed. The Blakean "forge" which is the locus of "What the anvil? What dread grasp,/Dare its deadly terrors clasp!" becomes for Di Prima the dark night of the soul: "who forged this night?"

Blake of course was a tremendous influence on the Beats: Di Prima herself would compose a heartfelt homage "For Blake" and Allen Ginsberg in 1948 in Harlem famously experienced a mystical vision of Blake chanting "Ah Sunflower, Weary of Time" and took him as his guru. A young musician named Jim Morrison from California would call his rock 'n' roll group The Doors after Blake's celebrated apothegm: "When the doors of perception are cleansed, everything will appear to man as it is—infinite," and Blake's influence can be seen in the lyrics of Morrison's songs as well as those of Bob Dylan.

The fraught mood of "Brass Furnace Going Out: Song, after an Abortion" intensifies in section four with a plethora of animal allusions: "your face dissolving in water, like wet clay/washed away, like a rotten water lily/ rats on the riverbank barking at the sight." References to otter, mosquito, lion, giraffe, fish, ant, snake, turtle, fly, maggot follow in a descent into a frightening jungle of the unconscious. The "brass furnace" of the title is both an enclosing womb and the fires of guilt, anguish, love, and regret. In section seven, the poem breaks out into open expostulation:

what is it that I cannot bear to say?
that if you had turned out mad, a murderer
a junky pimp hanged & burning in lime
    alone & filled w/the rotting dark
if you'd been frail and a little given to weirdness
or starved or been shot, or tortured in hunger camps
it wd have been frolic & triumph compared to this—

I cant even cry for you, I cant hang on
that long

Amy L. Friedman in "'I say my new name': Women Writers of the Beat Generation" argues that Di Prima recapitulates here the concerns of the Beat trajectory in Ginsberg's *Howl*—"if you had turned out mad," "a junky pimp"—and in her poem "the lost generation is the aborted child, the sense of fury the product of the emotional aftermath." "Brass Furnace Going Out" illustrates Di Prima's ongoing and courageous voicing of central issues in the experience of women which are often consigned to silence.

Two other writers significant in Di Prima's development during this phase were John Wieners and Frank O'Hara. Wieners arrived in New York after being released from a mental hospital in Boston: his *Hotel Wentley Poems* was published in 1958. Di Prima encountered it at Paperback Traffic on Sixth Avenue and read the entire text, "recognizing many of the effects I was also at work on: the street language flowing so smoothly it seemed effortless, the almost-cliché shining and made new. A taut nervy lyricism that fooled you—it looked so easy." Wieners had a particular interest in the Tarot and

Robert Duncan in his review of both *The Hotel Wentley Poems* and *Ace of Pentacles* entitled "Taking Away from God His Sound," observed:

> John Weiners has reference to the Tarot cards as emblems of poetry. Turning to that Tarot deck drawn by Pamela Coleman Smith for the Order of the Golden Dawn under the direction of A. E. Waite—the Tarot then of Yeats's poetry, of Eliot's The Waste Land and of Charles Williams' The Greater Trumps—I find that a hand of light emerges from the shadow upholding in its radiance the "Ace of Pentacles," gold upon which the magic sign of the Son is engraved.

Many American poets including Sylvia Plath, Anne Sexton, Alice Notley, Ted Berrigan, Phlip Whalen, Philip Lamantia, Robert Creeley, Charles Olson, and T. S. Eliot allude to Tarot, and as we shall see, by the mid-1960s, Di Prima would also make a serious study of Tarot. Wieners would remain a close friend over the next decade, becoming a member of the "extended family" Di Prima established with Alan Marlowe at the Hotel Albert in 1967.[35]

As for O'Hara, Freddy Herko had been the roommate of Vincent Warren who became O'Hara's lover, and Di Prima also worked as stage manager when O'Hara's *Awake in Spain* was performed at the Living Theater's Monday Night Series in August 1960. O'Hara looked after her two-year-old daughter Jeanne and Di Prima visited O'Hara during the evenings or on Sunday mornings.[36] In preparing issues of *The Floating Bear*, Di Prima noted that she would sometimes obtain O'Hara's manuscripts in a unique fashion:

> We got hold of manuscripts all kinds of ways besides in the mail. For instance, I would go over to Frank O'Hara's house pretty often. He used to keep a typewriter on the table in the kitchen, and he would type away, make poems all the time, when company was there and when it wasn't, when he was eating, all kinds of times. There would be an unfinished poem in his typewriter and he would do a few lines on it now and again, and he kept losing all these poems. They would wind up all over the house. He was working full time at the Museum of Modern Art, and he never paid much attention to what was happening. The poems would get into everything and I would come over and go through, like, his dresser drawers. There would be poems in with the towels, and I'd say, "Oh, hey, I like this one," and he'd say, "OK, take it." Very often it would be the only copy. My guess is that huge collected Frank O'Hara has only about one-third of his actual work.

Di Prima responded to his easy, conversational, intellectual, and humorous poems—Richard Howard has described O'Hara's later work as "interim reports . . . notes on getting through the pleasures and palliations of a

much-befriended existence, newsy, fretful and of course entertaining"—
which seemed to effortlessly incorporate into their flow the seemingly
insignificant details of quotidian experience as well as chatty gossip
concerning his friends and the famous. Gregory Corso thought "Frank
had fire all right, and very metropolitan—I liked that about him. When
he mentions his friends' names, he is not name-dropping. In other words
people he was associated with, that was his life, and he incorporated
them into his work." Di Prima published several O'Hara poems in her
magazine *The Floating Bear* including "Now That I Am in Madrid and
Can Think," "Mary Desti's Ass," "Song (Did you see me walking by the
Buick Repairs?)," "Cohasset," "Beer for Breakfast," "For the Chinese New
Year & Bill Berkson," "St. Paul and All That," "Pistachio Tree at Chateau
Noir," "Adventures in Living," and "Hotel Particulier." While it may seem
that O'Hara and the Beats had little in common, O'Hara mentions Gary
Snyder's stay in Japan in his poem "Les Luths," Allen Ginsberg in "Post
the Lake Poets Ballad" and LeRoi Jones in "Personal Poem."[37] O'Hara
died on July 25, 1966, and would inspire a number of elegies by fellow
poets, including Allen Ginsberg's "City Midnight Junk Strains." Three days
after O'Hara's death from her home in Kerhonkson, New York, Di Prima
composed "For Frank O'Hara: An Elegy": she refers to O'Hara as her
"big brother" who took her to art openings, walked with her in Tompkins
Square, frequently bought her lunch which she promised to reciprocate
once she "got a little richer," and to whom she contributed onion bread
for their Sunday brunches on 9th Street. She renders homage to her friend,
expressing gratitude for the "things you taught without teaching, a style
you gave me/mirrored back in the green clarity of your eyes."[38]

While composing "For Frank O'Hara: An Elegy," Di Prima was immersed
in Hindu philosophy as we may observe in the poem's opening:

Bells like thunder are sounding in the air, the rain
it falls after how many weeks, streams are flowing
beginning to flow, Indra has slain the dragon
the taxi backed over you: a simple horror
* * * * * *

yours a prana, an energy that wanted out
the new age is softer than you or I or
* * * * * *

or Freddie or Larry or Roi—anachronisms, we are being wiped out
like Lhasa, like the Forbidden City
like Tokyo now 90% new—that which must not survive
into the new age:
certain forms of porcelain, minds, a time of love is coming

The poem begins with falling rain, causing streams to flow: in Hinduism, the dragon Vritra who is blocking the river's course is slain by Indra. O'Hara perished on Fire Island, thus the reference to "the taxi backed over you," while prana in Hindu philosophy is the cosmic life energy which we find in the Vedas and Upanishads. This term appears frequently in Di Prima's work, and Paul Deussen in *The Philosophy of the Upanishads* has noted:

> No natural phenomenon bears so ambiguous a character, none appears to be derived so immediately from the most intimate essence of things and so fully to reveal it, as the phenomenon of life, manifested in the activity of all the vital organs (pranas), but above all in the process of breathing (prana) which determines the life itself. Hence as early as the Brahamana period the central significance of prana (breath or life) was discussed together with its superiority to the other pranas (vital forces, as the eye, ear, speech, manas), and its identity with Vayu, the god of the wind as the vital breath of the universe, was discussed.[39]

For Di Prima, this ancient emphasis on prana as spiritual energy is significant in two ways. First, as Norman Mailer pointed out in his essay "The White Negro"—a manifesto now rightly criticized due to its reductive essentialism regarding ethnicity—prana was an energy which the counterculture valued because

> to be with it is to have grace, is to be closer to the secrets of that inner unconscious life which will nourish you if you can hear it, for you are then nearer to that God which every hipster believes is located in the senses of his body, that trapped, mutilated and nonetheless megalomaniacal God who is It, who is energy, life, sex, for, the Yoga's prana, the Reichian's orgone, Lawrence's "blood," Hemingway's "good," the Shavian life-force.

Secondly, prana has analogues to Charles Olson's Projective Verse poetics which would influence both Allen Ginsberg's and Di Prima's emphasis on the breath as unit of the line of verse and on reciting poetry by the rhythm of breath rather than conventional metrics. Breathing exercises in yoga are called pranayama and Di Prima practiced yoga while at Timothy Leary's Millbrook and had a favorite teacher with whom she was studying. Thus the practice of meditation and performing breathing exercises becomes assimilated into an innovative Beat poetics in which spiritual and artistic disciplines merge. Lhasa, holy capital city of Tibet and home of the Dalai Lama, is also invoked as is the Forbidden City, the imperial palace of the Ming Dynasty. Di Prima places O'Hara in the same category as other friends Freddie Herko, painter Larry Rivers, and LeRoi Jones whom she believes may also all be "wiped out" as "anachronisms" before the new age arrives.

The poem is noteworthy not only for its moving homage to O'Hara, but also for the ways Di Prima began to more methodically incorporate her studies in Eastern thought into the texture of her poetry.

Di Prima's "multiculturalism" is apparent in *Various Fables from Various Places* (1960), a volume she edited containing fables selected from Spain, Russia, Medieval Europe, the Malay Peninsula, England, Africa, India, China, Italy, Scotland, Ancient Greece and Rome, France, and Tibet. In her afterword "About Fables," she declares:

> As for what a fable is; I don't know. All I have made is a rough guess: that it has something to do with the qualities of the human personality, whatever that means; and with the success or failure of the different choices you make or don't and the different things you do or try to do or don't do.[40]

From the beginning of her career, Di Prima possessed a powerfully mythopoeic imagination—which bears full flower in her masterwork *Loba*—and drew sustenance from a variety of sources, refusing the ethnocentric bias of those who celebrate only the achievements of their own culture. As we shall also see in Chapter 5, Di Prima's course "The Hidden Religions in the Literature of Europe" which she taught at the New College of California undertook a cross-cultural, historical investigation of humanity's archetypal religious symbolism from prehistory to the present. C. G. Jung was the great predecessor in this "multiculturalism" through his studies of world mythological traditions and their relevance for his theory of archetypes and exploration of the psychology of the unconscious. Jung influenced not only Di Prima, but also set the precedent for the Beats in his attraction to Eastern thought and his search for a rapprochement between various spiritual traditions. For example, in his *The Red Book* (2009), Jung's drawing of Philemon—a character from Greek and Roman mythology—depicts a dream from 1913. In the upper left corner of the painting there is a quotation from the *Bhagavad Gita*, while the text at top is in Greek: PROPHETON PATER POLUPHILOS PHILEMON and Jung's own script is in German.[40] Here we have a confluence of Judeo-Christian, Indian, European traditions, illustrating Jung's desire to forge a new syncretic belief system. Jung's fascination with Gnosticism, alchemy, astrology, the *I Ching*, mandalas, synchronicity, flying saucers, and the paranormal find exact parallels in the Beats. Jung's studies of alchemy were continued not only in the work of Di Prima, but in Kenneth Rexroth, Robert Duncan, Michael McClure, and William Everson (Brother Antoninus) as well. Furthermore, the Eranos conferences presided over by Jung—where Henry Corbin, Mircea Eliade, Gershom Scholem, and Joseph Campbell lectured on subjects as diverse as Kabbalah and Ismaili mysticism—set the stage for the Californian Esalen Institute where ideas of expanded consciousness were explored. Frederic

Spiegelberg, Alan Watts, and Aldous Huxley were significant figures in bringing to California what would evolve into the "New Age" or Human Potential movement which intersected with Di Prima's own trajectory when she finally settled on the West Coast in the late 1960s.

Thus the 1950s were a significant period in Di Prima's development during which she began to seriously explore the philosophical questions which would occupy her throughout her life. However as a woman loosely associated with the Beat movement, it was not always easy to publish her work. As Johanna Drucker has observed:

> The ways in which work gets seen, distributed, accorded significance and deemed worthy of critical recognition continues to divide along gender lines. . . . If one of the features of the modern avant-garde was to pretend to the autonomy and self-referential value of the work, then one of the most significant projects of the contemporary scene has got to be the undoing of that mythic autonomy in recognition of the complicity of (still male dominated) power relations as they structure the ongoing production of literature as its own critical history. If I am interested in anything with regard to that "legacy," it is with overturning its controlling lineages and traditions, the need to be positioned within a canon which was never mine either in my formation as a writer or in my presentation of my self socially. . . . Unfortunately, the legacy of the avant-garde, such as it is, has been to perpetuate, rather than change, the very terms of canon formation and evaluation so conducive to a male-dominated and masculinist scene—now all the more perversely fashioned as it mistakenly represents itself in the name of the "feminine."

An example of what Drucker is here chronicling is the appearance in 1960 of Don Allen's groundbreaking *New American Poetry*, which included Philip Lamantia, Gregory Corso, Allen Ginsberg, and Jack Kerouac; however, Di Prima was conspicuously absent. She had submitted to Donald Allen poems such as "The Jungle"—it would later appear in *The New Handbook of Heaven* (1963)—which Di Prima felt to be as artistically successful as some of the work Allen included by LeRoi Jones from *Preface to a Twenty-Volume Suicide Note*. Di Prima believed she had been excluded because she was cast in the role of "the invisible mistress"—she had an affair with Jones while he was married to Hettie Cohen—thus there was animus against her for extra-literary reasons. However, her poem "Blackout" was included in the volume *Beat Coast East: An Anthology of Rebellion* (1960)—later collected in *The New Handbook of Heaven* (1963)—and she was also published in the important underground magazine edited by Irving Rosenthal in Chicago, *Big Table*, in Spring, 1960. Entitled "The New American Poets Issue," her untitled poem beginning "I am a woman and my poems/are woman's"— later to be named "The Practice of Magical Evocation"—appeared alongside

William Burroughs, John Ashbery, Robert Creeley, Allen Ginsberg, Charles Olson, Robert Duncan, Gregory Corso, Harold Norse, Michael McClure, and Gary Snyder. She also was published in Don Allen's later anthology, *The Postmoderns: The New American Poetry Revised* (1982).[41] As the 1960s began, she would continue striking out on her independent path through a male-dominated literary establishment.

3

Tell all the gods we're turning back to find them:

From *Dinners and Nightmares* to Paracelsus, Alchemy, and Tarot, 1961–67

During the early to mid-1960s, Di Prima engaged in a variety of literary pursuits: editing journals, establishing a theater to produce plays, running her own printing press, and publishing prolifically. In this chapter I discuss her third book, *Dinners and Nightmares* (1961), *The New Handbook of Heaven* (1963), as well as her continuing immersion in the *I Ching* which would result in *The Calculus of Variation* (written 1961–65; published 1972). Di Prima's deepening and wide-ranging spiritual quest can be traced in her initial trips to California in 1961 and 1962 where she met Zen master Shunryu Suzuki, her discovery of Tibetan saint Milarepa (ca. 1052–1135 CE), beginning studies of Sanskrit, as well as her move in 1965 to Rammurti Mishra's ashram in Monroe, New York. She spent a meditative sojourn in 1966 at Kerhonkson, New York, writing *Kerhonkson Journal* which reflects her deepening studies of Hinduism, as well as time in Timothy Leary's psychedelic Millbrook community. I shall explore another important turning point when Di Prima discovered the alchemist Paracelsus and contributed a thoughtful introduction to his works. Finally, during her stay in New Mexico in 1966, Di Prima became absorbed in Tarot as well as Heinrich Cornelius Agrippa (1486–1535) the German astrologer, occultist, and author of *De Occulta Philosophia Libri Tres* (1533) which led her to a serious study of the Kabbalah: I trace these influences in both her verse and prose.

A sense of the wide range of subjects which engaged Di Prima during the early 1960s may be gauged by a letter written to her friend Peter on February 21, 1961, which she further dates "end of the Lupercal"—an archaic pre-Roman apotropaic festival to purify the city held in February—asking him for books including: Leo Frobenius, Ezra Pound, Robert Grosseteste, Roger Bacon, texts on Medieval Science (she specifies the subjects of light, space, and alchemy), a Provencal Dictionary, Chinese classic texts, *Manyoshu or Book of a Thousand Leaves*, Herbal and Bestiary texts, as well as a Middle Latin Dictionary. This latter volume Di Prima likely utilized as she worked on *Seven Love Poems from The Middle Latin* (1965) which contains her hip, lively, and bawdy version of a lyric included in the famous *Carmina Burana*, "Sevit aure spiritus." The Lupercalian dating of her letter reveals another aspect of Di Prima's evolving mythic imagination for she had recently purchased a fourteen-volume edition of Sir James Frazer's (1854–1941) *The Golden Bough* (1906–15). Although Ludwig Wittgenstein famously criticized Frazer for his misunderstanding of the role of magic in "primitive" cultures—Wittgenstein thought Frazer more "savage" than the supposed "savages" he failed to properly interpret—Di Prima was interested in *The Golden Bough* primarily as a treasure box of fascinating anthropological lore. Here she learned about equinoxes, solstices, cross-quarter days, as well as festivals held in honor of these cosmic events during "pagan" times. Of course, "pagan" was the word used by Christians to disparage "heathen" peoples or the mythological belief systems of the ancients. Just as words such as "superstition" or "magic" are employed as pejorative terms in relation to what is considered to be the "correct religion," so too a rich and archaic substratum of cultural traditions was demeaned in favor of the new "monotheistic" religions—Christianity, Judaism, and Islam. The archaic spiritual mythologies spoke to Di Prima as they did to her friend Charles Olson who saw the gods of the Maya as "not at all inventions, but . . . disclosures of human possibilities, in other words, human necessities."

Di Prima would also study Martin P. Nilsson's *Primitive Time-Reckoning* (1920) which specifically devotes several individual chapters to "Solstices and Equinoxes. Aids to the Determination of Time," "Artificial Periods of Time. Feasts," "Calendar Regulation," and "The Calendar-Makers." The influence of Nilsson's explorations of "pagan" time is apparent in Di Prima's "Revolutionary Letter Number Fifty-Nine" from *Revolutionary Letters* (1971). Here she encouraged her readers to "secret celebration of ancient season feasts & moons./Rewrite the calendar." She held celebratory parties on Wednesday evenings beginning with the winter solstice, 1963, to mark the calendar's seasonal turnings, reflecting her increasing fascination with "neopagan" ritualism and "witchcraft" which La Monte Young, A. B. Spellman, Cecil Taylor, James Waring, Freddie Herko, Merce Cunningham, and Brion Gysin—the close friend of William S. Burroughs—attended. One recalls Ralph Waldo Emerson's memorable warning in "Self-Reliance" that modern humanity had lost touch with Nature:

> The civilized man has built a coach, but has lost the use of his feet. He is supported on crutches, but lacks so much support of muscle. He has a fine Geneva watch, but he fails of the skill to tell the hour by the sun. A Greenwich nautical almanac he has, and so being sure of the information when he wants it, the man in the street does not know a star in the sky. The solstice he does not observe; the equinox he knows as little; and the whole bright calendar of the year he is without a dial in his mind.

Thus Di Prima was striving in authentic Emersonian fashion to "tell the hour by the sun," to observe and sanctify cosmic time. Her exhortation to "rewrite the calendar" reflects the desire of both the Beats and hippies to dissociate themselves from Western, Christian, linear clock-time. They sought to abandon the modern slavery to "technological-industrial" chronometry—"scientific" and "efficient" practices in the management of employees in modern factories were promulgated by Frederick Winslow Taylor (1856–1915) and became known as "Taylorism"—in favor of "primitive" sacred cyclical time which changes in relationship to the motion of the planets and procession of the seasons. At the beginning of the film *Easy Rider* (1969)—the updated version of Jack Kerouac's *On the Road*—before Billy and Wyatt set out on their journey across the American continent, Wyatt takes off his wristwatch and throws it on the ground. The Beat relationship to archaic time—Gary Snyder rejected dating his poems in terms of the Gregorian calendar in favor of conceiving of history in terms of the thousand-year cycles of Jurassic, Cretaceous, Mesozoic—symbolized a rejection of the increasing despoliation of the planet through pollution, the depletion of natural resources and an affirmation of a new ecological awareness which affirmed a less anthropocentric view of reality.

During her parties, at midnight, Di Prima and her friends would throw the *I Ching* and read stories from Milarepa. Brion Gysin later told Di Prima that during the early 1960s, "the most important thing going on for me in New York was coming up to your house on Wednesday nights." These evening gatherings were a way to create a countercultural sense of shared artistic and spiritual aims. Although Di Prima does not appear to have sought to belong to a conventional witch's "coven," in a sense by studying in such depth archaic conceptions of time and celebrating pagan rituals, she was now initiating one of her many efforts at alternative forms of communal sacrality. What happened during these evenings is recounted in Di Prima's "Notes on the Solstice" (1969; 1975) which she described as "the notes for a series of ritual events for 12–13 people." A typical evening involved: casting incense into the fire in honor of the ancestors; throwing an orange covered with cloves into the fire in honor of the sun; gathering the demons of the house by walking through it with frankincense, drums, and bells; stopping the procession at the house's door which is opened. Lentils are then cast outside "and the demons (hungry ghosts) rush out to devour them." The door is then loudly shut and a mandala is painted upon it with pitch; the people return to the hearth, throw into the fire written upon a scroll the name of their "private demon(s)," burn logs of white birch, followed by "music, drugs and dancing all night RAM'S HORNS AT DAWN." Di Prima was anticipating a later cultural trend, since "Neopaganism" would become a central feature of the counterculture during the mid- to late 1960s.

T. M. Lurhmann points out in her study of witchcraft in contemporary England that the witches' covens

> meet on (or near) days dictated by the sky: the solstices and equinoxes and the "quarter days" between them, most of them fire-festivals in the Frazerian past: Beltane (1 May), Lammas (1 August), Halloween (31 October), Candlemas (2 February). These are the days to perform seasonal rituals, in which witches celebrate the passage of the longest days and the summer's harvest. Covens also meet on the full moons— most witches are quite aware of the moon's phases—on which they perform spells, rituals with a specific intention, to cure Jane's cold or to get Richard a job. Seasonal ritual meets are called "sabbats," the full moon meetings, "esbats."

Indeed, Di Prima's manuscript notebooks reveal during this period that she kept a careful record of these four witches' Sabbaths with only a slight variation of Luhrmann's nomenclature, listing Candelmas, February 2; May Eve, April 30; Lammastide, August 2; and All Hallow's Eve, October 31. Robert Graves's *The White Goddess* would further deepen Di Prima's familiarity with pagan traditions, and as we shall see in Chapter 4, her readings in both Frazer and Graves would supply a rich source of material which she mined during the composition of *Loba*. Di Prima would also frequently employ *spells*—"rituals with a specific intention"—in her poetry, such as her cycle of poems dedicated to her close dancer friend, *Poems for Freddie*.

One of her important works of the early 1960s, *Dinners and Nightmares*—dedicated "to my three pads & the people who shared them with me"—is divided into five sections: "What I Ate Where," "Nightmares," "Memories of Childhood," "Conversations," and "More or Less Love Poems." An expanded edition published in 1998 contains two additional chapters: "What Morning Is," included at the beginning and as conclusion "Some Early Prose." The book may be interpreted as an anthropological inquiry into the counterculture by an insider who also acts as an informant concerning the odd and intriguing behaviors of this new tribe of young people. A culture is composed of the ways a given group creates art and mythology, makes music, prepares food, encounters the sacred, behaves toward parents, children, spouses, and lovers, establishes kinship rules and employs language. The newly emerging counterculture's "hip" language, artistic, musical, and literary activities and their questioning of gender and sexual roles are all explored by one of the first writers to make poems from "cool" language. The first section is in prose, broken up into brief tableaux beginning with "What I Ate Where" in which Di Prima describes the sparse diet (the text has scattered references to American junk food brands: Oreo cookies, Kraft cheese, Lipton soup, Pepperidge Farm) on which she and her fellow impoverished bohemians subsisted. Potatoes in tomato sauce is rather memorably described as "menstrual pudding."[1] As in *This Bird Flies Backward*, Di Prima again employs hip lingo:

> I remember sitting there with this cat who was half Cherokee with a Spanish name, a beautiful cat with those cheekbones and lovely eyes . . . and there was that in my stomach. I mean that feeling that happens when you are about to go to bed with a cat for the first time, the sense of adventure the quick in the air, and I drank pernod being unconsciously pregnant and knowing how another winter chalked up.

The sound of these sentences is new in American literature for we have a description of erotic possibility told from a young woman's point of view forcefully and unambiguously: "that feeling that happens when you are about to go to bed with a cat for the first time." The man is a "cat"—being a "cool cat" was a term of high approbation—and he is being admired and apprised in ways which conventionally would be "male" ways of judging a female: "those cheekbones and lovely eyes." The woman knows what she wants and she takes it guiltlessly and with pleasure.

In a passage concerning the police we are given a veritable cornucopia of "with it" lingo—*fuzz, man, wow, pad, drag*: "Fuzz he said fuzz is looking for me. Oh I said oh man what a drag. Like I can't go to my pad he said . . . Like he said wow I said to Ben. He just said wow kind of."[2] Here "like" employed as a discourse marker seems a precursor to Valleyspeak—the language of young women in California's San Fernando Valley—while "kind of" also functions similarly to "like" in conveying the emotional tentativeness and confusion of the situation. *La vie bohème*—there are allusions to Proust, Blake, Redon, Virgil, Byron, and Shelley—however is often far from romantic. Rats in the kitchen, bugs in a new apartment appear, but a robust, lively sense of ironic humor prevails as in Di Prima's description of getting hooked on Oreo cookies which she eats copiously, helping her to "get through january. to get through january in manhattan is hard, to get through january and february the same year almost impossible."[3]

The prose is swiftly moving, often composed in lower case, à la e.e. cummings. One also notes a childlike, innocent, pre-hippy tone reminiscent of Richard Brautigan: "and then i went out and brought back from the snow pastrami sandwiches and ale and yes more oreos and we waited for it to get dark," as well as a touch of the confiding, onrushing voice of Holden Caulfield in *The Catcher in the Rye* (1951) when Di Prima chronicles her return after Swarthmore to her family home: "There were dozens and dozens of family dinners that happened to me after I left school . . . mostly they were the dinners of holidays, of thanksgiving and Christmas and easter and birthday parties. Some of them were weddings and one that I remember was a funeral but I won't tell about that not this time." Nancy M. Grace has noted in her essay "The Beat Fairy Tale and Transnational Spectacle Culture: Diane di Prima and William S. Burroughs," the "once upon a time," fairy-tale quality in *Dinners and Nightmares*, observing that "the tale makes sense as a form that might attract Beat writers, many of whom were philosophically committed to the concept of childhood as a pure state of being and also identified magic and wonder as counters to the horrors of the nationally and globally focused Cold War."[4] The conflicts described earlier surface when our narrator has dinner in a fancy Chinese restaurant with an "Old Family Friend" and upon returning to her apartment "vomited for the first time in my life from anger and cried for the millionth time in my life from anger I scarcely ever cry from anything else."[5] Holden was perhaps a pre- or proto-Beat in his wounded innocence: like Holden, she also becomes nauseated when confronting hypocrisy, cruelty, and ugliness in the "adult world." The autobiographical narrative also reveals the young Di Prima we have met in earlier chapters: this is a brainy young woman who studies ancient Greek, calculus, and medieval philosophy in her spare time, challenging conventional gender roles by leading an independent life, having a child on her own, and dedicating herself to creative pursuits. She describes family celebrations with many aunts, a large Italian family with seventeen cousins; she wears Levi's, not a dress—much to her mother's consternation. This chapter's close is understated as she leaves the family matrix for her apartment: "then I would say some cool things to my brothers, take the food and go back to my part of the world."[6]

Di Prima also includes details of her literary experimentation. One afternoon she is waiting for a lover to arrive and when he doesn't show up, productively employs the time to compose a play: "I took out a pair of dice and made some rules and began to write a play by chance, which is a good way to pass time and not very difficult, and at the time I called it six poets in search of a corkscrew, which was a title that had been hanging around." This intelligent humor is typical of the book as a whole—here obviously riffing on Luigi Pirandello's great play *Six Characters in Search of an Author*. She tells us that the play was later performed and called *Paideuma*—and indeed it was staged at New York's Living Theatre in 1960—the title is from Ezra Pound's adaptation of the term employed by German anthropologist Leo Frobenius (1873–1938) which Pound defined as "the active element in the era, the complex of ideas which is in a given time germinal, reaching into the next epoch, but conditioning actively all the thought and action of its own time."[7]

The "Nightmares" section is divided into thirteen prose/poems which recount absurd, surrealistic dreamlike, black humor episodes, sometimes of only one sentence in length as in "Nightmare 6": "Get your cut throat off my knife" or "Nightmare 13": "It hurts to be murdered"—recounting the darker side of megapolitan life. One recalls the wry, black humored twenty-seventh entry in Bob Kaufman's *Jail Poems*: "There, Jesus, didn't hurt a bit, did it?" One episode which later appeared in Paul Goodman's anthology *Seeds of Liberation* (1964)—"Memories of Childhood"—describes a youthful encounter with a man possessing an hydrogen bomb, revealing how reality and imagination began to blur for sensitive young people during the fearful, postatomic 1950s. The "Conversations" are stripped-down dialogues in the manner of Hemingway, with no punctuation save for periods at the ends of sentences or quotation marks indicating dialogue which is rendered as bare "he said," "she said." "No Saviors for this Race" depicts a discussion about the Soviet invasion of Hungary in 1956. Di Prima later recalled how during high school she "experienced the sudden closing down of the American horizon that was the Korean War. One's boyfriends suddenly draft-age. Then the post-war madness." It is clear that the aftermath of the Second World War, Hiroshima, Nagasaki, Hungary—all contribute to the Cold War angst of this turbulent period. Gregory Corso memorialized America's use of atomic weapons in his famous poem "Bomb" and Di Prima records the initial tremors of the planetary crisis which would compel the Beat generation to search for new forms of spiritual experience and philosophical wisdom. Thus the book's various sections illustrate youthful American lives from a number of perspectives. Several sketches depict young artists discussing their work: Jackson Pollock, Alexander Calder, Baudelaire's *Les Fleurs du Mal*, the letters of Van Gogh to his brother Theo, and Wanda Landowska's performance of Bach's *Goldberg Variations* weave in and out of their conversations. These allusions to politics, literature, art and classical music will recur in *Memoirs of a Beatnik* (1969).

In the 1950s, young women such as Di Prima rebelled against the conformist lives that had been prepared for them. As Wini Breines has observed in her essay "The 'Other' Fifties: Beats and Bad Girls":

A subterranean life, acted out or dreamed about, was generated by a culture that penalized girls and young women who were unable or unwilling to fit the model of the perky, popular teenager eagerly anticipating marriage and motherhood. The rigidity of what was acceptable in that culture made some young women feel discontented and unreal, as if their lives had not yet begun. The parameters of feminine beauty, personality, intelligence, and ambition were narrow enough that a minor deviation meant exclusion and discomfort and, often unintentionally, became a wedge that grew into insurgence.

Being a smart, Italian American radical did not exactly set Di Prima up for the conventional life depicted in *Leave It to Beaver* or *The Donna Reed Show*. As we have seen in Chapter 1, Di Prima had already in high school been a member of a group of eight young women calling themselves "The Branded" who defined themselves in opposition to the expectations of the dominant culture. They were black, white, Italian-American, heterosexual, bisexual, lesbian, smart, interested in books and ideas, practicers of the occult, defiant of the "place" women were told to occupy. We see the "insurgence" of a pre-1960s women's liberation sensibility reflected in *Dinners and Nightmares* when in one exchange, a female artist tells her male partner she is weary of washing the dishes: she is as busy as he, but "just because I happen to be a chick" is expected to do all the chores. The narrative closes: "I got up and went into the kitchen to do the dishes. And shit I thought I probably won't bother again. But I'll get bugged and not bother to tell you and after a while everything will be awful and I'll never say anything because it's so fucking uncool to talk about it. And that I thought will be that and what a shame. Hey hon Mark yelled at me from the living room. It says here Picasso produces fourteen hours a day."[8] Mark is clearly oblivious to the notion that his partner might be able to be as creative as Picasso were he to take responsibility for a few household duties. And we also note a style which we recognize today—"because it's so fucking uncool to talk about it"—which sounds now as stark and compact and declarative in a radically honest way as it did more than a half-century ago.

Di Prima thus was ahead of her time in suggesting the stultifying roles foisted upon women as well as in her open depictions of gay life. There were widespread persecutions and "witchhunts" of people considered sexual "deviants" as well as communists during this period and the FBI conducted surveillance of homosexuals through the 1970s. One "Conversation"—"And Face the Day"—considers questions of gender and sexuality. Brad tells the nameless girl that his parents are "all worked up about the queer bit again," and she responds: "Shit man I said nearly everybody's bisexual." At the close Brad tells her: "I love you he said but I'm queer," to which she responds: "I touched the hollow in his face, just under the cheekbone. I know I said don't worry. It's not important."[9] This scene is reflective of Di Prima's own sexual orientation. She was bisexual and many of her male friends were either gay or bisexual including Freddie Herko, Frank O'Hara, and Alan Marlowe, whom she would marry in 1962. Di Prima recalled: "For me and for some of the people I knew, it didn't really matter what the sex of somebody—if you wanted to sleep with them, you did. Sex was a way of learning, a journey into someone, so you came closer to them and knew them and their life better. And if they were a woman or a man or they liked this or that, that was just part of it, that is, what you were learning. It wasn't so much, 'Now I'm being gay, now I'm being straight.' At least that's how it was for me." Di Prima's attitude toward sex and gender recall what has been argued concerning the ancient Greeks: they did not have categories for "homosexual" or "heterosexual" and that only later did separating and sorting people according to sexual preference become a historical imperative.

A significant undertaking of Di Prima's during this period was editing with LeRoi Jones—he would change his name in 1967 to Amiri Baraka—*The Floating Bear*, one of the era's most influential underground publications. Di Prima had been reading *Winnie the Pooh* to her daughter Jeanne "in which The Floating Bear was an upturned umbrella and 'sometimes it was a boat, and sometimes it was an accident.' I figured our magazine would be like that." Of thirty-seven issues published, Baraka coedited the first twenty-five. Baraka had experience with publishing at the Totem Press and *Yugen* and hence had developed a great deal of skill. Di Prima noted that he "could work at an incredible rate. He could read two manuscripts at a time, one with each eye. He would spread things out on the table while he was eating supper, and reject them all—listening to the news and a jazz record he was going to review, all at the same time." Baraka himself recalled in his *Autobiography* that it "was coming out regularly and became the talk of our various interconnected literary circles. It was meant to be 'quick, fast, and in a hurry.' Something that could carry the zigs and zags of the literary scene as well as some word of the general New York creative ambience." Bookstores did not carry *The Floating Bear*: it was sent by mail free to those who desired it.[10] Di Prima was one of the prime movers in what would become the efflorescence of underground publishing during the 1960s. As Ron Loewinsohn has remarked in "After the (mimeograph) revolution":

> But more important than the quality of their contents was the fact of these magazines' abundance and speed. Having them, we could see what we were doing, as it came, hot off the griddle. We could get instant response to what we'd written last week, & we could respond instantly to what the guy across town or across the country had written last month. Further, many poets who didn't stand a Christian's chance against the lions of "proper" publication in university quarterlies or "big-time" magazines could get exposure &, more importantly, encouragement &/or criticism. For all its excesses it was a healthy condition.[11]

One important contributor to *The Floating Bear*—Charles Olson (1910–70)—would become a significant figure in Di Prima's career. In 1951, Olson taught at the experimental arts school in North Carolina, Black Mountain College, becoming its rector from 1951 to 1956. As we have seen, his influential essay

"Projective Verse" (1950) emphasized the creation of poetry which measures the syllable and emphasizes movement by the breath of each line rather than conventional meter as well as the precise placement of words on the page as in a musical score. One may observe Olson's influence in the patterned ways Di Prima often organized the appearance of her own poems. Olson's rejection of "traditional American values" also appealed to Di Prima for he sought wisdom in sources as diverse as ancient Sumeria and Apollonius of Tyana—about whom he composed a play. The two poets would also ingest LSD together. Like D. H. Lawrence, Olson would find sources of spiritual and physical power in the culture of the Maya and Aztecs of Mexico: Olson spent six months—from December 1950 to July 1951—in Lerma in the Yucatan studying Mayan glyphs with the help of Alfred Tozzer's *A Maya Grammar*. Olson wrote Creeley who would edit his *Mayan Letters* (1953): "I have no doubt . . . that the American will more and more repossess himself of the Indian past." In his essay "Human Universe," first published in Cid Corman's *Origin* no. 4, Winter 1951–52, Olson includes a lovely passage in praise of the modern descendents of the Maya whom he encountered on the buses which took him on his archaeological investigations:

> When I am rocked by the roads against any of them—kids, women, men—their flesh is most gentle, is granted, touch is in no sense anything but the natural law of flesh, there is none of that pull-away which, in the States, causes a man for all the years of his life the deepest sort of questioning of the rights of himself to the wild reachings of his own organism. The admission these people give me and one another is direct, and the individual who peers out from that flesh is precisely himself, is a curious wandering animal like me—it is so very beautiful how animal human eyes are when the flesh is not worn so close it chokes, how human and individuated the look comes out of a human eye when the house of it is not exaggerated.

Olson sought in the Maya, in ancient Sumeria, in his play about Apollonius of Tyana for the intuitive, direct contact with spiritual and sensual reality he found absent in modern America.

There are echoes of Olson's ideas in Di Prima's celebrated poem "Rant" in which she declaims: "History is a living weapon in yr hand/& you have imagined it, it is thus that you 'find out for yourself'/history is the dream of what can be, it is/the relation between things in a continuum/of imagination." The phrase Di Prima quotes—"find out for yourself"—alludes to Olson's reference in "Letter 23 Maximus broke it" which ends: "I would be an historian as Herodotus was, looking/for oneself for the evidence of/what is said." In *The Special View of History*, Olson points out that for Herodotus, the ancient Greek *historin*—from which we derive *history*—"appears to mean 'finding out for oneself,' instead of depending on hearsay." If Di Prima learned from Olson, Olson was also grateful to the younger poet for she recalled that Olson found *The Floating Bear* extremely useful:

> I remember that the last time I saw Charles Olson in Gloucester, one of the things he talked about was how valuable the Bear had been to him in its early years because of the fact that he could get new work out that fast. He was very involved in speed, in communication. We got manuscripts from him pretty regularly in the early years of the *Bear*, and we'd usually get them into the very next issue. That meant that his work, his thoughts, would be in the hands of a few hundred writers within two or three weeks. It was like writing a letter to a bunch of friends.

The first issues contained twelve pages and were produced on a mimeograph machine at Robert Wilson's Phoenix Book Shop: *The Floating Bear* was distinctive because it included work by writers from a variety of "schools"— New York, San Francisco Renaissance, Beat, and Black Mountain.[12]

The Floating Bear began as a bimonthly containing approximately six sheets and the first mailing list included about one hundred recipients: authors published included Gregory Corso, Edward Field, Gilbert Sorrentino, Robert Creeley, Jack Kerouac, John Wieners, Denise Levertov, John Ashbery, Allen Ginsberg, Robert Duncan, Gary Snyder, Frank O'Hara, and Charles Olson—two of his brief "Maximus" poems appeared in the first issue. Di Prima sent a copy to the Trappist monk Thomas Merton who responded by sending postage stamps to help her effort since he had no money. When *The Floating Bear* published William S. Burroughs's "Roosevelt After the Election" in its ninth issue—the text is a parody of F. D. R.'s Cabinet officials whom Burroughs depicts being compelled to undergo intercourse with a baboon—Di Prima was pursued by the FBA for alleged "obscenity":

> When the Supreme Court overruled some of the legislations perpetrated by this vile rout, Roosevelt forced that august body, one after the other, on threat of immediate reduction to the rank of Congressional Lavatory Assistants, to submit to intercourse with a purple assed baboon, so that venerable, honored men surrendered themselves to the embraces of a lecherous snarling simian, while Roosevelt and his strumpet wife and the veteran brown nose Harry Hopkins, smoking a communal hookah of hashish, watch the lamentable sight with cackles of obscene laughter.

LeRoi Jones was arrested on October 18, 1961, and his mailing lists were confiscated as well. Di Prima herself had been in the practice of never answering her door before noon since she had expected likely visits from law enforcement. The day of Jones's arrest, she and her young daughter went up the fire escape to Freddie Herko's apartment while the FBI knocked on the door. When Di Prima heard them leave, she returned to her apartment, got dressed up to go to court, and Freddie explained to her daughter that "mom has to go downtown and explain some stuff to some very stupid men who didn't understand something she had published." The grand jury ultimately threw out the case.

Over the years, Di Prima would develop a continuing relationship with Burroughs and their intellectual paths converged on a number of levels. When she began living with Alan Marlowe, Herbert Huncke and Burroughs visited and they ingested LSD together, experiences which would appear in a book she composed between 1961 and 1964, *The Calculus of Variation*: "the LSD illumination. Torn through, all shapes of matter." At a 4:00 p.m. performance at the American Theatre for Poets on February 14, 1965, Burroughs arrived wearing a three-piece suit, a topcoat and fedora and carrying a briefcase. He played tape recordings of the North African Joujouka music of which he was fond combined with cut-up sound of pneumatic drills, static from a radio, and his voice reading text from newspapers. He read excerpts from *Junkie*, *Naked Lunch*, *Nova Express* and also played a cut-up tape of *Dutch Schultz's Last Words*. Di Prima mimeographed and collated the text because Burroughs wanted the audience to have a copy: she handed them out as they left the theater. As we shall see in the following chapter, in the mid-1970s when Di Prima's friendship with Burroughs deepened, they engaged in frequent discussions regarding magic and the occult. In "Revolutionary Letter Number Forty-Five," she counsels that those involved in political struggle must "take hold of the magic any way we can/and use it in total faith/to seek help in realms we have been taught to think of/as "mythological"/to contact ALL LEVELS of one's own being/& loose the forces therein/always seeking in this to remain psychically inconspicuous/on the not so unlikely chance/ that those we have thought of as "instigators"/are just the front men for a gang of black magicians/based "somewhere else" in space/to whom the WHOLE of earth is a colony to exploit/(the "Nova Mob" not so far out as you think)." The "Nova Mob" is an allusion to Burroughs's *Nova Express* in which Inspector Lee and the Nova Police battle the Nova Mob led by Mr Bradly-Mr Martin to wrest away from them their control of reality—the "gang of black magicians" who seek to exploit planet Earth as their "colony." [13]

In addition to her publishing and editing ventures, Di Prima also founded—with James Waring, John Herbert McDowell, LeRoi Jones, Alan Marlowe, and Fred Herko—the New York Poets Theatre in order to produce one-act plays composed by poets. [14] She planned to stage the music of her friend McDowell, dances by Herko, Waring's choreography as well as her own and others' plays. [15] Located on East Fourth Street between the Bowery and Second Avenue at the East End Theatre, a typical weekly schedule would feature: Monday and Tuesday, dance evenings; Thursday, music evenings; Friday through Sunday evenings, new drama; on alternate Sundays, poetry readings. In the gallery, Di Prima exhibited collages by Ray Johnson (1927–95) as well as photographs by Jack Smith. A section of LeRoi Jones's *The System of Dante's Hell* was staged, as well as Michael McClure's *The Pillow*. The last act of Robert Duncan's *Faust Foutu* and plays by Barbara Guest and Wallace Stevens were performed. When the Poets Theatre was closed "by order of police," it reopened as the American Arts Project and staged Michael McClure's *The Blossom, or Billy the Kid*, with sets by George Herms in June/July 1964. This was a notable event because the evenings opened with audiotapes of Antonin Artaud's radio play *To Have Done with the Judgement of God*. Replete with screams, cries, and clashing gongs, its scatological anti-Catholicism caused the French authorities to cancel its premiere on February 2, 1948, and Artaud would die a month later. The text was a favorite with Philip Lamantia and Robert Duncan in San Francisco and Artaud would become a significant figure for the Beats in his explorations of madness, experiments with drugs and celebrated sojourn among the Tarahamura Indians in Mexico. Other notable theatrical events were chronicled by Ed Sanders, poet and musician in The Fugs who had met Di Prima when she worked at the Phoenix Book Shop. Sanders recalled a flier Di Prima typed for the week of March 3–9, 1965: "March 3 saw Brion Gysin's 'Permutations and Permutated Portraits,' plus Robert Filliou, 'Street Fighting/Whispered Art History.' Then March 4, at midnight, Dick Higgins performed 'Requiem for Wagner the Criminal Mayor.' On Monday, March 8 were The Fugs, 'Tuli Kupferberg, Ed Sanders, Kenneth Weaver in a new rock-and-roll program.' The next day, March 9, Allan Kaprow gave a talk called 'The Techniques and New Goals of Happenings.'"

Movies were shown as well: in 1964, Jack Smith's *Flaming Creatures*, *Andy Warhol Films Jack Smith Filming Normal Love* and Jean Genet's *Un Chant d'Amour* led to a court case alleging obscenity.[16] Indeed, the experimental and avant-garde films of the 1950s and 1960s began to accelerate the techniques of cinema into new dimensions and it became possible to think of a great film as having the same potential for depth, originality, and emotional power as any other work of art. Indeed, the concept of the *auteur*—the notion that a film director possessed a degree of creative autonomy and control over his/her work such that a film may indeed be considered an artistic production of the highest order—began to become widespread. Directors such as Stanley Kubrick, Werner Herzog, Federico Fellini, Akira Kurosawa, Rainer Maria Fassbinder, cinephiles often awaited their new works with the expectancy formerly reserved for the latest work of a distinguished composer, writer, or painter. Ingmar Bergman in his autobiography *The Magic Lantern* spoke of cinema as a route to oneiric timelessness: "Film as dream, film as music. No form of art goes beyond ordinary consciousness as film does, straight to our emotions, deep into the twilight room of the soul." Di Prima in her devotion to film certainly was aware of the potentialities of this relatively new art form and thus showing films along with performing plays was a complementary way of organizing her programs.

Because of her wide-ranging contacts in the literary world, Di Prima began to reach out personally to many authors she had known only through correspondence and professional association. San Francisco was the place Allen Ginsberg had premiered *Howl* in 1955 and California had long been a central locus of radical philosophical exploration where Taoism, Theosophy, Vedantism, Hinduism, and Zen Buddhism had been practiced. During the early 1960s, Di Prima made the first of several trips to California—in August 1961 and again in September 1962. During the first visit she traveled with her four-year-old daughter Jeanne, staying with Michael McClure and his wife at their apartment at 2324 Fillmore Street. Poet Philip Whalen (1923–2002), a Buddhist who became a close friend, played host, showing her California's exotic flora and fauna. An episode later recounted in *The Calculus of Variation* (1972) describes his attentive presence: "Phil Whalen . . . walks among bonsai trees in the old part of the city. Phil Whalen pointing them out: fifty years old . . . . Phil, his robe is off, all to the navel. He sits under a tree, beside his staff, which lies on the ground. He sees what he looks at." Of course *seeing what you look at* is a concise description of the goals of Zen Buddhist practice. Michael McClure arranged for her to also meet Robert Duncan, who was not thrilled about the encounter until he saw Di Prima combing out her long, striking, red hair: a close friendship now commenced.[17]

Duncan's immersion in Theosophy, Gnosticism, magic, and mystical experience spoke deeply to Di Prima, who as we have seen from childhood had a profound affinity for these topics. Duncan had been adopted by Theosophists as an infant, and in *The H.D. Book* (2011)—his ambitious study of poet Hilda Dolittle (1886–1961)—Duncan remembered his childhood as a time when he would overhear his parents speak of ancient Egypt, clairvoyance, reincarnation, Plato, and the lost continents of Atlantis and Lemuria. Furthermore, they believed—as would Duncan himself—that

> God was not a god, but from His Being He sent out teachers or gods. True teachers—Christ, Hermes, or Lao-Tse—were Light Beings, messengers of the Sun itself, a Sun to which our sun but referred . . . the theosophy of Plutarch, of Plotinus and Pseudo-Dionysius the Areopagite, the hermeticism of Pico della Mirandola, with The Light of Asia and the Bhagavad-Gita, joined in the confusion of texts and testimonies of libraries that could include accounts written by trance-mediums of travel to past time or far planets, manuals of practical astrology and numerology, or Max Heindel's *The Rosicrucian Cosmo-Conception*.[18]

As we shall see in the following chapter, Di Prima's friendship with Duncan would continue during the early 1970s and his influence became increasingly discernible in her poems devoted to esoteric topics. During this time she would also make a translation of Robert Fludd's (1574–1637) Latin Rosicrucian texts.

This West Coast sojourn was immensely significant in Di Prima's development since she would gradually combine her New York Beat sensibility with California's emergent hippie culture which was flourishing in the Bay Area as well as Los Angeles. Topanga Canyon near the Pacific Ocean became an enclave of bohemian creativity and Di Prima would spend time there with actor and artist Dean Stockwell (to whom she would dedicate her poem "Nightspore" celebrating the Canyon's landscape) and George Herms. She met several authors including Philip Lamantia, Lew Welch, Kirby Doyle, David Meltzer, and Wallace Berman, as well as artists Jay DeFeo—she saw DeFeo's celebrated masterwork "The Rose" (created 1958–66) at her apartment—Marjorie Cameron and Bruce Conner (1993–2008). Just as the Beats in New York had fraternized with the Abstract

FIGURE 3.1 *Robert Duncan. Photo courtesy of Stanford University Libraries.* © *Allen Ginsberg Estate.*

Expressionists, so too it is noteworthy that when Allen Ginsberg premiered *Howl* in San Francisco on October 7, 1955, it occurred in the Six Gallery which had previously been called the King Ubu Gallery where the paintings of Robert Duncan's partner Jess Collins had been exhibited. Denis Johnston in *Precipitations: Contemporary American Poetry as Occult Practice* has pointed out that artists such as Collins, Bruce Conner, Jay DeFeo, and George Herms all "drew on a hodgepodge of occult and religious sources, as did the filmmakers Stan Brakhage, Harry Smith, and Kenneth Anger. Likewise, among practitioners of the 'New American Poetry' such as Helen Adam, Robert Duncan, Robert Kelly, Philip Lamantia, Diane di Prima, John Wieners, and Allen Ginsberg, occultism proved a topical source of interest as well as a means by which to define their process." Richard Candida Smith has traced alchemical symbolism in "The Rose" via DeFeo's readings in the work of C. G. Jung—De Feo, Conner, and Berman were also (like the Beats) ardent admirers of William Blake—while Conner declared that he and his fellow artists "were interested in a spiritual quest. It was a time when people would die or go to jail for their art." Conner was speaking of his friend Wallace Berman, publisher of the important underground magazine *Semina* which appeared in nine issues from 1955 to 1964. Michael McClure called *Semina* "a real outlaw act, as complex as outlaws in the Old West, as sexy and cool and hip and pop—and at the same time religious." Berman was immersed in Kabbalah (which would become a preoccupation of Di Prima's) and his Ferus Gallery in Los Angeles was raided by the police for "obscenity." David Meltzer, a student of Kabbalah, compiled an anthology of Kabbalistic texts, *The Secret Garden*. Herms was a pioneer in the evolution of Californian assemblage sculpture whom Di Prima would later invite to New York in the spring of 1964 to design sets for Michael McClure's *The Blossom, or Billy the Kid*.

When Di Prima visited Herms at his cottage, she noted that its front yard "was surrounded by indescribable 'junk sculptures,' 'assemblages' the art world called them later. All the glowing objects of the local dump—phosphorescence of decay and change—were brought into relation here so that their magickal essence stood revealed. George Herms lived here with his wife Louise and their child Nalota, who was a bit younger than Jeanne." We note here again Di Prima's invocation of alchemical phosphorus as well as Aleister Crowley's "magick." Herms also provided illustrations for a sequence of Di Prima haiku poems which were published in 1966, the cover work for *L.A. Odyssey* (1968) and he had also taken several photographs of Freddie Herko, three of which Di Prima would include in her *Freddie Poems* (1974). Like Di Prima, the assemblage artists studied Hinduism, Buddhism Native American culture, and astrology. Herms, for example, incorporated astrological materials into his wall-mounted assemblage *Saturn Collage* (1960). Rebecca Solnit has noted that compared to their East Coast colleagues, California artists were "a hermetic tribe of icon-makers" who were "concerned with religious and drug-induced experience . . . . Berman and Herms made art that reflected the state of transcendence central to such experience, a state that blurs traditional distinctions between beautiful and ugly, sacred and profane, precious and worthless. In one way or another, this state of transcendence seems to have been an important goal in the arts of the time." The West Coast artists in many respects were unique and just as she had become part of the artistic community in New York, so too in California Di Prima would be at ease within the world of the visual arts. One might argue that just as Zen strives to improve one's ability to look straight at the world without preconceptions—without the filters which categorize objects and events as either "sacred" or "profane," "special" or "common"—so too California artists wanted to view the world before them as it was, to show the observer what had always been before his or her eyes but which they had so taken for granted that they never indeed *perceived* what it was they were looking at.

Marjorie Cameron (1922–95) was an intriguing figure employing symbolism in her art derived from studies of British occultist Aleister Crowley (1875–1947), whose works, as we have seen, Di Prima also perused. Cameron's infamous untitled drawing—known as "Peyote Vision"(1955)—depicting a fierce, alien-like creature engaging in canine-style sexual intercourse with a female whose snake-like forked tongue flares out extended in ecstasy, led to the closing of Wallace Berman's exhibition at the Ferus Gallery in 1957. By all accounts, Cameron was a mysterious, wild, and tragic personality whom Di Prima met through Berman: he had used a photograph of Cameron's face on the cover of the first issue of *Semina*. Di Prima took to her immediately, noting her green eyes and vibrant red hair. Upon leaving the Bermans where she had been staying during her trip to Southern California, Di Prima had inadvertently left at their house a carved lingam-and-yoni sculpture which she had employed as an altar. She called the Bermans, telling them to give it to Cameron. Di Prima was aware that she was about to set out for the desert for "a magickal retreat" and that her friend would experience challenging times during this event requiring the help she could derive from the sculpture. Di Prima reported that fifteen years later, Cameron informed her that indeed the carving had been of great use to her during that difficult period of her life. Cameron's works have recently been rediscovered, and Di Prima devoted a poem "For Cameron" included in *Loba* to her memory: "How was woman broken?/ Falling out of attention./Wiping gnarled fingers on a faded housedress/Lying down in the puddle beside the broken jug." She laments the decline of her friend and the ways women become trapped in unfulfilling relationships: "Where was the slack, the loss/of early fierceness?/How did we come to be contained/in rooms?/ Which room/holds the jewels which buy us/& for which we have/other uses?" One can see why Di Prima would include this poem in her archetypal epic *Loba* since Cameron represented Woman in yet another of her many incarnations as artist/magician and seer.

Another important figure whom Di Prima met during her second trip to San Francisco in September 1962 was Shunryu Suzuki Roshi (1904–71), who recently founded the San Francisco Zen Center with a branch in the city called Sokoji at 1881 Bush Street, as well as a mountain center in Tassajara. The Buddhist community in California began as early as 1905, when—according to Rick Fields in *How the Swans Came to the Lake: A Narrative of Buddhism in America*—the Japanese Zen master Soyen Shaku arrived in San Francisco. D. T. Suzuki—who emerged as one of the strongest influences on Beats such as Gary Snyder—acted as Shaku's interpreter. For Di Prima, the encounter with an authentic representative of this venerable tradition was transformative. For the first time in her twenty-eight years, she had a direct encounter with a profound place within herself.[19] Di Prima had recently been studying Heinrich Zimmer's *Philosophies of India* where Zimmer describes the *guru*, and she wondered if she would ever find an inspiring teacher. Suzuki would be the first of several gurus who became central to Di Prima's spiritual life: later she would study with Chogyam Trungpa and Lama Tharchin Rinpoche. Upon meeting Suzuki, she trusted him completely and decided to become his pupil. Di Prima also recognized as she participated in Zen *sesshin*—or extended retreats—as well as *dokusans*—private interviews with Suzuki—that there was a continuity between her activities as a writer and spiritual practice:

> The instruction given at my first interview was to form my deepest question in such a way that it would express the totality of my understanding, as it was at moment, to my teacher. The bow, the question, asked the same thing of me that the poem did: that I render utter trust to myself, as I was, knowing that I knew more than I knew. This surrender to what Roshi called Big Mind is what I had felt from the beginning to be required of me as a writer: it was with this understanding that I came to the cushion.[20]

As with Jack Kerouac's concept of "spontaneous bop prosody," Di Prima sought freedom within discipline. She allowed herself to know that she knew more than she knew—to let the unconscious speak without interference, surrendering and trusting the moment of inspiration just as she did during her Zen meditation.

During this trip, Di Prima also continued her writing projects. Before leaving for California, she began composing a play entitled *Whale Honey* concerning the death of Percy Bysshe Shelley enacted by just three characters: Byron, Mary Shelley, and Shelley himself. She continued working on *Whale Honey*—like *Murder Cake* another playful, *koan*-like title—while staying at Stinson Beach with her lover Alan Marlowe, whom she now agreed to marry and with whom she would have a child named Alexander: Shunryu Suzuki performed the marriage ceremony.[21] Suzuki's influence on Di Prima's inner life may be seen in the fact that when Di Prima left California to return to the East Coast, she took with her a *zafu*—the round cushion employed in *zazen* meditation. Upon arriving in New York, she found a new apartment at Thirty-Five Cooper Square. Due to her poverty she was compelled to place as a deposit a Jim Dine assemblage the artist had given her. She had continued her friendship with the owner of the Phoenix Bookstore, Robert Wilson, who left a vivid account of Di Prima's colorful life during this period:

> She was living at the time with her third husband, Alan Marlowe, in a condemned building—quite illegally, of course—in what is now called the East Village. Actually it was on Cooper Union Square, just a few houses south of the Cooper Union Building . . . . Diane was there not only with her husband, but her three children from prior attachments. As well as an enormous number of hangers-on, musicians, poets, various ex-lovers of her bisexual husband, and all too often, simply spongers. Virtually none of them had jobs or could in any way contribute money to the communal establishment, but somehow Diane always managed to supply food and shelter for anyone who came knocking at her door.

This situation would be repeated a few years later when she lived in the Hotel Albert in a similarly communitarian fashion.

Di Prima would now discover the work of the most celebrated Tibetan saint, Milarepa (1028/40–1111/23 CE), also much admired by Henry Miller. A romantic figure, Milarepa studied sorcery and black magic to avenge wrongs done to his family and sought salvation through Buddhist study for his violent acts. His master Marpa compelled him to undergo difficult trials which he successfully overcame. Marpa also taught him the wisdom of the Tantric master Naropa (1016–1100 CE). His karma thus purified, he led a life of solitude in Himalayan mountain caves, wearing only a cotton cloth against the cold. At the Orientalia Bookstore, Nicol Cernovich gifted her with a deluxe two-volume set of *The Hundred Thousand Songs of Milarepa*. In her poem concerning her relationship with LeRoi Jones, "For the Dead Lecturer"—the title derives from Jones's eponymous poetry volume published in 1964—Di Prima writes: "I have heard you creaking/ over the roof at night to steal my books/coming in thru the telephone wires/just when my head/was empty/When Milarepa and other Tantric wisdom/was clambering thru my skull." Di Prima now began rising in the morning, burning incense as she recited her mantra—"I take my refuge in Shiva and Kali"—reading Milarepa, and sitting for a half hour on her *zafu*. One may thus see how Di Prima continued to incorporate both in her writings and daily life an intense syncretic spiritual practice. Indeed, this thoughtful attention to meditation became inextricably bound up with her poetics, for the symbolism of her poems often derived from visions Di

Prima experienced during these deep interior voyages. She kept in touch with Shunryu Suzuki through Richard Baker—a poet from the Midwest whom Di Prima had known through correspondence regarding *The Floating Bear*—and Baker sent Suzuki's responses back to her. This relationship with Suzuki was one of the primary reasons Di Prima would later return to settle permanently in California in 1968.[22] As we shall see, Buddhism as well as Chinese philosophy—the *I Ching* in particular—became central aspects of Di Prima's life as well as oeuvre.

Di Prima's next major writings chart her transition from the hip, cool 1950s scene to the 1960s mystical sensibility and she attributed at least one reason for this stylistic shift to her ingestion of peyote. After this trip, she began composing poems which would become *The New Handbook of Heaven* (1963) published by Dave Haselwood's Auerhahn Press in San Francisco—the title itself indicating a shift to a new orientation. There is a leap in technique and thematic density demonstrated in these poems, which will continue with *The Calculus of Variation*. Di Prima revealed that her poems now

> broke open to long lines like those in *The New Handbook of Heaven*. That book started after the peyote trip in '59 in my apartment on the Lower East Side. Jimmy [Waring] also helped as a teacher of mine. He said to follow precisely wherever the poem went—"the graph of the moving mind" (that's Philip Whalen's phrase), rather than this thing that I was doing earlier of cut, cut, cut, and make it sparse. I think I was doing that to learn certain techniques. This wasn't about technique now, it was about really following and being obedient to consciousness, as Robert Duncan liked to put it. That started in 1959.[23]

The condensed lines each seem a separate thought charting the opaque movement of consciousness, one moving after the other: the poems constitute a radically different approach from the learned philosophical poems such as "John Dee," "Paracelsus," and "Tsogyal" and the poems cast in the direct, declarative, and transparent mode of *Revolutionary Letters*. Di Prima commenced writing following the beginning of her affair with LeRoi Jones—she rapidly composed at this time all five sections of the final extended poem "The Jungle," first published in *Yugen* 7, 1961. She thought of *The New Handbook of Heaven* as a book of love poems to Jones, conceiving it as a kind of dialogue between them.[24] It is noteworthy that Di Prima imagined their relationship as a mythic archetype which she derived from her reading of Heinrich Zimmer's *The King and the Corpse* where she encountered the Grail story of Lancelot and Guinevere. She perceived

> that in a reversal of roles that was usual with me, I was Lancelot to Roy's Guinevere. It was I who had the task not to hesitate when he appeared suddenly, as he often did, in a gallows-cart in front of me. Not to hesitate

for the barest second, not to miss a step—as Lancelot did in the story—but to leap on the cart beside him, share his fate. Whatever that might be. I leaped. I was acrobat in life as well as in art. I leaped often enough that it felt like a way of life.

It is typical of Di Prima's imagination to perceive relationships between literal reality and the world of symbolic archetypes, as we shall see later in her masterwork *Loba* as well as in her autobiographical *Recollections of My Life as a Woman*. The myth tells the *true* story, the deeper story, the symbolic narrative of how we are to be made whole again. We also recall that Di Prima had often cited Jean Cocteau's belief that an artist must be an "acrobat" in order to constantly be ahead of his or her audience. So too, in her love affair, she sought to "leap" like Cocteau. She conceived of her love for Jones in spiritual terms: he was the "Beloved as Godhead. . . . We were each to the other the door into boundless space."[25]

Cocteau returns in the poem "Vector" which is dedicated to him and contains a pattern of astronomical language—*space, void, stars, atoms, constellations, light*—which recurs throughout *The New Handbook of Heaven*. A "vector" is a term from mathematics and physics indicating a quantity having direction as well as magnitude, especially as determining the position of one point in space relative to another. Di Prima begins: "this: to Xplode/the love affair with space./that the void penetrate/make talons/make like fangs/slip in/mist is an incarnation much desired/the modeling of light . . . the stars/are always blackest on the other side of the void." Primal, sexual language is juxtaposed with cosmic imagery, as revealed in the next verse: "if I cd get hot pants for you, not just/the affable desirings of warmth/how we are friends!" There is also a reference to the Eumenides or the Furies: "I'm in headlong flight from something I will meet/the hand in my back, just below the shoulderblades/Eumenides?/the stars/with streaming hair/scream laugh awake/my feet haven't touched the ground in years/a gentle wobbling motion/side to side." *The Eumenides* is the final play of Aeschylus's trilogy *The Oresteia* in which Orestes, Apollo, and the Erinyes go before Athena and eleven other judges to decide whether Orestes's killing of his mother, Clytemnestra, makes him guilty of the crime of murder. Orestes is tormented by the Erinyes, or Furies. The lovely close illustrates Di Prima's increasing technical mastery:

> and the light focuses
>   is gently led
>   thru prisms, lenses
> comes at last to point
>   & burns
>   the paper smokes
> all space is smoking & my hair streams back

light flat like on snow
                coming head on
                hits
like an open hand on the back of the neck
cuts steps in ice, all you get is hit more times
cut steps   the hand is gold
                  light streams out from it
                or seems to
        the secret is:
                  LIGHT NEVER STREAMS OUT
only back.
           I always hear a raincoat
hands in the pockets pull back
        (it's never buttoned)
and I walk forward out of it
        unembarrassed[26]

Di Prima often voiced her admiration for Cocteau's ability to create magic—or Crowleyian "Magick"—in his films, and here she weaves an elaborate mosaic of light imagery familiar to us from her studies of Robert Grosseteste which stands at once for cosmic mysteries as well as the trance a gifted director—"prisms, lenses"—can create in his or her audience through chiaroscuro play of light and dark. There is also a pattern of classical allusion in many poems such as "The Jungle" in which the Eumenides return as well as the Cyclops juxtaposed with contemporary allusions to nuclear holocaust: "to drop the fucking thing & watch it burn/if it were in my hands, the atomic war wd be past history./how cosmic chill/. . . . I walk with every beast that walks/to take the dragon/ thru the city gates/neck with the cyclops, etc./Eumenides, if one face turns/ away/and the wind, which we must/swallow, whatever we will." In "Blue Nirvana" we are told of "a map of Greece I hung in my 1st pad," while in "Archive" the Trojan war appears in an allusion to "a toy horse w/20 toy men inside."[27] In other works such as "The Beach," we find another poem charting her love affair with Jones. The narrative shifts between two images: a railroad station and the beach. The final scene depicts a "monster lobster" escaping from a picnic basket and walking "home" to the ocean. This image is counterpointed with a scene at a railroad station, where two lovers are parting. And in "Lord Jim," the speaker of the poem is attracted to something "very beautiful" that she is determined to be closer to.[28] With *The New Handbook of Heaven*, Di Prima employs more polished, clear images and demonstrates a richer imagination, moving beyond the strictly personal toward a technical mastery of language as well as a merging of erotic and mystical themes which will define her work of the next decade.

Di Prima had a clear affinity for Buddhist and Chinese philosophy which became important influences during this phase of her career. In 1960, inspired by *Music of Changes* (1951) for solo piano by John Cage who had been experimenting with aleatoric or "chance" methods of musical composition, she obtained a two-volume edition of the *I Ching: The Book of Changes*, the classic ancient Chinese divination text made up of sixty-four combinations of six unbroken lines (yang/masculine) and six broken lines (yin/feminine) representing a variety of states of being in constant transformation. The oracle is consulted by creating a hexagram through casting three Chinese coins six times.[29] The interplay between determinism and free will, past and future, order and randomness, rationality and irrationality, suffering and joy in the *I Ching* is beautifully evoked by Jorge Luis Borges in "Para Una Version Del *I King*": "Do not give up. The prison is dark,/Its fabric is made of incessant iron,/But in some corner of your cell/You might discover a mistake, a cleft./The path is fatal as an arrow/But God is in the rifts, waiting." A. C. Graham in "Rationalism and Anti-Rationalism in Pre-Buddhist China" has provided an insight which may serve as a gloss on Borges's poem and on the relationship between chance and divination:

> If the hexagrams thrown up by chance carried unambiguous instructions they would of course, except by lucky accident, be grossly misleading; but since they offer only enigmatic auspices and an almost unlimited latitude to correlate with a variety of images, the diviner's interpretation in the light of his personal situation becomes a meditation on his circumstances opened up to new perspectives. The effect will be to break down preconceptions and give binary thinking a fresh start.[30]

Breaking free of the strait-jacket of "binary thinking" is precisely what the Beats set out to do. The "divinatory arts"—*I Ching*, Tarot, and astrology—all play with an interweaving of chance and fate in the mysterious unfoldment of human destiny: the Beats, as did the Abstract Expressionists, thus began to evolve an aesthetic—"action writing/action painting"—founded on emphasizing spontaneity, randomness, improvisation, and the experience of each moment's intensity as it unfolds in time. There is a spiritual freedom involved in giving up one's attempt to totally *control* the flow of experience. As Di Prima noted in her 1965 essay on Paracelsus, the *I Ching* represented the harmony between soul and cosmos which characterized ancient philosophical thought. It also reflected "the theory of what Jung calls 'synchronicity,' presupposing 'a peculiar interdependence of objective events among themselves as well as with the subjective state of the observer' at any given moment. It is, of course, the axiom on which astrology, as well as alchemy in this higher sense—and all magic—is predicated." William S. Burroughs affirmed that "there is no such thing as a coincidence." Burroughs taught writing both at the City College of New York and Naropa where he considered the relationship between magic and literature with his students: "Writers operate in the magical universe. . . . I give my writing students various exercises to show how one incident produces a similar incident or encounter. You can call this process synchronicity and you can observe it in action." The *I Ching* became a popular text in the United States during the 1960s and 1970s, praised by figures such as Arlo Guthrie, Ken Kesey, and Bob Dylan. Allen Ginsberg composed a poem with the catchy title "Consulting *I Ching* Smoking Pot Listening to the Fugs Sing Blake."[31]

The *I Ching* appears in several of Di Prima's works of the 1960s and early 1970s. For example, her play *Poet's Vaudeville* demonstrates her chance and collage method of composition and contains an allusion in Section IV to "Hexagram #21. Biting thru."[32] This refers to *I Ching*, "Shih Ho/Biting Through. . . . This hexagram represents an open mouth . . . with an obstruction between the teeth. As a result the lips cannot meet. To bring them together one must bite energetically through the obstacle."[33] She also devoted several poems to the topic, including "I Ching" dedicated to her friend, the jazz pianist and poet Cecil Taylor—in her volume *Pieces of a Song*: "mountain & lake/the breakup/of configurations/all the Persian rugs in the world are doing a dance."[34] In *Revolutionary Letters* (1971)—a book as we shall see in the following chapter devoted to accomplishing a political and spiritual revolution in America—she alludes to Hexagram #33: "retreat, says the *I Ching*, must not be confused/with flight, and furthermore, frequently, it furthers/ONE TO HAVE SOMEWHERE TO GO."[35] In "Revolutionary Letter Number Forty-Five": "And it seems to me the struggle has to be waged/on a number of different levels:/they have computers to cast the *I Ching* for them/but we have yarrow stalks/and the stars."[36] Bob Dylan—to whom Di Prima dedicated the *Revolutionary Letters*—in 1965 praised the *I Ching*: "The biggest thing of all, that encompasses it all, is kept back in this country. It's an old Chinese philosophy and religion, it really was one. . . . You don't have to believe in anything to read it, because besides being a great book to believe in, it's also very fantastic poetry."[37]

Yet the work most deeply influenced by the *I Ching* is *The Calculus of Variation*, composed from 1961 to 1964, but not published until 1972. The title combines Di Prima's mathematical training—"Calculus"—with "Variation," a musical term ("Theme and Variations") also implying "change." Calculus is the mathematical study of change—from Latin *calculus*—a small pebble used for counting, and the calculus of variation is a field of mathematical analysis which deals with maximizing, or minimizing fundamentals, which are mappings from a set of functions to the real numbers. Both Isaac Newton and Gottfried Leibniz made discoveries in this discipline. In the *I Ching*, there are four primary hexagrams: Chien (consisting of six yang lines); K'un (consisting of six yin lines); T'ai (three yin lines above three yang lines); and l'il (three yang lines above three yin lines).[38] At the opening Di Prima presents eight trigrams with descriptions:

Ch'ien: The Creative Heaven Father; *K'un*: The Receptive Earth Mother; *Chen*: The Arousing Thunder First Son *K'an*: The Abysmal Water Second Son; *Ken*: Keeping Still Mountain Third Son; *Sun*: The Gentle Wind Wood First Daughter; *Li:* The Clinging Fire Second Daughter; *Tui*: The Joyous Lake Third Daughter. The volume opens with a page on which a large empty circle appears and contains an untitled first section followed by nine chapters: "The Dragon"; "The Southwest"—this section appeared originally in *The Moderns*, edited by LeRoi Jones in 1963; "The Eldest Son"; "The Abysmal: A Prophecy"; "The Mountain"; "The Quarrel"; "The Feast"; and "The Joyous". Di Prima explained her method of composition:

> What I actually was doing was just following, looking at the wall and letting the images arise and following any image only as far as it went, not trying to make sense out of it, not trying to complete the sentence and going on to whatever next image arose . . . like another form of meditation. Not making anything out of the stuff, but just letting the images happen.[39]

This recalls the notion of *mindfulness*: a now popular mode of attentive spiritual introspection and receptivity in which the mind observes itself without commenting internally upon what occurs, analogous to Martin Heidegger's *Gelassenheit*. Heidegger derived this concept from the term for "letting go" or "releasement" in Meister Eckhart (1260–1327): Eckhart—to whom J. D. Salinger alludes in *Franny and Zooey* (1961)—was also the subject of a Di Prima poem. Thus the "aleatoric" or chance aspect of the *I Ching* became a method of literary composition, allowing the subconscious to find each "image" without forcing, letting mind float free in a calm, free, associative, meditative zone. James Laughlin at New Directions wanted to publish *The Calculus of Variation* but told Di Prima she would require an editor to revise the text: Di Prima declined, because she saw her work as a "received text" and wanted to leave it in its original "unrevised" state in order to preserve its unmediated nature.

The first four-page section opens: "postulate a woman. Blue light behind her unexpected bluer than turtles," and several keywords recur throughout— blue, light, roof, woman, turtles. Friends and colleagues such as Merce Cunningham, Frank O'Hara, James Waring, LeRoi Jones, Phil Whalen, John Wieners, and Freddie Herko also weave their way through the text. This "gossipy" aspect of Di Prima's style—her tendency to bring the actors, writers, dancers, and artists she knew into the texture of her writing—may be due in part to the influence of Frank O'Hara whose frequent invocations of famous American icons—"Lana Turner Has Collapsed!"—and listing of his friends' names formed a notable aspect of his style. On the following page we find: "the woman turned, forsaking her background, and began to walk slowly forward. The blue light receded & darkened. Purple. Dusk.

Lice dropped from her wool cloak, a hundred hands hacked at her pedestal. Turtles, crying like geese, flew into a transom." Thus permutations are now applied to the opening sentence, with "woman," "blue," "turtles" returning. There is no stable center of identity established, but then we encounter an "I" who confides autobiographical, graphic details employing hip talk familiar to us from *Dinners and Nightmares*: "the cat who I fucked by firelight, just by firelight. The never having seen his face by day. How many times have I seen deep into the sky, I mean stars and everything?" The fleshly facts are juxtaposed by a lyrical, childlike, innocent sweetness: "how many times have I seen deep into the sky, I mean stars and everything." This is followed by "phil whalen talking about the kinds of trees, and newyorkhick me," recounting the moment during Di Prima's 1961 visit to California and her meeting with Whalen. A surrealistic passage follows, perhaps inspired like the other dreamlike, transcendent lyrical flights throughout the text by Di Prima's experiments with peyote and LSD: "She crossed her hands on her breast & looked over her shoulder. There was a green vine trailing from the top of her head. at the end of each of her fingers a small mouth opened, showing a tongue. All the tongues moved. The road was paved with transparent, ruthless eggs." The "transparent egg" recalls the center panel of Hieronymous Bosch's famous triptych "The Garden of Earthly Delights." There is also a pattern of sacral symbolism—"she crossed her hands on her breast"—and this ritual language recurs throughout. This section closes surprisingly: "had a turtle once, fed it lettuce, damn thing died. Gave it cod liver oil from a dropper, its own kick."[40] Thus the significance of the turtle imagery is revealed, with a typical Di Prima comic turn.

The second section—titled after the Chinese symbol of the thunderstorm's dynamic force, "The Dragon"—opens: "In the black kingdom the shoes of the goddess are glass. The foam of the inner circle." This line sets the tone of oracular sacredness which follows and "light" is constantly intoned: "the light is waiting for him"; "the darkening of the light"; "flies buzzed in the slanting light." Derived from "Ch'ien/The Creative"—"the movement of heaven is full of power"—this is a direct quote from the *I Ching*, and more evocative lyricism returns: "what god was not born from a river?" "that the sea gave birth to heaven, the rocks are from another cosmos." There is also a pattern of classical imagery which we have seen Di Prima also employed in *The New Handbook of Heaven*: "Minerva carries the grain in Italy, the other gods hold lamps, step aside for her. into the plowed earth the maidens drop new cherries." A primal power accumulates through repetition and compression of a recurring set of images:

The white world rolls toward the jadeite paws of the dragon . . . between the concentric spheres of heaven the chaff is caught. The light cannot get thru. They move more and more slowly. The dragon, caught there, is slowly being crushed. The light that gets thru to earth now, this warm light, is fire and flood, and not the light of heaven. On what wheel has that light stopped? . . . they are painting the sky, the horrible end of the dragon . . . the desire of matter to touch all parts of heaven.[41]

In another passage, Di Prima elaborates her pattern of light imagery, but now in juxtaposition with an allusion to Homer: "it is within the eye that light begins/and going out, meets the object. OR light streams out from the object and wanders, seeking always the beholder. . . . boughs of trees. And sandals, aglaos, departing. " Hermes/Odysseus is *aglaos= splendid*: "shining feet the swift sandals." It is also clear that Di Prima is already incorporating Gnostic ideas into her work—a theme we shall see more insistently developed in her essays of the 1970s and in *Loba*—the light from which human beings have been exiled and which they seek to find again: "The light cannot get thru." There is a dense pattern of allusions to courtly love, to the phrase from Dante *directio voluntatis*—which also appears at the end of the book—which Ezra Pound speaks of in connection with Confucius's will, or direction of the will (*Chih*). These serious passages are interspersed occasionally with typically Di Prima humorous surreal flights: "he spends his moments of lucidity pouring coffee into alarm clocks: making salami sandwiches for meteors"; or "the marx brothers huddled in the cromlech"—the four great American comedians spending time in a megalithic tomb. Her friend Gregory Corso in "Marriage" was a virtuoso of the funny surreal pairing—"Radio Belly!," "Cat shovel!," "Radio brains!" Allen Ginsberg also frequently made effective use of such imagery, as did of course the master American surrealist, Philip Lamantia.

This section provides the basic structure of *The Calculus of Variation*: Gnostic and mythological strands are woven throughout as well as passages describing pregnancy, childbirth, and the struggles of women. Cernunnos, a Celtic horned god revered in neopaganism as symbol of the cycle of life, death, and rebirth, appears. According to Naomi R. Goldenberg in *Changing of the Gods: Feminism and the End of Traditional Religions*: "In witchcraft, the Horned God's duty is to make love to the Goddess and delight her. Witches often picture him as Pan, the half-man, half-animal nature god of Greek mythology. He is very dear to the Goddess but is never meant to rule her as a husband or master." When Christianity became dominant in pagan Europe, Cernunnos/Pan became transformed into the devil who also sports twin horns. As we shall see in Chapter 5, allusions to pagan traditions such as the Celtic festival *Lughnasa* appear in other Di Prima works such as *The Ones I Used to Laugh With: A Haibun Journal, April–May 1992*.

Loba also appears in *The Calculus of Variation*, and recurs in Di Prima's eponymous epic poem (1978; 1998) and Di Prima describes reading Milarepa (ca. 1052–1135) the great Tibetan yogi. Her intense mystical practice appears in several accomplished passages: "a heaven that sucks us upward like a whirlpool. Body and soul, like the sun on melted snow, as we rise our parachutes close, we close our eyes. the awkwardness of our bodies in space. The ones who crash against the colorless spheres. THE ONES WHO PASS THROUGH." These inspired flights are balanced by casual, personal, and autobiographical touches such as this allusion to Frank O'Hara: "frank at the museum, not quite like everyone else." The form of this section is unified by returning at the close to the *I Ching* Dragon: "nevertheless the dragon didn't make it . . . the moon dips into the tides to bring him water."

In section eight, "The Feast," we return to autobiographical elements such as the solstice celebrations involving her friends, including the great dancer Merce Cunningham, which we have described previously: "WINTER SOLSTICE Merce has no demons, he says. He is a satyr. He walks in coffee grounds to the edge of the roof. He flaps his arms & leaves, his coat is open. Over his shoulder 'I had a lovely time.'" Di Prima mentions this incident in her autobiography as well as in interviews: that Cunningham had no need of purificatory rituals for he had "no demons." As we have seen, each section also has at least one religiously inflected ritual passage. Here we find: "Prayer—Matins That I might waft in the god, pour slowly out, glittering . . . That the flesh might become word . . ." And again this sacred invocation becomes part of an autobiographical tapestry: "In his great silken robes John Wieners paces. Walks in the tower room like Haramchis"—Harmachis is an Egyptian god of the dawn and early rising sun. Buddhist and Hindu spiritual traditions are also evoked: "The attributes of atman . . . Krishna emerging from the shadows, pipe in hand. Krishna in all the corners of the room," as well as a clear allusion to the *Bhagavad Gita*: "Detachment, they told us, from the fruits of action." Di Prima also refers directly to the *I Ching*: "The book of changes end 'before completion.' The threads of light

FIGURE 3.2 *Cernunnos—Gundestrup Cauldron. Photographers: Roberto Fortuna and Kira Ursem. Source: National Museum, Denmark, C6562-74. Creative Commons Attribution-Share Alike 2.5 Generic license.*

are drawn together. The threads of joy focusing in my hand. The moving off. Cycle begins again. Before completion. Creative (tick them off now, on your fingers) Creative, receptive, arousing, abysmal, still. The gentle, the clinging, the joyous, But it ends/before completion." This refers to the hexagram #64, Wei Chi, and she again includes her friends as the symbolic "threads": "I think of you, John Wieners, one thread there. Bob Creeley, George, Louise, and my good husband. CIRCLETS OF LIGHT AROUND ALL OF YOUR BROWS. The Sport of Brahma, we are in its hands/the way of heaven turns like a ferris wheel . . . Hello Phil Whalen . . . Where is Kirby Doyle?"

Finally, we can see how Di Prima's themes throughout continued the Beat emphasis on a visionary poetics and also began to lay the groundwork for the hippie revolution which attained full flower a few years later: "That I'd rather again/my children would marry Indians, weave baskets/keep all the cornfeasts/learn no arithmetic/beyond that which is good for household matters RATHER WE STOP THE HARVEST FEASTS AND TREMBLE at mooneclipses. Tell all the gods we're turning back to find them." Here we note a desire to move away from the spiritual emptiness of modern life to embrace a direct connection with earth and stars. The phrase "tell all the gods we're turning back to find them" is a succinct statement of the hunger of youth for a more sustaining relationship to the sacred than that provided by institutional, conventional, orthodox, monotheistic religions. A new pagan "polytheism" began to evolve during the 1960s. As Henry Corbin has observed: "By confusing Being with a supreme being (*ens supremum*), that is by making of *Esse* an *ens supremum*, monotheism perishes in its triumph. It elevates an idol just at the point where it denounces such in a polytheism it poorly understands. Only a negative theology (apophatic) is able to encompass by indirection the mystery of Being (*Esse*). But official monotheism never had much love for negative theology." And E. M. Cioran in *The New Gods* (1969; trans. 1974) emphatically encapsulated the 1960s sensibility: "Surely we were more normal with several gods than we are with only one. If health is a criterion, what a setback monotheism turns out to be! . . . With all due respect to Tertullian, *the soul is naturally pagan.*" We also see in Di Prima the turn toward the Native Americans as inspiring models and an emphasis on a Thoreauvian simplicity—"keep all the cornfeasts"—an early example of what would become a major strand in the intellectual life of the counterculture. Di Prima returns throughout her work to a compassionate understanding of Native American life and culture. The final section of the book—"The Joyous"—includes a section originally published in Hettie Jones's anthology *Poems Now* (1966) as "Ode to Elegance." Here Di Prima closes the work with an invocation to Kali: "a cosmos comes to birth/let the pure pain tear your throat till you spit blood/cry out! rejoice!/that which comes to birth/even the goddessmother cannot dream of/we climb from rung to rung, a circular/undeviating golden, perfect ladder, of ages, long forgotten, to be told/over and over like a string of prayerbeads/'the ferrswheel has started up again.'" Employing the structure of the *I Ching* as a framework, *The Calculus of Variation* encapsulated many of the major themes which preoccupied Di Prima during the early 1960s and set the stage for her later explorations.

In March 1963, Di Prima's friend, the poet Paul Blackburn, began to organize poetry readings at *Le Metro*, a coffee house on Second Avenue and Joe Brainard (1942–1994) in his underground classic *I Remember*, recalled a scene captured in a famous photograph: "Diane di Prima sitting on top of a piano reading her poems." She also continued her publishing ventures by founding the Poets Press. To accomplish letterset printing, she purchased a Davidson 214 machine and went to printing school for a week—she was the only female in the class—and learned how to operate it. Poets Press would publish books by Jean Genet—Di Prima translated Genet's play *The Man Condemned to Death* (1963)–A. B. Spellman, Audre Lorde, and Kirby Doyle from her apartment at 54 East Fourth Street and later from her home in Kerhonkson, New York: both *Huncke's Journal* (1965)—by Herbert Huncke (1915–96), the street hustler and one of the connections for Burroughs, Ginsberg, and Kerouac to New York City's underworld—and John Ashbery's *Three Madrigals* (1968) also appeared under the Poets Press imprint. Di Prima described the Huncke book—which contained eleven line drawings by Erin Matson and featured a brief introduction by Allen Ginsberg—as a "technical tour-de-force" which was extremely time-consuming: "Since it was prose, I wanted it to look like prose, with a justified right-hand margin. The way to do that with an 'executive' typewriter was to count the hairline spaces that were needed to even out the margin of a particular line. You then pieced out said hairline spaces among the word breaks of the line, writing the numbers onto your typewritten copy. Then you retyped the whole page, adding the tiny spaces with the space bar as you went along. Each line was different, of course—it was a nerve-wracking process."[42] Several of the Poets Press books featured a back cover depicting the ouroboros—a dragon eating its own tail—and above the sun to left and the moon to the right. The ouroboros is a symbol of alchemy and the ceaseless cycle of creation and destruction in the universe.

Di Prima became associate editor of *Signal* magazine (1963–65) and continued her engagement with the politically "radical" avant-garde literary and artistic scene in New York, serving as contributing editor for *Kulchur* magazine, and becoming a member of the Advisory Committee—along with Allen Ginsberg, Peter Orlovsky, Paul Krassner, and Ed Sanders—of the New York City League for Sexual Freedom which "demanded 'respect for sexual freedom as a fundamental civil liberty.'" In an essay published in *The Nation* on May 4, 1964, entitled "Fuzz's Progress" Di Prima observed that "the term 'harassment of the arts' is relatively new but it has actually become a byword in New York and other cities of this country. Four theaters alone have been closed: writers and painters are spending more time in the courtroom than at the typewriter or easels." In her "Theatre Poem #1," Di Prima lamented in her typical mock-tragic mode: "How can I be serious when there are so many cops at the door/threatening me with papers or asking to see my papers/like in a Merle Oberon movie . . . ." The 1950s and early 1960s were a key time in the battle against censorship as D. H. Lawrence's *Lady Chatterly's Lover* as well as Henry Miller's *Tropic of Cancer*, and of course Allen Ginsberg's *Howl* were subjected to court trials but ultimately were ultimately ruled not to be "obscene."

This concern over freedom of expression—worry over both censorship by the authorities and her own possible self-censorship—may be seen in some of the works Di Prima was creating during this period. For example, in the poem "I Get My Period, September 1964," the speaker confides to her husband that the arrival of her menses ("How can I forgive you this blood?") angers and saddens her since he has both been refusing her sexually and her menstruation symbolizes the suffering occasioned by not having the child for which she yearned. Composing "I Got My Period" during this time of repression—the title itself would have been considered taboo—caused Di Prima a degree of anguish. She acknowledged that "when it gets scary, especially when you're a younger writer, is when you are writing about something that nobody has written about before . . . . That felt scary to write because nobody had been writing about that stuff in 1964." This poem—along with "The Practice of Magical Evocation," "Brass Furnace Going Out," as well as her harrowing accounts in *Recollections of My Life as a Woman* and in the poem "Nativity" in *Loba* describing the way her first pregnancy was handled by the hospital where she gave birth to her daughter Jeanne—illustrates Di Prima's courage in giving voice to topics concerning sexuality, pregnancy, childbirth, and abortion which hitherto had been considered largely forbidden subjects for literature.

Di Prima also now made contact with Andy Warhol's circle, becoming friends with filmmaker and photographer Billy Name (William Linich; 1940–2016)—he would visit Di Prima during her stay on Observation Drive in Topanga Canyon, California in 1962/1963—while Prima's friend Freddie Herko appeared in several Warhol movies. As we have seen, Di Prima had a passionate interest in film beginning during adolescence which she continued through her relationships with several avant-garde filmmakers such as Stan Brakhage (1933–2003), Jack Smith (1932–89), and Warhol. The Beats had all been involved with various aspects of film: Ginsberg, Corso, and Kerouac appeared in Robert Frank's classic *Pull My Daisy* (1959); William S. Burroughs produced several films with Anthony Balch including *Towers Open Fire, Bill and Tony, Bill Buys a Parrot* and provided the voice-over to *Witchcraft Through the Ages*. Thus Di Prima's fascination with film was typical of the Beat movement and she would be directly involved in filmmaking as a performer. According to Reva Wolf's *Andy Warhol: Poetry, and Gossip in the 1960s*:

> Another film that Warhol screened at the American Theatre for Poets in order to reach its regular audience features Diane di Prima and Alan Marlowe. The fact that di Prima and Marlowe ran this multipurpose theater would not have been lost on viewers of the movie. Warhol filmed the short episode-like movie of di Prima and Marlowe (the title of which is at present uncertain) soon after 29 January 1964, when di Prima sent a letter to the artist that alluded to his interest in making a film of the couple: "come see us & shoot a Day in Our House like you said & show the Alan & me pornography." Warhol ended up filming di Prima and Marlowe for around three minutes, rather than for the originally planned length of one day. Di Prima recalled, "He came and shot a movie. It was a very short movie. A three or five minute movie of me and Alan. Alan is in bed, and he's covered by a tiger skin, which he's stroking the tail of in a very obviously suggestive manner. I get on the bed in a black leotard and tights and kind of trample him. It was a tiny room."

The fourth part of Di Prima's play *Poet's Vaudeville* (1963) "Love" contains a reference to the marriage bed and animal skin imagery that appears in Warhol's film: "I'll make a sheet of your skin/To lie on wi/my husband."[43] However, Di Prima would never find Warhol's work of any interest: she later recalled that his "aesthetic was so far from mine that I didn't know what to do with it." She also performed in director Jack Smith's (1932–89) *Normal Love* (1963)—also variously called *The Pink and the Green Film*, *The Rose and Green Horror*, *The Drug Film*, *The Moonpool Film*, *The Great Moldy Triumph*, and *The Great Pasty Triumph*—which Smith never completed. Claes Oldenburg designed a huge, three-tiered wedding cake where a pregnant and bikini-clad Di Prima—she gave birth the following day to Alexander, her child with Alan Marlowe—disported among a crowd of other female dancers whom Smith referred to as "chorus cuties." Andy Warhol has a cameo role as he wanders onto the scene with his camera filming the festivities.[44] The production of the film involved the cast of monsters from classic Hollywood horror movies—including the Werewolf, the Spider, and the Mummy—and crew in an act of spontaneous performance. Andy Warhol noted how Smith "used anybody who happened to be around that day, and also how he just kept shooting until the actors got bored." Di Prima had already made forays into Dadaesque absurdism in her plays and her involvement in "camp" underground cinema is an extension of a trajectory which was already implicit in her work. Indeed, Jack Sargent has pointed out that "Allen Ginsberg has suggested that camp and Beat culture are related, both through their shared political dissidence, and because of their shared investment in the 'homosexual community.'"[45] For Di Prima, her esoteric spiritual orientation, radical politics, and commitment to gender equality and sexual freedom were all connected in both her art and life.

As we have seen, several of Di Prima's male friends and lovers were gay. Jennifer Doyle describes "queer friendships between men and women as a form of attachment that can disturb both the presumption of an 'us' and a 'them' and the opposition of desire and friendship." Di Prima's decade-long close friendship with Freddie Herko illustrates the complex nature of such relationships in which our "normal expectations" of conventional gender roles are challenged. Doyle further emphasizes the relevance of "the insights of queer scholarship on friendship, romantic intimacy, and the political importance of nurturing forms of relationality outside domestic and patriarchal structures."[46] Steven Watson argued that Di Prima "provided a constant in his [Herko's] life. They had lived together, been neighbors, and shared a lover (Alan Marlowe). They even staged a very private wedding, exchanging cheap silver rings before a Brancusi statue in the Museum of Modern Art . . . 'the feeling was that we would help each other out, try to take care of each other in the craziness of our lives, wherever we went.'"[47] Following Herko's dramatic suicide at the age of twenty-nine on October 27, 1964—strung out on drugs he listened to a recording of Mozart's *Coronation Mass in C*, danced nude in his room, and proceeded to leap from his window—Di Prima composed two works in his memory: *Spring and Autumn Annals* and *Freddie Poems*.[48] Begun the week following Herko's death in the form of a letter or journal and completed a year later, Di Prima titled *Spring and Autumn Annals* after the ancient Chinese method of keeping court records—alluded to by Ezra Pound in his *Cantos*—and only sections of the entire text have appeared in *Niagara Frontier Review*, *Evergreen Review, Restau: A Journal of Passage*, and *The Outsider*. Donald Allen had previously suggested that Di Prima compose a book employing the changing seasons as its structure, and she now naturally fell into a pattern of reminiscing about the various times she had spent together with Herko during their long friendship.[49] In the closing section of one excerpt published in the renowned underground magazine, Jon Edgar and Gypsy Louise Webb's *The Outsider*, Winter 1968–69, Di Prima touchingly recalled:

> Yes, this morning it was my birthday and I got up, went downstairs to the mail, and remembered that no one would remember that it was my birthday. A courtesy Freddie and I kept for one another. The keeping of the feasts. Each other's birthdays. Last year the wooden altar that stands in my study. Fragile last work of his hands. So that I pretended (finding a pink sleeveless polo shirt of his for the trip ahead) that Freddie had brought me a present after all. Tears in my head, in my answers all day to Alan.[50]

Their relationship provided a safe haven, a shared sense of belonging for them both and one notes "keeping the feasts" and the "wooden altar" which

Freddie had created—aspects of Di Prima's private spiritual practice which symbolize the sacral nature of their friendship. The employment of altars in neopaganism is a central aspect of creating a "ritual space." One also recalls a famous saying of John Keats's celebration of "the holiness of the heart's affections," and within the counterculture, love and friendship were an essential necessity since gifted young people often felt—as they perhaps throughout history always have—alone, adrift, estranged, and vulnerable in a world of adults they felt did not understand them and a society which rejected their values. Most of the Beats had come from dysfunctional backgrounds and indeed, the great hippie exodus of the 1960s toward San Francisco was also composed of many youths who had broken from their families and who sought escape and then an entrance into a nurturing community with others of like sensibility.

Poems for Freddie—composed from 1957 to 1966 and first published by Poets Press in 1966 and again in 1974 as *Freddie Poems* by Eidolon Editions—is a moving sequence of friendship/love poems. The style of the cycle is often emotionally naked and direct, in marked contrast to some of Di Prima's other more formal and intellectually dense poetry. They chronicle a variety of conflicting feelings concerning Herko: a kind of "survivor's guilt" following his suicide is expressed in "I Stay Home From A Party at John McDowell's" from January 1966: "How can I help being mad at you/my friends, who were Freddie's friends/ when I see how you thrive."[51] Yet one poem in the sequence—"Formal Birthday Poem: February 23, 1964" which begins "dear Freddie, it's your birthday & you are crazy/really gone now, crazy like any other old queen"—shocked Frank O'Hara when Di Prima read it at New York University: she replied that unfortunately the poem was merely expressing what everyone already knew to be true.[52] The volume, however, opens more gently with "Prelude": "Lad if I love you better than I should, think how thru/wasted tides I watched you grow." Born just two years after Di Prima in 1936, she however sees Herko as a "lad" and plays the role of sheltering mother to her child, or older sister to younger brother. One is sometimes reminded of the cycle of Catullus's poems to Lesbia, in which we witness the *sturm und drang* of a volatile relationship as in the "The Animal Trainer" where—as in Catullus—we see her plotting ways to make Freddie care about her: "one of the ways to win you is to leave you . . . I sit here grumpy/weighing the pros & cons."

Jose Esteban Munoz in *Cruising Utopia: The Then and There of Queer Futurity* has commented on Di Prima's admiration for the magical qualities of Herko's dancing:

Di Prima believed in Herko's performance despite its excess, its corniness. She never hesitated to describe the artist's work as romantic vectoring on the magical. At another point, she refers to a performance memorializing the life of Sergio, an Italian friend of Herko's and di Prima's husband

(and Herko's ex-boyfriend), Alan Marlowe, explaining, "When Freddie danced *For Sergio* at the New Bowery, he made a dance that was also a ritual. He magically 'did' something. Transformed something. It seems so simple now. But at that point many of us were groping our way backward to art as magick."[53]

These "magical" feelings evoked by dance and music are also described by Di Prima in her review of one of Herko's performances along with David Gordon and Yvonne Rainer—these artists pioneered in their break with traditional narrative structure what we now call "modern dance"—on July 6, 1962, at Judson Memorial Church which she published in *The Floating Bear* #21. On a hot summer day, three hundred people arrived at the church for a three-hour concert which included Rainer's "Dance for 3 People and 6 Arms," Gordon's "Mannequin Dance" as well as Herko's performance which occurred on roller skates. Di Prima noted the "high" which great dancing and music can create in the audience:

> Fred Herko's work still less clearly defined than those two. Seems to come from more varied places. His dances happen inside his costumes a lot. "Once or Twice a Week I Put on Sneakers to Go Uptown," a dance to Satie where he traveled around the stage his feet carried him, his arm made an occasional very simple gesture, he wore a kind of lampshade on his head. & "Like Most People" he performed inside one of those mexican hammocks (bright colored stripes) & Cecil Taylor played the piano. It was some of Cecil's very exciting playing, and after a while the dance started to work with it, and the whole thing turned into something marvelous & unexpected . . . . At this distance, the evening retains its excitement, the high one feels being in on a beginning: these people working out of a tradition (all three are, or have been, members of James Waring's Dance Company, all three have studied with Merce Cunningham & have been highly influenced by both of these masters) yet in each case doing something that was distinctly *theirs*, unborrowed, defined.

Indeed, creating a feeling of what Di Prima calls the "unexpected" was the aim of these performances and the dividing line between dance, theater, and "Happenings" began to become indistinguishable. As RoseLee Goldberg has observed: "By 1963 many artists involved in live events were actively participating in the Judson Dance Group concerts. Rauschenberg, for instance, who was responsible for the lighting of *Terrain*, created many of his own performances with the same dancers, making it difficult for some to distinguish whether these works were 'dances' or 'happenings.'" The key in all of these forms of artistic expression was to allow enough spontaneity and "uncontrol" to "happen" and thus evoke moments of magical transcendence.

We may observe these magical—we recall here Di Prima's interpretation of Aleister Crowley's "magick" in relation to the art of dance—qualities in *Poems for Freddie*. For example, "Prelude" concludes: "Helpless I bring your saddest happy birthday these/emptyhanded spells for sandstorm days." Indeed, the notion of *spells*—the use of a sequence of words to achieve a magical effect—calls up the supernatural powers inherent in poetic language itself. Di Prima would compose several poems in this genre including "A Spell for Felicia, That She Come Way" and "A Counterspell for Millbrook: First Day of Winter." S. J. Tambiah famously argued in the "Magical Power of Words" that people in premodern cultures considered language and magic as connected for words can directly influence the universe. T. M Luhrmann has observed that spells are employed by covens of witches in order to

> raise energy by calling on their members' own power, and that this energy could be concentrated within the magic circle, as a "cone of power," and directed towards its source by collective imagination. The first step in a spell was always to chant or meditate in order to change the state of consciousness and so have access to one's own power, and then to focus the imagination on some real or imagined visual representation of the power's goal.

An example of a putatively ancient Basque spell: "Eko, eko, azarak/Eko, eko, zamilak/Eko, eko, Cernunnos/Eko, eko, Aradia." And of course we are familiar with the famous opening of Shakespeare's *Macbeth* Act IV, scene I: "Double, double toil and trouble/Fire burn and caldron bubble/Fillet of fenny spoke,/In the caldron boil and bake" (ll. 10–14). The wizard Gandalf in Tolkien's *The Fellowship of the Ring* frequently employs spells to achieve a variety of ends, including creating light and fire. In addition to spells, Di Prima employs other methods to summon supernatural forces as we see in the following poem "Invocation" where she calls on the "guardian dead/ who to my youth brought peace/who ward off madness." She also turns to Homeric language as previously in *The New Handbook of Heaven*, naming them "goodly comrades/fellowship/that gave all gifts I wield." She will ask for the help of these comrades, not for herself but rather for "my brother." She asks that they "hear my crude songs for this festival, and for the love/ they bear stand with this boy."

Freddie Poems reflect not only Di Prima's conception of art as magic but also her new, vibrant mid-1960s explorations. Several poems in the book reflect her recent discovery of *The Tibetan Book of the Dead*. This text— along with the *I Ching*, Hermann Hesse's *Siddhartha*, and Aldous Huxley's *The Doors of Perception*—became a central source for young spiritual seekers during the 1950s and 1960s. The actual name of the text is *Bardo Todol*, or in transliterated Tibetan *Bar do thos grol* or "Liberation in the

Intermediate State through Hearing" and Padmasambhava, the famous Indian master of Tantra, is said to have been its author. As we shall see in Chapter 5, Di Prima will return to Tibetan traditions in her intricate poem "Tsogyal," the consort of Padmasambhava and queen of Tibet. In Di Prima's *Freddie Poems*, a reference to *Bardo*—the transitional state between death and rebirth in Tibetan Buddhism—occurs in "November Poem" from 1964 which alludes to Herko's leap to his death: "Well, now that you're gone . . . Your gifts: The great Bardo Thodol, that leap itself . . ." Andy Warhol in *POPism: The Warhol Sixties* recalled that for twenty-six nights after Herko's suicide, "the group at Diane di Prima's apartment met formally to read the *Tibetan Book of the Dead*. The ritual involved making sacrifices, and most people pulled out a few of their hairs and burned them."[54] Typically, *The Tibetan Book of the Dead* is read next to the body of deceased for forty-nine days in order ensure the soul a positive journey. According to Giuseppe Tucci in *The Religions of Tibet*:

> In the *Bar do thos grol*, in the literature that is which is dedicated to the technique of transformation of the life-principle at the moment of death, photism is a fundamental element. The consciousness of the spiritually mature person becomes identified with the light which shines out at the time of death, it perceives the identity between that light and its own radiant essence.

Thus we again observe how Di Prima incorporated spiritual questing into her writings as well as the ways she practiced rituals to mark significant turning points in her own life as well as those of her friends. In another poem, "Freddie's Monologue" we note the Hindu imagery which also distinguishes this phase of Di Prima's development: "*WALK INTO THE EAST RIVER TO BATHE, CRYING OUT TO KRISHNA*." "Song for My Spooks" alludes to "the end of KaliYuga, dark time on a dark planet." In yet another poem, "February 23, 1966, di Prima describes "pictures of Kathakali in this magazine./I want to tell you what I've found out about Shiva/to take you with me to visit Felicia and Kirby/in the woods; in their hotel on Tomales Bay/where we will eat clams and swim, you'll play your flute." Thus both the *Spring and Autumn Annals* and *Freddie Poems* memorialize her intimate friendship with Herko. In her autobiography, Di Prima remembered : "And no one will ever see me like he did. I already knew this . . . . How tender and scared we both were, two battered kids trying to make sense of the world, make some beauty in it."

Of course the magical and mythic focus of Di Prima's work reflected early 1960s turbulence when conventional certainties and pieties of the Establishment were being challenged on a number of fronts. The great anthropologist Claude Levi-Strauss argued in *La Pensée Sauvage*—which appeared in English as *The Savage Mind* (1962) but a better translation is *Wild Thinking*—that the myths of so-called primitive cultures contained wisdom in no way inferior to that of our "civilized" world, while philosopher of science Paul Feyerabend in *Against Method* (1975) questioned the dominant, special status science enjoyed in contemporary life. In his earlier 1964 essay "Knowledge without Foundations" Feyerabend made similar arguments in favor of "mythic thinking," asserting that

> a myth is by no means a dreamt up construction that is superimposed upon the facts without being in any way connected with them. Quite the contrary, a good myth will be able to cite many facts in its favor and it will sometimes be more firmly rooted in "experience" than are some highly appreciated scientific theories of today . . . a myth is therefore a system of thought which is supported by numerous very direct and forceful experiences, by experiences, moreover, which seem to be far more compelling than the highly sophisticated experimental results upon which modern science bases its picture of the world.

In "Revolutionary Letter Sixty-Three"—we will analyze the *Revolutionary Letters* in the following chapter—Di Prima also critiques science, in a manner which strongly recalls D. H. Lawrence, for destroying the magical vision of the "living cosmos": "Check Science: whose interest does it serve?/ Whose need to perpetrate/Mechanical dead (exploitable) universe/Instead of living cosmos?/Whose dream those hierarchies: planets & stars/Blindly obeying fixed laws, as they desire/Us, too, to stay in place . . . ./What point in this cosmology /but to drain/Hope of contact or change /oppressing us w/'reason.'"[55] Di Prima creates an analogy here between the "hierarchical" view of the universe with the heavenly bodies "blindly obeying fixed laws" and the desire of the world's powers-that-be—"they"—who seek to repress humanity through their "reasonable" laws which are actually unjust within fixed, tyrannical social systems. Di Prima here also continues the tradition of William Blake's animadversions against the purely "rational" trend of European thought during the Enlightenment. Isaiah Berlin has observed that for Blake: "'Art is the Tree of Life . . . Science is the Tree of Death.' Liberate the spark—that is the great cry of all persons who feel strangled and suffocated by the new tidy scientific order which does not respond to the deeper problems of the human soul." Di Prima was thus highly receptive to the "irrational myths" of alchemy, Tarot, astrology, and magical practices. As for C. G. Jung, these alternative systems of thought would provide her with a set of symbolic archetypes which helped in building a framework for interpreting her spiritual experiences.

In addition to these challenges to the hegemony of a purely scientific understanding of the cosmos, during the 1960s, American society was undergoing seismic shifts: John F. Kennedy's assassination on November 22, 1963, increasing US involvement in the Vietnam War, as well as the burgeoning Civil, Women's and Gay Rights movements were all reflected in the themes of Di Prima's work. Di Prima saw America as undergoing a period of cataclysmic change and that the country would at some point have to repay its karmic debts for its ethical violations. As she declared in "Revolutionary Letter Number Ten": "These are transitional years and the dues/will be heavy./Change is quick but revolution/will take a while./ America has not even begun as yet./This continent is seed." In a sense, the outer chaos seemed to drive her ever more powerfully to seek an inner fulcrum, an interior center which would provide an order and peace which was so lacking in the "real world." Young people began to turn avidly toward non-Western sources while American hippies contributed to make J. R. R. Tolkien's *The Hobbit* and *The Lord of the Rings* trilogy bestsellers. Indeed, the archetypal structure of Tolkien's mythology as a spiritual allegory has been recently affirmed through the creation of a set of Tarot cards employing figures from the narrative on each individual card. "Magic" and "Mystery"—as in the title of the Beatles's *Magical Mystery Tour* (1967)— were two concepts which in many ways defined the countercultural hunger for deeper sources of sustenance than those provided by conventional religion which lay in ancient Greek mystery cults, in Egyptian mythology, in paganism, and in occult and esoteric knowledge of the Medieval and Renaissance poets and philosophers. Indeed, by the mid-1960s many young people seemed to be carrying on a full-scale love affair with Renaissance magical traditions. "Renaissance Fairs" were held every spring near Los Angeles in which renaissance life was recreated. Frances Yates had argued that the works of Shakespeare himself were permeated with occult themes: "Hamlet's melancholy is the inspired melancholy with its prophetic visions. Shakespeare's preoccupation with the occult, with ghosts, witches, fairies, is understood as deriving less from popular tradition than from deep-rooted affinity with the learned occult philosophy and its religious implications." Di Prima registered these impulses in her work. Her encounters with Paracelsus, Heinrich Cornelius Agrippa, John Dee, Tarot, and Kabbalah led to a decades-long exploration of alchemical and occult texts, culminating in a course she would offer beginning in 1980 at the New College of California entitled "The Hidden Religions in the Literature of Europe," which I shall explore more fully in Chapter 5.

Felix Morrow, the publisher of University Books—who had also brought out an edition of Milarepa's work—asked Di Prima to contribute an introduction to a proposed two-volume reprinting of alchemical writings of Paracelsus—Philippus Aureolus Theophrastus Bombastus von Hohenheim (1493–1541). She composed the essay while in residence at Ananda Ashram in Monroe, New York, founded in 1964 by Shri Brahmananda Sarasvati as the country center of the Yoga Society of New York. As with John Dee a decade later, this research would bear fruit in a marvelous poem "Paracelsus" in which Di Prima describes alchemical creation: "Extract the juice which is

FIGURE 3.3 *Aureolus Theophrastus Bombastus von Hohenheim [Paracelsus].*
Reproduction, 1927, of etching by A. Hirschvogel, 1538. Wellcome Library, London.
Wellcome Images, http://wellcomeimages.org. Copyrighted work available under
Creative Commons Attribution only license CC BY 4.0.

itself a Light/Pulp, manna, gentle/Theriasin, ergot/like mold on flame, these
red leaves/bursting/from the mesquite by the side/of dry creekbed."

In her essay, Di Prima emphasizes that although Paracelsus's Europe was
wracked by political and social upheaval "it had not yet been fragmented
as it is today. The unity of the microcosm and the macrocosm, the harmony
between the courses of the stars, the cycles of the seasons, and the spiritual life
of man was not in question." Here she is echoing her friend Robert Duncan,
who in his essay "Rites of Participation" spoke of "the correspondences
that haunted Paracelsus, who saw also that the key to man's nature was
hidden in the design of the larger Nature." Jean Seznec in his classic text
*The Survival of the Pagan Gods: The Mythological Tradition and Its Place
in Renaissance Humanism and Art* has remarked on the difference between
Paracelsus's view of humanity and prior philosophies:

In a world system all parts of which are interconnected, with no single
creature possessing an existence independent of the cosmos, man's
position is impossibly humiliating. To be sure, the bonds which attach
man to the universe are undeniable: but they now cease to be thought
of as a form of imprisonment. Marsilio Ficino still adheres to the notion
of "superior" powers with dominion over "inferior" beings (the stars
sending their influences down toward the earth). Nicholas of Cusa no

longer accepts this subordination of earth to sky; he sees only harmony and correlation, not dependence. Paracelsus goes even further: he suggests that the influence may operate in the other direction—from man to stars, from *soul* to *thing*, from the inner world to the outer. "It might be said that Mars has more resemblance to man than man to Mars, for *man is more* than Mars and the other planets."

As she immersed herself in alchemical texts, Di Prima "began to understand that everything meant more than I thought; that people used to think in a multilayered way. There was no simpleminded way to read, say, a text from the 1500s."[56] Alchemical and occult themes appear in earlier British and American literature. For example in Mary Shelley's—one of Di Prima's favorite writers—*Frankenstein: A Modern Prometheus*, the "monster's" creator Victor immerses himself in the lore of both Paracelsus and Heinrich Cornelius Agrippa. So too, Nathaniel Hawthorne's celebrated short story "The Birth-mark" (1843) concerning the "man of science" Aylmer—a chemist who is actually an alchemist—and his secret experiments on his wife Georgiana alludes to both Agrippa and Paracelsus. Paul Feyerabend in his posthumously published *Philosophy of Nature* (2016) observed that

> Heinrich Cornelius Agrippa, Johannes Trithemius, the legendary Faust— they all refer to the fact that reason has its limits and occasionally requires support from a mysterious, magical, and yet reliable source, namely experience. According to Agrippa, formal qualities "are called occult qualities, because their causes are hidden, and because human intellect cannot entirely investigate them—whereby the greater number of philosophers attained this from very long experience, rather than from searching by reason". . . . This magical source is usually combined with certain useful actions to result in discoveries and practical progress: the call for experiments rose in the occultist tradition and in alchemy long before the arrival of Bacon's philosophy, which reinterpreted it for very different objectives.

Di Prima composed several poems on alchemical subjects, including "Prophetissa" which begins with an epigraph from Maria Prophetissima, known as Mary the Jewess (ca. second century CE), considered the first alchemist, about whom Di Prima most likely learned from alchemist Michael Maier—whom she taught in her "Hidden Religions in the Literature of Europe" course—and his book *Symbola Aureae Mensae Duodecim Nationum* (1617) which contains an engraving depicting Maria. The epigraph reads: "Two from One/Three from Two/and out of the Three/ the Four, as the first." When read aloud, the lines clearly have a spell-like power and the three sections of Di Prima's poem explicate Maria's gnomic utterance. Maria's riddle fascinated C. J. Jung as well who discussed it in

Psychology and Alchemy and in several other works. Jung acknowledged the relevance of alchemy to our modern understanding of the psyche, arguing in *Mysterium Coniunctionis* that

> alchemists, with but few exceptions, did not know that they were bringing psychic structures to light but thought that they were explaining the transformations of matter . . . there were no psychological considerations to prevent them, for reasons of sensitiveness, from laying bare the background of the psyche, which a more conscious person would be nervous of doing. It is because of this that alchemy is of such absorbing interest to the psychologist.

And most significantly, in *Aion* Jung developed an argument concerning the relevance of alchemical thought to our awareness of the existence of a "deep Self": "For the alchemist it was clear that the 'centre,' or what we would call the self, does not lie in the ego but outside it, 'in us' yet not 'in our mind,' being located rather in that which we unconsciously are . . . which we still have to recognize."[57]

Di Prima immediately understood these texts as though Paracelsus had composed them specifically *for her*. She felt a sense of recognition similar to what one experiences in the presence of a great work of painting, literature, or music, since even the obscure sections seemed inevitably *true*—an encounter with authenticity which she also felt when she first met Shunryu Suzuki. Paracelsus's writings opened up the world of alchemy and she saw them as

> some of the most gorgeous texts in the world. It's the science of transformation. There are laws of energy that pertain whether you are talking about metals or galaxies or human consciousness. . . . I'm not interested in the purely descriptive, but in using words to evoke, or suggest things beyond that. So I think they can be expressed. In the way they were expressed say in the *Hieroglyphic Monad* by John Dee—which reads as if he was doing a text of geometric theorems like Euclid, but when you start getting under the surface you start to realize . . . reading an alchemy text is for me like reading language within language within language. And it's also about what can't be said outright and has to be encoded, and that's how that's done-but not in any facile Language Poetry way. I guess I got caught because it's so utterly beautiful.[58]

Indeed, we may observe that from the beginning of her intellectual life, Di Prima gravitated toward the idea that Nature holds a secret code, a hidden message, a meaning which lies behind the surface, a symbolic language she seeks to understand. Thus when she traveled to New Mexico in 1965, she now also began to experiment with Tarot cards which led to episodes of lucid dreaming. She experienced this phase of her life as a return—as we have seen in Chapter 1—to her experiments with the occult and paranormal while she was at Hunter High School: this "magical" strand in her thinking now returned in full. As we shall see in the following chapter, the Tarot would lead her to the study of the Tree of Life and Kabbalah, as well as the work of Heinrich Cornelius Agrippa. A revelatory passage in her manuscript "Structures of Magic and Techniques of Visioning" from October 23, 1978, describes the ways she began to draw the strands of her studies together:

> I'm interested in the combining of the Tarot—the Tree as it was worked out by the Golden Dawn people and later people in terms of changing my point of view or my perspective so that my way of seeing the world is in terms of correspondence, so that everything has a thickness of dimensionality instead of linearity, so that blue also means Jupiter and also means whatever planet it means, [and Wheel of Fortune card and lapis or sapphire] so that everything moves thru several dimensions at once like certain so-called "primitive" languages do: both because it's a way of seeing and because it's a way of using words and image that seems to me breaks down the necessity for metaphor in the old sense and makes all that stuff obsolete. I really want to enter that head and live there, not just have it as a quaint old idea, the idea of correspondence.

Di Prima seeks to perceive the "idea of correspondence" as a living reality rather than simply as an intellectual construct, as "a quaint old idea."

Di Prima also had begun to seriously study Hinduism and from January to September 1966, relocated with Alan Marlowe and her three children to "a big, drafty old farm house with 14 rooms" in Kerhonkson, New York. *Kerhonkson Journal: 1966* (1971) contains twenty-six poems arranged chronologically through the seasons, beginning with the first snow of sinter, through the dark of the moon in February, the spring equinox, the full moon of May, the summer solstice.

Out of New York City and now surrounded now by Nature, the poems teem with pine trees, ponds, valleys, hayfields, corn farms, birds, the Catskill mountains, green moss on rocks, field mice, fireflies, crickets, and a variety of exotic insects. During her stay at this bucolic location, Di Prima was able to devote time to meditation as well as hatha yoga and there are a number of references to Shiva in the poems "Hymn," "Poem to a Statue of Shiva in the Garments of Kali," and "Hymn to Shiva." Di Prima entered into a kind of "bhakti relationship to Shiva"—*bhakti* signifies in Hinduism the "loyal devotion" or "loving devotion" to a god such as Vishnu or Shiva—believing "there's a point where human love can be translated into a kind of religious experience that has nothing to do with what you're getting out of the experience of love in terms of material goodies." In the

lovely "Hymn to Lord Shiva," Di Prima attains a lofty degree of lyrical and
visionary power:

> burn it my lord as you
> burn the stars as you will
> burn the earth as the sun
> wheels burning thru the heavens so hurl
> burning and wheeling thru the spaces
> of night, my heart, till it plunges hissing
> into the black unfathomed sea, till
> extinguished, turned to ash, it filters thru
> dark waves which are
> your gentle, pulsing life.

"Hymn to Lord Shiva" dramatizes a seemingly effortless synthesis of
human and divine love, a unity of human microcosm with natural universal
macrocosm—stars, earth, sun, heavens, spaces of night, sea, waves—the
fires of *eros* burning, becoming the devotional fire of transcendent yearning.
The chanting repetition of "burn" and "burning," "wheels burning" and
"burning and wheeling" creates a hypnotic and erotic mood. Di Prima will
return to this sweet *bel canto*, erotically orgasmic style in poem "Kali-Ma"
in *Loba*, an adaptation of Ramprasad Sen. The self now burns away to ash,
returning to the source of life. In another poem, "Hymn," Di Prima also
invokes Shiva—this time in connection with Egyptian gods: "O Set O Ptah
who is Shiva O dark ones/Here in the heat of a Kerhonkson summer."[59]
One may note in passing that Di Prima would begin during this period
to frequently employ apostrophe in her verse—another striking example
is the opening of "Prayer to the Ancestors: "O you who burn forever
wheeling/like stars across our night, thin hands/like flame held in the
winds . . ." She accomplishes this quite unselfconsciously and effectively to
indicate—like Walt Whitman who declares in "A Patient Noiseless Spider,"
"O my soul"—that she is approaching the precincts of the sacred. Set is
the Egyptian god of storms and disorder while Ptah brought the world
into being through his thought. Ancient Egypt was of absorbing interest to
virtually all the Beats—Gregory Corso studied hieroglyphics and composed
"The Geometric Poem" on Egyptian mythological themes; Philip Lamantia
studied R. Schwaller de Lubicz's theories of esoteric Egyptian architecture;
and William S. Burroughs based his novel *The Western Lands* on the
Egyptian quest for immortality.

    Kerhonkson Journal is not without struggle, for there are several poems
recounting her often estranged marriage to Alan Marlowe, she notes the
escalating war in Vietnam, calls out Robert McNamara by name, records
the Buddhist nuns who set themselves afire, protests the murder of Patrice
Lumumba in the Congo. The farmlands surrounding her are being sprayed

OYEZ ANNOUNCES

Kerhonkson Journal happened between January and late September of 1966, while I lived with Alan Marlowe and my three kids on a road called Pataukunk in the Rondout Valley, which lies between a single ridge known as the Shawangunk Mountains, and the beginning of the Catskills. The nearest town was Kerhonkson, which ran along one side of the road for about a block and a half, starting with an abandoned railroad station and ending with a shiny new real estate office. We had a big, drafty old farm house with 14 rooms, and almost an acre of land. The rest of the

KERHONKSON JOURNAL
by Diane Di Prima
farm that had gone with the old house had been bought by speculators and was slated to be sliced into half-acre lots for some kind of development. We watched them cut into the hills from our back windows. We had a small print shop in the house with us, and passed the time printing and collating Poets Press books, walking, writing, and meditating and doing hatha yoga. For both Alan and me, it was our first serious experiencing of yoga, of macrobiotics, of peace and quiet. Our first house away from the city. In a lot of ways the most reasonable and balanced life I ever led — it gave me a glimpse of what might have been possible in a saner world. By the fall the landscape around us had nearly been destroyed, and on either side of us a garish crackerbox house stood facing the road, waiting to be bought.

Diane di Prima

Available from: Serendipity Books, 1970 Shattuck, Berkeley, Calif. 94709
Price — $2.00

FIGURE 3.4 Kerhonkson Journal *Announcement. Creative Commons License.*

with poisonous herbicides. Yet she turns to B. K. S. Iyengar's *Light on Yoga* (1966) for wisdom and in perhaps the loveliest poem in the volume and one of the greatest in the Di Prima canon—"Buddhist New Year Song"— she breaks out into ecstatic song. She describes Planet Earth as "this sullen and dingy place that we must make golden/make precious and mythical somehow, it is our nature,/and it is truth, that we came here, I told you,/from other planets;/where we were lords, we were sent here/for some purpose." The human soul as Joni Mitchell sang in "Woodstock" is golden and made of star-stuff and the meaning of our lives is the journey back to the Garden.

Di Prima would later read Arthur Avalon's—the pen name of Sir John Woodroffe (1865–1930)—*Hymns to the Goddess* which she gave to John Wieners who planned in turn on loaning the book to Charles Olson. She read several weighty tomes on Hindu Tantra while at Kerhonkson and thus was prepared to help Olson when he wrote to her with questions concerning Hindu and Buddhist thought as well as where he could find more Goddess materials. Another text of Woodroffe's which became important to both Beats and hippies due to its exposition of the *chakras* and *kundalini* in Tantra was *The Serpent Power*. Jeffrey J. Kripal has noted that

> the chakras or "energy centers" of various Hindu, Buddhist, and Taoist systems of yoga were a central feature of the American counterculture and are now staples of the New Age and metaphysical scenes. In what is probably the most historically influential version of these in the West, the Hindu Tantric system set out in Sir John Woodroffe's *The Serpent Power*, an occult feminine "Energy" or Shakti called the "Coiled One" or Kundalini is imagined as a sleeping serpent coiled up at the base of the spine. Once aroused, the serpent power spirals up from the anal and genital centers through the stomach, heart, and throat regions into the "third eye" and core of the brain, the *brahmarandhra* or "portal of cosmic being," and then explodes out the top of the skull through the "crown chakra," through which the mystic realizes his or her true nature as an immortal energetic superconsciousness. Shakti and Shiva, Energy and Consciousness, are now realized, and erotically united, as One.

Di Prima emphasizes Olson's curiosity concerning these traditions in her essay *Old Father, Old Artificer: Charles Olson Memorial Lecture* (2012), where she describes three enlightening visits she had with the poet in 1966, 1967, and 1968. Olson "wanted everything I knew about Eastern thought" and Di Prima suggested he read Heinrich Zimmer's *Philosophies of India* and *The King and the Corpse*, as well as Chatterjee and Datta's *An Introduction to Indian Philosophy*. Olson was also curious about the new generation's quest to open consciousness through entheogens. During the summer of 1966, Di Prima drove from Kerhonkson and spent a few days in Vinalhaven with the painter Raphael Soyer and his wife, went on to Nova Scotia, and then continued on to meet John Wieners in Gloucester. There she met Olson for the first time and they took a forty-eight-hour LSD trip together. The six-foot-seven Olson astounded the revelers before embarking on this psychedelic experience by first eating three filet mignons, at least one sizable lobster, a dozen cobs of corn and drinking two bottles of Mouton Rothschild served by their hospitable host Panna Grady.[60]

In another poem, "Jacob's Ladder," Di Prima yokes ecological concerns to her relationship with concepts from Hindu thought such as the *chakras*. The poem opens with a description of the sawmills near Mt Shasta in

Northern California—"dismembered corpses of trees"—and as she travels toward the summit,

> the Mountain
> pierces thru to this matter universe from another dimension.
> from how many other dimensions? The way the Hindus tell us
> chakras are body places where the etheric
> body is joined to the physical; so mountain chakra Mt Shasta joins
> this ravaged matter place to the world of spirits.
> Angels climb up & down from the cloudy moon.

Mt. Shasta—14, 162 feet in height—is renowned as a mythical locus in esoteric lore where the remains of the lost continents of Atlantis and Lemuria are hidden and vortexes of spiritual energy are concentrated: above its peaks, clouds wander in the shape of angels and elusive lights pulsate. "Chakras"—as we have seen above from Sanskrit "wheel" or "circle"—are energy points/nodes in the body, while the "etheric body" is a Theosophical term indicating the "aura" of the human organism. Di Prima invokes at the close the story of Jacob's Ladder (Gen. 28: 40–49) famously illustrated by William Blake, to suggest a communication between earth and heaven, between the "ravaged" environment and the higher world from which "Angels climb up & down."

Timothy Gray has argued in *Urban Pastoral: Natural Currents in the New York School* that Di Prima's journey West "had a profound effect not only on her psyche but also on her poetry, which discarded the harsher style of the New York Beats and edged closer to the ecological and mystical poetics favored by San Francisco Renaissance writers." Indeed, Di Prima's poetry during this phase would increasingly give voice to the nascent ecological movement of the 1960s and 1970s—here set within the context of both Biblical and Hindu symbolism—in order to call attention to the necessity to ameliorate our destructive relationship to the natural world. In "Trajectory," produced as a broadside in 1970—the year of Earth Day—Di Prima speaks of "the wounded Earth" and laments that "now is no star seen/as it was seen by our fathers/now is no color on the hills, no brightness/in the bay. Now do sea creatures rot/with oily fur/with oily feathers choke on black sand." As we shall see in *L.A. Odyssey*, Di Prima had been horrified by the oil-polluted waters of the Pacific Ocean during her visit to Southern California. And "Trajectory" closes with an allusion to Chinese Buddhism: "the hungry ghosts like a wind/descend on us." In Sanskrit the *pretas* are ghosts of the deceased which wander looking for drink and food, emaciated in appearance with distended bellies: this concept is translated into English as "hungry ghost." Thus Di Prima again situates her critique within the context of ancient spiritual tradition in order to emphasize the existentially cosmic situation facing the modern world.

Di Prima visited Ranchos de Taos in New Mexico for a time in 1966 where—as we shall see in the following chapter—she became involved in studying the Tarot. She also traveled to Monroe, New York—a town in the Catskills—visiting Timothy Leary's (1920–96) commune in Millbrook where she would live with Alan Marlowe and daughter Jeanne above the bowling alley in rooms which had vaulted ceilings and hardwood floors for six months from 1966 to 1967. Leary and Richard Alpert—later Ram Dass—had founded the Harvard Psilocybin Project and both were removed from their positions at Harvard for their activities at the close of the academic year in 1963: Leary would spend years in flight from the legal authorities. It was at Millbrook that Di Prima experimented most intensely with LSD to achieve higher states of consciousness and also pursued studies in Hatha Yoga.[61] Her Poets Press would publish Leary's *Psychedelic Prayers* in 1966. She combined her visionary and practical goals in a clever fashion: Di Prima had begun learning Sanskrit and discovered "that if I set my course before I got high, I could learn those irregular Sanskrit verbs in fifteen minutes when I was on the re-entry part of the trip, or I could use the peaking time to investigate this or that about the space between the worlds, or wherever I wanted to go."[62] She also vividly described a celebratory Thanksgiving in her essay "The Holidays at Millbrook—1966" in which she returns to her love of dance in her description of Bali Ram, a Nepalese temple dancer:

> Bali was in full costume, about to begin a dance recital in the "music room" when I came in, and I immediately sat down to watch. He is a great dancer, and today he danced the dedication of Shiva—with which he opens all his concerts—particularly well. He changed, did a narrative dance from the Mahabarata, changed again, and danced the Nataraja, which I had never seen before. In it, he actually portrays Shiva doing his dance of the destruction of the cosmos, and ends in the pose on all the statues of the dancing Shiva: one hand raised in the "have no fear" mudra, the other pointing to his lifted foot, which represents liberation/enlightenment. I have never found any of Bali's dancing as moving as I did today.

Later, during the evening's festivities, Allen Ginsberg sang a *kirtan* accompanied by his finger cymbals and the whole assembled group joined in to sing "Hare Krishna," "Hare Om Namo Shivaya," and "Om Sri Maitreya." Leary would be arrested in December 1965 in Laredo, Texas, for possession of marijuana and again at Millbrook in April 1966 in a raid led by G. Gordon Liddy, who later would gain infamy for his role in Richard Nixon's Watergate scandal: Di Prima and Allen Ginsberg created the Timothy Leary Legal Defense Fund to help their friend with his legal troubles.

While at Millbrook, Di Prima composed a moving poem "Ode to Keats" which summons up the memory of Freddie Herko, her concerns that LeRoi

Jones in Harlem will be murdered like Malcolm X: she implores Keats to come visit her in her solitude as he had previously during her adolescence. She also prepared a manuscript by Philip Whalen he had planned to publish with Poets Press—*On Boar's Head*—but Whalen received an offer from Harcourt Brace just before Di Prima was ready to go to print. According to Whalen's biographer Daniel Schneider, she "felt betrayed, sold out to "the Big Press," and she literally trashed the pasted-up boards—typesetting, original calligraphy." However the two remained friends and in the 1970s and 1980s lived nearby one another in San Francisco.[63] Hettie Jones also edited *Poems Now* (1966) published by Kulchur Press in New York containing work by Di Prima, Larry Eigner, Gerard Malanga, Ray Bremser, and others, while artist George Herms published under his Love Press imprint in Topanga Canyon Di Prima's book *Haiku* (1966) decorated with woodblock illustrations he carved from cherry and pear wood. The project had begun in the spring of 1964 when, as we have seen, Di Prima had invited Herms to New York to design sets for *The Blossom, or Billy the Kid* by Michael McClure. This was the twenty-nine-year-old Herms's first trip to New York and he stayed in a small eight-foot cubicle located in the Lower East Side. His illustrations accompanied fanciful poems such as "can't sleep: inside my/skull an unborn poem/is starting to kick at night"; "no roaches in it/and it's better than nothing/yesterday's coffee"; "this armless woman/silently in the blind night/waits the hands of Mars"; and an open mailbox with nothing in it inscribed "POET" with the accompanying haiku: "the empty mailbox/more sorrow there/than in my empty apartment."

Two other writers with whom Di Prima had continuing relationships were John Wieners and Audre Lorde. Wieners became part of her and Alan Marlowe's "extended family" while living at the Hotel Albert on University Place and 10th street in Manhattan.[64] Di Prima recalled that for ten years, Wieners was one of her closest friends and she arranged for the performance of his play at her theater. During this period, Di Prima also sought to promote the work of her friend Audre Lorde, to whom she declared: "Now, we really have to do this book of yours, so get your things together and we'll get them out." Thus Poet's Press published Lorde's first book of poetry, *The First Cities* (1968) to which Di Prima contributed an "Introduction," pointing out that "in these poems the past does a cartwheel and becomes the future. But where is the present do you dare put a hand on it? Bumpy roads, wobbly vehicle, but she gets thru." *The First Cities* went to the printers in 1967 and while this literary birth transpired, Di Prima on Christmas Eve went into labor: she called on Lorde who came to deliver Tara, her new baby.[65] Later, in 1976, Di Prima would also publish under her Eidolon Editions imprint seven of Lorde's poems entitled *Between Our Selves*. As she had collaborated earlier with LeRoi Jones, so too Di Prima made common cause with the struggle of African Americans for justice. And as we have seen, Di Prima was ahead of her time in advocating a feminism which went beyond the confines of White bourgeois women to include demands for equality by lesbian, gay, bisexual, and queer people of all ethnicities. Again like Gloria Anzaldua, Di Prima refused to be narrowly categorized and fixed into a "social construction" of selfhood. Pushing the barriers and limits in her spiritual life was matched by her desire to avoid being constricted into conforming to the performance of a single "role" in her understanding of the paradoxes and multiplicities of human "identity."

Di Prima published a twelve-page chapbook the following year—*Hotel Albert*—chronicling her time in the quasi-commune of her residence. The cover depicts in outline Nataraja—Shiva as cosmic ecstatic dancer—and the holograph text is illustrated with Di Prima's own fanciful drawings. The Tarot and *I Ching* continued to power her imagination as we see in the opening poem, "Fragment, for Alan and John":

O blessed and questionable creatures, tall
as the figures on a tarot card, gone
to hear Donovan on this rainy sunday
the lightning out of season
heralding changes too deep
to cast shadows

Next to "figures on a tarot card," Di Prima has sketched a card with a figure upon it and after the phrase "heralding changes," she inserts the symbol for Hexagram #63, "After Completion," thus again illustrating her intimate familiarity with the *I Ching*. The book is noteworthy because it ushers in a shift from the Beat to Hippie generation—folksinger Donovan appears as well as an allusion to Tarot—both signs that we are now entering the Age of Aquarius. Another aspect of *Hotel Albert* revealing a new countercultural sensibility is an allusion in "Anthropological Note" which begins: "According to the Osage, it is the spirits of the dead/who first see the signs of spring."[66] Di Prima—like many other youthful Americans during the 1960s—was discovering the magnificent treasures of Native American culture, which continues in her epic poem *Loba*.

However, beginning in the mid-1960s, the Tarot begins to regularly appear in Di Prima's work. The colorful and vivid symbolism of the Waite-Rider deck complemented and merged easily into the psychedelic imagery which became prominent in rock 'n' roll posters during the mid- to late 1960s. The first card games began in the West in 1375: Tarot's origins are in Northern Italy of the fifteenth century where the deck was used only to play games. Later there was an attempt by Antoine Court de Gebelin in *Le Monde Primitif* (1781) to associate the wisdom of the god Thoth/Hermes of the ancient Egyptians with the symbolism of the Tarot, and during the occult revival in England, the Hermetic Order of the Golden Dawn correlated the deck with esoteric knowledge: intellectual giants such as W. B. Yeats pursued studies in the Tarot. Yeats kept a pack in his rooms while staying at 18 Woburn Buildings, an unpublished notebook of his from 1900/1901 is filled with Tarot charts and his writings feature the Wheel of Fortune, Death on Horseback, Sun, Moon, the Tower, Fool, and Hermit.[67] It was the French occultist Eliphas Levi who noted that the sacred language of Hebrew contained twenty-two letters which correlate to the twenty-two paths of the Tree of Life and the twenty-two trumps. Aleister Crowley—whom as we have seen Di Prima studied—in *Magick in Theory and Practice* (1930) and *The Book of Thoth* (1944) also was a major contributor to the reevaluation of Tarot for contemporary life. Charles Williams (1886–1945)—a member of the Inkings with J. R. R. Tolkien and C. S. Lewis—authored a Tarot novel *The Greater Trumps* (1950) which would fascinate the great Canadian literary scholar Northrop Frye.[68]

The Tarot's influence was pervasive in the counterculture: Duncan, Spicer, John Wieners, and of course Di Prima herself were all absorbed in studying it. According to his biographer Tom Clark, Charles Olson had contemplated a collaboration with his artist friend Corrado Cagli of poems and drawings on the theme of Tarot as well as "a full-scale book on the occult mythic framework of the tarot (to include in its embracing scheme 'major arcana-gods, minor arcana-demiurges, arcana-man'); he initiated a new offensive upon the catalogs and stacks of the Library of Congress, combing through all available readings on the history of hermetic magic."[69] Both Robert Duncan and Jack Spicer had a deep interest in the subject. In his notebook composed circa 1958, Spicer sketched out "A Plan for a Book on Tarot" in which he planned to explore Tarot as a "parascience," arguing that "a parascience can become a science; alchemy can become chemistry; astrology can become astronomy; fortune-telling, after a century of patient scientific observation, could become a new means of understanding time and necessity in the universe."[70] Spicer advocated interpreting the Tarot from what we might view today essentially as a "pre-structuralist" approach for he believed "that the individual card has no meaning solely in itself but only in relation to the cards around it and its position in the layout—exact analogy to word in a poem."

The new propulsive energies of the late 1960s bore fruit in one of Di Prima's best-known poems, "Rant, from a Cool Place," composed in January 1967 and bearing an epigraph from Erasmus: "I see no end of it, but the turning upside down of the entire world." The apocalyptic sense of Bob Dylan's famous chant "the times they are a changin'" propel the opening verses of "Rant" which combine the revolutionary fervor of the times with a plea to Americans to abandon their addiction to consumerism: "We are in the middle of a bloody, heartrending revolution/Called America, called the Protestant reformation, called/Western man,/Called individual consciousness, meaning I need a refrigerator/and a car/And milk and meat for the kids so I can discover that I don't/need a car/Or a refrigerator, or even milk, just rice and a place/with no wind to sleep next to someone." As Henry David Thoreau famously counseled, "Simplify, simplify," and Di Prima also wants us to live simply, so that others may simply live. This theme recurs in Jack Kerouac's *Dharma Bums* when Japhy Ryder—a literary portrait of Gary Snyder—delivers his famous lecture on abandoning materialism:

> See the whole thing is a world full of rucksack wanderers, Dharma Bums refusing to subscribe to the general demand that they consume production and therefore have to work for the privilege of consuming, all that crap they didn't really want anyway such as refrigerators, TV sets, cars, and general junk you finally always see a week later in the garbage anyway, all of them imprisoned in a system of work, produce, consume, work, produce, consume. I see a vision of a great rucksack revolution thousands or even millions of young Americans wandering around with rucksacks, going up to mountains to pray.

Di Prima has mastered an utterly plain American speech which becomes the language of poetry. She opposes the rampant materialism of American consumer culture with a desire to "come to that blessed definable state/ Known as Buddhahood, primitive man, people in a landscape/together like trees, the second childhood of man." Yet this vision of a new spiritualized world is opposed by the Establishment "waiting to get Tim Leary/Bob Dylan/Allen Ginsberg/LeRoi Jones." When Jones/Amiri Baraka was arrested during the riots in Newark in 1967, Di Prima and sixteen other poets including Ashbery, Duncan, Corso, Creeley, Koch, Ginsberg, and Olson composed a letter to protest his sentencing to prison for possessing firearms. While the FBI and police were pursuing such dangerous radicals, the US military was committing "genocide in Southeast Asia," and Buddha returns not as the "great stone Buddhas" of Asia and but rather at the poem's finale "'all beings are from the very beginning Buddhas'/or glowing and dying radiation and plague we come to that final/great love illumination/'FROM THE VERY FIRST NOTHING IS.'"[71] The great Japanese Zen Buddhist Hakuin Ekaku's (1686–1768) "Song of Zazen" is the source of "all beings are from the very beginning Buddhas"—another favorite Hakuin quotation for Di Prima is "What remains to be sought? Nirvana is here before me/This very place the Lotus Paradise, this very body the Buddha"—and the poem closes on the hope for a "great love illumination."

Buddhist themes became more prominent as Di Prima gradually made the shift to a permanent life on the West Coast. She had undertaken several trips from New York to California in the early 1960s, and in 1967 began a twenty thousand mile journey around America. Travelling in a Volkswagen bus through Vancouver, Seattle, San Francisco, Los Angeles, and Ranchos de Taos, she read her poetry at a variety of venues including discotheques, storefronts, galleries, and universities. With Alan Marlowe she gave birth to her third daughter Tara during this time. Accompanied by the singer John Braden—a lover of Marlowe's—they stayed with poet Lenore Kandel on Chestnut Street in North Beach. Kandel was the only woman to speak from the stage along with Timothy Leary, Allen Ginsberg, Gary Snyder, and Michael McClure at the famous "Human Be-In"—the name of the event carried the double meaning of "human being" but also that the experience of the moment should be celebrated—in San Francisco on January 14, 1967, where she read "To Fuck with Love," a celebration of the divine power of sexual love.

The poem was included in Kandel's *The Love Book*: the cover depicted a Tibetan scroll on which the Adi Buddha—in Vajrayana the "primordial Buddha"—and his Shakti are in the *yab-yum*, or intercourse position. City Lights Bookstore in North Beach and the Psychedelic Book Shop in Haight-Ashbury were both raided by police in November 1967: staff were arrested on grounds of "obscenity." The trial, which began in April 1967, ended in a guilty verdict which was appealed and overturned in 1974. Kandel had been a student of Buddhism from her early adolescence and became an important figure as Di Prima began to make the transition from East Coast Beat to the now-burgeoning California hippie counterculture. Di Prima recalled that Kandel "was right in the thick of it. Lenore was wonderful as the woman on the scene, the matriarch, and she made it so clear that I was welcome; otherwise, it could have been very different."[72] Kandel provide a sanctuary

FIGURE 3.5 *"Kandel & Leary," Lenore Kandel and Timothy Leary talking at Gathering of the Tribes of San Francisco Human Be-In, 1967. © 1967 Larry Keenan.*

for Di Prima as she set out to find a new arena for her spiritual explorations.
As Di Prima revealed in her "Preface" to Kandel's *Collected Poems*:

> For several months, I had lost my power to dream. This is fact. Perhaps
> I set out on this Quest because I was no longer dreaming. I woke in
> the morning with no treasures from the kingdoms of Night. Then one
> afternoon I returned to her apartment from the beveled glass and flashing
> ocean light of the San Francisco streets, to find the room Lenore had
> lent me had been changed: clouds hung in the air, and sharp bits of mica
> flashed and swam before me as if space were some viscous substance.
> Something not empty.[73]

Di Prima's *Notebooks* are filled with her dreams and the ability to plunge
into the fecundating nightworld of the unconscious was essential to her
creative imagination. As we shall see in the following chapter, Di Prima was
now entering on yet another phase of her spiritual quest, and California
would indeed provide her with many "treasures from the kingdoms of
Night."

4

The Age of Aquarius
and the Wolf:

Revolutionary Letters, Monas Hieroglyphica, Loba, 1968–79

Di Prima declared her move to California was motivated by a desire to both continue the serious study of Zen Buddhism with Shunryu Suzuki and to work alongside the Diggers in Haight-Ashbury who sought an egalitarian society liberated from money and capitalism. The creative efflorescence which marks this stage of Di Prima's career is remarkable. In this chapter I discuss *Revolutionary Letters* (1968; 1971; 1974; 1979), a central text in the Di Prima canon to which over time she continually added poems as well as the quasi-autobiographical *Memoirs of a Beatnik* (1969) and a poem cycle devoted to her stay in Los Angeles, *L.A. Odyssey* (1969). In 1969, Di Prima began studies at the Tassajara Zen Mountain Center where in 1970 she met Chogyam Trungpa. I then turn to her explorations of Gnosticism and alchemy as well as *Loba* which Di Prima began to compose in 1971: *Parts I-VIII* were published in 1978. During the early 1970s, she moved to Marshall, California, near Point Reyes where Robert Duncan would influence her turn toward Renaissance occultism: several Di Prima works during this phase were inspired by Paracelsus, John Dee, and Heinrich Cornelius Agrippa. In 1974 she began teaching with Allen Ginsberg at the Naropa Institute in Boulder, Colorado, and delivered an important lecture entitled "Light/ and Keats." In 1975 she produced *Whale Honey*, a full-length play and also wrote a fascinating "Preface" to John Dee's *The Hieroglyphic Monad*—Dee's text was first published in Latin in 1564—as well as the poem "John Dee" which I discuss in detail as well as her 1979 lecture at the Minneapolis Jung Society in which she developed her ideas about Henry Corbin and angels.

Because Di Prima shared many of the same spiritual interests as Beats such as Ginsberg, Burroughs, Lamantia, Corso, and Snyder—Buddhism, Hinduism, Native American culture, Gnosticism, Tarot, astrology, and magic—in many ways, she became a bridge between the Beats and hippies. Her later developing interests in alternative medicine and healing merged with the "New Age" and human potential movement which had one center in Northern California at the Esalen Institute. However, although Di Prima shared the pacifist and idealistic dreams of the California hippies, it must be said that—like the artist Robert Crumb who kept an ironic distance from the San Francisco scene—one could not identify her as a hippy. While Di Prima was hardworking, disciplined, and bookish, the hippies tended in general to reject the life of the mind. Many were well read, but it is not untrue to claim a degree of anti-intellectualism in the movement. The misuse of drugs, a tendency toward laziness, and a general lack of interest in strenuous thought and cultural curiosity characterized many members of the movement.

As we have seen in the last chapter, by 1968 Di Prima was ready to make a permanent move to the West Coast. She recalled a humorous moment of self-revelation while at a New York literary party with W. H. Auden and Marianne Moore: "But I mean being a literary person is not fun . . . . It was 1968, and that night I just knew that if I didn't get out of New York and away from the literary world someday I was going to wind up on that couch like Marianne Moore in a little black silk hat."[1] One may also observe a shift from Beat to the new hippie sensibility in comments Di Prima made to Charles Olson. During her last visit with him while living at the Hotel Albert with "a large extended family," Di Prima told him,

> What I'd seen when we drove West the year before, and even more what I'd found on a recent reading trip—the really *new* quality the sixties had brought—an excitement in the air: the music, the color everywhere, the people, the art. Feeling of dawn finally breaking. We now so readily forget or dismiss what those days were like—but that quality truly permeated the mid-and late sixties.

After returning to the United States in 1967, following more than a decade studying Zen in Japan, Gary Snyder had a similar reaction upon beholding the new scene: "So I got to see the way all those kids looked, and they were a pretty sight. There was a lot of color in the clothing, a lot of invention and imagination in the way everyone was doing things. The girls were stunning. The guys looked great too. And they were all friendly with each other."[2] It is noteworthy that both poets noted the colors, electric excitement, and spirit of brotherly and sisterly love which permeated the mood of the mid- to late 1960s. The word *psychedelic* derives from ancient Greek *psyche*=mind/soul and *delos*=manifest/visible. Thus the new consciousness would express itself in a literal manifesting of the joyous, hitherto repressed colors of the soul as well as what Walt Whitman called "the body electric" as California's Age of Aquarius began.

Di Prima chose perhaps the most tumultuous year of American political and social change—1968—to make her permanent move to California. It is perhaps difficult a half-century later to imagine the intense divisions ripping the country apart during the 1960s: the people of the United States were anything but united. The war in Vietnam escalated as John F. Kennedy and later Lyndon B. Johnson increased troop levels and intense bombing campaigns began. The use of napalm—a viscous and vicious jelly which stuck to the skins of its victims and burned them horribly—became widespread. George Wallace of Alabama ran for president on a segregationist platform. In April 1968, Martin Luther King, Jr., was assassinated; in June, Robert F. Kennedy was gunned down in Los Angeles; in August, the Democratic National Convention erupted into chaos as police rioted in the streets of Chicago. Drug laws had become increasingly punitive and homosexuality was still considered by the psychiatric establishment a mental illness. A massive oil spill in Santa Barbara, California, would be yet another indication of ecological destruction which would lead to Earth Day: on April 22, 1970, twenty million people demonstrated during a national day of recognition the necessity to preserve the environment. The great work Henry David Thoreau had published more than a century previously in 1849—"An Essay on Civil Disobedience"—became newly relevant. Thoreau of course had dedicated his life to the preservation of nature and fulminated against materialism and the total absorption in economic goals which began to mark the American temperament. Thoreau described a country which at the time was fighting an absurd war—The Mexican American War—and riven by the moral depravity of slavery. He had famously refused to pay his taxes, spending a night in jail to protest this pernicious institution. So too, America in 1968 was beset by war and racial injustice. Thoreau also was strongly attracted to Native American culture, and so too America's young now turned to indigenous peoples for wisdom. Thus an extreme collision developed between what was called "The Establishment"—the conservative leaders who were supporting war, racism, unbridled capitalism, and ecological destruction—and the counterculture which challenged these actions and sought a new world of peace and justice. This conflict is graphically dramatized by the close of the film *Easy Rider* in which the two motorcyclists played by Peter Fonda and Dennis Hopper are gunned down by Southern rednecks in their pick-up truck.

This at once chaotic—yet also heady and transformational time—is reflected in Di Prima's poetry and prose of the period. As the Beat period transformed into the hippie era, Di Prima would be at the forefront of the women who would create the new consciousness. As Gretchen Lemke-Santangelo has observed, women such as Di Prima, Lenore Kandel, Carolyn Adams, Rain Jacopetti, and Marylyn Motherbear Scott had all been "attached either to the Beat subculture or its allied avant garde literary and artistic circles during the 1950s and early 1960s. More experimental, idealistic, and playful than many of the Beats, they moved fluidly across the boundaries of bohemia to lay the foundation of a new counterculture." In California, Di Prima would also find in the Bay Area a plethora of women involved in breaking through the domination of males in the literary world. Judy Grahn would establish the Women's Press Collective; Susan Griffin developed a conference at the University of California Extension devoted to women poets; alta founded Shamless Hussy Press; and Joanna Griffin and Sande Fini established the Bacchanal reading series.

In June 1968, Di Prima settled into a house at 1915 Oak Street in San Francisco with fourteen rooms on the Panhandle of Golden Gate Park where she paid $300 a month rent, sharing the place with several fellow residents. She was embraced by the community, by poet Lenore Kandel, as well as by Moe Moskowitz, proprietor of Moe's Books in Berkeley—a legendary meeting place for students and local literati—where Di Prima often visited to buy and sell books. In her poem "Memories of Moe," she described Moskowitz as "a one-man welcoming committee" who let her "know from the start that I was part of the tribe." The Diggers—founded in Haight-Ashbury in 1966 and comprising thirty-five communal houses— were across the street from her house, providing free clothing, sustenance, and shelter for the impoverished: food was delivered three times weekly in Di Prima's VW bus. Their name derived from a radical agrarian movement in seventeenth-century England: the modern American Diggers believed "every brother should have what he needs to do his own thing." Robert P. Sutton observed that the Diggers did not believe in conventional religion, but rather approached it "as something spiritual, such as the idea of karma

FIGURE 4.1 *"Diane di Prima Digs in San Francisco." Courtesy: Nathan Gelgud.*

yoga (without the meditation), service, and doing good works."[3] She had been working rapidly on her *Revolutionary Letters*, mailing them regularly to the Liberation News Service: they were then distributed to two hundred free newspapers throughout Canada and the United States. Di Prima also performed the poems, sometimes with musical accompaniment, "on the steps of City Hall, while my comrades handed out the Digger Papers, and tried to persuade startled office workers on their way to lunch that they should drop out and join the revolution."[4] The first selection was published in 1968 in Ann Arbor by Artists Workshop Press and by the Poetry Project, St. Mark's Church in New York City with the notification: "Free poems. No copyright. May be reprinted by anyone," as well as "Power to the people's mimeo machines!" *Revolutionary Letters* was then published by Long Hair Books in London in 1969 and subsequently appeared several times under the City Lights imprint as Number 27 in their *Pocket Poets Series*: the first and second editions in 1971, third in 1974, and fourth in 1979. Di Prima added to the book over the years and an expanded edition containing ninety-three poems was published by Last Gasp Press in San Francisco in 2007.[5]

Dedicated to Bob Dylan and to her grandfather, Domenico Mallozzi, the volume combines the prophetic, mystical, and anarchic. She wrote the book as part of her political activity during the late 1960s because she felt most people found her poetry "too intellectual" when she attempted to read it on the street: for example, she noted that her poem "Goodbye Nkrumah" contained references to Shiva, the death of Buddha by eating mushrooms, and Miles Davis. So the *Revolutionary Letters* were composed "almost as theatre, as street theatre." She wanted an immediate response from her audience and to make a direct emotional impact through the spoken voice. Thomas Albright has noted that one of the Beats's great "achievements was taking art out of the academies, museums, and concert halls into the streets, coffeehouses, and nightclubs—Beat poets declaimed on street corners and table tops." And to continue the anarchist imperatives of her grandfather Domenico, Di Prima ultimately had to literally take to the streets. As Jesse Cohn has observed in *Underground Passages: Anarchist Resistance Culture, 1848-2011*: "Quite frequently, the mutual understanding of anarchist poets and their audiences could be verified, as anarchists tended to favor the oral circulation of poetry in face-to-face settings."[6] The 1960s were a time of manifestos, proclamations, Buddhist sutras—Allen Ginsberg and Gary Snyder both composed poems with political messages in sutra form—and idealistic fervor. Poets did not feel comfortable inhabiting ivory towers but desired to declare publicly their egalitarian themes in order to effect social change and to re-establish the direct connection to their readers Walt Whitman had achieved with *Leaves of Grass*.

Thus *Revolutionary Letters*—as we shall see with *Loba*—was an evolving, open-ended, extended work, created by a process of steady accretion over decades. The title indicates that these are "letters" addressed directly to "the people," and are hence composed in a conversational style. The rubric also provides a kind of general category allowing Di Prima to contribute poems in a number of styles on subjects which she had been pursuing such as the *I Ching*, Buddhism, Hinduism, Giordano Bruno, and Kabbalah as well as seemingly mundane issues such as eating healthy foods. Here she again yoked spiritual and communitarian visions—she had by now thoroughly integrated a radical politics firmly anchored within a thoughtful appreciation of world traditions. She has also mastered a flowing, American style which freely combines colloquial speech with an often-exalted, Whitmanesque openness of soul. D. H. Lawrence famously praised Whitman for his journey down the "Open Road," and so too Di Prima sings here often in her finest *bel canto* style. For example in "Number Twenty-Eight," she announces: "O my brothers/busted for pot . . . we are approaching your cells, to cut you loose/to march triumphant with you, crying out to Maitreya, across the Pacific." Here colloquial "busted for pot" is found next to the formal nobility of the Beethovenian "O my brothers"—one remembers Schiller's "Ode to Joy" in the Ninth Symphony "*Alle Menschen werden Brüder*"— and "crying out to Maitreya, across the Pacific." Di Prima's friend Lenore Kandel—as we have seen in the previous chapter—was devoted to Buddhist studies and had herself composed a poem entitled "Hymn to Maitreya in America." Maitreya, which in Sanskrit is "The Benevolent One," is the successor to Gautama (Sakyamuni) Buddha and will appear in the future on Earth, achieve total enlightenment, and teach the pure dharma. Maitreya

> now abides in Tusita heaven as a Bodhisattva, awaiting the proper time for him to take his final rebirth . . . the teachings of the current Buddha Sakyamuni would flourish for five hundred years after his death, after which would follow a one-thousand-year period of decline and a three thousand year period in which the dharma would be completely forgotten. At the conclusion of this long disappearance, Maitreya would then take his final birth in India in order to establish the Buddhist dispensation anew.

Thus Di Prima's fellow revolutionaries who have been arrested for marijuana possession—"O my brothers/busted for pot"—await the cleansing appearance of Maitreya whom she invokes "across the Pacific."[7] The liberation of Americans unjustly jailed for the slightest infraction of marijuana laws—Neal Cassady, "Dean Moriarty" from Jack Kerouac's *On the Road*, for example, was put in prison for possessing two joints—is tied to a celebration of Maitreya as symbol of a new world about to be born.

Another important influence on Di Prima who appears in *Revolutionary Letters* is the Neapolitan Giordano Bruno, the "heretic" included by G. W. F. Hegel in his survey of the history of Western philosophy *Vorlesungen über die Geschichte der Philosophie* and beloved by both James Joyce and Walt

Whitman. At the age of twenty-one, Joyce reviewed a biography of Bruno, who is the most frequently mentioned philosopher in his final masterwork *Finnegans Wake* (1939). In his essay, the young Joyce wrote that Bruno's

> idea of an ultimate principle, spiritual, indifferent, universal, related to any soul or to any material thing, as the Materia Prima of Aquinas is related to any material thing, unwarranted as it may seem in the view of critical philosophy, has yet a distinct value for the historian of religious ecstasies. It is not Spinoza, it is Bruno that is the god-intoxicated man. . . . His mysticism is little allied to that of Molios or to that of St. John of the Cross; there is nothing in it of quietism or of the dark cloister: it is strong, suddenly rapturous, and militant.[8]

It is evident from Joyce's vivid phrasing and adjectives the qualities that attracted Di Prima to Bruno are: "religious ecstasies," "god-intoxicated," "mysticism," "strong," "rapturous," and "militant." And Di Prima's affinity for Bruno was also shared by Walt Whitman who declared in his introduction to *Giordano Bruno: Philosopher and Martyr*:

> As America's mental courage is so indebted, above all current lands and peoples, to the noble army of old-world martyrs past, how incumbent on us that we clear those martyrs' lives and names, and hold them up for reverent admiration as well as beacons. And typical of this, and standing for it and all perhaps, Giordano Bruno may well be put, today and to come, in our New World's thankfulest heart and memory.

Whitman, as did Di Prima, saw Bruno as a "martyr" from the "Old World" who died for a cause and celebrates his memory in America's "New World." Bruno challenged the notion that the fixed stars existed on an outer sphere. Rather, he conceived of stars as themselves suns possessing their own system of planets extending ceaselessly into an infinite universe containing infinite inhabited worlds moving in an uncentered space. In *De l'infinito universo e mondi* (1584), Bruno argued—anticipating our contemporary science fiction speculations—not only that these other worlds must be more spectacular than ours, but that they also contain creatures superior to those existing on our own flawed planet. He agreed with Copernicus because, as Mircea Eliade has noted,

> He thought that heliocentrism had a profound religious and magical meaning. While he was in England, Bruno prophesized the imminent return of the occult religion of the ancient Egyptians as described in *Asclepios*, a famous Hermetic text. Bruno felt superior to Copernicus, for, whereas Copernicus understood his own theory only as a mathematician, Bruno claimed that he could interpret the Copernican celestial diagram as a hieroglyph of divine mysteries.

As we have seen earlier, Bruno believed a sacred source of wisdom lay in ancient Egyptian thought. British scholar Frances A. Yates (1899–1981)—whose works Di Prima read with intense fascination—noted Bruno's fervent belief that "the truth which is coming to light is the truth which was suppressed by false Mercuries (that is by the Christians), magical truth, Egyptian truth, the sun as the visible god, as Hermes Trismegistus called it." Mercurius—the central symbol in alchemy—is equivalent to Greek Hermes, and alchemists make a strict distinction between common mercury—Hg—and philosophical mercury, Mercurius, which they call "our Mercury." The alchemical text *The Golden Tract* emphasized that "our mercury is not the mercury of the vulgar herd."[9]

Giordano Bruno appears in "Revolutionary Letter Fifty-Nine" as a symbol of spiritual rebellion—a sublime "militant" as James Joyce asserted—as well as a profound thinker who was far ahead of his time:

> What we need to know is laws of time & space
> they never dream of. Seek out
> the ancient texts: alchemy
> homeopathy, secret charts
> of early Rosicrucians (Giordanisti).[10]

Di Prima counsels America's young—in a time of war, racism, social unrest, and increasing ill-health due to the consumption of excessive meat, sugar, soft drinks, and junk food—to turn to the healing knowledge of Paracelsus's homeopathy. The theme of proper nourishment recurs throughout the book, as in "Revolutionary Letter Three" where she counsels the young to keep stores of brown rice, whole wheat flour, cornmeal, kidney, or soy beans, sea salt, dried fruit and nuts, squash, coconuts, and healthy oil. Warren J. Belasco in *Appetite for Change: How the Counterculture Took on the Food Industry* cites Di Prima's role in the movement to challenge the processed food industry and the theme of "living simply so that others may simply live" threads its way throughout the *Revolutionary Letters*. Di Prima also alludes in "Revolutionary Letter Fifty-Nine" to ancient alchemical texts and to the *Giordanisti*. She most likely learned about the Giordanisti from Yates's *Giordano Bruno and the Hermetic Tradition*: she would teach this text as well as other Yates works such as *The Occult in Elizabethan Times* in her course at the New College of California. According to Yates, Bruno believed his ideas would particularly appeal to the Lutherans, for "he had begun a new sect in Germany, and if he could get out of prison he would return there to organize it better, and that he wished that they should call themselves Giordanisti."[11] Yates would emerge as a central influence on Di Prima's developing historical understanding of the hermetic tradition, while Bruno became her hero both for his cosmological thought—as we have seen he believed in the plurality of worlds—and for his imprisonment and death at the hands of the Church as a "heretic."

In "Minnesota Morning Ode: for Giordano Bruno," Di Prima announces that "The City of the Sun is coming!," invoking Bruno as her "brother, waiting in prison/eight years to be burned, to find the sun at last/on the Campo de Fiori . . . here in this Christian place, where Christ the Magus/& Christ the Healer are both forgotten, where the veil/of the temple is rent, but no resurrection follows." We return here to solar imagery, to the sun as symbol of spiritual illumination, to Bruno's "Egyptian truth." For Di Prima, Christianity as a state religion had excluded the notion of Christ as magician and physician of the soul, concentrating instead on doctrines of sin, guilt, and punishment. But she promises the City of the Sun will be made a reality: "I will build it/on this spot. I will build it at Attica/& Wounded Knee/on the Campo de Fiori, at the Vatican/the strong, bright light of flesh which is the link/the laughter, which transmutes."[12] Di Prima alludes to philosopher and astrologer Tomasso Campanella (1568–1639) who like Bruno had been imprisoned due to his revolutionary ideas. Campanella's utopian *Citta del Sole* was conceived in accordance with hermetic ideas and is the source of Di Prima's phrase "The City of the Sun is coming!" There is also an echo in "I will build it/on this spot" of William Blake's "Jerusalem"—"And I will build Jerusalem in England's green and pleasant land"—but now utopian America will be founded by renewing the places of political struggle during the 1960s such as Attica prison in New York where from September 9 to September 13, 1971, inmates rose up in a bloody rebellion. And on February 27, 1973, approximately two hundred Oglala Lakota occupied Wounded Knee, South Dakota, in protest of the deplorable conditions at the Pine Ridge Reservation. Of course in the phrase "the laughter, which transmutes," the verb *transmutes* alludes to the alchemical metamorphosis of base metals into gold, just as America will be transformed through the activism and strength of its youthful dreamers into the New Jerusalem. In a text Di Prima required in her Hidden Religions course—Northrop Frye's classic *Fearful Symmetry: A Study of William Blake*—Frye argued that

> to the alchemic visionary, gold, the material of the New Jerusalem, was the quintessence of the mineral world, that is, the dead or opaque part of the creation, the "Hermaphroditic Satanic world of rocky destiny." A process of transforming metals to gold would be a redemption of this world: it would symbolize, or even cause, by some form of sympathetic magic which the writer does not pretend to understand, the resurrection and apocalypse of man. The ultimate object of alchemy . . . was exactly what Blake said the object of his art was, "to Restore what the Ancients call'd the Golden Age."[13]

We may note here the ways Di Prima has effortlessly synthesized her political and social ideas within the context of a variety of intellectual *topoi* including Blake, alchemy, the New Jerusalem, Campanella, and Bruno.

In another poem included in *Revolutionary Letters*, "April Fool Birthday Poem for Grandpa" Di Prima again invokes Bruno, now in conjunction with the stars and her anarchist grandfather Domenico. As we recall from Chapter 1, these images formed a kind of emotional, imaginative, symbolic complex—*Bruno/stars/grandfather/anarchic communalism*—during her childhood. Di Prima's grandfather's message continues to inspire as she now celebrates the "peace and love" litany of the new generation: "the love you told us had to come or we/die. Told them all in that Bronx park, me listening in/spring Bronx dusk, breathing stars, so glorious/to me your white hair . . . /young men with light in their faces/at my table, talking love, talking revolution/which is love spelled backwards, how/you would love us all, would thunder your anarchist wisdom/at us, would thunder Dante and Giordano Bruno, orderly men/bent to your ends." These lyrical and moving verses again bring Giordano Bruno whom she learned about at the age of seven in the early 1940s into the present ecstatic yet turbulent 1960s, as "young men with light in their faces"—again we have the double meaning of "light" as material and spiritual energy—earnestly seek to bring about radical social justice. Di Prima also cleverly observes that if one reverses letters two-to-five of "*revol*ution," we obtain the word *love*, thus indicating that the ultimate purpose of the youthful rebellion of the 1960s is to bring humanity together in euphoric love. The phrase also seems a response to and variation of the final verses of Amira Baraka's "In Memory of Radio" where Baraka plays with the relationship between the words "love" and "evil": the latter is a near palindrome of the former. Thus again we may observe how Di Prima connects her spiritual studies with her revolutionary dreams, continuing the quest of Jack Kerouac in *On the Road* to discover a New Jerusalem in America. The American novelist John Crowley has populated his novels *Aegypt* and *The Solitudes* with figures such as Bruno and John Dee. Ed Park has noted that although these thinkers have traditionally been considered "marginal" figures in intellectual history, in Crowley's work they are cast as "countercultural heroes" who represent "alternate histories and modes of knowledge" and were the authors of "foundational works officially suppressed but never quite extinguished."

Di Prima continues this program of reconstructing American society under the aegis of a new visionary philosophy in "Revolutionary Letter Sixty-Eight: Life Chant" which begins with an epigraph from *The Tibetan Book of the Dead*: "may it come that all the radiances will be known as our own radiance."[14] This new infusion of inner courage taken from a revered Buddhist source inspires her to proclaim—as in "Minnesota Morning Ode"—"we begin the work/may it continue/the great transmutation/

may it continue/a new heaven & a new earth/may it continue/may it continue."[15] "Transmutation" here again alludes to the alchemical quest to transform lead into gold, which for Di Prima—as for C.G. Jung—symbolized the struggle of the human psyche to evolve into a higher plane of consciousness. One notes the chanting repetition—"may it continue"—the call and response which Di Prima began to develop in her interaction with the audiences to whom she declaimed her poetry. Another dramatic example is "Revolutionary Letter Forty-Nine": "Free Julian Beck/Free Timothy Leary/Free seven million starving in Pakistan/Free all political prisoners/Free Angela Davis . . ./Free Sitting Bull/Free Crazy Horse . . ./ Free Galileo & Bruno & Eckhart. . . . Every doctor brainwashed by AMA a political prisoner . . ./Free yourself/Help to free me/Free us/DANCE."[16] Di Prima alludes here to Julian Beck (1925–85), director of the Living Theatre who was in frequent collisions with legal authorities as were Timothy Leary and Angela Davis (1944–), the African American philosopher and leader of the Communist Party USA who was fired from her teaching position at UCLA; the brave Native American heroes Sitting Bull (ca. 1840–77) and Crazy Horse (ca. 1831–90) who fought against their oppressors; spiritual geniuses such as the German mystic Meister Eckhart (ca. 1260–1328) to whom she devoted a poem and whose concept of *Istigkeit* or *is-ness* would influence Aldous Huxley in his mescaline researches; scientific and theological rebels such as Galileo and Bruno; and doctors who resist alternative medicine because they are under the hegemony of the American Medical Association.

During the 1970s, feminism, gender roles, and gay rights were becoming central in American culture. Kate Millett's *Sexual Politics* and Germaine Greer's *The Female Eunuch* both appeared as the decade began in 1970. The acceptance of women into the literary canon began to become noticeable during the early 1970s: for example, John Giorno's "Dial-A-Poem" event at the Information Exhibition at the Museum of Modern Art from July 2 to September 20, 1970, in which visitors could call a phone number and hear a poem included poets Kathleen Cleaver, Barbara Guest, Lenore Kandel, Bernadette Mayer, Diane Wakoski, Anne Waldman, and Di Prima. Di Prima's work was also included in two important collections of poetry by women: *Rising Tides: 20th Century American Women Poets* and *No More Masks: An Anthology of Poems by Women*, both published in 1973. Issues of social justice for women and gays, the burgeoning sexual revolution, and challenges to the patriarchy also occur throughout *Revolutionary Letters*. For example, Di Prima in "Revolutionary Letter Number Forty-Nine" declaims: "Every housewife a political prisoner . . . . Every faggot hiding in bar a political prisoner/Every junkie shooting up in john a political prisoner/Every woman a political prisoner/Every woman a political prisoner." Di Prima repeats the last verses twice to emphasize the subordinate roles women have been compelled to play: housewives chained to their circumscribed roles are equally political prisoners who must be liberated, a theme we have seen adumbrated earlier in *Dinners and Nightmares*. Di Prima began composing the *Revolutionary Letters* before the Stonewall riots which began on June 28, 1969, at the Stonewall Inn in Greenwich Village—the beginning of the gay liberation movement. Homophobia was omnipresent in America and public opinion was very slow to change. Some members of the gay community opted for complete separation from the straight world. However, it has been pointed out by Eric Keenaghan that *Revolutionary Letters* "articulates a coalitional ethos informed by Di Prima's New Left activism. Unlike her more highly regarded contemporaries such as Judy Grahn, Adrienne Rich, and Audre Lorde, she did not abandon that coalitional spirit, even temporarily, for lesbian separatism in the mid-1970s." As we have noted earlier, Di Prima did not engage in "identity politics" in the sense that she conceived of her activity as essentially humanist and anarchist in orientation and indeed was essentially supporting a "coalitional ethos" in both her work and her life.

The book also registers the shift from Beat lingo to the new, *groovy* California hippy argot, as in "Revolutionary Letter Eleven" in which Di Prima documents her "on the road" trip with writer Kirby Doyle:

drove across
San Joaquin Valley
with Kirby Doyle
grooving
getting free Digger meat
for Free City Convention
grooving
behind talk of Kirby's family[17]

Di Prima would pay tribute to Doyle in a late poem and Doyle's own "An Unfinished Letter" which is dedicated to her exhibits their shared interest in the magical universe: "Beloved Sister,/Baby, I'm trying to get home. I am trying to swing the vessel/toward the center of the Universe. /All my ancestors are in me./I have carried the left eye of Ra to keep the night awake." The San Joaquin is the great, central agricultural region of California and the repetition of *grooving* signals the easy, free mood of this road trip which also includes observations concerning the Diggers as well as Doyle's family life. California can be free and easy under the sun, the automobile taking you where you want to go as in Kerouac's *On the Road*, and Di Prima is here clearly enjoying a new life in stark contrast to the uptight, frantic pace of life in Manhattan. Although the word *groovy* originated in the jazz culture of the 1920s and was in use thereafter, it had become commonplace by the 1960s.

Thus throughout *Revolutionary Letters* the emphasis is on spontaneity, on colloquial language as employed in daily speech, poetry at the service of a democratic vision of a transformed culture. Di Prima wanted her work to reach as many people as swiftly as possible which was achieved through syndication to the underground newspapers through the Liberation News Service. As Ammiel Alcalay observes in "R.D.'s H.D.": "Here we can see another form of lineage: a direct line leading from an initiative like *The Floating Bear* to the underground press, breaking through the Cold War policy of communication as propaganda to the counterculture's call for communication as empowerment, exploration, and kinship."[18] This direct connection to the reader was also accomplished through Di Prima's publication of a variety of poems in the format of colorful broadsides—a large sheet published by small publishers with the poem printed on just one side of the paper. During the 1960s, broadsides became a common means of disseminating not only lyrical poems, but also of promulgating political, social, and environmental ideas to oppose the Establishment. Some of the broadsides Di Prima created include in 1967, "Hymn"; in 1971, "So Fine," "Prayer to the Mothers," "After Completion," "Revolutionary Letter Number 21"; in 1976, "Darkness Invocation" and "The Bell Tower"; and in 1980, "How Shall I Win You to Me." Other broadsides intended to oppose the escalation of the war in Vietnam such as Gary Snyder's "A Curse on the Men in Washington, Pentagon" were also compelling political statements. "A Curse" was published in 1967 by the Communication Company, an anarchist publishing collective in San Francisco distributed during the Summer of Love that year: Allen Ginsberg believed the broadside "helped initiate flower-power era mass peace-protest 'Levitation' of Pentagon, the demystification of its authority."[19]

One of Di Prima's greatest poems—which emerged during the time Di Prima was working with the Diggers as well as the Black Panthers in San Francisco—"Revolutionary Letter Number Twenty" is dedicated to Huey Newton (1942–89) who founded the Black Panther Party for Self Defense with Bobby Seale in October 1966—is "Canticle of St. Joan," dedicated to Robert Duncan. Divided into four sections, it opens with a remarkable dramatic monologue featuring allusions to an array of sources: Christian (*St Michael, grail*); pagan (*wood, spruce, and holly*); Buddhist (the serpent *naga*); and Tarot (*ace of swords*). Joan of Arc declares:

> It is in God's hands. How can I *decide*
> France shall be free? And yet, with the clear song
> of thrush, of starling, comes the word, decide
> For human agency is freely chosen. I embrace
> the iron crown, the nettle shirt, as I
> embraced our lord god in the darkling wood
> He of the silver hooves and flashing mane
> Who shall be nameless.
> Nameless as spruce and holly, which endure.
> Holy St. Michael, but the ace of swords

is bitter! And the grail
not to be drunk, but carried into shelter.
The dragon, my naga, purrs, it lays its claws
about the bars which will soon close around me.

In her poem "A Counterspell for Millbrook: First Day of Winter," composed
while Di Prima was living at Timothy Leary's retreat, she again invokes
holly and "pagan" religious feelings while casting on the day of the winter
solstice a *spell*—a magical incantation—against dark forces inhabiting the
house: "we will bring music/will worship/watching the deer run at sunset/in
the clearing, white tails high/Will worship among the spruce trees, bringing
holly/O Thor, O Woden/Older Druid gods/Turn the black wills, pain and
madness/from this house." Part 3 of "Canticle of St. Joan" goes on to roar
with martial music as Joan exclaims in her eagerness for battle—"Where
is my helmet? Battle/is what I crave, shock of lance, death cry, the air/filled
with the jostling spirits of the dead"—which recalls Ezra Pound's own
stirring hymn to war, a dramatic monologue by troubadour Bertran de
Born—"Sestina: Altaforte"—depicting a warrior who longs to hear clashing
swords, to behold the vivid colorful banners, to rush with mad joy as he
heads into fierce battle, and to watch the fields turn crimson with blood.

Joan announces that "GRAIL IS BLOOD IS HOLLY/red with our
sorrow as we reclaim the ground/free to lie again with the horned man, the
overlords/must build their edifices elsewhere." The holly tree was believed
by the Celts to ward off evil and increase fertility, while the "horned man"
here is again Cernunnos, the Celtic god sacred in neopaganism whose duty,
as we saw earlier in *The Calculus of Variation*, is to delight the Goddess by
making love to her. In the final fourth section, Joan goes to the fire: "The
cross was ours before you holy men, its secret/there, where the two sticks
meet, you cannot fathom./I hear the cart creak home that brought me, the
driver/won't even stay for this end—leap, pirouette./Inside the grail is fire,
the deep draught/melted rubies, blood of the most high god/whose name is
Satan, and whose planet earth/I reclaim for the Bundschuh, sons of men."
Satan of course is here praised as the admirable Lucifer=*lux fero*=Latin
"light bringer" rather than the evil figure of Christianity. Jeffrey B. Russell
observes in *A New History of Witchcraft: Sorcerers, Heretics and Pagans*
that during her trial, charges of witchcraft were not the main thrust of the
accusations against Joan of Arc. Rather, "Joan was condemned—for political
reasons of course—on charges of heresy, not of witchcraft." Di Prima turned
to several sources for her knowledge concerning Joan's spiritual interests,
including the groundbreaking work by Margaret Murry, *The Gods of the
Witches* (1931). Murry emphasizes that Joan came from Lorraine which
as a remote district was "still Pagan," and points out that one of the main
accusations against Joan was "that she had dealings with the faeries" and
that "she had held communication with 'evil spirits' at the Fairy Tree."

So too, Di Prima clearly seeks to foreground these "heretical" aspects of Joan's thought, her immersion in the hidden religions. Di Prima revealed that her intention indeed was to depict St. Joan

> as a continuum of the natural magical religions of Europe and as a practitioner of the same and therefore someone who heard voices, and so on. Had trances. And someone for whom there wasn't necessarily a devil but a horned god. And someone for whom the woods themselves were the temple. That's why she says, "the cross was ours before you holy men."

An important text for Di Prima which she required in her courses at the New College of California was Norman Cohn's *The Pursuit of the Millennium: Revolutionary Millenarians and Mystical Anarchists of the Middle Ages* (1957; 1970), a book which became newly relevant and was reprinted during the spiritual and political uprisings of American youth during the 1960s and early 1970s. Cohn reviews eschatological and apocalyptic ideas current in medieval Europe and describes the radical movements of southwest Germany

> which were known collectively as the *Bundschuh*—a term meaning a peasant's clog and having the same significance as the term *sans-culotte* during the French Revolution . . . its object was nothing less than a social revolution of the most thorough-going kind. All authority was to be overthrown, all dues and taxes abolished, all ecclesiastical property distributed amongst the people; and all woods, waters and pastures were to become communal property. The flag of the movement showed Christ crucified with on one side a praying peasant, on the other the peasant clog, above it the slogan: "Nothing but God's justice!"

Thus Di Prima connects the *Bundschuh* movement (1493–1517)—the poor who died fighting against injustice—with Joan of Arc's communitarian goals. We recall that Di Prima during the late 1950s in her letters had speculated concerning the ways medieval concepts were being recapitulated in contemporary America, and here during the late 1960s we may observe the same trope of the millennial "Age of Aquarius"—the sense that history was moving toward a new revelation, a vital revolutionary society, some rough beast was slouching toward Bethlehem to be born—which characterized the apocalyptic thought of earlier times. "Canticle of St. Joan" is a striking example of the ways Di Prima reclaims the "pagan" substratum of Joan of Arc's courageous life. In a sense, Di Prima identified personally with Joan in her role as a politically radical woman, willing to die for a cause, highlighting her role as warrior for the poor and dispossessed—but in the tradition of "the natural magical religions of Europe" rather than as a representative of official, orthodox, institutional Christianity. Joan of Arc recapitulates Di Prima's own desire to synthesize her esoteric spiritual beliefs with revolutionary political commitments. Furthermore, in reclaiming Joan as an icon of female power, Di Prima is performing the same kind of reconceptualizing of the role of women throughout history which she will undertake in *Loba*.

As Joan of Arc lived during times of intense political turmoil, so too Di Prima was witness to the violence of the times which she recorded in her works during this period. As the violence in Vietnam continued to escalate, Di Prima noted the carnage in several eloquent passages in *Spring and Autumn Annals*:

> The war in Vietnam has started. World War III . . . I shall print a thousand STOP AMERICA NOW signs, in red ink. . . . We are bombing Laos, are bombing Vietnam, are bombing Santo Domingo. We are spreading all kinds of rumors: that Mao is dead, that Chou En Lai is a devil, that we have been sent by God to save the world. By killing it, by poisoning the air, the water, the wheat, defoliating the jungles, perhaps we speak nothing but the truth. Perhaps we have indeed been sent by God. Perhaps we are saving the world, by turning its face back to the Mystery, away from the black cloud science, back to the only knowledge that can save it now. The redemption of the earth thru blood and tears. Thru alchemy.

In what appears to be a massive act of rationalization, Di Prima suggests here that the horror which America is unleashing on the world is analogous to the alchemical stage of *nigredo* which is "the initial, black stage of the opus alchymicum in whch the body of the impure metal, the matter for the Stone, or the old outmoded state of being is killed, putrefied and dissolved into the original substance of creation, the prima materia, in order that it may be renovated and reborn in a new form." Corruption must precede regeneration, thus the eerie "redemption of the earth thru blood and tears." As part of her opposition to the conflict, Di Prima edited *War Poems*, published by her Poets Press in 1968 and containing protest poems by Gregory Corso, Robert Creeley, Robert Duncan, Allen Ginsberg, LeRoi Jones, Michael McClure, Charles Olson, Joel Oppenheimer, Gary Snyder, Philip Whalen, as well as four of her own, including "To the Unknown Buddhist Nun Who Burned Herself to Death on the Night of June 3, 1966." Here Di Prima laments: "you with your shaved head and can/of kerosene. Under what driving form/of ecstasy? I pray to taste it once/your soaked robe chilly in the spring night wind."[20] The poem suggests a kind of mystical illumination which may accompany acts of supreme self-sacrifice in devotion to a noble cause—again as in the cases of Giordano Bruno and Joan of Arc, affirming a link between martyrdom and transcendence. A similar antiwar volume entitled *Thunderbolts of Peace and Liberation* appeared in England in 1969 containing work by a variety of poets including Di Prima, Lawrence Ferlinghetti, and Gary Snyder.

Di Prima's work as a playwright was not neglected during this period: on March 10, 1968, her play *Monuments*, directed by James Waring, was among the last works performed at the important theatre, Caffe Cino which was established in 1958 in Greenwich Village and where Off-Off-Broadway began. The play consisted of eight monologues, three of which were acted each night. Like Di Prima's other plays, the texts are highly lyrical, surreal, and sometimes comic, juxtaposing the sacred and profane, sublime and quotidian in equal measure. For example, "Handgrenade," for Alan Marlowe, opens with "KAN JI ZAI BO SATSU GYO JIN HAN YA HA RA MIT TA JI SHO KEN" which the uninitiated might not recognize as the Japanese translation of the *Heart Sutra*—"Hymn to the Perfection of Wisdom"—the most widely recited of Mahayana Buddhist sutras. This opening blast is followed immediately by: "The plastic buildings are melting around me. I set a match to them, and they collapse like celluloid. Not even any flames. Hello. Hello. What I mean to say is, that I am a poet, clearly, and in excellent physical shape." Several paragraphs later the speaker informs us that "Form is the emptiness, and emptiness is the form"—well-known lines from the *Heart Sutra*—followed by: "My long hair grows out of my shaven head. The Gemini again, taking off two ways at once. I have eaten brown rice for 24 days and nights, nevertheless I would like a chocolate éclair." Astrology appears here with "Gemini" and the transcendent and comically mundane are—as is often the case with Di Prima—thus placed in close juxtaposition. "John's Words" is dedicated to singer John Braden which includes allusions to "shadows of great druid women," and to Merlin and Morgan le Fey: when he acted in the play, Braden also sang a song to the lyrics Di Prima provided, "The Death of the Hermit." One of the monologues entitled "Zipcode"—which Di Prima composed for herself to perform—asked whether she would ever "sit in a bay window in San Francisco, looking at the rain and writing another novel," a dream which had now been realized. The critic Ross Wetzsteon complained:

> At first glance, Diane di Prima's *Monuments* seems a very simple theatre piece—eight monologues written specifically for and in a sense about the people who perform them. But immediately a problem arises—are they performance pieces, or character sketches, or self-images or Miss di Prima's images of the performers' self-images? This isn't merely a quibble of definition, for the answer determines the very mode of our response— by what criteria does one judge them?[21]

Indeed, as with Di Prima's other plays, *Monuments* seems poetry set on the stage rather than drama in the conventional sense of human interactions leading to conflict and possible resolution. Yet as we have seen, Di Prima's plays derive from the early "Happenings" staged by John Cage at Black Mountain College and her scripts should be understood as posing a similar challenge to conventional dramatic form: her plays are, indeed, *Happenings*. The stage exists solely to provide a locus where events and words take place. However, *Monuments* does catch precisely the mood of the late 1960s, in which deep spiritual longings were often suffused with a giddy innocence, with the dreams and childlike, joyful humor of now omnipresent Flower Children.

A significant Di Prima work of this period containing five poems—*L.A. Odyssey*—was composed between July 28 and August 5, 1969, and issued in holograph by Poets Press: George Herms created the cover illustration. Di Prima composed the text for Robert Wilson at the Phoenix Bookstore to earn money to repair her car during a drive from San Francisco to Los Angeles: 125 copies were printed at an instant print shop and soon "a hundred signed and numbered copies of a brand new 'limited edition' of *L.A. Odyssey* were on their way to New York for Bob to sell to his mysterious stable of 'collectors.' The debt was paid, a bit more money would be coming in, and we ambled back up the coast to San Francisco."[22] The first—"Elegy for M.R." laments the increasing despoiling of Earth: "I always cry in Los Angeles, last year/I cried for the planet, hearing news/of G.E. on Navaho reservation, I cried/for the lost green earth. . . . I cried/for grandchildren of my children, done out of/their inheritance, cried/for the big trees trucked out of the mountains." A year later, as we have seen, the first Earth Day was celebrated to address the need to halt the increasing despoiling of the planet's resources. This ecological elegy combined with sympathy for the destruction of Native American culture by greedy mega-corporations such as General Electric also chronicles her physical response to the smog covering Los Angeles—"no oxygen—the body mobilized/for desperate smog survival signals/anxiety-sorrow."[23]

The following poem—"Rooftop, Hollywood" continues the threnody: "I breathe death,/in your streets walk glittering zombies, the clock/sings loud at the day-grey night yellow dome which/has cut us off/from the living god, your sea rolls, dead, phosphorescent/pitifully restless, onto the oil black sands."[24] The denizens of Southern California resemble the living dead zombies of a Hollywood horror movie, the surrounding polluted air creating a "yellow dome" separating a doomed humanity from a blue sky. Di Prima sustains a lofty lyrical tone, smooth enjambment carrying the movement of the verse forward. In her autobiography *Recollections of My Life as a Woman*, this image of a befouled Pacific Ocean reappears as Di Prima recalls this same scene but now in connection with time she spent with poet Jack Hirschman (1933–) and his wife Ruth. While they spent an evening together in conversation and drinking wine, Di Prima noted the great oil rigs furiously pumping in the ocean. As they all walked the beach, the sand had been blackened by oil spills and the waves of the sea were churning with a fiery phosphorescence. Observing oil pumps darkening the sea, rendering the waves phosphorescent must have been particularly troubling to Di Prima. Alchemists conceived of light as symbolic of the spirit, and phosphorous was intriguing because it appeared to trap light: it glows in the dark. In her poem "Phosphoros," Di Prima quotes as epigraph Philalethes, the pseudonym of the American alchemist George Starkey (1628–65) who influenced Isaac Newton: "Watch carefully that you may see the Day-star arising with deliverance" and opens: "The morning star casts light on all/ the towers on the hill./We consort w/angels/We are the prey of beings/ who break us open to extract the seed/The mineral sperm which flows/like vapor from our hearts." Phosphoros is the morning star or Venus, in Greek *phos*=light; *pherein*=to bear and Lucifer is the Latin equivalent=light bringer. The poem ends again with a quotation: "The sky was green as morning/& the dew/lay golden on the grass." However in "Rooftop, Hollywood," this phosphorescent incandescence is not a light-bringing event, but rather the sign of environmental destruction. One recalls Allen Ginsberg's "Sunflower Sutra," in which he bemoans with Jack Kerouac the oil-begrimed waters of the Pacific where the two poets "sat down to cry."

The perspective shifts from Earth to outer space in "Full Moon in Aquarius: 3 Takes" commemorating the moon landing on July 20, 1969—the poem was begun eight days later on July 28: "there is/shit on the moon, there are/landing platforms and cameras, and what else/they don't say, already we manufacture/deadly energy shield of disenfranchised metal/to break the moonbeams/when they come to earth." Charles Bukowski (1920–94)—a poet one might not easily associate with Di Prima who however has several stylistic and philosophical connections with her—composed a story entitled "The Absence of the Hero" published in 1969 affirming the gap between America's technological achievements and the horror of its social injustice which features similar imagery: "Then I took yesterday's newspaper, some dull shit about men landing on the moon. . . ." Di Prima then continues "werewolf/where will you /go for refuge now/what stopping place/for souls on their way/out?" Di Prima's devotion to paganism and "witchcraft" during the 1960s is signaled here by the werewolf whose natural relation to moon's force—witches were also believed to be able to shape-shift into the form of a wolf—is now ruptured by humans upsetting the universe's fragile balance as they wield a "deadly energy shield of disenfranchised metal." Di Prima's experience may be interpreted as a 1960s version of Henry Miller's account of his travels across America with painter friend Abraham Rattner from 1940 to 1941, *The Air-Conditioned Nightmare* (1945). After ten years in Paris, Miller found his native land horrifying. Upon arriving in Detroit, he exclaimed: "The Duraluminium City! A nightmare in stone & steel. Terrifyingly new, bright, hard—hard as tungsten. Glitter of cruelty. Tough to be a beggar here in winter. The city of the future! But what a future! . . . *Bomb Detroit out of existence!*" So too Di Prima has created in her opening three poems a pensive commentary on the devolution of American society, its ecological destruction, consumerism, soullessness, and military adventurism disguised as "space exploration."[25]

The fourth final part of *L.A. Odyssey* seeks to redeem this apocalyptic vision through turning to art's magic, in particular the paintings of Willem de Kooning (1904–97). The poets of the "New York School" were famously fully engaged with the art world: Frank O'Hara worked as a curator at the Museum of Modern Art and created poems about artists such as "Ode to Willem de Kooning" and "The Mike Goldberg Variations"; James Schuyler was also a curator at the Museum and published art criticism; Kenneth Koch composed a poem "To and About Willem de Kooning," and a play inspired by Larry Rivers; John Ashbery wrote prolifically about art. The artists reciprocated: Larry Rivers painted a portrait of Ashbery and Elaine de Kooning created one of Frank O'Hara; Willem de Kooning provided an illustration for O'Hara's "In Memory of My Feelings"; Jasper Johns created a lithograph entitled "Study for *Skin with O'Hara Poem.*" Di Prima, as we have seen, was equally enamored of artists, having known—among many others—Jasper Johns, Jim Dine, Franz Kline, Andy Warhol, and Willem de Kooning. De Kooning had several connections with the Beats: both the Abstract Expressionists and the Beats spent time at the Cedar Tavern at 24 University Place in Greenwich Village. On March 2, 1959, de Kooning attended a poetry reading by Frank O'Hara and Gregory Corso at the Living Theatre at 14th Street and Sixth Avenue: in the small audience were also the painters Franz Kline, Allen Ginsberg, and Jack Kerouac. De Kooning visited Corso in Rome during a visit there in 1959. Kerouac became acquainted with de Kooning, Franz Kline, and Larry Rivers. Dore Ashton observed that they would all congregate both at the Cedar Tavern and at the Eighth Street Club, established in 1949, and known familiarly as "The Club":

> It was not unusual to see Kerouac and Kline with a group of younger artists drinking at the Cedar and finishing up the night at Kline's studio. Whenever there was a party at the Club the Beats turned up, sometimes high on marijuana, sitting in the rear of the loft while the artists—still faithful to liquor—danced and bellowed loudly.

The Beats, writers who influenced them, and those with whom they were associated all made art: Allen Ginsberg, Gregory Corso, William S. Burroughs, Jack Kerouac, Lawrence Ferlinghetti, Robert Duncan, Kenneth Rexroth, Henry Miller, Kenneth Patchen, Charles Bukowski, and Di Prima herself. Allen Ginsberg studied art with Meyer Schapiro at Columbia University and became fascinated by Paul Cézanne's paintings and their "cosmic vibrations," composing the poem "Cézanne's Ports"; Gregory Corso composed a sequence of St. Francis poems based on Giotto; Lawrence Ferlinghetti wrote "Short Story on a Painting of Gustav Klimt," "Seeing a

Woman as in a Painting by Berthe Morisot," among many others. Thus Di Prima's engagement with the work of Willem de Kooning was in no way idiosyncratic among her fellow writers and she saw a natural connection between modern art and her own work as a writer, declaring: "I grew up with gestural work, with Abstract Expressionism. I like kinesthetic work, work with a lot of movement, body in it." Her poem "De Kooning Xhibit: L.A. County Museum" is divided into six sections containing a cycle of ekphrastic poems describing a variety of the great artist's works: "Elegy 1939," "Pink Angels," "Woman, Wind and Window 1950," "Excavation 1950," "Woman I-1950-52," and "Door to the River 1960." Di Prima is returning to de Kooning in Los Angeles more than decade following the efflorescence of Abstract Expressionism in New York in the 1950s when she had become acquainted with the artist in New York during the period she and Amiri Baraka were lovers. As with jazz, the Abstract Expressionists placed an emphasis on the spontaneous, energetic, creative moment. De Kooning taught at Black Mountain College in the summer of 1948. He had lived in extreme poverty in New York: there were times when he had to paint with enamels because he could not afford pigments. His freewheeling lifestyle—he was a notorious womanizer, imbibed copiously and was arrested in Provincetown, drunk and nude on the beach—did not prevent him from working as long as a year on one painting, constantly revising and repainting.[26] It is understandable that Di Prima would be receptive to de Kooning, with his evocations of *Magna Mater*'s cosmic, creative power as well as the aggressive force of the female, themes which would preoccupy her as she began *Loba* two years later in 1971. Di Prima had always been fascinated by artists and is herself a watercolorist and collagist. In *Recollections of My Life as a Woman* in describing her love affair with Bonnie, a painter, Di Prima emphasized the profound pleasure she obtained observing an artist in the act of painting and the mysterious act of creation as forms took shape out of nothing. Painters and paintings form the subject matter of many of her poems. "So Fine" opens with a description of one of Leonardo Da Vinci's most famous works : "In the postcard, the *Girl with an Ermine*/turns her head, her hand/& the animal's pause in archetypal gesture, & she might be fifteen." And Di Prima's poem "On the First Day of Spring I Visit the Museum" begins with arresting verses: "fortified by a Kline and 2 Gustons I clean the house:/cots return to the closet, dust retires/under the bed." Viewing the works of Franz Kline and Philip Guston supplies the energy required to undertake the labors of spring cleaning in a light-hearted manner.[27]

Di Prima describes de Kooning's "Elegy 1939" with great precision, illustrating the same sensitivity in her interpretation of works of art she had demonstrated in her earlier studies of dance: "There was, then, this time: a pause/in the conflagration/in which forms were balanced, outrageous/pink against green, fish shapes or tits/touching in greeting, the tension/between

foreground and moving back-/ground in which I sprouted." "Elegy 1939"
echoes the oval shapes in the paintings of de Kooning's friend Arshile Gorky
(1904–48), and Di Prima notes how the objects de Kooning depicts may be
seen as either female breasts or floating fish. The cryptic final verse which
ends "in which I sprouted" introduces Di Prima herself into the painting,
for several poems which follow move back and forth between the present
exhibit which she is viewing in 1969 and her past life in New York. Several
poems in the de Kooning sequence bear witness to Di Prima's Buddhist
and Hindu studies for there are allusions to the *tandava*, *karma*, and
Kali. For example, "Pink Angels ca. 1945" is "a whirl of/quick charcoal,
the green/turned yellow, *tandava*/dance of angels, dance of destruction."
Here again Di Prima's reading of religious texts supplies her with a rich
source of poetic allusion: the *tandava* is Shiva's divine dance of creation
and destruction of the universe. "Pink Angels" was completed in 1945. De
Kooning often attended films and his wife Elaine recalled that newsreels
depicting the horrors of the Second World War were shown; Di Prima
has clearly appreciated how the "angels" here also perform a "dance of
destruction." Di Prima returns to this theme of the angels and apocalypse in
her poem "Prayer to the Ancestors" in which she sings of those "who saw/
the stars on fire blooming & going out, who hear/& heard the angels of
apocalypse before/we even charred the earth, who tremble (forever)/on the
brink of some/unthinkable liberation."

   She also turns to her memories of the 1950s when she and LeRoi Jones
became acquainted with de Kooning in her evocation of "Woman, Wind
and Window 1950" which is vividly rendered: "now it is white and the
colors of paper/broke loose, the forms drift the paint/drips, it is not unlike/
what hung on my walls and Roi's/a few years later, a touch/on my arm in
the windy music/we stood by the window to listen/I turned, pink female
flesh/engulfed/engulfing, that time/engulfs me still, it sucks me into its
maw. . . ." There is a considerable amount of white in "Woman, Wind
and Window 1950," with dripping lines of paint in the fashion of Jackson
Pollock. Again as in "Elegy 1939" where Di Prima brings herself into the
poem—"in which I sprouted"—she recalls a vivid period of her life. It is
ambiguous what has transpired: "a touch/on my arm . . ." Who is doing
the touching? Is it LeRoi Jones, someone else, or a nonhuman contact?
Windows are clearly discernible in the upper left of the painting and the
music is "windy" to which she listens: thus the poem's title "Woman,
Wind and Window." The white face on its side in de Kooning's painting
has an open mouth—Di Prima's "maw"—and the repetition of "engulfed,"
"engulfing," "engulfs" emphasizes a feeling of being swallowed by the mass
of "pink female flesh" as well as being overcome by time and memory. The
poem deftly moves between the painting, the actual past, and the ways the
imagination can reconstruct the past, re-experiencing it in relationship to
the painting. The following poem is devoted to one of de Kooning's largest

paintings, "Excavation" which is a massive 80 by 100 inches in size. Di Prima alludes to both Franz Kline and Jackson Pollock, noting in de Kooning's work "a touch of Pollock/there a year when you wanted/to do the Kline thing." Seeing "Excavation" stirs recollections of a party at de Kooning's "loft on Broadway" with Bill Berkson, Frank O'Hara, and "LeRoi/stoned playing jazz with Larry"—the painter Larry Rivers—"all of us/immersed in karma like tarpits fossilizing/our small knowledge." Here again the concept of karma—the law of cause and effect in which the actions of our present lives determine the situation we will face in our next incarnation—combines with an allusion to the La Brea Tar Pits in Los Angeles (near the art museum where Di Prima was viewing the de Kooning exhibit) in which the bones of many prehistoric animals are fossilized. Thus the psychic "excavation" which de Kooning conducted in order to produce such a complex and rich canvas which the viewer must study carefully to find its hidden meanings is analogous to the archaeological excavation which resulted in the discovery and interpretation of the fossils in the La Brea Tar Pits.

Finally, in "Woman I—1950-52," Kali is invoked: "O woman/great fury seated/among your peers, destroying/whatever you look on, tooth/and nail, O Kali/among women, who looked on me/so often at the Museum/of Modern Art/high heeled avenger, 'fierce in your/great austerities.'"[28] Kali— the magnificent Hindu goddess—is often depicted in iconography dancing or standing upon the prostrate body of her consort Shiva, and Di Prima would study the Tantric traditions associated with Kali which found a place in several of her later poems, most notably in a sequence dedicated to Kali in *Loba*. The last phrase in quotation marks comes from verse 41 from "The 108 Names of the Holy Tara": "Who terrifies Death even, fearsome, terrible, fierce in your great austerities." Hugh B. Urban has commented that for the American counterculture, such imagery "turned into a powerful weapon to criticize the dominant sociopolitical order, which is perceived as repressive, bankrupt, and corrupt. With its emphasis on the terrible, erotic Mother Kali, Tantra seemed to offer a much needed antidote to a hypercerebral Western world that had lost touch with the powers of sex, femininity, and darkness." For Di Prima, de Kooning's "Woman I—1950-52" was replete with hidden significance which she intuitively connected to her Buddhist and Hindu studies. Gods and goddesses of course are exteriorized symbolic forms of internal psychological forces, and American youth were struggling in the 1960s to rebalance *yin* and *yang*, father and mother, male and female, light and dark in new, healthier psychological patterns. Indeed, as we have seen, Di Prima's questioning of traditional marriage and the often stultifying roles men and women have been compelled to occupy had been a central focus of her work from the beginning. Indeed, in discovering the power of Kali, she is putting into practice her succinct apothegm from *The Calculus of Variation*: "tell all the gods we're turning back to find them." Young people in America now need to refind the abandoned gods of prior times and resuscitate their meaning for contemporary humanity and as companions and psychic familiars in their own individual spiritual quests.

Di Prima would return to her memories of the 1950s in another significant work appearing in 1969—*Memoirs of a Beatnik*—which had a curious genesis. Di Prima had met the owner of Olympia Press, Maurice Girodias (1919–90)—the son of Jack Kahane (1887–1939) whose Obelisk Press had published Henry Miller's *Tropic of Cancer*. Girodias would publish Vladimir Nabokov's *Lolita*, William S. Burroughs's *Naked Lunch*, Gregory Corso's sole novel *American Express* as well as work of Jean Genet and Samuel Beckett. He offered Di Prima to ghost-write the sex scenes for two books—*Of Sheep and Girls*, by Robert M. Duffy and *Love on a Trampoline*, by Sybah Darrich—both of which appeared in 1968 in "The Traveller's Companion Series." Before she left New York for California, Girodias asked her if she would create an erotic book of her own: thus Di Prima embarked on the composition of *Memoirs of a Beatnik*—a potboiler, written because she needed the money. Although she now had some practice churning out erotic-prose-for-hire, when she sent the manuscript to Girodias, he constantly complained there were insufficient sexual scenes, so Di Prima dutifully conceded, adding more and more as requested. As Nancy M. Grace has observed, the book gives us "a bifurcated story: one a fictive erotica and the other a nonfictive representation of Beat New York, the former overpowering the latter." *Memoirs of a Beatnik* is perhaps her best-known work, and Di Prima is thus in the rather curious situation of being a kind of female Henry Miller, since many know her for this erotic book rather than her wide-ranging philosophical explorations. So too, Henry Miller was fascinated by theosophical, esoteric, and Eastern religious figures such as Madame Blavatsky, Milarepa, Paracelsus, Ramakrishna, and Vivekananda, devoting several essays and passages in his books to these subjects, yet many remember him solely as the author of "dirty books" such as *Tropic of Cancer, Tropic of Capricorn, Sexus*, and *Quiet Days in Clichy*.

Fred L. Gardaphe has emphasized the fact that *Memoirs of a Beatnik* should be seen as the first important autobiography by an American woman of Italian descent and that "it should be considered as a precedent against which one might better read the sexual personae of Italian American women like Madonna and Camille Paglia."[29] Gardaphe correctly situates Di Prima as the predecessor of an Italian American cultural critic such as Paglia, whose works *Sexual Personae, Vamps and Tramps* and *Sex, Art and American Culture*—like Di Prima's and Gloria Anzaldua's—push against the restrictive limits within which discussions of gender, sexuality, creativity, and our understanding of what it means to be a woman have been conventionally conducted. Christopher Gair agrees with this assessment, declaring that *Memoirs of a Beatnik* "represents di Prima as being able to manipulate a fluid sense of self that is defined as an ongoing process of re-invention able to outwit male efforts to categorize her." If the book declares

Di Prima's independence from the sexual mores defined for her generation by her parents and American society during the post–Second World War era, she also emphasizes the bohemian/Beat milieu in which she moved before and after her time at Swarthmore, returning to several of the same characters described in *Dinners and Nightmares*. At the opening, we are informed that her place in the West Village is decorated with "our low bed, the only furniture in the room was made of skids stolen from nearby paper companies and painted a flat black. They served as both chairs and tables, and no cushions broke the austerity of the furnishings, no draped Indian prints and antique velours such as we have become accustomed to in the sixties."[30] One notes here that Di Prima is narrating her memoirs of the 1950s from the vantage point of the 1960s, comparing the "austerity" of her youth to the more vibrant, colorful, psychedelia of a later era.

In Chapter Two, this contrast is again made explicit when comparing a gay bar on MacDougal Street—"Swing Rendezvous"—with the present:

> The Swing was a haven because it was off-bounds, a meeting place for outlaws. Now, in the midst of "gay liberation" the social stigma has gone out of homosexuality, and with it the high, bitter romanticism that made it so debonair . . . .Gayness can no longer be used to hold the world at bay, put down the society around you, signal your isolation and help you stand clear. It is no longer a component of black magic: Cocteau, Genet, or Kenneth Anger.[31]

Because of her central role during the Beat 1950s, Di Prima is able to subtly distinguish and analyze shifts in attitudes prevalent at the time she composed the *Memoirs*. As in *Dinners and Nightmares*, she again invokes touchstones significant to the counterculture: Federico Garcia Lorca, J. S. Bach *Cantatas*, Wilhelm Reich, Oswald Spengler, Brahms's *Requiem*, Hieronymus Bosch, Dylan Thomas, J. D. Salinger, Jean-Paul Sartre, Tallulah Bankhead, Aleister Crowley, Hermann Hesse, Alexandra David-Neel, Peter Kropotkin, Ezra Pound, the Modern Jazz Quartet, Miles Davis. One is reminded of the album cover of the Beatles's *Sgt. Pepper's Lonely Hearts Club Band* (1967), which depicts a similar array of fabulous cultural icons for young people during the 1960s. And just as the Beatles portrayed several Indian gurus on their cover, so too Di Prima refers to Eastern thought. For example, in Chapter Eleven she describes the "love affair" she had with Manhattan, with

> the strange cemetery downtown at Trinity Church, of Wall Street in the dead of night, Cathedral Parkway on Sunday afternoons, of the Chrysler Building gleaming like fabled towers in the October sun, the incredible prana and energy in the air, stirring a creativity that seemed to spring from the fiery core of the planet and burst like a thousand boiling volcanoes in the music and painting, the dancing and the poetry of this magic city.[32]

Prana—which we have encountered previously in *The Kerhonkson Journal*—
in Sanskrit is wind, breath, or vital force and in Tantra, these winds travel
through a network of channels—"nadi"—in the human body.[33] As we shall
see later, Di Prima would also incorporate these concepts in poems such as
"Tsogyal," devoted to the great female Tibetan Buddhist spiritual figure.

One notes as well in the above passage an echo of Jack Kerouac's style—
the onrushing, long, ecstatic sentences of *On the Road*—and in the final
Chapter 14 Di Prima renders homage to Ginsberg as well. As we have seen
earlier, she had read *Howl* and "knew that this Allen Ginsberg, whoever
he was, had broken ground for all of us—all few hundreds of us—simply
by getting this published . . . . we read *Howl* together, I read it aloud to
everyone. A new era had begun."[34] *Memoirs of a Beatnik* then concludes
with a highly imaginative, funny scene involving Ginsberg, Kerouac, and Di
Prima in bed together during which Di Prima describes Kerouac attempting
to have intercourse with her "in Tibetan yab-yum position."[35] *Yab yum*
literally means "father-mother" and in Vajrayana iconography depicts
female and male deities in sexual intercourse, either sitting, standing, or face
to face.[36] Kerouac would include Di Prima's friend Lenore Kandel's practice
of *yab yum* in his novel *Dharma Bums* where she is depicted as "Princess,"
a friend of "Japhy Ryder"—Gary Snyder. Di Prima's again incorporates
her intellectual investigations—here in an effervescent and light-hearted
fashion—into her writings.

Maria Farland in her essay "'Total System, Total Solution, Total
Apocalypse': Sex Oppression, Systems of Property, and 1970s Women's
Liberation Fiction" studied the connection between Beat poverty and the
"penchant for liberatory experience." Farland argues that for the Beats
"the source of sexual repression was bourgeois morality—or, for those such
as William Burroughs and Norman Mailer who followed the teachings
of Wilhelm Reich, the repressive economic structure. Thus in Di Prima's
Memoirs, bohemian poverty provides the preferred social milieu for erotic
experimentation . . . . For Di Prima's generation, sexual experimentation
appeared to be in a kind of inverse relationship to possessive individualism
and private property." This reminds us of connections between Di Prima
and Henry Miller or Herbert Marcuse in his *Eros and Civilization* who also
saw the pleasure of an open and joyous sexuality as part of a revolt against
bourgeois materialism and the life-denying structures of modern society.
Indeed, Di Prima conceived of sexual freedom as deeply connected to the
history of revolutionary, antinomian movements, asserting that "the secret
tradition tends also to be the tradition of anarchism, and the tradition of
equality between women and men and the tradition of sexual freedom. And
it's often a tradition of property held in common, also. Tribalism. These
things are linked all through European history."

In 1969, Di Prima's father died and her Poets Press also published *John's
Book* by husband Alan Marlowe, whom she would divorce that same year.

Introduced by Robert Creeley, the book's cover by Daniel Entin depicts Di Prima, John Braden, and Marlowe robed and hieratic with sacred necklaces in quintessentially fashionable late 1960s style.

The androgyny ushered in by the Beatles in the early 1960s—men wearing long hair, colorful Madras shirts, the freedom to be "sensitive" and nurturing, the emphasis on the previously supposedly "feminine" world of inner spirituality—all of these aspects of male behavior began by the end of the decade to be felt throughout the counterculture. Di Prima during this period also was continually harassed by the FBI and decided to retreat from the city. She resided from late 1969 to early 1970 at the Black Bear Ranch, an eighty-acre commune in a forest north of San Francisco in Siskiyou County: while there, Di Prima learned of the death of one of her closest friends, Charles Olson. The commune was founded in 1968 by Richard Marley who called it a "mountain fortress in the spirit of Che Guevara," and it is the subject of Jonathan Berman's documentary film *Commune* (2005). The turn toward communal living during the 1960s may be seen as another

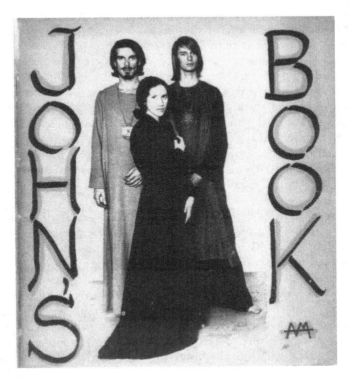

FIGURE 4.2 *Alan Marlowe, Diane di Prima, John Braden. Courtesy: Daniel Entin Studio.*

way Native American tribal practice influenced the counterculture, along with experimentation with peyote, donning love beads and head bands. In her role as poet/shaman she desired a direct experience of a communal life outside the urban environment to peel away the false layers of societal conditioning to actualize an authentic self. As J. Boekhoven in *Genealogies of Shamanism* has observed: "Humanistic and transpersonal psychologists were crucial for the genealogy of shamanism, as they constructed an image of shamans as individuals with distinct self-actualizing qualities. As wounded healers, shamans had experienced a valuable mystical breakthrough through which they had attained a more authentic and integrated, and less inhibited frame of mind." This is precisely what Di Prima hoped to incorporate into American cultural life and she turned to the "archaic" to find sustenance and inspiration for the new revolution. Boekhoven also returns to the theme of the "wounded healer": as we saw in Chapter One, this is an aspect of the shaman's evolving mystical sensibility and defined Di Prima's own gravitation toward the life of art, poetry, and "self-actualization"—as defined by Abraham Maslow, the quest for an authentic self at the summit of the "hierarchy of needs." Once our basic requirements for food, shelter, and clothing have been met, as well as our need for social affiliation and usefulness, we seek to fulfill ourselves through actualizing our deepest potential to become what we are meant to be. Of course, there is also a central ambiguity in this quest for a "real self" for a Buddhist, since Buddhism denies the existence of a "self." Gary Snyder in his poem "Avocado" wittily compares the large round seed of the avocado to one's own original nature. Although it is smooth and seemingly pure, it is nevertheless slippery. You think it is something that you can plant in the ground, but when you try to hold it in your hands, it slips away through your fingers.

The anthropologist Victor Turner (1920–83) also expounded his concept of *communitas* which he saw the Beats and hippies as exemplifying:

They stress personal relationships rather than social obligations, and regard sexuality as a polymorphic instrument of immediate communitas rather than as the basis for an enduring structured social tie. . . . The "sacred" properties often assigned to communitas are not lacking here, either: this can be seen in their frequent use of religious terms, such as "saint" and "angel," to describe their congeners and in their interest in Zen Buddhism. . . . The hippie emphasis on spontaneity, immediacy, and "existence" throws into relief one of the senses in which communitas contrasts with structure. Communitas is of the now; structure is rooted in the past and extends into the future through language, law, and custom.

Turner correctly places the countercultural movement within the context of an anthropological understanding of the ways societies create ideological structures which then naturally set into motion opposing minorities who—as he puts it—choose to "'opt out' of the status-bound social order."

Thus Di Prima left for the commune to experience *communitas* and to experiment with the ideas she had been advocating in *Revolutionary Letters*: "If I'm going to write about going back to this more primitive way of seeing the world and living in it I should really do it!" In San Francisco, Di Prima had been studying Zen with Shinryu Suzuki at Tassajara Zen Mountain Center. She believed that Suzuki

> saw no contradiction between revolution and Zen, and neither did I. . . . There's no way we win, because the ghettos can be napalmed as easily as Vietnam can be napalmed . . . and it began to be clearer and clearer that you really have to understand the forces behind stuff rather than blindly react to stuff. . . . What I said one day was "Actually, none of it's important except poetry, magic and zazen."[37]

Di Prima began to feel responsible for the poor and oppressed whose lives she was attempting to rescue and protect: if blacks and Hispanics and Native Americans were to rise up as she was advocating in the *Revolutionary Letters*, the mood in the late 1960s led her to believe they would be crushed as mercilessly and relentlessly as the US Army was destroying Vietnamese civilians and villages.

Di Prima's poetry composed following her return to San Francisco in the early 1970s is marked by her deepening studies of Buddhism. Richard Hughes Seager in *Buddhism in America* has observed that the period from approximately 1963 to the mid-1970s

> are likely to be looked back upon for some time as the most important turning point in American Buddhist history. At around that time, convert Buddhism in this country grew from a small community of seekers preoccupied primarily with Zen to a far larger and more differentiated community, as people in the burgeoning counterculture went in search of spiritual alternatives and found them in Zen, Nichiren, Tibetan, Theravada, and other kinds of Buddhism, whose teachers they discovered among immigrants to this country and overseas.

In the same year—1970—as the birth of her second son, Rudi, Di Prima met the Tibetan Buddhist Chogyam Trungpa (1939–87) and depicted the daily lives of her two gurus—Shunryu Suzuki and Trungpa—in "Tassajara, Early 1970's": "Suzuki watering the rocks so they wd grow/Trungpa & his young wife talking in the garden/the thump of huge mallets making mocha/in a hollowed-out tree stump/to the rhythm of Japanese & American folksongs/on New Years' Eve/It was the chanting that rose & fell like waves from the zendo/Crickets among the lanterns that outlined

the paths/It was the small silver bell that clanged you awake." One notes
the haiku-like, image laden style, each verse presenting a vivid picture to
the reader's mind. By placing Trungpa and Suzuki together in the garden,
Di Prima symbolizes the ways she has combined both Tibetan Vajrayana
and Japanese Zen Buddhist wisdom into her own practice. In addition,
Japan and America—mortal enemies during the Second World War—had
begun a process of reconciliation. Although during the War Japanese-
Americans had been viewed as a threat and interned in concentration
camps, traditions of Zen culture were now incorporated into American
literature and thought—the poet Gary Snyder had spent a decade studying
at a Zen temple in Japan—and now Di Prima hears together the "rhythm
of Japanese & American folkongs." The present quest is for enlightenment,
symbolized by ringing the bell which will "clang you awake." This evolving
syncretism of differing traditions may also be seen in Di Prima's poem
"Tassajara, 1969":

> Even Buddha is lost in this land
> the immensity
> takes us all with it, pulverizes, & takes us in
>
> Bodhdharma came from the west.
> Coyote met him.[38]

Here Di Prima—a recent East Coast transplant—muses upon the immensity
of the American West and recalls the legend of Bodhidhama who is said
to have brought Chan Buddhism to China "from the West." So as Chan—
or Zen—comes to California, it also meets an indigenous wisdom, that of
the Coyote mythology of the Native Americans. For Di Prima, spiritual
traditions can live together in harmony and out of them a new, syncretic
philosophy may come to fruition.

   As we have seen, Di Prima is a special sort of spiritual voyager, for she
frequently balances her serious, solemn side with a life-affirming, ironic,
and self-deprecating wit—qualities sometimes lacking in persons with a
yearning for what William Wordsworth called "something far more deeply
interfused." For example, another poem dealing with her Buddhist studies—
"I Fail as a Dharma Teacher," laments:

> I don't imagine I'll manage to express Sunyata
> in a way that all my students will know & love
> or present the Four Noble Truths so they look delicious
> & tempting as Easter candy . . .
> * * *
> Alas this life I can't be kind and persuasive
> slip the Twelve-part Chain off hundreds of shackled housewives

present the Eight-fold Path like the ultimate roadmap
at all the gas stations in Samsara

But, oh, my lamas, I want to
how I want to!
Just to see your old eyes shine in this Kaliyuga
stars going out around us like birthday candles
your Empty Clear Luminous and Unobstructed
Rainbow Bodies
swimming in and through us all like transparent fish.[39]

Sunyata is the concept of "emptiness," while the Four Noble Truths and the
Eight-fold Path are central tenets of Buddhism. "Twelve-part chain" refers to
the *nidanas—nidana* means cause or link—the doctrine in which each link is
asserted as a primary causal relationship between the connecting links. This is
the mechanistic basis of repeated birth, *samsara*, and resultant *dukkha*—the
First Noble Truth that all life is suffering—starting from *avidya* (ignorance). It
is one application of the Buddhist concept of *pratityasamutpada* (dependent
origination). "Rainbow bodies" refers to the teachings of Dzogchen—"great
perfection"—a tradition begun by Padmasambhava who brought it to Tibet
in the eighth century, which holds

the axiom that the mind, as self-existing intelligence, is by nature pure
and undefiled. Because, however, this is not recognized, beings wander
in the cycle of existences—samsara. A method for breaking out of this
cycle is direct experience of "naked," or "ordinary" mind, which is the
basis of all activities of consciousness. This is the gateway to primordial
knowledge, the union of emptiness—sunyata—and clarity. . . . Their
goal is realization of the "rainbow body," i.e., the dissolution of the
physical body—that is, of the four elements that constitute the body—
into light.[40]

Di Prima expresses these aspects of Tibetan thought with a deft and humorous
touch, indicating that she has not yet reached the sacred higher levels of
awareness toward which she strives, yet in so doing acknowledging—with a
profane and comical American quotidian image—that there are many "gas
stations in Samsara."

Di Prima's energetic researches into Buddhist thought and into a variety
of other philosophical sources may be seen not only in her verse and prose,
but in her prolific *Notebooks* which she continued to regularly create. These
are often extremely appealing aesthetic objects in themselves containing
striking collages, as we see in the opening pages of the *San Francisco
Notebook 2*, which Di Prima created from August 30, 1971 to March 1972.
The opening of the *Notebook* contains one of the famous Tahitian paintings

by Paul Gaugin and beneath a quotation from William Blake's *Jerusalem*: "I
give you the end of a golden string;/Only wind it into a ball,/It will lead you
in at Heaven's gate/Built in Jerusalem's wall . . ." Next we find an illustration
of Blake's prophetic books and beneath a sculpture of Sogyo Hachiman—or
"Hachiman in the guise of a monk"—the syncretic Buddhist/Shinto deity.
The next entry contains a Native American kachina doll beneath which
Di Prima has inscribed "The Ideal Becomes What Nature Was" which is
a quotation from Friedrich Hölderlin's *Hyperion*, followed by *I Ching*
notations which are omnipresent throughout the *Notebooks*. The following
pages recount a meeting with Kirby Doyle, annotations from Laura de
Witt James's book *William Blake and the Tree of Life*, and narratives of
dreams. The *Notebooks* as we saw earlier with Di Prima's *Diary* contain
a wealth of information concerning her daily life as well as the constantly
curious, impressively wide-ranging and probing nature of her intellectual
investigations.

FIGURE 4.3 *San Francisco Notebook. Courtesy: University of North Carolina at
Chapel Hill.*

During the early 1970s, the quest for mystical illumination, for "light," which began with her studies of Robert Grosseteste as well as her work in Zen and Tibetan Buddhism, resurfaced when Di Prima began reading H.D.—Hilda Dolittle (1886–1961)—in 1971. Between 1973 and 1978, Di Prima lived in the tiny town of Marshall—population about fifty people—north of San Francisco on the Pacific Ocean at Tomales Bay where Robert Duncan often visited her. Phyllis Stowell—who had come to interview Di Prima—recalled that her

> house was a shaky green structure hanging onto the bank by rotted supports and tilting with a nervous slope over the water on pilings infested with powder post beetles. Diane, with a mixture of forbearance, annoyance and amused acceptance, showed me where the termites entered and left above the windows, windows that looked out to the gently drifting water, ducks, gulls, and across the bay, green hills.

Stowell noted her books on Native American literature, Tarot, mysticism, and Madame Blavatsky who Di Prima declared "was the grandmother of us all." As always, she had little money, the refrigerator and hot water heater were in disrepair, but the favorite food of her family was brown rice, so the food bills were minimal. While residing in Marshall, she worked on *Loba*, created collages, and kept her journals. Perhaps due in part to Duncan's influence—he had embarked on a major study of H.D.'s poetry, to be published posthumously as *The H.D. Book* (2012)—Di Prima also began reading deeply in the famous "Imagist" poet whose career was closely linked with Ezra Pound. She perused *Tribute to Freud*, and was struck by H.D.'s idea of the "event out of time." In recollecting her life, H.D. singled out certain past experiences: "Memories too, like the two I have recorded of my father in the garden and my mother on Church Street, are in a sense super-memories, they are ordinary, 'normal' memories but retained with so vivid a detail that they become almost events out of time, like the Princess dream and the writing-on-the-wall."[41] Di Prima claimed that she did not find this concept "in any of the rest of her published work. And yet the idea as I have interpreted it—the event, inner or outer, whose power and numinosity place it *outside* the flow of linear time—has stayed with me since my first reading of *Tribute to Freud* in 1971."[42] Di Prima's engagement with H.D. continued over the next decades and she gave several talks on her work. As we shall see in Chapter 5, Di Prima responded intensely to H.D.'s preoccupation with angels and visionary experience: her own fascination with this topic found expression in her 1988 lecture on "H.D. and Angel Magic." This obsession with angels is typical of Beat literature, beginning with Allen Ginsberg's "angel-headed hipsters" in *Howl* and is prevalent in the work of Gregory Corso and Philip Lamantia.

As was the case throughout her career, Di Prima's literary work and commitment to social justice were intertwined during the early 1970s. In April 1972, she participated in a City Lights Poets Theater event held at Fugazi Hall in North Beach to aid Greek resistance to the military junta which had been instituted in the cradle of democracy. She was joined by Helen Kazantzakis as well as Kay Boyle and Lawrence Ferlinghetti who read his poem "Forty Odd Questions for the Greek Regime and One Cry for Freedom." On October 11, 1973, she read her work at Bard College: early work from *The New Handbook of Heaven*, poems about Willem de Kooning from *L.A. Odyssey*, sections from *Loba*, and also the inspiring "Revolutionary Letter Number 49" with its rallying cry to free America's imprisoned revolutionaries. She also began a six-year stint of teaching poetry in schools, including reform schools, in Wyoming, Montana, Arizona, and Minnesota as well as in prisons and reservations.[43] While in Wyoming teaching Native Americans pupils, she witnessed unparalleled degrees of suffering and began to have a series of dreams. She reported that in one episode "there was a she wolf. She was supposed to hunt me through this labyrinth. When I decided to split and not wait to be hunted, she turned into a guardian who just followed behind me." Di Prima began composing the opening poem "Ave"—"O lost moon sisters/crescent in hair, sea underfoot do you wander/in blue veil"—in December 1971 without intending to create a long work: the following February she began working on the poem—which would become *Loba*—in earnest.[44] *Loba* was published in several editions: *Loba Part I* (1973), *Loba as Eve* (1975), *Loba Part II* (1976), *Loba Parts I-VIII* (1978), a longer edition containing Books I and II in 1998, and excerpts appeared in *City Lights Anthology* (1974) and *Ms. Magazine* (May 1977). During this phase, Di Prima continued her teaching career when she conducted community poetry workshops at Intersection for the Arts in San Francisco from 1971 to 1975. She began to work with students developing images from their dreams, offered erotic writing seminars for women and led classes on individual poets including William Carlos Williams, Ezra Pound, Robert Duncan, Allen Ginsberg, Charles Olson, Gertrude Stein, and H.D. She also began another publishing venture—Eidolon Editions—in 1974.[45]

The struggle for Native American justice had continued during the 1960s and early 1970s and Di Prima's experience witnessing the anguish of children in the Bureau of Indian Affairs schools provoked her to political action. In October 1974, Di Prima confessed to feeling increasingly disgusted with the traditional Thanksgiving holiday and desired to declare solidarity with "some of the desperate and righteous struggles" of Native peoples, arguing that "what we are about to discover is the power of collective non-consuming." But instead of the "Be-Ins" or "Love-Ins" of the 1960s, she proposed a "FAST-IN." Di Prima argued that if "each concerned family set aside what they usually spend on Thanksgiving food and drink, and contributed that sum to some portion of the Indian struggle, this futile festivity could turn instead into a strong and useful act." This sensitivity to the plight of the Native Americans is expressed in Di Prima's poem, "American Indian Art: Form and Tradition":

Were we not fine
were we not all fine
in our buckskin coats, the quillwork, the
buttons & beads?
Were we not fine
were we not all fine

O they have hung our
empty shirts in their cold
marble halls. They have
labeled our baskets, lighted
our masks, disassembled our pipes
in glass cases.
        (We flashed in those colors
thru the dark woods over the dun plains
in the harsh desert)
        Where
do they hang our breath? our
bright glance, where is our song now
our sorrow?

                     Walker Art Center, Minneapolis

Di Prima employs the repetition characteristic of Native American song—"were we not fine"—recalling a poem such as "She Had Some Horses" by the Native American writer Joy Harjo in which the phrase "she had horses" is repeated continually: "She had some horses./She had horses who were bodies of sand./She had horses who were maps drawn of blood./She had horses who were skins of ocean water." Di Prima evokes the vanished lives of the Plains Indians: the title is based on the eponymous exhibition held at the Walker Art Center in Minneapolis—"American Indian Art: Form and Tradition" which was subsequently published under this name as a catalogue—and raises the controversy concerning the robbery of Native American artifacts and sacred objects for purposes of display in museums. Di Prima contrasts the proud beauty of the destroyed cultures, concentrating on specific visual details—"buckskin coats," "quillwork," "buttons & beads"—with the "cold/marble halls" of the museums. Although the Native Americans are still very much alive, their arts and culture have been appropriated by their invaders and exhibited as if they were dead animals stuffed by taxidermists, their vibrant culture "catalogued" under the dull, sterile academic rubric: "American Indian Art: Form and Tradition."

Another significant development during this period was Di Prima's teaching in 1974 at the opening session of the Poetics Program at the Naropa Institute in Boulder, Colorado—she would continue her professional association with Naropa until 1997.[46] As we have seen, Di Prima met Allen Ginsberg in 1957: over the decades the two poets pursued similar political and philosophical pathways. Chogyam Trungpa had asked Ginsberg to create a writing program at Naropa which would ultimately be named the Jack Kerouac School of Disembodied Poetics where Di Prima, William S. Burroughs, Gregory Corso, Ed Sanders, and Anne Waldman would teach. By 1976, BA and MA programs in Buddhist studies had been established as well.[47] Di Prima began regularly attending Chogyam Trungpa's lectures, whom she had met previously at Tassajara in 1970. They developed a close friendship: Di Prima recalled that she "would have a formal meditation interview with Trungpa every summer. He was helping me, but I was still practicing Zen—I was still committed to Suzuki's teaching. I practiced Zen until 1983." Her friendship with William S. Burroughs deepened during this period and they discussed magic and occult subjects together. Indeed, three great Renaissance "magicians"—Paracelsus, Heinrich Cornelius Agrippa, and John Dee—would begin during this phase to become central figures in Di Prima's increasingly learned visionary poetics.

She delivered an important lecture at Naropa in 1975—"Light/and Keats"—in which she returned to the poet who had become her hero during adolescence, John Keats. Di Prima conceives of Keats not as the romantic poet in love with nightingales and "easeful death" but rather as an initiate of the esoteric traditions. In a way, she had taken Keats as one of her "gurus" from an early age, just as Allen Ginsberg had adopted William Blake and Gregory Corso Percy Bysshe Shelley as spiritual exemplars. Di Prima's interpretation of Keats has been recently corroborated by Jennifer Wunder, who in *Keats, Hermeticism, and the Secret Societies* argues that his work derives from Rosicrucian, Masonic, Hermetic, and alchemical sources.[48] One thinks of Keats's famous letter about the earth being the crucible of "soul-making" in which through a spiritual/alchemical process of transformation, the coal of the unshaped human soul is transformed into a diamond through the suffering of life. In one of her best-known poems—"Rant"—we encounter an allusion to Keats's conception: "There is no way out of the spiritual battle/the war is the war against the imagination/you can't sign up as a conscientious objector/the war of the worlds hangs here, right now, in the balance/it is a war for this world, to keep it, a vale of soul-making." Di Prima focuses in her lecture on his letters of December 22, 1817, and October 27, 1818, in which Keats expounds his concept of "negative capability"—letting the "self" drop away and a receptive emptiness take its place, a characteristic Keats associated with Shakespeare who himself had no fixed "identity" or "personality" which allowed the playwright to become the locus of the creation of thousands of other "characters." Di Prima agrees with Keats's notion that "with a great poet the sense of Beauty overcomes every other consideration, or rather obliterates all consideration." The act of writing requires a "loss" of self which can be seen in relation to the Buddhist idea of *satori* or Zen Buddhist enlightenment. When Keats says "not myself goes home to myself" he expresses the central paradox of creativity, suggested also by Arthur Rimbaud's *J'est un autre*—"I is another."[48] When the Muse visits, the poet must be in a state of passive receptivity—or as Di Prima puts it—"to make yourself a fine enough organism to most precisely receive." It is noteworthy that Ginsberg, Corso, and Di Prima took British romantic poets as guiding spirits and also interpreted their work within an esoteric framework. In each case, they sought to assimilate and adapt their nineteenth-century poetic *gurus* into a contemporary American context through a close study of their esoteric symbolism as well as by continuing their tradition of visionary poetics.

In the lecture she also explored her deepening fascination with alchemy and Gnosticism—which as we shall see influenced *Loba*—as well as the metaphysics of light which had intrigued her since her studies of Robert Grosseteste in the late 1950s:

> It seems to me . . . that the actual stuff poetry is made out of is light. There are poems where the light actually comes *through* the page, the same way that it comes through the canvas in certain Flemish paintings, so that you're not seeing light reflected *off* the painting, but light comes through, and I don't know the tricks that make this happen. But I know they're there and you can really tell when it's happening and when it's not. And I think it's not very different from the light of meditation. So what I'm beginning to suspect that what makes it happen is *the way sound moves in you*, moving your spirit in a certain way to produce a certain effect which is like an effect of light.[49]

Heinrich Cornelius Agrippa (1486–1535), the illustrious German occultist—Christopher Marlowe wrote that Faust compared himself to Agrippa, proclaiming that he "will be as cunning as Agrippa was/Whose shadowes made all Europe honor him" (*Faust*, ll. 144–46)—became significant for Di Prima in understanding the Kabbalah as well as her theorizing about inspiration and *light*: how art can *illuminate*.[50] In "Light/ and Keats," she cites Chapter XXV from the Second Book of Agrippa's *De Occulta Philosophia* regarding music: "Singing can do more than the sound of an Instrument . . . . It moveth the affection of the hearer by his affection, and the hearer's fantasy by his fantasy, and mind by his mind, and striketh the mind, and striketh the heart, and pierceth even to the inwards of the soul." Agrippa leads Di Prima to speculate on the human body itself as a kind of musical instrument: "And so, there is a way, to me, that the most high aim of poetry is to create that sense of light."[51] She ponders the visceral, transcendent emotions which great art stirs in us, goose-bumps and physical, bodily sensations of ecstasy: Emily Dickinson famously said she knew a literary work was true poetry if it made her feel as if the top of her head was being blown off.

In another central passage in "Light/and Keats," Di Prima clarifies her deepening preoccupation with Gnosticism and alchemy:

> I'm totally influenced by Gnosticism, if in it you include all those heresies, because I feel that's my heritage. My tradition. That I come out of Europe that's almost completely forgotten what it was because the Church did such a good brainwashing job, but that was a place of strong shamanism, of medicine religions, out of which grew this Gnostic root. . . . I have to say that the Gnostic position is very strong in Pound, very strong in Robert Duncan; it runs like a thread through the Romantics, and it's here, now. So, who was wiped out in 500 A.D.? "Straining at particles of light in the midst of a great darkness"—that's Keats. "In the gloom, the gold gathers the light against it"—that's Pound.

The Gnostics believed true enlightenment came not through institutions or a professional clergy, but rather through direct knowledge of the divine— hence *gnosis*, ancient Greek for knowledge. The divine spark in humanity was trapped in matter, and our life's purpose is to release the light within. Henry Corbin—the great French scholar of Islamic mysticism who would influence Di Prima's later work—believed that contemporary humanity was in exile on planet Earth, "but refuses, or is unable, to recognize that fact. . . . Living in this world, the 'gnostic' is a 'stranger' to it, because he has at least discovered the true nature of his condition, and knows that his true home is elsewhere." Di Prima's studies led her to believe that the Gnostics and alchemists

> began to get a glimmer that maybe, just maybe, spirit is trapped in matter for a reason . . . ? More than just to climb out again. That maybe there's a way to take the whole thing with us. To truly transform the matter universe. And at this point, alchemy becomes a serious business. It deals with the question, which is still the question, the real millennial question: how to make paradise on earth. How to transform the matter universe so that the spirit, which has fallen into matter finally, like yeast in bread, fills everything.[52]

Agrippa was also responsible for leading Di Prima toward the Tarot which she began studying while staying in Ranchos de Taos, New Mexico, in 1966 where she spent two months. During this time she also received a $5,000 grant from the National Endowment for the Arts to produce four more poetry books with her Poets Press. Northrop Frye pointed out in *The Critical Path* that during the 1960s, young people

> had been educating themselves, partly through the film, with its unparalleled power of presenting things in terms of symbol and archetype, and partly through the oral tradition of popular contemporary poetry . . . there has grown up a new tolerance for schematic patterns in thinking, of a kind that . . . is deeply congenial to poetry. Astrology, Tarot cards, the I Ching, maverick writers like Velikowski or Gurdjieff, all have their student following.

The Emperor, Fool, Magician, High Priestess, Empress, Hierophant, Lovers, Chariot, Hanged Man, Moon, Sun—the Tarot supplied a set of archetypal symbols which the Beat and hippy generations employed to interpret the meaning of their experience within a cosmic framework. Di Prima's friend Gregory Corso among the Beats was perhaps the most deeply involved with Tarot as we see in his homage to Edgar Allan Poe, "Nevermore Baltimore" in which he invokes a lady reading Tarot cards, "scrying" in her crystal ball— the technique employed by John Dee to make contact with the angels—who tells Corso on his thirty-eighth birthday tales of Parsifal, the Egyptian gods Nut and Sin and interprets for him the meaning of the "eight wands" which refers to a Minor Arcana Tarot card in the popular Rider-Waite deck depicting Ace of Wands through Ten of Wands, as well as Page, Knight, Queen, and King of Wands.[36] A. E. Waite (1857–1962) was a prolific Brooklyn-born occultist living in England who became a member of the Hermetic Order of the Golden Dawn and edited the alchemical writings of Paracelsus for which Di Prima would compose an Introduction. Allusions to the Tarot also began to surface in Bob Dylan's compositions. Not only does the exotic, luxurious, formal and slightly archaic style of Corso's "Nevermore Baltimore" sound very much like lyrics of a Dylan song, on the back cover of his 1976 album *Desire*, Dylan featured "The Empress" from the Rider-Waite deck.

Di Prima worked daily with the Waite deck of Tarot cards and studied Kabbalah. Frances Yates in *The Occult Philosophy in the Elizabethan Age*—a required text in the course Diane di Prima would teach at the New College of California—has explained the origins of Kabbalah:

> It was believed that when God gave the Law to Moses he gave also a second revelation as to the secret meaning of the Law. This esoteric tradition was said to have been passed down the ages orally by initiates. It was a mysticism and a cult but rooted in the text of the Scriptures in the Hebrew language, the holy language in which God has spoken to man. Out of Cabalist studies of the Hebrew text there developed a theosophical mystique, nourished on elaborate search for hidden meanings in the Scriptures, and on elaborate manipulation of the Hebrew alphabet.

One may thus understand Kabbalah as yet another means by which to delve beneath the "letter" for clues which might indicate what the letter stands for: the world is a sign system. Throughout her career, Di Prima sought to fathom precisely these "hidden meanings" which seemed to lie tantalizingly beneath the surface appearance of things. The universe presents itself to us on two levels: the Book of Scripture and the Book of the visible world. In both cases we have an outward "exoteric" level of language, of signs and symbols which cloak an inner, esoteric secret realm of meanings. Thus the need for a hermeneutics, a method of *interpretation* to reveal the significance of the languages of Scripture as well as of the visible world.

Indeed, several American poets during the rise of the counterculture turned to Kabbalah for inspiration. The work of the celebrated scholar of Kabbalah Gershom Scholem began to become known to American poets such as David Meltzer, Jack Hirschman, Jerome Rothenberg, Nathaniel Tarn, and George Quasha. These authors also became aware of the allusions to Kabbalah in Pico della Mirandola and the transmission of this body of knowledge through William Blake, the Hermetic Order of the Golden Dawn to W. B. Yeats and Charles Williams. Di Prima herself was now inexorably led toward Kabbalah through her studies of Tarot: she would fall asleep, dream about a specific card and as with the genesis of *Loba*, dreaming allows entrance to the unconscious where creative connections can be accomplished. This immersion in the cards' symbolism gradually led Di Prima by the early 1970s to discover the Tree of Life and "then everything fell into place."[53] In her encounter with Renaissance occultists, Di Prima was uncovering a link in a long chain of mystical thought in Germany which had its roots in ancient Neoplatonism, in Kabbalistic lore, and in the texts of Hermes Trismegistus. Christian Knorr von Rosenroth (1636–89) published in the tiny town of Sulzbach-Rosenberg two volumes of his *Kabbala Denudata: Sive Doctrina Hebraeorum Transdendentalis et Metaphysica Atque Theologica* (1677–78). Meister Eckhart (1260–1328) sought immediate access to God by means of meditating and prayer. Johannes Reuchlin (1455–1522) in *De arte cabalistica* (1517) disseminated the notion of accessing God through the ten emanations extending down through each level of creation in the Tree of Life—a concept as we shall see which became significant in Di Prima's esoteric symbolism—while Sebastian Franck would translate the *Corpus Hermeticum* (1542). In our own time, German Dadaists such as Hans Arp studied Jacob Boehme, and Hugo Ball familiarized himself with the apophatic theology of Pseudo-Dionyisus the Areopagite. And the turn toward Eastern thought by Hermann Hesse in books such as *Siddhartha* would have a direct influence on the evolution of hippie culture in the United States.

Heinrich Cornelius Agrippa was born in Nettesheim near Cologne, and his *De Occulta Philosophia Libri Tres* devotes a significant section to Kabbalah and these ideas inspired Di Prima to a new bout of creativity. Harold Bloom in *Kabbalah and Criticism* has noted that Kabbalah through history was combined with other conceptions: "Christian popularizations of Kabbalah starting with the Renaissance compounded Kabbalah with a variety of non-Jewish notions, ranging from Tarot cards to the Trinity." Di Prima emphasized this historical evolution of Kabbalah into a variety of different formulations when she announced that she was "not talking about Judaic Kabbalism; I'm talking about Kabbalistic magic which grew out of the Renaissance, transmitted by Cornelius Agrippa and others." One reason Agrippa may have appealed to her is due to his particular emphasis on the feminine aspects of the Kabbalah. According to Johanna Drucker, Agrippa "extolled the superior virtues of *Shekhinah*, the female counterpart of God, while also asserting that Eve was closer than Adam to the perfection of the Divine being represented by the Tetragrammaton"—the Tetragrammaton— in Hebrew the *Shem ha-Mephorash*—is the four letters *YHWH* for the Divine Name, *Yahweh*.[54]

Hermetic Kabbalists such as Agrippa and John Dee correlated the twenty-two Tarot cards (known as "The Major Arcana") to twenty-two letters of the Hebrew alphabet and twenty-two paths of the Tree of Life. The Tree of Life was central to activities of Samuel MacGregor Mathers's Hermetic Order of the Golden Dawn (1888–1903). As we recall from Chapter 1, a member of the group—the British occultist Aleister Crowley (1875–1947)— founded Thelema in 1904 and Di Prima would include readings about the Golden Dawn as well as Crowley on her course syllabus for "The Literature of the Hidden Religions of Europe." Joseph Leon Blau has pointed out that for Jewish religious philosophers "the concept of God became more and more refined, more and more remote, less and less human" leading to the idea of the ten emanations through which The Infinite—or *Ein Sof*— manifests itself. These are called the *sephirot* and first or highest of the Tree is known in Hebrew as *kether* or crown.[55] The influence of Kabbalah and the Tree of Life would appear in Di Prima's *Revolutionary Letters*. In "Number Fifty-Seven" of the *Revolutionary Letters*, after detailing how humanity is progressively moving away "from the light/our bodies sprout new madnesses," Di Prima envisions an oncoming end-time: "we sprout new richness of design/baroque apologies for Kaliyuga/till Kether calls us home/ hauls in the galaxies like some/big fish." *Kali Yuga* is the final apocalyptic age of the four cycles in the Sanskrit scriptures, yet here there is hope that our whole galaxy will return to its primal beginnings, gathered in "like some big fish." Here again we note Di Prima's effortless syncretism in combining Hindu and Kabbalistic conceptions and thus creating her own unique and individual style.

In "Revolutionary Letter Number Seventy-Seven," she again emphasizes the Tree of Life as part of her being, as incarnated in her own body: "The root of my brain/(the actual stem and medulla)/is the Tree of Life./It is the story we have all been telling/The story of the journey and return/It is all

about Light/and we never stop telling it."[56] Thus for Di Prima, Agrippa was
a central text in her understanding of Kabbalah which she connected to
social transformation: again, personal and political change and evolution
are inseparable. As Joseph Dan observed in *The Christian Kabbalah: Jewish
Mystical Books and Their Christian Interpreters*: "Agrippa followed Pico
and Reuchlin, but went further in two main respects. He declared that
magic and kabbalah are the best means to the understanding of God and
the universe in all their aspects; and he claimed that kabbalistic knowledge
endows the practitioner with magical powers which can be of service to meet
human needs."[57] Jorge Luis Borges—who studied Kabbalah in great depth—
summarized its philosophy: "In each one of us there is a particle of divinity.
This world, evidently, cannot be the work of an all-powerful and just god,
but it depends on us. This is the lesson the Kabbalah gives us—beyond being
a curiosity studied by historians and grammarians." Borges's insight precisely
describes Di Prima's goal: she saw the purpose of the shaman/magus/poet as
harnessing magical and poetic energies to both help humanity and to aid the
Creator in completing the act of creation. As we shall see below, the purpose
which Di Prima attributed to John Dee's work she also defined as her own
poetic task: "This is the Work which the magus, partaking of the divine,
furthers: the redemption and transmutation of the worlds."

It is extraordinary the amount of work Di Prima continued to accomplish
during the mid-1970s. Her *Selected Poems: 1956-1975* appeared in 1975
featuring a cover by George Herms. In addition to her labor on *Loba*, the
many additions to the *Revolutionary Letters,* her lecture in 1974 on "Light/
and Keats" and a 1976 seminar on Charles Olson's *Selected Writings*—both
at Naropa—she also undertook a translation of the Latin Rosicrucian texts
of Robert Fludd (1574–1637) and delved into yet another Renaissance
magus, John Dee (1527–1608/9): mathematician, astronomer, occultist,
adviser to Queen Elizabeth II and one of England's "learned astronomers."
Rudolf II (1576–1612), Holy Roman Emperor and member of the House of
Habsburg, gathered many eminent minds to his court in Prague, including
Tycho Brahe, Johannes Kepler, alchemist Michael Maier (whom Di Prima
also studied), and John Dee. Over a period of three decades, Dee assembled
the greatest personal library in England, consisting of four thousand volumes,
and also owned his own astronomical observatory as well as alchemical
laboratory. Lewis Spence memorably portrayed him:

> Living in comparative solitude—practising astrology for bread, but
> studying alchemy for pleasure—brooding over Talmudic mysteries and
> Rosicrucian theories—immersed in constant contemplation of wonders
> which he longed to penetrate—and dazzled by visions of the elixir of
> life and the Philosopher's Stone, Dee soon attained to such a condition
> of mystic exaltation that his visions became to him as realities, and he
> persuaded himself that he was the favoured of the Invisible.

This "mystic exaltation" of course was a state much desired by the Beats and the quest for sources in Medieval and Renaissance thought which might aid in the attainment of such states of consciousness was one of the factors which led them to study these often arcane and recherché works.

By the late 1570s, Dee, who had been influenced by Agrippa's "angel magic," became preoccupied with communicating with angels through scrying—or summoning up visions in a crystal ball—and on December 22, 1581, conducted his first significant "angelic conversation." In October 1958, in London, William Burroughs—who as we have seen shared Di Prima's interest in magic—purchased a stainless steel dowsing ball. Its shiny surface allowed Burroughs and his friend Brion Gysin to employ it for divinatory purposes: incidentally, Gysin would register in Paris in 1962 a patent "Dreamachine" capable of creating stroboscopic "flickers" which would become a common accompaniment at LSD hippie gatherings. As we shall see in the following chapter when I shall develop this theme more fully, Di Prima would devote one of her lectures to the topic of "angel magic." The counterculture had cultivated a particular obsession with angels, and one might speculate that with Friedrich Nietzsche's declaration that Gott ist tot—"God is dead"—modern humanity's hunger for the divine was met with a deafening silence. Perhaps the angels could carry messages to an absent divinity and help us again make contact with the vanished sacred. Yet in the modern world, even angels are threatened with cosmic disaster as Di Prima's friend, poet Lenore Kandel lamented in her poem "First They Slaughtered the Angels" which depicts the ritual killing of angels by slitting their throats, binding their fragile legs with wire as their wings beat like chickens in their death throes. Yet Kandel ends the poem with the affirmation that no more angels shall be murdered, "not even us."

While living at Tomales Bay in January 1975, Di Prima composed a "Preface" to Dee's dense Monas Hieroglyphica, The Hieroglyphic Monad (1564) which contains twenty-four "Theorems" with accompanying illustrations. Peter J. French argues that in this weird and complex text, Dee's main purpose was to depict "the gnostic ascent to the One, to God. . . . Dee was attempting to discover a symbol that would embody the entire universe and, when understood and engraved within the psyche, would enable men to achieve that gnostic regenerative experience of which Nous spoke to Hermes Trisgmegistus." Dee quotes from the text attributed to Trismegistus, the Tabula Smaragdina—the Emerald Tablet—in "Theorem XIV":

It is therefore clearly confirmed that the whole magistery depends upon the Sun and the Moon. Thrice Greatest Hermes has repeatedly told us this in affirming that the Sun is its father and the Moon is its mother: and we know truly that the red earth (terra lemnia) is nourished by the rays of the Moon and the Sun which exercise a singular influence upon it.

The fourth declaration of the *Emerald Tablet*, as translated by Sir Isaac Newton is: "The Sun is its father, the moon its mother, the wind hath carried it in its belly, the earth is its nurse." *Monas* in ancient Greek is "one" or "unity" and Dee's sign of the *Monas* is composed from the characters of the seven planets. The astrological orientation of many young people during the 1960s: we recall the lyrics to the musical "Hair," *when the moon is in the Seventh House/And Jupiter aligns with Mars/Then peace will guide the planets/And love will steer the stars*—pervades Dee's work. In her essay, Di Prima analyzes Dee's monad which depicts above an upper semicircle the moon, and at center a circle with a point in the middle as sun; underneath is a cross and at bottom, Aries is symbolized: a half-figure-eight representing the four elements as well as birth, crucifixion, and resurrection. There are also planetary symbols of Saturn, Jupiter, Mars, Venus, and Mercury. Furthermore, Frances A. Yates in *The Rosicrucian Enlightenment* points out that "different formations of the four lines of this cross can turn into a sign for both three and four, both triangle and square" which explains why Di Prima in her poem "John Dee" emphasizes the numbers three, four, and the multiple of the two, "dodecahedron." In her analysis, Di Prima posits that

> Dee's monad represents the alchemic process and simultaneously the genesis and evolution of the cosmos. This is the Work which the magus, partaking of the divine, furthers: the redemption and transmutation of the worlds. To "raise," as Dee has it, "the element of Earth thru Water into the Fire." Whether, in the Jacob's ladder reaching from heaven to earth, the planes of manifestation are envisaged as ten, as in the Tree of Life; as four: "natura, horizon temporis, horizon aeternitas, horizon mundi supersupremi," as in Johannes Pistorius, Dee's contemporary; or simply as three: terrestrial, celestial and supercelestial (Agrippa, et al.); it is in all cases cabbalistic truth that the same forces operate and the same forms manifest on each separate plane (level) (sephirah). Mathematics is uniquely the clearest and most flexible expression of the relations between these forces and forms.
>
> The monad is Dee's expression of these relations: it is diagram, at once, of process and goal. From the point in the center of the circle, the entire glyph unfolds, theorem by theorem; yet it was always there; was produced instantaneously; and we feel that its shape is inevitable.[58]

As we have seen, Di Prima's "Jacob's Ladder" returns to the theme of a "ladder reaching from heaven to earth" within an ecological context and this is a typically highly packed, dense piece of Di Prima prose indicating the depth of her erudition as demonstrated by her reference to Johann Pistorius (1546–1608) who compiled a text *Artis Cabbalisticae* (1587) published in Basel.

Di Prima declares that "mathematics is uniquely the clearest and most flexible expression of these forces and forms," an idea which will find expression in one of her greatest poems which was inspired by the *Monas Hieroglyphica*, "John Dee," which contains three sections. Section 1 opens:

Thru the transparency of water is the explication of light
This light is a mean toward the manifoldness of numbers
which are nothing but the implicit, infolded upon itself & transparent
This is the circle of the world, a perfect window of crystal

Dee in his "Preface" to Euclid's *Elements* (1570), remarks: "Yet from these grosse and material thynges, may we be led upward, by degrees, so, informying our rude Imagination, toward the conceivyng of *Numbers*, absolutely (:Not supposing, nor admixtyng any thing created, Corporall or Spirituall, to support, conteyne, or represent those *Numbers* imagined:) that at length, we may be able, to find the number of our owne name gloriously exemplified and registered in the booke of the *Trinitie* most blessed and aeternall." Numbers show forth the structure of the divine and Dee believes

FIGURE 4.4 *Title page of John Dee's* Monas Hieroglyphica *(1564). Courtesy: Special Collections and Archives, Cardiff University.*

that the secrets of God's creation are discovered in the proportionate forms of geometry. The four elements thread their way through the poem—we have "water" here in section 1—in order to illustrate Dee's desire to "raise the element of Earth thru Water in the Fire." Section 2 continues with geometrical imagery: "The angles of the dodecahedron enfolding the infinite maze/Like the hollow space in an egg, teeth of gears/that wind us back before the beginning, this perfection/was with him/at the creation of the world." Dee conceptualized the egg as a symbol of the heavens: planets orbiting within it form an oval shape, and *ovum* is also the alchemical vessel, thus "the hollow space in an egg."[59] Part 3 closes the poem and ends in a lovely "theophany":

> March of archangels, theophany
> of implicate wings, dimensional
> space yielding to space in a depth
> that requires no sounding. Trace them
> like frost on the glass our tears
> make of the heavens[60]

As in the imagery of her earlier poem "Vector," Di Prima again employs the cosmological language of "dimensional," "space," "depth," to suggest the final "divine appearance" or *theophany*, as the wings of the flying archangels become visible. Finally, we perceive the "trace" of the angel wings in a pattern as on a window where the water of our tears of spiritual yearning create a frosty shape of the heavens we view beyond. As we shall see, angels will begin to increasingly preoccupy Di Prima in the coming decade.

Di Prima's essay on Dee coincides with her deepening friendship with Robert Duncan during the 1970s. In "R.D.'s H.D.," Di Prima recalled: "It is 1975. I am living in Marshall, California, in a small house on Tomales Bay. Robert has been here often. Last year he came and sat at the kitchen table breathlessly reading us the just-completed *Dante Etudes* . . . Robert has promised me a copy of his tape of H.D. reading from her *Helen in Egypt*."[61] It is during this period—from 1976 to 1978—that Di Prima began teaching classes at the Dance Palace in Point Reyes. One workshop she conducted

> was a mix of writing and collage . . . images from dreams and collages in poems. . . . Then it became clear people wanted to get into more specific material, so I began to move into the western mystical tradition— information about the Tarot and Tree of Life. We started to do workshops in what is loosely called magic that would feed into either making collages or writing exercises.[62]

She also made her first trip abroad, attending the International Poetry Festival in Rotterdam and meeting her old friend, poet Ted Joans, in Paris.[63] She contributed her broadside "The Bell Tower" to the *No Mountains Poetry*

Project in Evanston, Illinois, where a variety of letterpress broadsides were printed by several poets including Charles Bukowski and Anne Waldman. It is an affecting, evocative, musical lyric marked by haiku-like images: "the wind does not die in autumn/the moon/shifts endlessly thru flying clouds/in autumn the sea is high."[64]

Another memorable broadside poem is "Darkness Invocation/Winter Solstice 1976." In 1976, the winter solstice fell on December 21, and here Di Prima celebrates the "pagan" Christianity of her grandmother *Lucy=Lux=Light* which we recall from Chapter 1:

It is from this deepest night
nadir of forgetfulness
sweet well of empty sleep
that the Child is born

no dreams
bring him to birth:
pain like a shower of meteors
we roll thru
in the intensest blue-black of our sky

& the golden one emerges
  ludens
from the depths of the well
   &
we sigh, for music

& seek to devour
to incorporate light, that gold
shine thru our flesh
(blue night for golden stars)
our black skies flower forever

that we forget no more[65]

For many years, Di Prima had collected illustrations of The Three Wise Men in order to understand the various ways they have been interpreted. They were Zoroastrian *Magi*, and our word *magic* derives from the Old Persian word *mageus*. Marsilio Ficino believed there were six major sages who expounded an esoteric, perennial wisdom: Zoroaster, Hermes Trismegistus, Orpheus, Aglaophemus, Pythagoras, and Plato. J. B. Allen has pointed out that the primacy of Zoroaster "was preeminently something that highlighted the centrality of the Epiphany and the Magi. The three wise Chaldeans who had come from the East, following a star, were the followers of Zoroaster . . . thus they symbolized the coming of the ancient wisdom to the cradle of a new philosopher-king-magus: the new Zoroaster." Thus, Di Prima again interprets Christianity within the framework of an archaic occult substratum and also returns to her grandmother Lucy's spiritual orientation. For her, "the child of course is the alchemical stone, or the principle of renewal or eternal life. . . . Every child is the Christ child in that sense, and that was the kind of Pagan Catholicism that my grandmother had."[66] Di Prima urges—as she does in several other poems we have considered—"that we forget no more" our divine origins among the stars and "that gold/shine thru our flesh." In addition, we note the colors Black, Blue, and Gold—all are stages in the alchemical process. Black is the *nigredo*, the dissolution of the old form of body or metal at the beginning of the Great Work; blue or azure is the mercurial water; and gold is of course the final goal of the transformation, both in the material and spiritual sense.[67] John Dee also correlates metal, color, and planet in the *Monas Hieroglyphica* as Black/Lead=Saturn; Blue/Tin=Jupiter; and Golden/Gold= Sun. The meaning of the ritual of transformation is that we remember our origin in the stars and the divinity of our flesh so that "we forget no more" our purpose on Earth.

In 1976, Di Prima participated in a political rally concerning California Proposition 15 regarding the construction of nuclear power plants where she read from the *Revolutionary Letters*. And the close of 1976 also brought a memorable event: on November 25, 1976, at the Winterland Ballroom in San Francisco, she recited her poetry along with Michael McClure, Lawrence Ferlinghetti, and Robert Duncan at the last concert of the musical group The Band. Martin Scorsese created a documentary entitled *The Last Waltz* (1978) to memorialize the event. Di Prima read "Get Your Cut Throat Off My Knife" from *Dinners and Nightmares*; "Revolutionary Letter #4"—"Left to themselves people/grow their hair./ Left to themselves they/take off their shoes./Left to themselves they make love/sleep easily/share blankets, dope & children . . ."; and a more recent and splendid poem, "The Fire Guardian." Dressed in a long, flowing black gown, Di Prima held the book in her left hand, informing the audience that "The Fire Guardian" is "all one sentence but it goes around in circles." She declaimed in a passionate voice, shaping the delivery of the lines with her right hand as she proceeded:

> on crumbling sandstone molecules
>   which dance
> in their sudden, expected brains
>   like stars
> thru ponderosa dance in ours
>   when we fall to sleep
> on bed of needles in the arms
>   of our own black pain & wake
> cresting again, riding invisible
>   soul-stuff (we call it joy)

FIGURE 4.5 *Di Prima reading at political rally in California, 1976. Courtesy: Pamela Mosher and Third Mind Books.*

A pattern of colors—blue, yellow, black—is counterpointed with light and shadow and a pattern of sense imagery: sight, touch, and in the final stanza with pain and joy. In the final section we are in the southwest with sandstone, ponderosa, and bed of needles as star and soul also speak to one another.

In 1977, Di Prima met Sheppard Powell who became her life partner. Powell—an artist and alternative healer—conducted seminars at the San Francisco Shambhala Center in their Nature of Healing and Practice of Meditation Series. Di Prima also contributed a brief essay to a volume of tributes to Kenneth Patchen, with whom she had corresponded in the 1950s. She recalled Patchen as the source of "Dark reaches of Albion Moonlight in all our brains. Gaunt shadows of futurity disguised as ghosts of the second world war," praising him as a "Clear voice of hope & wrath, loved traveler-gone-before, who gave us courage, & does."[68] She taught workshops in Point Reyes and the following year, studied psychic reading with Helen Palmer and cofounded *The Gold Circle*, a community devoted to studying visualization, meditation, and magical practice.[69] T. M. Luhrmann in *Persuasions of the Witch's Craft: Ritual Magic in Contemporary England* has documented the centrality of these practices to magical activity. Luhrmann defines "creative visualization" as

"seeing" vivid mental images. Like the meditation, visualization is explicitly part of the magical technology, the means by which the magic works. The mental image is often thought to be the link between the subtle, ethereal energies of magical ritual and the physical world, so that the skill in "bringing the power through" depends directly on the ability to visualize. When magicians learn how to visualize, they understand— or at least, their concepts allow them to understand—themselves to be learning to use the mechanism which makes the magic work. Every training manual emphasizes the need for imaging proficiency.

Thus Di Prima began to incorporate these techniques in her teaching and we can observe that her literary, spiritual, and magical activities had been incorporated together in her life and work.

She also reconnected with Audre Lorde with whom she had been friends at Hunter High School: Lorde stayed with Di Prima, spoke at a rally and women's march and Di Prima dedicated her poem "Narrow Path into the Back Country" to Lorde which commemorates Lorde's 1974 voyage to Dahomey: "You are flying to Dahomey, going back/to some dream, or never-never land/more forbidding & perfect/ than Oz. . . . Well, we carry/ pure-land paradise within, you carry it to Dahomey, from Staten Island."[70] "Pure Land" refers to a branch of Mahayana Buddhism which is based on Buddha Amitabha and holds that since humans will never inhabit an uncorrupted world, we must strive to be reincarnated on another plane known as the "Pure Land." Thus Di Prima connected again to her friend within the context of her spiritual studies and honors her trip back to her African homeland. However, the most important literary achievement of 1978 was the publication of *Loba, Parts I-VIII*. Sections of the poem had been published in 1973, 1975, and 1976, and an enlarged edition appeared in 1998 which now divided the poem into two "Books" in which the *Parts I-VIII* of the 1978 edition now comprise "Book One" and a new additional *Parts 9-16* comprise "Book Two." Each stage of the poem's development therefore registers various spiritual and mythic influences which Di Prima had been absorbing during each phase of composition.

Loba commenced with a dream Di Prima experienced in Wyoming while teaching in a Native American school. She was being followed by a gigantic, white wolf which she recognized as "a goddess that I'd known in Europe a long long time ago."[71] As an Italian American, it appears she was at least in part making an unconscious connection with Rome's founding myth: Romulus and Remus suckled by a she-wolf. Di Prima derived the title *Loba*—or female wolf—from Ezra Pound's troubadour poem "Piere Vidal Old" (1909). Pound tells us at the opening that his poem will deal with "Piere Vidal, the fool *par excellence* of all Provence, of whom the tale tells how he ran and, as a wolf, because of his love for Loba of Penautier." In one of her homages to Pound entitled "for E.P.," Di Prima reveals Pound as one of the intellectual forces behind her poem: "who else in these years/has glimpsed the goddess moving in the dark/the loba in the swollen forest where wind/scatters virtu." As the feminist movement gained momentum during the 1960s and 1970s, the time was ripe for an ambitious poem presenting a revisionary version of the role of women in myth, history, art, literature, and religion. In a sense, just as canines have been "domesticated" from their primal forms as wolves, so too men from archaic times had attempted to "domesticate" the female. Di Prima retells the myths we have been told about women, asserting women must lay claim to all of their potentialities as creative human beings. Alicia Ostriker has remarked in *Stealing the Language: The Emergence of Women's Poetry in America* that beginning in the 1960s, American women poets began the serious exploration of "revisionist myth" in which the traditional historical narrative of male supremacy is "altered." Ostriker argues that

> these poems generically assume the high literary status that myth confers and that women writers have often been denied because they write "personally" or "confessionally." But in them the old stories are changed, changed utterly, by female knowledge of female experience, so that they can no longer stand as foundations of collective male fantasy or as the pillars sustaining phallocentric "high" culture. Instead, they are corrections; they are representations of what women find divine and demonic in themselves; they are retrieved images of what women have collectively and historically suffered; in some cases they are instructions for survival.

So too *Loba* represents Di Prima's version of the narrative sweep of female experience—as Robert Graves subtitled *The White Goddess* it is "a historical grammar of poetic myth"—through the millennia.

The initial lines suddenly began speaking to her in dictation. George Steiner, in *Grammars of Creation*, describes this moment "when the compositional process is in spate, when formal obstacles seem to yield so that the pen can scarcely keep up with the informing rush, poets, novelists, composers tell of working 'under dictation.'" Di Prima confirms this is often true for her as well. Now, compelled to write down the lines, she herself was initially puzzled about their meaning: "if he did not come apart in her hands, he fell/like flint on her ribs . . ." This reads as a kind of Zen *koan*, a gnomic statement that may or may not hide deeper meanings. Perhaps this initial kernel or germ contained riddling dualities the work itself would seek to explore: she/he, passive/active, creative/destructive. One either "comes apart," disintegrates, merges; or one "falls like flint," like a hard piece of stone. It is also noteworthy that "he fell . . . on her ribs" evokes the Genesis myth of Eve's creation from the rib of Adam. Robert Graves, whose *White Goddess* and *King Jesus* were significant texts for Di Prima, also composed a brief work entitled *Adam's Rib* (1955) which elaborates an alternative version of the Genesis narrative. The received version of the creation of Adam and Eve is actually a misreading of a picture—the Canaanite icons captured by Hebrews who then overran Hebron—of one man killing another with a curved knife (hence the rib) in a quarrel over a woman. This may explain the violence of "like flint on her ribs," a transposition of the elements of this scenario. These seemingly opposed energies exist within men as well as women, and *Loba* constructs and deconstructs polarities constantly. The work conceptualizes woman from multiple perspectives: lover, pregnant, giving birth, Wisdom figure, feral wolf—the first poem opening Part One concludes, "she grinned/baring her wolf's teeth"—spiritual goddess, Mother, in old age; and in her numberless incarnations as Aphrodite, Nut, Inanna, Astarte, Lilith, Isis, Ishtar, Cerridwen, Urania, Kali, Brigit, Iseult, Beatrice, Persephone, the Virgin Mary, Guinevere, Heloise, Juliana of Norwich, and Bag Lady. *Loba* in its earliest incarnation was an inspiration to other poets such as Robert Creeley who wrote Di Prima on March 12, 1974: "At present am working on text called MABEL: A STORY, sort of reverse side to LOBA in fact, trying to locate multiple projections of 'senses' of 'women' from diversity of random takes."

Also suggested throughout *Loba* is what Leon Surette in *The Birth of Modernism: Ezra Pound, T.S. Eliot, W.B. Yeats and the Occult* has called Pound's "mystical eroticism." Surette argues that "for Pound the eroticism of the troubadours was not figurative but literal. . . . This reading of the erotic aspects of Gnosticism and the troubadours is plainly contrary to Mead's purely symbolic understanding. . . . Mead would have regarded Pound's literal understanding of the steamy Gnostic myths and accounts of erotic rituals as depraved." Surette finds this eroticism evident in Pound's early poem "Piere Vidal Old" from *Exultations* (1909):

> Not only does he invent a nighttime tryst between the troubadour Vidal and his lady, la Loba of Penautier, but he describes it in terms that bring together love, death, and valour in a manner that might have made Virgil blush. La Loba approaches Vidal through the dark forest dressed in a green "mantel" made of flimsy mousseline "wherethrough her white form fought." There were no words spoken, for "Hot is such love and silent,/ Silent as fate is . . ./Stark, keen, triumphant, till it plays at death." Vidal, of course, is not silent, for this is a poem of reminiscence. He expostulates, "God! She was white then, splendid as some tomb." Not content with comparing her to a tomb, Vidal continues: "Half-sheathed, then naked from its saffron sheath/Drew full this dagger that doth tremble here." We do not learn why he draws his dagger, for "Just then she woke and mocked the less keen blade . . . Was there such flesh made ever and unmade!"

On this reading, Di Prima's verses "if he did not come apart in her hands, he fell/like flint on her ribs" are variations on this erotic encounter in which Pound's "dagger" and "blade" are transformed into the "flint" of Di

Prima's rendering. The sexual theme indeed is carried throughout *Loba*, and continues the poet's celebration of mystical *eros*.

Lynn Keller in *Forms of Expansion: Recent Long Poems by Women* divides extended poems into three types: (1) epic, (2) lyric, and (3) radically experimental, situating poems such John Berryman's *Dream Songs*, Robert Lowell's *Notebook 1967-68* and Di Prima's *Loba* in the "lyric" category. Keller argues that

> where contemporary epics offer a sweeping worldview and cultural critique, lyric sequences treat narrower portions of a culture, more confined history, or more inward perspectives. The usually brief units from which sequences are composed may be held together only loosely by subjectivity of theme but . . . appear in a hypotactic structure; elements in one lyric section will enhance an understanding of lyrics that follow.[72]

Loba is indeed structured as a sequence of separate lyric poems representing a kind of encyclopedic mythic history similar to Sir James Frazer's *The Golden Bough*. For example, in "Four Poets Speak of Her" from Book One, Part Four, Di Prima turned to *The Golden Bough* for the dying king around whom a religious coven would form and who became the Goddess' consort.

Loba also displays a counterpointing of "I" and "You": Self and Other, Poet and Reader. Di Prima subtly places her poem in the great American cosmic, Transcendentalist tradition: Henry David Thoreau, Ralph Waldo Emerson, and Walt Whitman were the magnificent genius mystical predecessors of the Beats in their devotion to what Whitman's disciple Richard M. Bucke named "cosmic consciousness" and to Eastern philosophy. Di Prima echoes Walt Whitman's encounters with his deepest soul in *Leaves of Grass*. For example, in Book One, Part Three in the lyric "Her power is to open what is shut/Shut what is open": "Her bower/lurks in the unseen muddy places/of yr soul, she waits for you under the steps/of yr tenement."[73] This is an urban updating of the ecstatic section 52 of Whitman's "Song of Myself": "I bequeath myself to the dirt to grow from the grass I love,/If you want me again look for me under your boot-soles"; and "Failing to fetch me at first keep encouraged,/ Missing me one place search another,/I stop somewhere waiting for you." This interchangeability of poet and reader as well as poet and hidden self recalls again the project of Whitman's *Leaves of Grass* in which Whitman addresses his audience directly as if they are an extension of himself and he is incorporated within them, just as he addresses his own Soul and Body as intimate partners. This is also a major theme in *Loba*, the Gnostic goal of uncovering the soul's identity which appears in the opening "Ave": "I walk the long night seeking you/I climb the sea crest seeking you . . . /I am you/ and I must become you/I have been you/and I must become you/I am always you/I must become you."[74] In Book One, as an epigraph at the beginning of Part Four, Di Prima cites *The Gnostic Gospel of Eve*—"I have come to know myself and have gathered myself from everywhere"—a fragment preserved by Epiphanius. Furthermore, an epigraph to the section of Book One, Part Four entitled "Loba as Eve," includes an excerpt from the *Gospel of Eve*: "I am Thou & Thou art I/And where Thou art I am/and in all things am I dispersed/ and from wherever Thou willst/Thou gatherest Me/but in gathering Me/Thou gatherest Thyself." Each verse supplies a title for every poem of the section. Thus "i am thou & thou art I" begins a searing lyric: "where tossing in grey sheets you weep/I am/where pouring like mist you/scatter among the stars/I shine/where in black oceans of sea & sky, you die/you die/I chant/a voice like angels from the heart." E. R. Dodds has observed that "the formula 'I am Thou and Thou art I' has often been used by Christian, Indian and Moslem mystics to express the identity of the soul with its divine ground," and cites the same passage "the Ophite *Gospel of Eve*" which inspired Di Prima.[75] It is clear that Di Prima has succeeded in condensing and synthesizing a variety of diverse sources seamlessly within the texture of her own original poetics in order to voice the drama of human striving and transcendence.

Di Prima varies pace and rhythm by including briefer lyrics to leaven longer narrative sections: the formal challenges of keeping a 314-page poem engaging as well as varied is solved by following the precepts of one of her masters Ezra Pound in his *Cantos*. For example, in "Hymn: The Other Face," from Book One, Part Eight, she fashions a pure imagistic lyric:

> *lucus*
> *lycos*
> grove of light
> thru which
> the white wolves
> glide
> silent
> their white breath
> flecking the leaves
>
>   * * * * *
>
> footfall padding
> silence on silence
> white on white
>
> thru trees of light
> light slants
> it spills
> on planes of light:
> forest floor

Through careful repetition and spacing of lines on the page, Di Prima creates a mysterious scene. By avoiding "the" and cleaving to a Poundian, haiku-like directness and simplicity—"grove of light," "trees of light," "planes of light"—she evokes white wolves' numinous presence as they soundlessly journey. The chanting of *light* also suggests an experience recalling the "Event out of Time" we encountered previously in H.D., which Di Prima relates to the underlying spiritual meaning of the Imagist movement. In her essay "The Mysteries of Vision: Some Notes on H.D." Di Prima argues:

> When I would suggest here that the Event Out of Time is the natural expansion of the Imagist idea of image—this is not to reduce these visionary occurrences in any sense but rather hopefully to expand our idea of Image, as it works in the later work of H.D. and of Pound, expanding naturally out from the early, "Imagist" manifestoes with their attempt to include an experiential poesis that was perhaps already moving out of bounds (out of definable boundaries) for at least H.D.—an attempt to include the barely visible: "what can be seen."[76]

Imagism as a literary movement thus was fundamentally anchored in a mystical phenomenology: no ideas but in things reveals to us directly the *Istigkeit*—the "Is-ness" expounded by Meister Eckhart—of reality and provides the basis for Di Prima's own visionary poetics.

Di Prima's lecture "Light/and Keats" (1974)—composed as she was working on *Loba*—begins to consider in depth the meaning of Gnostic thought for her life and work. She argues that meditation and mantras are part of the Gnostic discipline of learning

> how to release the spirit from matter, and send it home. Probably the mystery cults taught even then that *this is not our home*, the material world is only a disguise to penetrate, an alphabet to read, to get at the true kernel of things . . . . No, this whole thing is a hideous monstrosity, it's a prison, a trap, the only thing we can do here is get out of here as fast as we can. If we could remember for one minute who we really are.

There are vivid references in *Loba* to the history of Gnosticism as in "Reprise" from Book One, Part Eight: "Stumbled keening/tongue cut out/eyes . . . hands . . ./stumbled keening/thru the forests of Provence/after the debacle of Montsegur."[77] On March 16, 1244, ten thousand troops attacked the castle of Montsegur, killing more than two hundred Albigensian "heretics." As we recall from Chapter 2, Ezra Pound believed the tradition of the ancient Greek Eleusinian mysteries was continued in "the song of Provence and of Italy." Akiko Miyake has remarked:

> Albigensians are consecrated by Pound in Canto 92/619 for their Eleusinian worship of the light and the sun in their mystical "Eleusinian" marriage. Pound inherited the Provencal tradition of worshipping light,

not only by writing "Alba," but also by absorbing passionately the works
of Plotinus, Grosseteste, and Erigena, who all identified the creation of
the world with the emanation of the celestial essence in the form of light.
For Pound, light embodies Plotinus's Soul in heaven, the divine creator of
the world as well as the celestial spouse in Rossetti's mystical marriage. In
Canto 92, Pound reaches the summit of a mountain in the third heaven
and mythically identifies the place as Mt. Segur, the headquarters of
Albigensianism and the sanctuary of the mystical marriage:

> O Anubis, guard this portal
> as the cellula, Mont Segur
> Sanctus
> that no blood sully this altar . . .

Di Prima carries on this Poundian tradition of interpreting the Gnostic
Albigensians of Provence at Montsegur as continuation of the metaphysics
of light propounded by the ancients as well as philosophers such as Robert
Grosseteste.

Finally, the body's passional, intuitional, and sacred power is intoned
in the opening sequence of Book One, poem ten: "If you do not come
apart like bread/in her hands, she falls/like steel on your heart. The flesh/
knows better than the spirit what the soul/has eyes for." D.H. Lawrence's
instinctive "blood knowledge" is evoked as well as a subtle play on "to
have eyes for someone"—now applied to the soul "knowing" what *it* has
"eyes for." The epigraph to Book One is from a Tlingit song: "It would
be very pleasant to die with a wolf woman It would be very pleasant."
The Tlingit are the indigenous inhabitants of Alaska, and Native American
mythology reappears in "Three More Sketches of the Loba." Here we
witness Loba's magical ability to—like Odysseus during his return to
Ithaca in *The Odyssey*—disguise herself when necessary by changing her
form: "she strides in blue jeans to the corner/bar; she dances/w/the old
women, the men/light up, they order wine . . . were it not for the ring of fur/
around her ankles/just above her bobby socks/there's no one/wd ever guess
her name": Loba can change from woman to wolf and back again and
often escape notice.[78] "Deer Woman," a tale by Native American author
Paula Gunn Allen describes men going to a bar where they meet females
whom they assume to be human until they notice their hooved feet. Jeffrey
B. Russell has observed that the "belief in shape-shifting or lycanthropy
was connected with witchcraft in Europe, and witches were believed to
have the power, with the Devil's assistance, to change their shapes and
take animal forms."[79] Thus the wolf symbol connects a substratum of
world mythology across a number of different cultural formations. As we
shall see in Chapter 6, Di Prima will considerably expand the scope of
Loba to include sources from a diversity of places and spiritual traditions

including ancient Egypt, the Tibetan Tantric traditions of Padmahansava and Tsogyal, Kali poems by the Bengali yogi Ramprasad, as well as Ishtar from Mesopotamian myth.

Di Prima closed the decade of the 1970s by participating in the City of Rome's International Poetry Festival in Ostia, Italy, in June 1979 along with Allen Ginsberg, Lawrence Ferlinghetti, Gregory Corso, and Yevgeny Yevtushenkko. Attended by some twenty thousand people, the festival was held on the beach and was called by Ferlinghetti "the Italian Woodstock." Ferlinghetti observed that "the Communist government of Rome backed the Roman *Teatro Beat* in inviting dissident writers from capitalist countries and establishment poets from the USSR." She also delivered a significant unpublished lecture on angels at the Minneapolis Jung Center in September 1979. The notecards for her lecture document the rich, associative power of her thinking as she draws together sources as diverse as Pico della Mirandola, John Keats, and Henry Corbin:

> The means by which the Soul rises to god thru the archangels is none other than the separation of the soul from the body—Pico goes on to say *not* the body from the soul. "Imagination" as a *creative* faculty—"What the imagination seizes as beauty" . . . etc, Keats Faculty of CREATING the worlds—i.e., tune into and then bridge the astral stuff.

She had been closely studying Henry Corbin's *Avicenna and the Visionary Recital* as well as *Creative Imagination in the Sufism of Ibn Arabi*: it is possible that Di Prima first learned of Corbin through Charles Olson who in the early 1960s had read his *Avicenna*.

Olson's "Grammar—a book," published in the May 1961 issue of *Floating Bear* #7 demonstrates he had also studied his "Cyclical Time in Mazdaism and Ismailism" and Corbin would influence Olson's "Maximus, at the Harbor."[80] Corbin had been a favorite of Robert Duncan, and more recently Harold Bloom in *Omens of Millennium: The Gnosis of Angels, Dreams, and Resurrection* (1996) has acknowledged his debt to the French thinker's genius. Corbin's ideas on the imaginal realm—in Arabic *alam al-mithal*—are expounded in his essay "Mundus Imaginalis, or the Imaginary and the Imaginal" in which he recounts his dissatisfaction with the word *imaginary* because as the word is presently employed, it is impossible for us not to understand it as signifying something "unreal, something that is and remains outside of being and existence—in brief, something utopian." Corbin instead chooses to describe the realm between the "empirical world and the world of abstract understanding" as "the world of the Image, *mundus imaginalis*: a world as ontologically real as the world of the senses and the world of the intellect, a world that requires a faculty of perception belonging to it, a faculty that is a cognitive function, a *noetic* value, as fully as real as the faculties of sensory perception or intellectual intuition."[81]

FIGURE 4.6 *Henry Corbin and Carl Jung. Courtesy: Association des Amis de Henry and Stella Corbin.*

For Corbin, the imaginal zone corresponds to the angelic realm, and in Di Prima's notes there are several memorable excerpts from Corbin's *Creative Imagination in the Sufism of Ibn 'Arabi* such as the following: "Since these Angel-Souls [*Animae colestes*] communicate to the Heavens the movement of their desire, the orbits of the heavenly bodies are characterized by an aspiration of love forever renewed and forever unstilled." Di Prima goes on to comment: "Angels as *links* between the sephira as if angels were the paths of the Tree Angels of the Tarot cards or: the Fool, Magus, etc *as* Angels (guides) The Letters as Angels."[82] Thus Di Prima strives to connect the various themes of her studies in diverse areas: from the Tree of Life in Kabbalah, to Tarot, to Corbin's angels. In a fascinating section of her *Notebooks* from July 6, 1983, Di Prima states that the card of today is "The Hierophant" and notes that she is reading again Corbin's *Avicenna and the Visionary Recital*. She then goes on to describe a walk she took through a grove of cedar trees during which she was accompanied by a huge crow which cawed loudly at her and followed her on her journey:

As I caught up to him, he'd begin to scream, take off and fly *around* me, screeching, in large circles. After the prescribed number of circumvolutions to fufill an apotropaic rite, he would perch again, stare again and make ready to swoop, circle once more. In this way, he followed me halfway home, stopping at what must no doubt be the edge of his area of guardianship. There he perched and watched till I was out of sight—and perhaps a long time after.

The entry then has the heading "Words for the Hierophant" with three pages of quotations from Corbin's *Avicenna*, beginning: "The realm of Light begins beyond, where the apparatus of cosmic power ends. Hence the soul must find the way of Return. That *way* is Gnosis, and on that way it needs a Guide. The Guide appears to it at the frontier where it has already emerged from this cosmos to return—or better to emerge—to itself." Di Prima then combines sections of her earlier powerful experience with the bird and Corbin's text in order to present her narrative within the context of an encounter with a Spiritual Guide. One may also consider Di Prima's studies of Corbin alongside her essay and poem about John Dee and his quest to decipher angelic language, for angels are humanity's messengers to the divine in a time of *deus absconditus*, *the hidden God*. Tom Cheetham has pointed out that

> the loss of the realm of the imaginal inhabited by the Angel of Humanity and the Angel of the Earth occasioned all the schisms that split the West. . . . In this history the place of the revealed Word is central, and the quest for the lost language of the angels is the fundamental task. It is the drama that underlies the unity of the three branches of the Abrahamic tradition.[83]

The animating impulse behind both Di Prima's poetics and her spiritual practice is to integrate a variety of philosophical traditions in order to heal the split between self and cosmos.

Di Prima also paraphrases a brief but trenchant phrase from *Creative Imagination in the Sufism of Ibn 'Arabi*: "The logical universe is nothing more than the dead body of an Angel." The passage from Corbin merits quotation since it summarizes in many ways Di Prima's own "metaphysics of light" which we have traced from the beginning of her career:

> In the Suhrawardian theosophy of Light, the entire Platonic theory of Ideas is interpreted in terms of Zoroastrian angelology. Expressing itself as a metaphysics of essences, the Suhrawardian dualism of Light and Darkness precludes the possibility of a physics in the Aristotelian sense of the word. A physics of Light can only be an angelology, because Light is life, and Life is essentially Light. What is known as the material body is in essence night and death; it is a corpse. Through the varying intensity of their luminescence, the Angels, the "lords of the species" (the Fravashis of Mazdaism), give rise to the different species, which the natural body can never account for. What Aristotelianism considers as the concept of a species, the logical universal, ceases to be anything more than the dead body of an Angel.[84]

Among the Zoroastrian *yazatas*—a term employed by Zoroaster himself to describe "a beneficent divine being"—the *Fravashi* signify an individual's personal spirit. And from *Avicenna and the Visionary Recital*, Di Prima paraphrases: "The soul has the experience that by acquiring consciousness of itself, it can know the angel" from Corbin's "At the frontier reached by the *Recital of Hayy ibn Yaqzan*, the soul has the experience that, by acquiring consciousness of itself, *Anima*, it can know the Angel." This is perhaps the ultimate experience, the *gnosis* for which the soul yearns: direct knowledge of light permeating the universe and the angelic movement of the soul into a transcendent reality.[85] As we shall see in the following chapter, this engagement with angels continues with Di Prima's studies of the poet H.D. What is abundantly clear from both *Loba*, her investigations of Corbin and angelism, as well as the impressive body of work she created during the late 1960s and 1970s is Di Prima's continuing commitment to fashion from a diverse body of sources her unique vision.

5

The Hidden Religions, H.D., Angels, and Tibetan Buddhism, 1980–92

In this chapter I shall discuss Di Prima's association with the New College of California where she taught from 1980 to 1987, developing a course entitled "The Hidden Religions in the Literature of Europe." She included in her syllabus a number of topics we have thus far encountered such as The Grail, Paracelsus, John Dee, The Hermetic Order of the Golden Dawn, the alchemist Michael Maier, W. B. Yeats, Aleister Crowley, Heinrich Cornelius Agrippa, and Giordano Bruno. She also began work on a poem cycle entitled "Alchemical Studies." In 1983, she commenced the study of Vajrayana Buddhism with Chogyam Trungpa and cofounded the San Francisco Institute of Magical and Healing Arts. From 1987 to 1993 she contributed a column to *Mama Bears News and Notes* in which she published chapters from her work-in-progress, the autobiography *Recollections of My Life as a Woman*. The time she spent in Wyoming teaching in Native American schools during the early 1970s is reflected in *Wyoming Series* (1988). Di Prima also delivered several important lectures, including "Role of the Hermetic in Poetry" at the Detroit Institute of Arts in 1982 and spoke at the twenty-fifth anniversary of the publication of Kerouac's *On the Road* on Kerouac as an immigrant writer. Di Prima appeared in the documentary *The Beat Generation: An American Dream* in 1987 and became increasingly involved with the work of H.D., composing several essays including "The Mysteries of Vision: Some Notes on H.D." in 1987; "Angel Magic" from 1988; and "R.D.'s H.D." delivered as a lecture in 1989. *Pieces of a Song*—a volume of selected poetry—was published in 1990. Finally, I discuss the ways Di Prima combined her interests in esoteric and occult thought with her Buddhist studies in *Seminary Poems* (1991) and conclude with *The Ones I Used to Laugh With: A Haibun Journal, April–May 1992*.

In 1980, Di Prima—along with Robert Duncan, Duncan McNaughton, David Meltzer, and Louis Patler—founded the Masters in Poetics Program at the New College of California which in some respects was a continuation of the Black Mountain curriculum. As Ammiel Alcalay remarks,

> New College's curricular initiative can draw very clear lines back to Black Mountain College (the early to mid 1950s, through the presence of Charles Olson, Robert Duncan, and Robert Creeley, along with their extraordinary students), and the various periods of activity at the State University of New York in Buffalo (often referred to as Black Mountain II), with Olson's brief but decisive two-year stay there beginning in 1963.[1]

A former student at the New College, David Levi Strauss, recalled the Poetics Program as "a very unusual mixture of classical poetics, Hermeticism, and other esoteric traditions, and structuralism and post-structuralism and recent Continental theory. Believe me, no one else was doing this at this time." Strauss stated that for Robert Duncan, Hermeticism and structuralism were connected because he "saw them both as ways of reading signs. Reading the world through signs," which precisely defines Di Prima's theoretical orientation as well. The curriculum which was developed was focused not on creative writing, but rather on poetics. David Meltzer taught Kabbalah, bringing to class translations by colleagues which had not yet been published.[2] An amusing interchange occurred when Di Prima discussed with Duncan possible topics for her own course offerings:

> "Robert, I think you should do a course that covers nonorthodox threads of thought in the West, maybe from the caves to the present. Give us some sense of continuity, how it all relates to one another, Gnosticism and the heresies and this and that." He said, "I think you're supposed to teach that, dear." I said, "Robert, I don't know anything about it." He said, "Well, that's why we teach, isn't it?"[3]

At Naropa in Boulder, Colorado, there had also been an innovative effort to teach literature within the context of spiritual traditions and one may note that this is indeed a unique way to envision teaching literature and poetics. The reign of the New Criticism had emphasized close reading of texts with no attention paid to historical context or biography of the author. Typically, university and college students take a required course in literature to fulfill their "general education" requirement; the curriculum for English majors has often been constructed around historical surveys from *Beowulf* to Beckett and since the 1980s, critical theory in the form of studies in structuralism, post-structuralism, Marxism, deconstruction, psychoanalytic, and Lacanian approaches has proliferated. More recently the emphasis has shifted to cultural and gender studies. Thus the approach at the New College—as well as

Naropa—was distinctive in its effort to consider literature within the context of an ongoing historical continuum of the spiritual and philosophical quest.

Although Di Prima, as we have seen in earlier chapters, had studied widely in Gnosticism, alchemy, Tarot, Buddhism, and Hinduism, teaching "The Hidden Religions in the Literature of Europe" allowed her to both delve more deeply into several areas she had previously explored and break new ground. For example, her syllabus lists the early scholar of witchcraft Margaret Murray: an Egyptologist, Murray was a significant figure in the development of neopaganism and believed witchcraft had roots in a nature religion which existed prior to the establishment of Christianity and had survived until the present—in an underground fashion—within the peasant society of Europe. Another text—G. Rachel Levy's *The Gate of Horn: Religious Conceptions of the Stone Age*—was also significant for Di Prima as she developed her ideas about early goddess worship. Poet Adrienne Rich described the ways Levy interpreted the Neolithic cave drawings:

> She sees the female symbolism and images in many of these paintings—some linear, some fully painted and gloriously immanent with power—along with the female statuettes found in the caves, as suggesting not just a "cult of the Mother Goddess" but a later identification of the caverns with the body of a Mother of Rebirth. She points out that the cave was not simply a shelter in the secular sense, but a religious sanctuary.

Thus Di Prima sought to avoid parochial reductionism and to anchor her understanding of the role of women in society in a close study of ancient cultures and texts. She included in her syllabus a wide range of challenging works including Grail texts; Henry Corbin, *Creative Imagination in the Sufism of Ibn 'Arabi*; Robert Graves, *The White Goddess*; Hans Jonas, *The Gnostic Religion*; Galileo, *Dialogue Concerning the Two Chief World Systems*; Northrop Frye, *Fearful Symmetry*; R. T. Rundle Clarke, *Myth and Symbol in Ancient Egypt*; Dion Fortune, *The Mystical Qabalah*; Frances Yates, *Giordano Bruno and the Hermetic Tradition* and *The Rosicrucian Enlightenment*; Ithell Colquhon, *Sword of Wisdom: MacGregor Mathews and the Golden Dawn*; Christopher McIntosh, *Eliphas Levi and the French Occult Revival*; John Michell (1933–2009)—a friend of William S. Burroughs—*The View Over Atlantis* (1969); Giorgio de Santillana, *Hamlet's Mill* and Norman Cohn, *The Pursuit of the Millennium*.

Di Prima described the course as follows:

> It begins with Rachel Levy's book *The Gate of Horn*, and carries on from guesses at prehistory like John Michell and *Hamlet's Mill* through the Paleolith and Neolith as constructed in various intuitive ways by people

like Gimbutas. Then we spend a month or so on the Gnostics, move on to the heresies of the Christian tradition, and then on to a long view of Alchemy, backwards and forwards from that Middle Ages point, and what the Renaissance was about in terms of the Magus as co-creator with God, and then on to the early Rosicrucians and the splintering-off of the continuity of the tradition in the seventeenth century, where one part of it becomes revolutionary thought and one part becomes what we now call holistic medicine—Hahneman [father of homeopathy] inherits the traditions of Alchemy via Paracelsus. . . . A couple of years ago I did a lecture course on Paracelsus, Dee and Bruno.

As we have seen, these traditions formed the background for Di Prima's own poetry and prose and several of these texts challenge the conventional narrative of human and scientific history. For example, de Santillana's *Hamlet's Mill* posits—as Paul Feyerabend has explicated in his posthumously published *Philosophy of Nature*—that

> there is some basic astronomical knowledge far older than the traditional history of astronomy and even the history of letters, knowledge that can be traced back to the late Paleolithic age and that was once available in an "international mythical language". . . . This basic knowledge either degenerated or was lost. Astrology is a late produce of this degeneration process, but like other products of degeneration, it contains valuable remnants that can be used to reconstruct the form and content of the ancient knowledge.

Di Prima also assigned David Kubrin's essay "How Isaac Newton Helped Restore Law 'n' Order to the West." Kubrin argues that there has been "a surprising amount of interest and belief these days in fields that seem, at first glance, to be totally antithetical to the scientific point of view: magic, alchemy, astrology, witchcraft, yoga, eastern philosophies, and occult studies in general. Why should this hostility to science emerge now?" Kubrin details how these traditions which had been submerged in the orthodox historical story were now being recovered by young people, asserting that it is "perhaps precisely the kind of wisdom necessary today, especially in the West, where there is a civilization which has become totally antagonistic to nature."[4] As we have seen, Di Prima also conceived of this "secret history" of intellectual and spiritual evolution as essentially aimed at human liberation and believed anarchism, gender equality, communal property, and sexual freedom were interlinked conceptions.

Guy Davenport has observed that "one of the continued themes from the poetry of Pound to that of the Projectivist School is a new sense of history. It is a sense that is always in touch with archaic beginnings." It is clear that Di Prima was constructing a model of the history of esoteric thought connected to political liberty stretching back to the beginnings of culture. As we shall see in the following chapter, the expanded version of *Loba* illustrates the ways Di Prima employed this knowledge in her understanding of mythic archetypes of woman throughout the centuries. Di Prima's approach to education—beginning with prehistory and providing a solid grounding in the intellectual evolution of humanity—recalls the polemics of Camille Paglia against contemporary university curricula and the dominance of post-structuralist thought in favor of a wide-ranging syllabus anchored in historical knowledge of art, literature, and the mythopoeic imagination of thinkers such as C. G. Jung and Erich Neumann. Indeed, the course in the hidden religions allowed Di Prima both to develop more fully her visionary poetics and to bring together the disparate strands of the historical quest she had undertaken since her early reading of Pound's *Cantos*—which she viewed as anchored in this same hermetic tradition—as well as the magical traditions represented by figures such as Paracelsus, Agrippa, Dee, and Bruno.

A key purpose of the course was to trace the links between early modern science and esoteric thought, and Di Prima assigned texts such as the essay noted above by David Kubrin concerning Isaac Newton (1642–1727). The great physicist has loomed large in debates concerning how to classify "pseudo-sciences" such as alchemy and astrology since as we have seen, Newton over several decades had demonstrated an intense interest in alchemy and composed a commentary on *The Emerald Tablet*, considered to be "the charter of alchemy." John Maynard Keynes famously declared that "Newton was not the first of the age of reason. He was the last of the magicians, the last of the Babylonians and Sumerians, the last great mind which looked out on the visible and intellectual world with the same eyes as those who began to build our intellectual inheritance rather less than 10,000 years ago." Newton's alchemical researches have recently attracted extensive scholarly attention and suggest that areas of knowledge formerly scorned by "modern science" are worthy of reevaluation.[5] Alchemical themes pervade Di Prima's work and it is clear that one of the purposes of her "Hidden Religions" course was to uncover common ground between "scientific" and "spiritual" questing and to perhaps suggest these two modes of cognition have more in common than is usually suspected. For example, commentators had often attempted to separate John Dee—the sober mathematician who had brilliantly expounded Euclid's geometry at the University of Paris—from the "crazy" John Dee who tried to communicate with the angels. So too, historians and philosophers of science had been hard pressed to reconcile Newton the genius who had discovered the elemental laws of physics and developed calculus with the Newton who pursued seemingly arcane, occult studies. For Di Prima, it was impossible to separate these two aspects of intellectual discovery and like one of her mentors Frances A. Yates, she sought to understand modes of cognition which since the Enlightenment had been relegated to second-class status.

In addition to her teaching at the New College of California, in 1981 Di Prima began working privately as a psychic and healer. Her life had always been devoted to integrating the imaginative with the practical: poetics and politics, magic and medicine. As Allen Ginsberg observed: "The poetic tradition has a lot of possibilities. Traditionally, it goes way, way back. The role of the bard, the role of the poet, has always been mixed up with the role of the priest, the role of the shaman, or the role of the teacher."[6] Gary Snyder had also explored the connections between poet and shaman, and virtually all the Beats—including Michael McClure, Philip Lamantia, and William S. Burroughs—were deeply conversant with Native American spiritual traditions. Thus Di Prima recalled that she began to

> do both healing work and trance visualization work for clients—people who felt they had a shadow in their life that was wrong, and so on. And in doing the visualization work, a few times I ran into forces (that's what I call them—I don't know what they were) that were way bigger than what I had been asked by my client to deal with. I would just put up a shield wall and call on larger forces to take care of them and go about my business. But I was aware that some of this work was kind of like Frodo in Tolkien's *Hobbit*: "If you shine a stronger flashlight, it's going to notice you!" So I started to wish I had a sangha, or other people I could sit with, just to ground myself after doing that kind of work.

In her healing room, she kept a magical altar where she conducted guided visualizations with pupils as well as Tarot readings. Di Prima viewed the Major Arcana cards as archetypal, "a series of steps in the psychic process, or a series of initiations" and her practices closely mirror the activities described by Sarah M. Pike in *New Age and Neopagan Religions in America*:

> Regular rituals are often conducted in small groups for any number of purposes, including healing and personal spiritual growth. They are usually held in circles and facilitated by ritual leaders who explain the purpose of the ritual, invite deities or spirits to be present, monitor the group's energy, and end the ritual in such a way that everyone returns to a normal state of consciousness. Ritual spaces are generally oriented in relation to the four cardinal directions and feature altars that hold statues of deities and symbols of water, air, fire, and earth.

From the Minor Arcana, Di Prima employed a cup, disc, sword, and wand to represent the four elements and twenty-five sub-elements; and from the *tria prima* of Paracelsian alchemy, she kept on hand a vial of mercury, a piece of sulfur from Sicily and a large crystal of solidified salt—thus the alchemical principles of mercury, sulfur, and salt. She would help her students "get into a hypnagogic state, enter the drawing for that particular sub-element and travel and come back to report where we've been."

The breadth of Di Prima's reading and studying—her bookishness as we have seen is one of her defining characteristics—of countless recondite sources is confirmed by the manuscript "Structures of Magic and Techniques of Visioning," which contains her class notes from October 23, 1978, where she explained the ways Tarot became integrated into her spiritual practice:

Tarot and Tree [of Life] as it was worked out by the Golden Dawn people and later people in terms of changing my point of view or my perspective so that my way of seeing the world is in terms of correspondences, so that everything has a thickness of dimensionality—instead of linearity, so that blue also means Jupiter and also means whatever plant, it means [and Wheel of Fortune card and lapis or sapphire] so that everything moves thru several dimensions at once like certain so-called "primitive" languages both because it's a way of seeing and because it's a way of using words and image that seems to me breaks down the necessity for metaphor in the old sense and makes all that stuff obsolete. I really want to enter that head and live there, not just have it as a quaint old idea, the idea of correspondence.[7]

This is a fascinating passage for Di Prima declares that she seeks to actually live out the ideas of correspondence—"as above, so below"—rather than think of it merely "as a quaint old idea." The theory of correspondence allows her to believe in a universe that makes sense, in which each element is part of and reflects a harmonious whole. Di Prima conceptualized her studies of Tarot in conjunction with her healing. In her "Foreword" to Angelina Hekking's *Seeds of Light: Images of Healing* (1990), Di Prima recalls the beginnings of her "psychic healing practice, which involved laying-on of hands and guided visualization."[8] This led to the founding of the San Francisco Institute of Magical and Healing Arts with Sheppard Powell, Janet Carter, and Carl Grundberg. As we shall see in the following chapter, the practice of visualization continued to play a prominent role in Di Prima's poetics.

On February 18, 1982, Di Prima delivered "Role of the Hermetic in Poetry" at the Detroit Institute of Arts. The notes for this lecture have been published: it is a dense and rich text, composed in a concise, telegraphic style, and replete with references to Rilke, Blake, Pound, Keats, Frost, and William Carlos Williams as well as to her favorite thinkers including Paracelsus, Jung, Ficino, and Bruno. "Role of the Hermetic in Poetry" touches on a number of key points in Di Prima's poetics and aesthetics including the role of the poet, the metaphysics of light, and inspiration. Regarding the function of the poet, she adduces several examples to illustrate her thesis, arguing "the poet like the Magus heals the rift between individual things and the One"; acts "as

co-worker with god in the unfinished creation of world," concluding that
the poet strives to "bring the archetypes to self-knowledge & so heal the
rifts in eternity." Di Prima also returns to her elaboration of the metaphysics
of light, quoting: "To live in the light of the inner sun suffices all things,"
followed by "moth with dust (light images)"—this may be an allusion to Stan
Brakhage's brief, one-minute-and-six second experimental film "Mothlight"
(1963) which captures images of moth wings against the light. She then
draws lines pointing to the right with five Latin terms arranged from top to
bottom: *fulgor, candor, lumen, lux, claritas*. For Robert Grosseteste, the first
form of light is lux, while reflected or radiated light is *lumen*, luminosity.
William K. Wimsatt, Jr. and Cleanth Brooks remarked:

> In Aquinas, as in most of the theological and aesthetic writers of
> his century and not only the Franciscans, we find the Plotinian and
> Platonic philosophy of light more radiant than ever. Claritas, splendor,
> resplendentia, fulgor, lux, lumine—such words recur throughout
> theological writing with almost as much frequency as words relating to
> form itself or to unity of being.

Di Prima continues to develop her interpretation of Giordano Bruno, turning
specifically to his ideas concerning the two types of inspiration. First, Di
Prima notes that Bruno believed the "divine spirit enters an ignorant person
who becomes inspired w/out understanding Cocteau's Orpheus getting
poems from the radio"; and secondly a "person 'skillful in contemplation &
possessing innately a clear intellectual spirit . . . comes to speak & act . . .
as chief artificer . . .' they are 'as the sacred thing'—assume the godform."
Di Prima alludes here to a passage from Bruno's *Eroici furori* upon which
Frances A. Yates comments in her *Giordano Bruno and the Hermetic
Tradition*: "In short, I think that what the religious experiences of the *Eroici
furori* really aim at is the Hermetic *gnosis*; this is the mystical love poetry
of the Magus man, who was created divine, with divine powers, and is in
process of again becoming divine, with divine powers." Attaining a state of
receptivity which will allow the influx of inspiration is a recurring theme in
Di Prima's poetics as we have seen in her earlier essays and interviews.

She also refers to Marsilio Ficino whom she taught in her "Hidden
Religions in the Literature of Europe" course: "Ficino (love) Eros links all
worlds is the stuff of the networks of correspondence Makes us ready to
receive (dictation, etc.) Duncan/Spicer/Calculus of Variation Poem moves
thru one . . ." This is from Ficino's *De Amore*, a commentary on Plato's
Symposium which he had written by 1469. Ficino writes that the "first
turning" of "Chaos"

> toward God we call the birth of Love. The infusion of the ray, the food of
> Love. The reaching out to God, the impetus of Love. The forming of the

Ideas, the perfecting of Love. The combination of all the Forms and Ideas we call in Latin a mundus, in Greek a cosmos, that is, an ornament. The grace of this world or ornament is Beauty, to which that Love, as soon as it was born, attracted the Mind; and it led the Mind, formerly ugly, to the same Mind made beautiful. Therefore the condition of Love is that it carries things off to beauty, and joins the ugly to the beautiful.

From this extract, we may see why J. B Allen has observed that Ficino was "the first of the Renaissance mages dedicated to the notion of a World Spirit and a World Soul"—the *spiritus mundi* to which W. B. Yeats refers in "The Second Coming." And from this passage—"the combination of all the Forms and Ideas we call in Latin a mundus"—Di Prima expounds the key concept: "Ficino (love) Eros links all worlds is the stuff of the networks of correspondence" and connects this insight to the state of receptive genius which love allows. She interestingly places her own work *Calculus of Variation* in this category of a "received" work, along with those of Robert Duncan and Jack Spicer. Thus she is drawn to Ficino for the inherent interest of the ideas themselves, but also for their relevance to her own work. As we saw previously with the final vision of Dante's *Paradiso*, for Ficino it is love which holds the universe together and it is again for Di Prima the motive force behind her visionary poetics.

As we have seen above with regard to Tarot, here again Di Prima invokes the "power of creative imagination"—at the close she quotes Keats: "I am certain of nothing but the holiness of the heart's affections & the truth of the imagination." Poiesis is a means of affirming the therapeutic role of the poet and artist. This idea recalls that of Nikos Kazantzakis who in *The Saviors of God* asserted that God needs humanity's help in order to complete himself/herself/itself. Di Prima acknowledges that it requires a "leap of faith" to believe that human life indeed possesses this meaning, that absurdity and chaos are not the fate of contemporary humanity. We can see the ways Di Prima's research studies flow directly into her poiesis in a poem dated February 12, 1981—"Studies in Light"—which mentions these forms of light:

claritas

sun
   caught in dew
flashing
a shapeliness
we stand out side of
candor

light
   a chorus swelling
filling out

       the contours of architecture
       cathedral
       palace
               theatre

                                    lumen

       light
       as a glyph that writes itself
       over & over, on the face
       of water, inscrutable
       perpetual motion

                                    lux

       needle point
       moving out
       from core
       of earth
       thinnest
       piercing rays

Claritas is the light of the sun, much loved by the Medieval and Renaissance philosophers Di Prima studied. As Umberto Eco has remarked, they "were enthralled by luminosity in general, and by the sun's light. Medieval literature is filled with joyous acclaim of the effulgence of daylight and of fire." One thinks of St. Francis of Assisi's celebrated "Canticle of the Sun." *Candor,* or the other hand, is whiteness from Latin *candere* to shine, glitter or glow which Di Prima associates with the light of a chorus singing in a cathedral, palace, or theatre. Robert Grosseteste's treatise *De Luce* had influenced Di Prima in the late 1950s and here she returns to his categories. Grosseteste writes: "When the first body, which is the firmament, has in this way been completely actualized, it diffuses its light (*lumen*) from every part of itself to the center of the universe. For since light (*lux*) is the perfection of the first body and naturally multiplies itself from the first body, it is necessarily diffused to the center of the universe." *Lux* and *lumen* are both forms of light, but have different properties and purposes. Di Prima is striving to integrate ideas from physics and cosmology within the framework of her experience and studies of the interior, contemplative world which she nurtures through meditation, visualization, as well as the incorporation of magical techniques within both her poetic and spiritual practice.

This absorption in Tarot, hermetic, and magical studies continued through the 1970s and early 1980s. After the death of Shunryu Suzuki in 1971, Di Prima continued to study Zen until 1983 at which point she sensed she had fulfilled her teacher's instructions and was now ready to pursue a new inner path. She encountered Chogyam Trungpa at Naropa during her teaching there in 1974—whom as we have seen she first met at Tassajara in 1970—attended his lectures and later decided to become his pupil.[9] In an essay she composed for the anthology *Beneath a Single Moon: Buddhism in Contemporary American Poetry* (1991), Di Prima noted she had come

> to the end of where I could go without a teacher. It became clear that I needed a tradition of Magick that was unbroken, dharmic, and explicit, and a master and sangha I could connect with. The Tibetan tradition, growing as it does out of *Bonpo*, is the Buddhism that most explicitly addresses the juxtaposition of the magickal view of the world and the dharma.[10]

Sangha refers to a community of Buddhists; however Di Prima did not desire to abandon her Western studies and told Trungpa: "I'm not prepared to give up Paracelsus for Padmasambhava. And he laughed and said, 'No problem.'"[11] Padmasambhava (fl. eighth century) was an important figure in transmitting Buddhism from India to Tibet. He and Ye Shes Mtsho Rygal (ca. 757–817), his Tibetan consort, recorded many teachings known as Gter Ma—or "hidden treasure texts"—which were then concealed and intended to be revealed later by a series of masters who were linked spiritually to Padmasambhava.

Di Prima turns to this Buddhist history in "Tsogyal," again employing the dense, learned, allusive style—spacing her lines as in a musical score following the example of Olson's Projective Verse—which marked her masterful homages to Paracelsus and John Dee:

> The central nerve is a white
> fire Do I dare speak
> of this? The whirling seed-
> essence flares
> co emergence
> the point
> where nothing has (yet)
> been defined
> The horse of prana rides on
> the nadis
> I ride
> that horse
>
> But this is as nothing to the Voice
> of the mantra
> rushing like breath
> thru the thousand and eight
>
> nerves, voice of the Guru
> flaring out

the dance I snake to the center
where bindu whirls
red/white
time/essence

so still
in this storm[12]

Tsogyal is seen as the first person in a single life to attain Buddhahood: reputed to be quite lovely, she escaped from an arranged marriage to pursue a spiritual life, becoming the consort of Padmasambhava.[13] According to Anne Carolyn Klein's *Meeting the Great Bliss Queen: Buddhists, Feminists, and the Art of the Self*, Tsogyal is regarded as an enlightened being as well as

> a manifestation of Sarasvati, the Indian goddess of sound and muse of learning and literature. She is also identified in some texts with the Bodhissattva Tara . . . Like all male and female enlightened figures in the Indian and Tibetan Buddhist pantheon, the Great Bliss Queen is a manifestation of wisdom and compassion. These qualities are inviolable, yet express themselves in a variety of ways.[14]

As we see above, Tsogyal was sometimes identified as "Tara" and Di Prima composed a poem in homage to Tara, a deity in Tantric Tibetan Vajrayana Buddhism. "Tsogyal" describes the *nadi*—the body's channels through which prana—or "winds"—flow, thus "rushing like breath." *Bindu* in Tantrism is either white, symbolizing male seminal fluid or red—the menses. The *bindu* can also be the point at which creation begins, or the mind's natural creative and empty state. Thus "the whirling seed-/essence flares" is both the moment of conception and creation of the universe. At the close, "where bindu whirls/red/white/time/essence," Di Prima again invokes the symbolism of female=red, male=white in relation to the "whirling" of the universe into time and being.[15]

Many monasteries in Bhutan perform dances in honor of Padmasambhava, thus the "voice of the Guru/flaring out/the dance I snake to the center." The poem is a dramatic monologue describing a Master who is an incarnation of female potency, and Di Prima included "Tsogyal" in her 1998 edition of *Loba*. Tsogyal here speaks tentatively in first person regarding her moments of transcendence, wondering whether she should reveal secrets which have been vouchsafed her: "The central nerve is a white/fire Do I dare speak of this?" Keith Dowman in *Sky Dancer* describes the experience as follows:

> In the Vase Initiation, at the height of sensual pleasure the red (female) and white (Male) bodhicittas interfuse, and retracted up the medial nerve in the spine, the focal points of psychic energy (cakras) are charged;

the sun and moon of each focal point is irradiated with light, and the entire psycho-organism is vitalized by a current of energy so strong that "concrete reality," the product of our normal dualistic mode of perception, dissolves, and the vision which is described in terms of Mahavajradhara, the Adi-buddha, overwhelms the initiate in his gnostic trance.

The sacralization of sexuality became a prominent feature of the counterculture and Mircea Eliade has analyzed the significance of Tantra in the quest for spiritual liberation, citing the *Guhyasamaja-tantra*:

> The Indian example shows to what degree of mystical refinement sacramentalization of the organs and of physiological life can be brought—a sacramentalization that is already amply documented on all the archaic levels of culture. We should add that the valorization of sexuality as means of participating in the sacred (or in India, of gaining the superhuman state of absolute freedom) is not without its dangers. In India itself, tantrism has provided the occasion for aberrant and infamous ceremonies. In the primitive world too, ritual sexuality has been accompanied by many orgiastic forms. Nevertheless, the example still retains its suggestive value, for it reveals an experience that is no longer accessible in a desacralized society—the experience of a sanctified sexual life.

Thus Di Prima's interest in Tantra may be seen as another avenue for seeking *gnosis*, or self-knowledge. Indeed, Giuseppe Tucci cited several of the great Gnostics in his observations regarding Tantra in his *The Theory and Practice of the Mandala*: "The aim of all the Tantras is to teach the ways whereby we may set free the divine light which is mysteriously present and shining in each one of us, although it is enveloped in an insidious web of the psyche's weaving. Mani, Valentinus, Bardesanes, and the author of the *Pistis Sophia* were moved by similar aspirations and they form so many bridges linking the ideas of oriental esoterism with Hellenistic *gnosis*."[16] Tucci invokes three of the great Gnostic thinkers—Mani, Valentinus, and Bardesanes—in order to connect ancient "oriental esoterism" and Gnostic traditions. Thus we see again how Di Prima has exhibited remarkable technical skill in shaping her extensive knowledge of Buddhism into a virtuosic poem.

In celebrating Tsogyal, Di Prima was seeking to place women centrally within the history of humanity's spiritual evolution. Religious and theological texts have typically been authored from the male point of view, and relegated women to a secondary role within orthodox institutional structures. The prevalence of female shamanism had also been ignored until the work of anthropologists such as Barbara Tedlock, who explored the subject in *The Woman in the Shaman's Body: Reclaiming the Feminine in Religion and Medicine*.[17] Di Prima was in the vanguard of the movement to reevaluate the role of women in forging new spiritual identities, declaring that women

> are in the forefront of figuring out what it is to be human. Because I don't think the guys have got the slightest handle on it yet. I'm not mad at them for that. I just think they are kind of slow. They've been caught by these structures, they've been caught by the analytic way, they've been caught by all the things that make their little male, white, supremacist world work on a temporary basis. They're in love with those things. So they're too slow to realize that there's endless potential to the imagination, to the human emotions. And art is only interesting when it's pushing at those boundaries.[18]

As Nancy M. Grace and Tony Trigilio argue, Loba compels "a reader to consider the possibility that masculinist myths of culture, language, reason, and immortality—as well as aesthetics—are acts not of knowledge but of ignorance and ego, repeatedly performed on the back of female silence, subjugation, and invisibility." Di Prima seeks to find a path toward the mysteries of existence which cannot be approached only through "the analytic way," but must be apprehended through the imagination, feeling, and intuition. Her decades-long work on Loba should be understood as her effort to redress the balance, to place the female principle—the goddess, the witch, the Magna Mater, the Great Mother—back in the primary role it enjoyed before being de-throned by the male, patriarchal God with a large "G." In "Prayer to the Mothers," Di Prima invokes the Mothers who still perhaps dwell "in the depths of the earth or on/some sacred mountain." She seeks their intercession in our troubled world and implores them to "wake us like children from a nightmare, give the slip/ to the devourers whom I cannot name/the metal men who walk/on all our substance, crushing flesh/to swamp." The Mothers may yet save us from the "metal men" of the modern world who are killing the environment with their "acid which eats clean" and their technological machines which pummel the life out of the cosmos.

This rewriting of the female role in spiritual history led Di Prima to a deeper consideration of H.D., who is known to many readers for her crystalline adaptations of Sappho: specifically, her ability to create from the poetic fragment a tantalizing sense of the ancient past as if Sappho's original voice had been caught forever in amber. Di Prima shared several characteristics in common with H.D. Like Di Prima, H.D. has also dropped out of College— Bryn Mawr; had a strongly mystical sensibility due to her Moravian religious upbringing; participated in séances and parapsychological experiments; and was also bisexual. H.D. immersed herself in the Kabbalah, Tarot, the wisdom of ancient Egypt, studied both Robert Graves and Margaret Murray, and in her poetry redefined the place of women in humanity's mythic imagination.

In her memoir documenting her relationship with Ezra Pound, *End to Torment*, H.D. recalled Pound giving her books by Blake, Swedenborg, Balzac's *Seraphita* as well as "a series of Yogi books," one of which was *Fourteen Lessons in Yogic Philosophy and Oriental Occultism* (1903)—all topics of central importance to Di Prima as well. In her five-section poem "For H.D.," Di Prima composed a dramatic monologue depicting H.D.'s spiritual struggles: "trophies of pain I've gathered. whose sorrow/do I shore up, in trifles? the weaving,/paintings, jewels, plants, I bought/with my heart's hope." Jo Gill has noted the influence of H.D. on a variety of women poets, including Di Prima:

> In later work, a distinctive and distinctively female speaking position re-emerges, but is dramatically rethought. It is presented by multiple personae or masks, by fragmented and dispersed subjectivities and, in many cases, by an unusual willingness to speak about female desire. Poets from Niedecker through di Prima and Atwood to Hejinian evidence the influence of H.D.'s work in this respect."

Erotic desire is of course a frequent topic of Di Prima's work and the employment of "multiple personae or masks" also supplied her with a method for the structure of *Loba* in which Di Prima "speaks through" the personalities of scores of historical and mythic incarnations of Woman. It is also noteworthy that Di Prima's has followed H.D.'s example in yet another regard for her latest enterprise (2016) has been a project to adapt the poems of Sappho, inspired by Anne Carson's *If Not, Winter: Fragments of Sappho* (2003).

H.D. had thus achieved a great deal beyond her early imagistic masterworks. Di Prima read her *Tribute to Freud* in 1971 and now devoted several essays to a study of H.D.'s thought and poetics. A Spring 1987 lecture delivered at the New College of California and published in 2011 entitled "The Mysteries of Vision: Some Notes on H.D." was the first of three Di Prima texts—with more projected—published by Lost and Found: The CUNY Poetics Document Initiative edited by Ammiel Alcalay and Ana Bozicevic.

Here she revealed her explorations "have proved to be the seed of a work now in progress, in which I propose to examine the visionary process in H.D.'s later works, from the vantage point of my own experience with visioning techniques and territories." She takes issue with the "materialist" approach to H.D. "subsumed under the various schools of feminism: lesbian and otherwise; as well as the various schools of poetic criticism."[19] Di Prima discusses H.D.'s final ambitious poems—*Trilogy, Helen in Egypt*, and *Hermetic Definition*—and the ways she interprets the meaning and significance of angels. H.D. devoted one of her great poems to the subject—"Tribute to the Angels" (1944)—in which Raphael, Gabriel, Azrael, Uriel, Annael, Michael,

FIGURE 5.1 *Ammiel Alcaly, Diane di Prima, and Ana Bozicevic, New York City, 2010. Photo courtesy:* Lost and Found: The CUNY Poetics Document Initiative.

and Zadkiel—each representing individual powers—appear. H.D. also declares her allegiance to the tradition of hermetic wisdom as symbolized in "Thrice-Great Hermes" whom she declares "is patron of alchemists." As Peter Gardella has observed:

> Beginning with an invocation of Hermes Trismegistus, patron of medieval alchemists, H.D. brought the angels of the planets one by one onto the stage, associating each of them not just with Jewish and Christian but also with Greek and Roman, Babylonian, and Egyptian myths. Michael, the regent of Mercury, was not just he who "casts the Old Dragon/onto the abyss" but also Thoth, an Egyptian god "with a feather/who weighed the soul of the dead."

Hermes is at once the patron of alchemists in his incarnation as Hermes Trismegistus—"Thrice-Great Hermes"—and of course messenger of the gods, an angel with winged sandals. And as H.D. created a syncretic fabric of world spiritual traditions in her poetry, so too would Di Prima—most powerfully, as we have seen, in *Loba*.

In one of her loveliest poems, "To a Student," Di Prima encapsulated the spiritual meaning of angels:

POEMS ARE ANGELS
come to bring you
the letter you wdn't
       sign for
earlier, when it was
      delivered
by yr life

The poet is also an angel, bringing to the reader a hidden—and vital—message which he/she has failed to recognize camouflaged in their experience previously. In *Kerhonkson Journal*, Di Prima included a poem "For Rilke": "Each single angel is different/Like babies/They demonstrate personality of necessity/They chortle, turning away in our arms/Or meet the direct gaze grasping at the air/I gave one my index finger and she held on/For twenty days, her white wings were getting dusty/They are like butterflies rather, I grow tired/Of watching them fly out to sea where they die in herds." Rainer Maria Rilke famously invoked angels at the opening of his *Duino Elegies*: "Who would hear me if I cried out among the angelic orders?" "Wer, wenn ich schriee, hörte mich den aus der Engel/Ordnungen?" And angel imagery as we have seen is pervasive in Beat literature, beginning most famously with Allen Ginsberg's "angel-headed hipsters."

Di Prima and the Beats had been predecessors in a quasi-obsession with angels which has preoccupied both popular culture and academics over the past three decades. Walter Benjamin (1892–1940) famously responded to Paul Klee's painting *Angelus Novus* in his "Theses on the Philosophy of History":

A Klee painting named "Angelus Novus" shows an angel looking as though he is about to move away from something he is fixedly contemplating. His eyes are staring, his mouth is open, his wings are spread. This is how one pictures the angel of history. His face is turned toward the past. Where we perceive a chain of events, he sees one single catastrophe which keeps piling wreckage upon wreckage and hurls it in front of his feet. The angel would like to stay, awaken the dead, and make whole what had been smashed. But a storm is blowing from Paradise; it has got caught in his wings with such violence that the angel can no longer close them. This storm irresistibly propels him into the future to which his back is turned, while the pile of debris before him grows skyward. This storm is what we call progress.

Robert Alter interprets this angel as

defining more sharply the disasters of secular modernity—the erosion of experience, the decay of wisdom, the loss of redemptive vision, and now, in 1940, the universal reign of mass murder. The angel here is not annunciating angelman but witnessing man, allegorically endowed with the terrible power of seeing things utterly devoid of illusion.

As humanity "progressed" toward the millennium, perhaps occasioned by the varying hopeful and apocalyptic expectations occasioned by this fateful date and by Walter Benjamin's warnings, several monographs appeared exploring the literary and spiritual meaning of the winged creatures: Massimo Cacciari, *L'Angelo necessario* (1992); Michel Serres, *Angels: A Modern Myth* (1995); Harold Bloom, *Omens of the Millennium: The Gnosis of Angels, Dreams and Resurrection* (1996); and more recently, Iona Cosma, *Angels In-Between: The Poetics of Excess and the Crisis of Representation* (2009). Angels fit neatly into the development of the hidden religions which had become central to Di Prima's explorations, and Giorgio Agamben in "Walter Benjamin and the Demonic: Happiness and Historical Redemption" commented upon the historical continuity linking these esoteric strands of spiritual history. In responding to Walter Benjamin's engagement with the "personal angel," Agamben observed: "Here we find ourselves before an extremely rich and yet coherent tradition which is present not only in Judaism but also (as idios daimon) in Neoplatonic mystics, late-ancient hermeticism, gnosticism, and early Christianity and which also has precise counterparts in Iranian and Muslim angelology." Agamben goes on to observe that "according to a doctrine that can be found in both Cabalistic texts and hermetic writings, the vision of one's own angel coincides with prophetic ecstasy and supreme knowledge." Agamben cites Henry Corbin and his exposition of these doctrines overlaps with our prior investigation of Di Prima's lecture to the Jung society.[20]

In Di Prima's engagement with H.D.'s angelology, she is interested in her account of meeting Azrael—in Hebrew "Help of God," the angel of death—and the angel's symbolic meaning for humanity which is perhaps

> on the verge of our own death as a species, the creation (not so conscious) of our own Azrael. The invitation to us as artists is to enter more planes, move in more dimensions than we humans had ever dreamed existed—and so of course we limit ourselves in new ways, hauling our white picket fences off into the warpings of relativist space: materialism, romanticism, feminism, historicity.[21]

As we have seen earlier, Di Prima viewed many contemporary critical approaches as reductive and seeks rather to situate H.D. within the context of the hidden religions. Di Prima conceives H.D.'s *Hermetic Definition* as a love poem to the journalist Louis Durand, which leads her to ponder the link between romantic love, religious ecstasy, and the poetic vocation:

> Hence the secret of the "love cults" thru the ages: to be "in love" is the severest discipline: it is thralldom, as any religious path is "thralldom," and can be chosen and even sought as such, as the troubadours, Sufis, fideli d'amore, etc. amply demonstrate. What we tend to forget is that poesis, especially visionary poesis, is a religious path, sought and chosen.[22]

In another late H.D. poem, *Helen in Egypt* (1961)—a work in which H.D. imagines an alternative version of the Trojan war in which Zeus removes Helen to Egypt to wait in safety until the war's conclusion—one specific passage made a powerful impression on Di Prima:

> If there is a single image for me of the "courage of the tenuous" it is the moment in *Helen in Egypt* when Achilles' eyes meet Helen's, across the battlefield and she on the Wall: "I counted the fall of her feet/from turret to turret;/will the count even yesterday's?/will there be five over?/this was a game I played,/a game of prophecy."[23]

We recall Di Prima's studies of Homeric Greek during the 1950s as well as the several references to Homer and to Greek mythology in *The New Handbook of Heaven* and many other works as well. Furthermore, H.D.'s revision of Homer's mythology to emphasize the feminine dimension of his epic would supply Di Prima with a precedent for the creation of her own "epic" in praise of Woman, *Loba*.

Robert Duncan died on February 3, 1988, and Di Prima composed a eulogy to be read at the San Francisco Dharmadhatu on February 21, recalling Duncan's "endlessly sharp perception and inquisitiveness: nothing got by him, there was nothing that he didn't want to know about—and it all got changed somehow, in that crucible, connections between things you had never dreamed of connecting, comparisons so off-the-wall, or so apt." And in a dream Di Prima recorded in her *Notebooks* on December 3, 1989, she recounted an emotional scene:

> I embrace Robert and feel w/all my body that no matter how I hold him & shelter him w/my body—there is no way I can keep death away—there is passion & grief in my holding him—then I burst out & say "We don't know what's best!/We don't even know what's what./We're like children who have to be told that it's bed time." While I am holding Robert & crying & saying this, he is saying over and over, as if summing up his life "I ALWAYS STROVE FOR THE HEART." I awake crying. But there is sweetness and connectedness in my crying. I have accepted in the dream that I can't hold death off—I have in some way again surrendered. As I recall the dialogue in winter dawn light I melt into tears again & there is a sweetness in it.

Duncan thus was clearly dominating Di Prima's imagination during this period and in 1989, she delivered a lecture entitled "R.D.'s H.D." interpreting his *The H.D. Book*, sections of which had appeared as single chapters in several publications during Duncan's lifetime: the complete volume finally appeared posthumously in 2011. She returns here to sacred love and the role H.D. played in Duncan's own spiritual quest, arguing that just "as the

troubadours took their model ((influence)) from the Sufi love cults, so too
Dante modeled his religion of love on their influence, as well as on primary
Sufic sources. But H.D. is also for Robert Duncan the Master Initiate,
Adept in the Mysteries, whither he sought to follow/and not follow her."[24]
Furthermore, in explicating H.D.'s influence on Duncan, Di Prima provides
a summary of several themes relevant to her own poetics throughout her
career:

> In the Poetics of Influence a study has yet to be made of the continuing
> force of what Duncan called the "magical cults": past Yeats and the early
> Golden Dawn years into the interbellum period. H.D. is active in many
> of these, in many ways: séance, angel magic (nascent in *Trilogy*, full-
> blown in "Sagesse"), "waking vision" and its exploration (her work with
> Freud can be seen as a working with a fellow magician), and deliberate
> evocation of "past life memory" (in "Vale Ave"). Here Robert Duncan,
> certain as he is that Poetry in itself is all the practice, all the religion and
> magic one needs (and for himself it may well have been), follows her to
> the threshold and hangs back.[25]

Di Prima traces here the genealogy of texts which she covered in her "The
Hidden Religions in the Literature of Europe." In studying the history of
magic with her students, the major texts included Frances Yates's *Giordano
Bruno and the Hermetic Tradition*, W. B. Yeats's *A Vision*, and the works of
British occultist Aleister Crowley.

Di Prima returned to H.D. and the relevance of angel names and meanings
in her work in an as-yet unpublished lecture delivered at Naropa in 1988
entitled "H.D.'s Angel Magic." She asserts that the last twenty years of H.D.'s
oeuvre—1943–61—represent her greatest poetry, observing that H.D.'s
Trilogy—composed of "The Walls Do Not Fall," "Tribute to the Angels"
and "The Flowering of the Rod"—was composed while the poet was in
London during the bombing of Second World War. "The Walls Do Not Fall"
contains Egyptian mythological figures such as Isis while simultaneously
chronicling the terror of the descending German V-2 rockets: H.D. connects
this "red-death" with the angel Uriel. Invocation is central to "Tribute to
Angels" in which a number of angels appear. Part Three—"The Flowering
of the Rod"—considers Mary Magdalene and the Christ myth. The main
purpose of this lecture, however, is to reorient the study of H.D.'s work
within its proper esoteric tradition, a task which Di Prima believes most
modern scholars have neglected:

> We haven't, so far, in the scholarship and studies, that have been going on,
> not much attention has been paid to what I'd guess we'll have to call for
> the lack of a better word, the "esoteric" in H.D. Most of the literary critics
> have shied away from it. And we're in the position that we've always

been in with our great minds, of wanting to take part of the package and leave the rest, like let's take Newton's laws of mechanics and forget his alchemy. Let's decide that poor John Dee was a great mathematician, but he must have gone crazy when he started conjuring. And to just bring them into the light of day, because I feel that we can't afford to go on ignoring that part of people's lives and work. I think we're at the point where this magic, or the spiritual, whatever you want to call it, the part of ourselves that we have been keeping out of the spotlight because of being caught in a few hundred years of Rationalism Civilization, has got to come back into the work.[26]

John Dee, whom Di Prima invokes here, is relevant to her discussion of angels since Dee—as we have seen in the last chapter—strove to understand angelic language. Di Prima points out that while in Antwerp, Dee was impressed upon discovering Johannes Trithemius's (1462–1516) treatise on cryptography, *Steganographia* (1606) which posited a way for angels to carry messages. Umberto Eco in *The Search for the Perfect Language* reports that in the third book of the *Steganographia* "there are clear descriptions of magic rituals. Angels, evoked through images modeled in wax, are subjected to requests and invocations, or the adept must write his own name on his forehead with ink mixed with the juice of a rose, etc."[27] Johanna Drucker observed that "Trithemius stated that messages to be transmitted secretly could be carried by spirits which had themselves to be called upon by means of unintelligible conjurations. He then provided an exhaustive record of the various spells to be used to bring forth spirits—who had names which resembled those of Hebrew angels."[28] With the aid of his helper Edward Kelly who "scryed" employing a crystal ball, Dee devoted years to transcribing the angelic messages he claimed to have received and credited Trithemius with inspiring him to compose the *Monas Hieroglyphica*.[29] In her lecture, Di Prima points out that Trithemius was also the teacher of both Agrippa—who dedicated his *De Occulta* (1510) to him—and Paracelsus. She underscores the significance of Adam McLean's publication of the first part of Trithemius's *Steganographia*, thus tracing the genealogy of angel magic from Trithemius to the Golden Dawn to H.D. Finally, for Di Prima, H.D.'s work reaffirms her belief that "poetry is magic . . . in the last years of this century, it seems clear to me that there is nowhere left for art to go than magic . . . the suffusion of spirit, drawing down of god forms, or drawing down of particular energies or powers, with the will to make change, this is what magic—this is what art—is for."[30]

As had become her custom over the three decades of her career, in the late 1980s and early 1990s Di Prima continued to divide her energies between composing poetry, writing essays and plays, creating her *Notebooks*, engaging in publishing ventures and developing ideas about poetics and the sources of inspiration through visualization. She had been at work on a cycle of poems entitled *Alchemical Studies*, and explained her process concerning the genesis and structure of the work in an interview from 1986:

> A lot of the poetry I'm writing now is stuff that at one point I once thought I'd go back and finish and then I realized that its nature is fragmentary—a lot of alchemical poems that are fragments, and they stop where they stop because I can't write part I don't know—they just stop. The book is called *Alchemical Studies*. But then, the question is, how do you bring this other stuff in? It's so thick and rich. Either it's going to just seep into the poem of itself, or there's going to have to be some kind of wedding, some conscious working of the images from visualizing in poem form—which doesn't seem likely. I don't work like that. Or the stuff as it is—what I jot down directly after a visualizing session—is already finished and I just haven't recognized its shape yet. Which often happens to me. I don't make sense of it, and I don't throw it out, and some ten years later, I pick the thing up and say, "Oh, this is this."

Di Prima had made a study of W. B. Yeats's *A Vision* and as we have seen, Yeats had been a member of Samuel Mathers's Hermetic Order of the Golden Dawn. During the time he stayed with Ezra Pound at Stone Cottage, Yeats read Heinrich Cornelius Agrippa's *De Occulta* and in *A Vision* published in 1925—the fruit of a prolific episode of automatic writing on the part of his wife George which occurred a few days following their marriage in 1917— Yeats discusses several of Di Prima's central areas of investigation such as Agrippa, John Dee, angels, and Kabbalah. Mathers had taught Yeats to depict Kabbalistic symbols on cards which would then be employed to create states of reverie. In raising the question of visualization, Di Prima alluded to Yeats's method of composition and its implications for her own practice:

> How do you begin to bring all the material which has begun to come in visualization back into the poem? That's something that Yeats never solved, and he's the only one I know of who came up against it so hugely, from *The Vision* on. There weren't so many poems toward the end of his life, and not so many of them brought in that information.

Thus we may observe in the mid-1980s the ways Di Prima continued to reflect upon her own visionary poetics which had marked her career from the beginning.

Di Prima took time out from her literary work to participate in the "River City Reunion Week" in Lawrence, Kansas from September 7 to 13, 1987. Participants included William Burroughs, Allen Ginsberg, Michael McClure, Robert Creeley, Anne Waldman, and Ed Sanders. Several films were shown, including Burroughs's *Towers Open Fire* and Robert Frank's Beat classic, *Pull My Daisy* (1959). Marianne Faithfull sang and Ginsberg recited *Howl*. During the 1980s, the Beats began to be rediscovered by a new generation of young people who found inspiration in their resistance to the destructive aspects of American capitalism and militarism. For example, Robert Siegel in an essay in *The Downtown Book: The New York Art Scene 1974-1984* included Di Prima in a list of authors who inspired the Punk rock musicians as well as experimental, outsider, performance artists and writers of the 1970s and 1980s: "One quality that kept the Beats on the mental horizon of Downtown writers was their problematic mixture of elements: women writing the body (Diane di Prima and Hettie Jones, among many others), issues of class and ethnicity (Allen Ginsberg and Gregory Corso), and the importance of race (Bob Kaufman, Amiri Baraka, and Ted Joans). Politics was everywhere, as was the primacy of oral performance over the written page." During the following decade as well, the Beats continued to be relevant. As Nancy J. Peters has observed:

> The renewed popularity of the beats in the nineties goes beyond nostalgia for a period that now seems innocent in its freedom of the road and for its pleasures of unrestrained sex and drugs. The 1950s and 1990s have much in common, both periods characterized by paradigmatic technological and economic change, government capitulation to corporate power, the rise of religious fundamentalism, and a media-imposed anti-intellectual culture.

As we have seen, it is precisely to these currents in American life to which Di Prima objected so powerfully.

Di Prima also now embarked on a new autobiographical work, *Recollections of My Life as a Woman*, and between 1987 and 1992, several chapters appeared in *Mama Bears News and Notes*, a Bay Area underground newspaper devoted to lesbian cultural and political issues. In 1987, excerpts from *Loba* also appeared in *Early Ripening: American Women's Poetry Now*, edited by Marge Piercy, and *Wyoming Series* (1988) was published by Di Prima's own press, Eidolon Editions. *Wyoming Series*—dedicated to "my teacher SHUNRYU SUZUKI who visited me in a dream and brought this poem"—is illustrated by five drawings by Di Prima herself depicting the Wyoming landscape.[31] Inspired by the period she spent teaching at Native American schools—a world of "broken motels" and "reservation shacks"—the sequence combines Buddhist, Native American, and angelic allusions. The poem begins—"In October all the Bodhisattvas come to Wyoming"—and this initial phrase is subjected to a variety of permutations throughout the brief thirteen-page chapbook: "At dawn the Bodhisattvas come to Wyoming," "In Wyoming the Bodhisattvas have turned to stone." The scene is fall hunting season, the Bodhisattva is "whispering warning to the antelope," hunters are depicted bursting with violent and erotic energy as they mate in motels: "In October the hunters feel fine, they are warm/w blood/they are warm w/whiskey/& able to make love/once more to their

women, who stroke them w/antlers/still red at the stump." Bodhisattvas
descend from on high, observing the vulgar scene and "gather fumes/of this
angry loving/to turn to pure sorrow/silver elixir they catch in/crystal vials/
to pour on the headless corpses of antelope/in the folds of raw, harmonious
hills." One recalls the film by Wim Wenders, *Wings of Desire* (1987) in
which Rilkean angels look down upon the melancholy scene in Berlin
below. Bodhisattvas here take up the "fumes" created by the hunters' "angry
loving," transmuting them into a sad "silver elixir"—this describes an
alchemical process in which volatile substances vaporize during sublimation
and become winged like angels—with which to perform a sacred ceremony
to honor the butchered antelopes. Unlike the Native Americans who prayed
to animals they were about to slay for forgiveness and respected them as
fellow creatures, American "sportsmen" slaughter then desecrate their prey.
And as was done in the nineteenth century to the vast herds of buffalo, they
then leave their butchered bodies—"antlers/still red at the stump"—to rot.

Di Prima now shifts to Native American mythology by invoking
"lizard-woman"—reptiles serve as symbols of survival in many indigenous
cultures—summoning her from the archaic beginnings of creation: "Here
lizard-woman works her tensile claws/into sands newly thrust/from sea-
floor./And time is a song the land sings." A dialogue ensues between the
ancient male midwife of death Mercy and female midwife of birth Severity.
Mercy declares "it doesn't pay to eat antelope/unless you know to eat
prana/instead of flesh." As we have seen previously, Di Prima again invokes
the Hindu concept of prana, or cosmic energy. Wyoming is a forbidding
landscape, yet "in the fall the air of Wyoming is full of angels," echoing
Richard Wilbur's famous poem, "Love Calls Us to the Things of This
world—"the morning air is all awash with angels." Like the Bodhisattvas of
Buddhist tradition, angels stand pitying watch over the desecration of the
land, "they lie in cold rivers/their wings crossed over their eyes. They are
singing requiem to hunters' children." Roger Gilbert has noted that

> the turn to religious themes and more archetypal or numinous imagery in
> the nineties by no means entailed a nostalgic reversion to traditional ideas
> of spiritual wholeness and redemption. The predominant tone of nineties
> poetry was not celebratory but elegiac. Thus its evocation of angels and
> other divine beings was continually shadowed or qualified by violence, loss,
> fragmentation, and entropy. Indeed much nineties poetry could be said to
> convey a distinctly Gnostic vision, in which deity is estranged from creation
> and material existence becomes a prison overseen by a malevolent demiurge.

So too, Di Prima's *Wyoming Series* published as the decade of the 1990s
was about to begin invokes a landscape marked what Gilbert names as
"violence, loss, fragmentation, and entropy" while lizard-woman here is also
an angel of sorts, since she "knows what she's doing/she out in the night/

bringing a message here, a warning here." In ancient Greek, the word for messenger is *angelos*, from which we derive "angel." A force of the universe, she is "jumping/Star-to-star" and in her work performs the magic function of preserving universal balance through her aesthetic sacred and cultural activity: "The hieroglyphs need to be traced/on the stone walls."

Di Prima cultivates an imagistic precision reminiscent of the brief Japanese tanka style which she invokes in the phrase "spun glass & tankas," a clarity and brevity of style practiced by Wallace Stevens in his vividly visual masterwork "Thirteen Ways of Looking at a Blackbird." "Among twenty snowy mountains/ The only moving thing/Was the eye of the blackbird./I was of three minds,/ Like a tree/In which there are three blackbirds." *Wyoming Series* also features an elegant method of musical repetition—"woman," "hunting," "rocks"— through permutation to portray creatures among the landscape:

> The woman was hunting/she thought she was hunting rocks.
> She searched out crevices in the butte for lizards
> Snow
>   lay on the edges of things
> Outlined the mountain.
>
> The woman was harvesting rocks.
> In the air above the water
> The deer & the woman drank news
>   from each other's eyes.

Linda V. Bamber in "Reading as a Buddhist" lists a number of American poets "seriously interested" in Buddhism including Allen Ginsberg, Philip Whalen, Gary Snyder, Robert Haas, W. S. Merwin, Kenneth Rexroth, Joanne Kyger, and Di Prima. She argues

> that High Modernism, of which Stevens is a stellar example, is an antecedent or influence on one strand of the poetry that reads so well from a Buddhist point of view. The modernists were acutely conscious of dismantling what Jacques Derrida calls the Western 'metaphysics of presence': God, Nature with a capital N, the stable, knowable, self-conscious Self—and so on and on. On the other hand, they, unlike many postmodernists, retained an interest in (and sometimes a longing for) these absolutes. They were both attracted and repelled by the possibility of a basis for identity, morality, meaning, and so on. The result was a dance of form and emptiness, an irresolvable alternation between affirming and denying the possibility of Being There. Just as Buddhists resist the temptation to cling to the Void, the modernists rejected nihilism as an alternate foundation. This created in their work a sense of constant movement, of no resting place, that is strongly reminiscent of Buddhist practice.

So too, for Di Prima the Wyoming landscape is bare; yet the atmosphere is suffused with a possibility of angelic visitations. She incorporates what D. H. Lawrence called the "Spirit of Place" by invoking Native American deer woman mythology in which women were able to metamorphose into deer in the last two verses, while in the final sections Di Prima draws the various thematic threads together, declaring that "In Wyoming the Bodhisattvas have turned to stone . . . . In Wyoming the giants still sing in windy canyons./The lovers hear them, it gives an edge to their dreams."

As the new decade began, Di Prima and Sheppard embarked on an enjoyable week vacation in Puerto Vallarta, Mexico, which Di Prima recalled as "quite wonderful: HOT sun and beach and sound of sea all night and millions of pelicans and frigate birds, and streetvendors with beautiful colors of stuff and melting liquid beautiful eyes of the folks, and millions of kids. He [Sheppard] went para-sailing and snorkeling. I gathered beach pebbles for ikebana." In addition, a collection of Di Prima's selected poems *Pieces of a Song* appeared in 1990 featuring a Foreword by Robert Creeley who recalled:

> Growing up in the fifties, you had to figure it out for yourself—which she did, and stayed open—as a woman, uninterested in any possibility of static investment or solution. Her search for human center is among the most moving I have witnessed—and she took her friends with her, though often it would have been simpler indeed to have gone alone.

The following year the cycle *Seminary Poems* was published: just as *Wyoming Series* is devoted to the memory of Shunryu Suzuki, this volume is dedicated to Tibetan Buddhist Chogyam Trungpa—the two gurus as we recall described in the poem "Tassajara." *Seminary Poems* developed from a three-month period of meditation and study which Di Prima spent at the Rocky Mountain Dharma Center in summer, 1988, and chronicles her deepening interests in Vajrayana Buddhism and in Trungpa's "crazy wisdom" philosophy which posits that as we keep asking spiritual questions, "we go deeper and deeper and deeper and deeper, until we reach the point where there is no answer . . . . This hopelessness is the essence of crazy wisdom."[32] The text is enriched with a Buddhist glossary included as appendix which defines terms such as *gomden*—a Tibetan mediation cushion; *lohan* [also spelled *luohan*], a Chinese practitioner who has become an *arhat*—a "perfected person"—in Hinayana Buddhism; *madyamika* which posits that neither the mind nor the world are either real or unreal; *yogacarin*—the "mind only" school of Buddhism. Di Prima pointed out that in

> Tibetan Buddhism, there is relative truth and absolute truth. Relative truth is about here, where we are, daily life, and the appearance of things. Absolute truth is about the emptiness (which isn't empty) and the constant

creative principle in that, which they call the dharmakaya. They fit comfortably together. In the same way, Tibetan Buddhism fits comfortably with my Paganism and other kinds of ritual magic. (I'm not talking about Judaic Kabbalism; I'm talking about Kabbalistic magic which grew out of the Renaissance, transmitted by Cornelius Agrippa and others). It's a seamless fit with no problems. So I have my Tibetan Buddhist practice, but if my daughter has a question, I will go to the Tarot cards.[33]

We may observe here how, by the early 1990s, Di Prima had continued the process of integrating Tibetan Buddhist practice with her studies in Renaissance magic—Paracelsus, Dee, Agrippa, and Bruno—with her knowledge of the Tarot. She did not find these traditions mutually exclusive, rather they enriched one another, continuing to provide a fecundating source of inspiration for her poetry.

The serious content of *Seminary Poems* does not prevent Di Prima from displaying her typical humor, for an opening "Swallow Sequence" reveals that a nest of birds had been removed by students from the shrine tent. Now they are wondering what to tell to the lohans: "when their new eggs hatch/ these swallows will teach their young/that Buddhists, like all humans/are not to be trusted." Addressing a bee which has flown into her quarters, she offers a koan-like apercu: "got in & now it's not so easy/to get out, huh, Bee?/Same for you as for me." The greatest philosophical question of all is transformed into a quick perception of the shared status of all sentient beings: no one gets out of here alive. In "Letter to Sheppard," another insect punctures humanity's spiritual pretensions: "Black moth walks on/*A Direct Path/to Enlightenment*/falls asleep on the slogan /'Don't act with a twist.'/ Cars pass on the dirt road." While in "Dawn Sequence," Di Prima notes:

birds
& alarm clocks
chirp
as the sun comes up

I pick my way thru the wildflowers
down the trail to the outhouse
farting all the way

like lemmings or monarch butterflies we gather
at the shrine tent
in the morning light

No matter the ambitions of earnest religious seekers, the fragile, funny human body announces its intransigent earth-bound facticity, compelling us to accept the essential humor and absurdity of our odd situation: on the one hand we reach for the stars; on the other we emit foul odors. As in the puzzling stories of Jorge Luis Borges, we are all caught in the labyrinth: or, as one of Chogyam Trungpa's clever koan-like apothegms has it: "The bad news is you're falling through the air, nothing to hang on, no parachute. The good news is, there's no ground." Trungpa died on April 4, 1987, and in her *Notebooks*, Di Prima memorialized the event by including a photograph of Trungpa and quoting his final will: "Born a monk, died a king/Such a thunderstorm does not stop./We will be haunting you along with the dralas./ Jolly good luck!"[34] *Dralas* are elements of the world—earth, air, water, fire for example—which reveal themselves to us their hidden meaning in epiphanic moments of awareness, an experience Trungpa believed we all commonly experience in childhood but lose as we become "mature adults."

Another work which emerged from Di Prima's spiritual and professional duties during this phase is *The Ones I Used to Laugh With: A Haibun Journal, April–May 1992*. These poems developed from an assignment she gave to her writing class in which they were instructed to compose a prose journal containing brief perceptions in the Japanese *haibun* style, a term first employed by the poet Matsuo Basho (1644–94) to describe a literary genre combining prose and haiku. Prima devoted her own haibun journal to her "relationship to poetry and creativity during that time."[35] The sequence begins on a melancholy note as she observes illnesses and deaths of friends, following haibun form through juxtaposition of prose and short verses. Four lines of prose describe how while writing the journal she learns of the departure of dear ones, then we shift to three verses: "Will they remove your lung?/I reach for the phone, my friend/Not knowing what news to hope for."[36]

Di Prima struggles to clear her desk to find time for composing poetry. In contemplating her partner Sheppard sleeping, she notices "his dharma text clasped to his heart," and then in the verse section elucidates: "The lojong slogans/clasped to your heart, you sleep/without thought of struggle/ Buddha shrine and magic altar glow/in the silent room."[37] The *lojong*—or in Tibetan *blo sbyong*—are a series of apothegms from twelfth-century Tibet designed to help people abandon selfishness and develop compassion for others.[38] Giuseppe Tucci remarks that

> the teaching aimed in the first place at the purification of the mind (blo sbyong), at the realization of the ethical and esoteric principles of Buddhism. Much less time was devoted to Buddhism's highly-developed theoretical side. Essentially this instruction was limited to leading the disciple to a better understanding of his own mind and to achievement of insight into "voidness" as the limiting state of things (mthar thug), together with compassion.

She perhaps envies her partner's ability not to be troubled by the compulsion to make art, and also may wonder whether an artist's life involves a degree of selfishness. Indeed, the function of the *blo sbyong* mind training exercises is "to transform the concept of self (atmagraha), characterized as a self-cherishing attitude into cherishing others, by contemplating the illusory nature of the self, the faults in self-cherishing, and the benefits that flow from cherishing others."[39] Now, instead of working on the poetry she "longs" to write, Di Prima turns her attention to composing an essay for a magazine on the Lughnasa—a Gaelic festival which marks the commencement of harvest. This ritual held a particular interest for Di Prima since Lughnasa—when the god Lug entered into a marriage with the earth goddess—is celebrated in Celtic neopaganism usually from July 31 to August 1. In Ireland, according to T. G. E. Powell in *The Celts*, "the centre of devotion at Lugnasad was not, apparently, the god himself [Lug], but the nature goddess, whether as Tailltu, in whose honour he was reputed to have founded the festival, or as Macha, who was entreated in Ulster at this time." Di Prima again shifts to verse: "the grey stones standing/ in green fields/boisterous with color" evoking·a medieval holiday gathering of people with flocks, "gentry and nobles, commoners and kings."[40] A few poems later reporting on a Van Morrison concert in Berkeley, she declares the singer "carries the tradition of the Celtic bard into this time, this place," and finally returns to this neopagan theme in *Loba* in "Point of Ripening: Lughnasa," where Di Prima hymns the "rich time when the harvest/is not for yourself/You no longer need/ to claim it."[41]

Astrology enters the poem when a meeting with a new friend who is an astrologer encourages her with news that she should "Let it explode/like the stars/these next five months"—her "current transit" has given her "license to go for it," the stars are now in alignment predicting a fecund creative phase.[42] Going to the theatre, seeing gifted dancers and witnessing moving music by the Bulgarian Women's Choir also reignite her desire "to return to this state of passion in the daily practice of poetry."[43] The men accompanying the choir play flute and bagpipes, reminding Di Prima of the "Land of Dionysus and/I nearly saw the hooves/on these short and randy men."[44] Di Prima's youthful dedication to the art of dance is reawakened. But it is the "egolessness" and "transparency" as well as "the trust between the women, the way they touched" which strike her so forcibly. She acknowledges that "I manage to write/but do I open my heart?" She beholds the Bulgarian women "Taking hands in a trio/or standing shoulder to shoulder—/how they cherish each other!"[45] The word "cherish" here is noteworthy, for as we saw above it is precisely this term which is employed in the Tibetan *blo sbyong* exercises emphasizing the "faults in self-cherishing, and the benefits that flow from cherishing others." We now return to our opening creative aporia as Di Prima clears her desk, sorts her letters, and prepares to compose, but the summer days are "dark as winter" and she closes with a verse tercet: "Do I have the heart for them/in the summer fog—/these stacks of dusty poems?"[46] Thus in a twelve-page sequence, we have traversed a condensed psychological territory: while undergoing a period of creative self-doubt, she finds both expression and release finally in giving voice to the experience itself and affirming it within the context of her larger spiritual quest. Mid-career during the 1980s and early 1990s, Di Prima continued to develop her unique genre of visionary poetics anchored in esoteric and philosophical studies. As we shall see in the following chapter, she has devoted her formidable energies in her final phase to extending and deepening the impressive reaches of her creative imagination.

6

Speech of the Heart:

Poet Laureate of San Francisco, 1993 to the present

Di Prima's final phase has been one of the most productive of her career: continuing to evolve and innovate, she has experimented with new genres of poetry and created several significant prose works. During the 1990s, she was engaged in two major projects: completing the second book of *Loba* published in 1998, and developing the autobiographical *Recollections of My Life as a Woman* (2001) which explores the first part of her life, with a promised sequel to follow. She studied with Lama Tharchin Rinpoche (1936–2013), a *Dzogchen*—"Great Perfection"—master of Vajrayana Buddhism, continued to do her painting, was named Poet Laureate of San Francisco in 2009, and the following year made a trip to Gloucester to honor Charles Olson on his 100th anniversary. She also lost several friends during this period, including the artist Ray Johnson (1927–95), Allen Ginsberg and William S. Burroughs in 1997, as well as Philip Whalen in 2002. I conclude with a discussion of *The Poetry Deal* (2014) and her failing health, which has limited her mobility in recent years. She however has continued to write prolifically and still has a significant number of unpublished books—she listed fourteen as of 2010—and incomplete manuscripts.

One unpublished text which Di Prima composed during this period—*Not Quite Buffalo Stew*—is a rollicking, surreal *jeu d'esprit*, a comic novella regarding a male drug smuggler named Lynx. Divided into fifteen chapters and set in San Francisco and Northern California, Chapter One opens: "The corner of Grandview and Buena Vista has the longest stoplight in Alameda. I was sitting there in the rain when I fell in love with this vegetarian witch from Oakland. She was half Nigerian and half Chinese and it turned out her

name was Dorothea." Rather like Dorothy in *The Wizard of Oz*, Dorothea
and Lynx embark on a psychedelic tour of the dreamlike landscape of the
archetypal unconscious. Di Prima allows her fantastic, witty imagination
full reign as a sequence of magical events ensue: the witch is somehow able
to enter Lynx's locked car door and when they get caught in traffic, a hang
glider from the Sierra Club arrives, plays his alto recorder, and all the cars
suddenly are thrown into reverse gear, thus escaping the congestion. The
text is packed with recherché allusions: Dorothea owns a manx cat named
"Nostradamus" as well as a macaque "Heraclitus" who has completed
"three linked Trees of Life" by "rearranging dead flies on a piece of flypaper."
Heraclitus is now working on a fourth Tree of Life and "Assiah is going to
be a little short"—Assiah is the last of the four spiritual worlds in Kabbalah:
Atziluth, Briah, and Yetzirah. Dorothea also wants to show Lynx the
"sylphs"—which originate in Paracelsus's idea of invisible beings of the air,
but complains that all she gets "are these ragged elementals": in Paracelsus,
the elementals in addition to Sylph/Air, are Gnomes/Earth; Salamander/Fire;
Undines/Water. In Chapter Three, Lynx and Dorothea race along the freeway
among allusions to the *Shiva Purana*—dedicated to Shiva and one of the
eighteen Hindu *Purana*—while Dorothea fires off memorable apothegms
such as: "Christ was the ultimate pagan . . . but that's tired news. A Celtic
Shiva will say what I'm trying to say." There are references to Gary Snyder,
Lew Welch, Michael McClure, Ernest Hemingway, Bob Dylan, and Frank
Herbert's novel *Dune*. Lynx confesses in Chapter Ten that he "married Isis"
and Chapter Eleven alludes to "the Ray of the Aeon" which derives from
Aleister Crowley—the First Aeon in Crowley's historical genealogy is of Isis
and the maternal, where the female aspect of the Godhead was revered.

We swiftly become aware that *Not Quite Buffalo Stew* has no plot: the
novella moves comically from one seemingly drug-induced hallucination to
the next—marijuana, hashish, THC—and at the close of Chapter Six: "The
stained glass window showed a cobra with peyote buttons for eyes. It was
holding out its hands to some fish with human faces. It was a cool design."
Chapter Twelve closes with a cryptic statement by Dorothea: "It is the moon
of the Worm . . . Moon of the Laidly Worm." This alludes to the Laidly
Worm of Spindleton Heugh, a Northumbrian ballad about a princess who
changed into a dragon. Chapter Thirteen depicts Dorothea with her son
Aristotle who needs help with his homework and turns to Tiriel—"Tiriel"
(1789) is a narrative poem by William Blake and is also associated with the
planet Mercury in Heinrich Cornelius Agrippa's *De Occulta Philosophia*—
to help him with his differential equations. In Chapter Fourteen, Lynx
enters a commune where there is a heated debate over whether the Velcro
on a Nike tennis shoe is reason enough to not allow the shoe entrance to
the commune. In the final Chapter Fifteen entitled "In Which Lynx Seeks
Enlightenment in the Sonoran Desert," amid talk of the Lower Astral
level, Lynx is told by "the Great Mentor in the sky" that "THIS IS YOUR

LAST CHANCE TO GET IT"—to understand the mystery at the heart of the novella. Yet Lynx and reader remain unenlightened as both text and philosophical quest end simultaneously: "The whole scene folded in two like a book being shut." *Not Quite Buffalo Stew* is a humorous send-up of the detective story genre, revolving around answering life's existential questions. Di Prima has composed an entertaining bagatelle in which many of the themes of her life's work are lightly handled—it is in fact a kind of disguised autobiography—and in which she again demonstrates how she can skate on the surface while revealing hidden depths.

In 1992, seventeen writers including Kathy Acker, Jack Hirschman, and Di Prima inaugurated "Wordland" where poetry as well as hip-hop were performed at the Women's Building in San Francisco, attracting hundreds of people at each reading. In 1993, Di Prima received an Award for Lifetime Achievement in Poetry from the National Poetry Association and the following year spoke at The Poetry Project at St. Mark's Church in New York, meeting again with Ted Joans.

She also contracted with Viking Press to write her autobiography. As we have seen, she had been publishing sections of this ongoing project in *Mama Bear News and Notes*—some of the material which appeared there was not included in the final version—and now devoted herself to shaping a first draft of what would become *Recollections of My Life as a Woman*. Confronting her past at times proved challenging, and her brother and her mother's younger sister were angry about the fact that Di Prima was revealing the hidden story of the Di Prima family. In Italian American culture, *omerta*—or silence—was expected of women, thus in opening up her private familial

FIGURE 6.1 *Diane di Prima and Ted Joans, The Poetry Project, St. Mark's Church, 1994. Photograph by Allen Ginsberg, © Allen Ginsberg Estate.*

anguish she was exposing herself to shame. Di Prima confessed that "along the way I did some therapy, especially when I felt I was breaking taboos or sharing family secrets."[1] She also continued working on *Loba*, completing Book II containing eight new sections: along with Book I, this added up to a total of 205 poems. While Book I was enriched by Gnostic, Greek, Hebrew, and Christian sources, Book II contains fresh material spanning a variety of traditions: Tibetan Buddhist as we have seen in the last chapter with "Tsogyal," Mesopotamia, the Indian goddess Kali, as well as Thoth/Tahuti from ancient Egypt.

The Sumerian goddess of fertility, love, and warfare is depicted in "Inanna: The Epiphany": "Before the first days, when no one numbered the moons/ Before the first nights, when no one named the hills/When no one mapped the rivers, or set sail on the seas/From the steppes she came/From the place of tall grass she came." Di Prima evokes a prelapsarian goddess-centered cosmos, a time before language and before humanity put names to things or mapped bodies of water: Nature as yet "undomesticated." Inanna's—known as Ishtar in Akkadian—warlike powers are emphasized as she rides a lion, carrying a sword and arrows. The lion is typically an emblem of thunder gods and Inanna's chariot is conventionally shown being drawn by seven lions, Inanna rides a lion, or is herself depicted as a lion. In the following poem "Theology Becomes the Body Politic," Di Prima asserts: "The King is expendable, but not the Queen/The King of Sumer is expendable, but not/the Queen of Heaven."[2] Judith Ochshorn has argued in *The Female Experience and the Nature of the Divine* that

> the warlike attributes of fertility goddesses were neither merely symbolic nor used as a literary device to further the action in myths, but were seen as very real and terrible. For instance, *The Exaltation of Inanna* is one of the earliest extant Accadian hymns from the end of the third millennium, part of a great cycle of hymns to the temples of Sumer and Accad and an important contribution to Mesopotamian theology . . . the hymn seems to imply the elevation of Inanna to equal rank with An, son of Nammu, the earliest and most potent god of the sky.

Inanna became a significant figure in magical circles and the evolution of the idea of goddess worship for she is yet another incarnation of the Persephone myth. As we saw earlier with the mysteries of Eleusis which celebrate Demeter as the bringer of grain, so too Inanna is a fertility goddess who descends into the underworld where Erishkigal—queen of the "Great Below"—is informed by the Netherworld's gatekeeper that she is seeking admission.

One of the students in Di Prima's "Literature of the Hidden Religions of Europe" course—Betty de Shong Meador—acknowledged Di Prima as a teacher who "gave dimension to the underground strand of a female-oriented spirituality." Meador would ultimately make a translation of the writings of Enheduanna (ca. twenty-third century BCE), a daughter of Sargon of Akkad and High Priestess of the Sumerian moon god Nanna, published as *Innana, Lady of Largest Heart: Poems of the Sumerian High Priestess*. Di Prima seeks to restore the goddess to the central position she occupied during Mesopotamian times before being dethroned in Hebrew and Christian myth by the patriarchal male God. C. G. Jung in his 1940 Eranos lecture "On the Psychology of the Concept of the Trinity" pointed out the banishment of the feminine from Christian representations of divinity. However, both esoteric Christianity and Gnostic doctrines sought to reintegrate the feminine—in the form of Sophia or Divine Wisdom—into a more democratic, inclusive conception of God.[3] Di Prima remembered her grandmother Antoinette's Catholicism as Mediterranean in its tolerant good humor. When her grandmother's Italian friends reported some fleshly transgression, Antoinette would tell them that since the Virgin Mary was a woman, she would deliver an appropriate explanation to God concerning the matter. From this, Di Prima concluded that the male God was lacking a sense of perspective, an essential wisdom which the female version possessed. Di Prima thus makes a distinction between an embracing, life-affirming vision of human life and the restrictive, punitive, and ultimately destructive forms of theology promulgated by the patriarchal tradition.

Di Prima not only adduces historical evidence for the power of women, she also includes the realities of women suffering in the modern world. In "Part 6: The Seven Joys of the Virgin," Di Prima reimagines the birth of Christ and brings autobiographical elements into the third poem of the sequence—"Nativity"—which follows "Annunciation" and "Visitation: Elizabeth and Mary." "Nativity" begins with a stark description of Di Prima's own experience of childbirth when she gave birth to Jeanne. The first section begins:

> Dark timbers of lost forests falling into my bed.
> My hairs stirring, not asleep. Did they fetter me
> With cat's paw, rock root, the beard
> (of shame) of woman? They fettered me
> w/leather straps, on delivery table. I cd not
> cry out. Forced gas mask over mouth,
> slave. I cd not
> turn head. Did they fetter me
> w/breath of a fish? These poison airs? I cd not
> turn head, move hand, or leg
> thus forced. They tore child from me. Whose?

The clue to deciphering this passage lies in Di Prima's autobiography, *Recollections of My Life as a Woman* where she recalls her experiences at the hospital which ministered to the poor of New York City, the Gouverneur. There she describes the scenes of mayhem: the shrieking and groaning of women about to give birth under severely straitened circumstances. Di Prima expressly asked not to be given painkillers so she could experience a natural childbirth, however the nurses strapped her to the table against her will, forcing a gas mask over her face which rendered her unconscious. Thus she memorialized this moment of "slavery" to demonstrate the oppressed status of women, even in twentieth-century America. She repeats "I cd not/ turn head" twice to indicate her trapped helplessness.

Just as Di Prima depicts the history of oppression of women and their physical and psychological vulnerability, we also encounter woman in her warrior role—as we have seen with Inanna—and in the final poem of Part One as Shiva: "the Loba/dances, she/treads the/salty earth, she/does not/ raise/breath cloud heavenward/her breath/itself/is carnage."[4] Shiva—whom as we have seen in Chapter Three with her poem "Hymn to Lord Shiva" Di Prima began to incorporate into her devotional life in the mid-1960s—also appears in the first poem of Book Two, Part Fifteen—"Kali-Ma"—which contains adaptations by Di Prima of songs by Ramprasad Sen (ca. 1718–75), Shakta saint and poet who composed tributes to Kali in Bengali: "Because you love the burning grounds/I have made a burning ground of my heart, O Kali,/That you, Beloved, may dance there unceasingly . . . O Mother, who dances on Lord Shiva's corpse,/Come, swaying to the sound of drums,/Enter my heart's ash:/I await you with closed eyes." The verses when recited aloud mimic the movement of the dance in their artful repetitions—"burning grounds/burning ground"—and the answering rhyme of the drumbeat "sound" with "ground." Kali—the Hindu goddess of Shakti or empowerment is a popular Beat subject: Allen Ginsberg devotes several passages to her in his *Indian Journals*; William S. Burroughs and Gary Snyder allude to her, while Philip Whalen in his poem "Souffle" (1957) memorably invokes her: "I believe/in Kali the Black, the horrific aspect/the total power of Siva/ absolute destruction." Kali is often depicted in iconography dancing on top of Shiva her husband, who lies prostrate upon the ground. There are clues in Di Prima's earlier poetry such as "Poem to a Statue of Shiva in the Garments of Kali" that Di Prima was beginning to confront Woman as Power, for the poem opens: "O there is evil in you as well as good/You sitting on my altar table/Showing your teeth," and goes on to invoke "O Durga Shiva." Durga is the Hindu warrior goddess associated with Shiva as his wife, capable of employing anger and violence to combat injustice: in depictions of Durga, each of her many arms bears a weapon. Di Prima has commented that during Zen practice she "actually experienced the true sense of my core feralness": this devouring side of Kali/the female is a complementary aspect of plenitude and creativity just as in Jungian psychology the Shadow (or "negative" aspects of the Self) is connected inextricably with our "positive" characteristics.[5]

Several of the Beats—including Philip Lamantia, Gregory Corso, and William Burroughs—studied the hieroglyphics, architecture, and mythology of ancient Egypt. Di Prima continues this tradition in Book II of *Loba* where she devotes poems to Tahuti—Thoth—the Egyptian god of writing whom she portrays as a secret lover of Isis.[6] Divided into eight sections, Di Prima describes Isis restoring the dead Osiris through the help of Tahuti/Thoth who is depicted as a Magus and Healer: "His incantations help her conceive the dead man's child, and later revive the infant Horus after his death in the swamp."[7] Tahuti/Thoth in section five appears "in headdress/or bird's head (mask)/Ibis/or man./Smith, beater of runes/into metal./Hence, scribe./My lord./He Who Walks/staff in hand/who chants/ the umanifest to Light." It is Tahuti who "makes Black Isis shine."[8] Again, we have a reconceptualization of myth—this time Egyptian—in which Di Prima reimagines the male energy of Tahuti/Thoth performing a mid-wife-like role as both "support" and *daimon*: this word is emphasized to suggest the male spirit as both Muse and creative helper of Isis.[9] One may also interpret this relationship as a reformulation of the horned god in Celtic mythology whose role is to serve as consort to the Goddess which as we have seen is a theme in witchcraft lore invoked by Di Prima's in *The Calculus of Variation*. Estella Lauter observed that "the Loba is a shapeshifter" for she takes the form of Eve, Mary, Helen, Guinevere, Lilith, and Tahuti/Thoth as well. The critical reception of the poem was positive and Lauter admires *Loba*, arguing however that it "badly needs the kind of cutting and shaping that Pound gave to Eliot's *The Waste Land*, and even then it would take longer to work its way into the culture than Eliot's work did. Yet at moments it is as moving as anything Eliot wrote. It simply requires a willingness to step outside the myth we have adopted about the linear progression of intelligent life, category by category. Di Prima's great triumph is to have created images that transcend categories of both wolf and woman."[10] Indeed, as we have seen in Di Prima's survey of the evolution of culture, she also proposes in *Loba* an alternative model for interpreting the meaning and shape of human history and woman's central role in creating a rich spiritual imagination.

Di Prima had always employed autobiographical elements in her work— *Memoirs of a Beatnik* (1969) being the most obvious (and largely fictional) example—and she now turned to a fuller exploration in *Recollections of My Life as A Woman* (2001). There was some struggle with her editor who Di Prima claimed tried to transform her "vernacular" into "standard" English.[11] She sought to preserve her purposely Brooklyn style inflected by her Italian American speech patterns—so she felt compelled to revise the manuscript again to shape the text back into accordance with her original intentions.[12] Di Prima's continuing awareness of her heritage may also be seen in her responses to fellow Italian American as well as Italian poets. In her "Afterword" to *Where I Come From: Selected and New Poems* (1995) by Maria Mazziotti Gillan, Di Prima comments upon the details marking the immigrant experience in America: "Where Maria Mazziotti Gillan 'comes from' is clearly imaged here: the fig tree, the basement kitchen, the ghetto streets of Paterson, the special espresso service with its tiny silver spoons, her father's demeaning jobs, the sacred tenacity of her people— their ways of being and of being together." And Di Prima also composed an "Introduction" (2001) to *The Seasons* by Italian writer Giuseppe Conte (1945–) whom she praises as a musical poet rooted in the Mediterranean's mythological traditions: "Because he does not seek poetry for his own ends, his relation to the world—to sea and sky, to gods and humans—is pristine and his voice is untrammeled. It is pure Song that we find on these pages, as it was in Sumer, and in Greece, and Provence, and will be again in the times to come."[13] As we have seen, Di Prima emphasized the ways the culture of Italy had dominated her childhood: its language, anarchist traditions, and especially literature—for example Giordano Bruno and Dante—which were fed to her as essential aesthetic and philosophical nourishment by her grandfather Domenico. During her time in New York in the 1950s, she also studied Ovid and Virgil and later produced a translation, *Medieval Latin Love Poems*. Italy and Greece—the world of bright sunlight, the intense pleasure taken in the senses, a pagan celebration of the joys of this world, as well as a tragic awareness of their inevitable evanescence—we can see these themes throughout Di Prima's work.

In an important lecture Di Prima delivered on November 11, 1994, at the annual meeting of the American Italian Historical Association— subsequently published as "Don't Solidify the Adversary! A Response to Rudolph Vecoli"—she pondered the meaning of being Italian American: her lecture was in response to Vecoli's paper "Are Italian Americans Just White Folks?" Here she revisits several episodes from her past regarding her Italian identity which she also considers in *Recollections of My Life as A Woman*. Di Prima observes:

> Although I am in no way a Marxist, nor even a political theorist, I need to say, to point out that when it was convenient for the ruling class to have Italian/Americans be an underclass (field hands, factory workers) that's what we were. At those times we were seen as black, or close to it. And now it's convenient to subsume at least some of us into the so-called "professional" classes, and all of us into the "white" category— even though to this day we are not truly seen or treated as white—we are excluded from the "multicultural" category and its accompanying "perks," as Mr. Gambini has just called them.

Di Prima goes on to reveal that when asked to check the box to indicate what "race" you are, she for years checked the "Other" box or would write in "Sicilian" in the blank space and "leave it for them to figure out themselves." Growing up, her parents "were not at all sure about the value of *italianita*." Because women at that time stayed at home, the stories she heard of discrimination were those told by her uncles and father. Yet Di Prima points out that it was also the Italian Americans themselves who were willing and eager to jettison their language, cuisine, and music—their cultural "identity"—in order to enter "the mainstream." Di Prima counsels that in order to preserve "Italian culture" for the next generation, there must be critical scrutiny of what is valuable and what is destructive in that culture. She cites the "patriarchy, sexual repression, and infinite amounts of dysfunction" in her own family and the "keeping of secrets." She also brings up the then recent 1991 case concerning Supreme Court nominee Clarence Thomas's sexual harassment of Anita Hill. Di Prima observes that in the Bay Area, "a large part of the African American community—the men, in particular, and among them some famous and honored writers—stated forcefully and frequently, that Ms. Hill had no business saying anything against a man of her own race, giving weapons, as it were, to the 'enemy.'" However, Di Prima points out that this attitude has kept minority communities in silence over abuse for too long, and she states in italics: "BUT—*the time has come when each and every ethnicity has got to name its demons if we are to come to any understanding at all*." She ends by suggesting the necessity to preserve what is good and the "old ways that nurture us as a people," but also asks if it is possible to let go of the "old habits and patterns that stand in our way, and in the way of further communication with others?" Di Prima wants to avoid both "assimilation" and "fossilization": "Neither oppressor nor oppressed; not Other, not We-Are-All-One. Just an easy and flexible *difference*, love of our traditions and pasts as we move forward against all odds toward whatever awaits us."

These themes regarding the Italian American community during Di Prima's childhood as well as her struggles within an American WASP culture also are treated in her autobiography *Recollections of My Life as A Woman* which chronicles the years from her birth in 1934 to the beginnings of her sojourns in California in the early to mid-1960s. The title alerts us to a complex yet playful sense of identity: her life "as a woman"—implying perhaps that being a woman is just one of the many roles she has played in the quest for selfhood. In her early sixties during the composition of the book, Di Prima was able to reflect with some perspective on her formative years and well as the Beat and hippie periods to fathom both their personal and cultural significance. Divided into twenty-one chapters with an "Afterword," Di Prima in the acknowledgments pays homage to one of the significant *gurus* of her later years, Lama Tharchin Rinpoche. The narrative takes us on a thirty-one-year-long spiritual journey, from her grandparents the Mallozzis to 1965 when she moved to Monroe, New York, to stay at Rammurti Mishra's Ananda Ashram. The opening pages are replete with references to *light* as Di Prima evokes the atmosphere of grandmother Antoinette's home:

> It was a house of dark and mellow light, almost as if there were fire and kerosene lamps, but to my recollection there was electric light, the same as everywhere else. It is just that the rooms were so very dark, light filtering as it did through papers shades and lace curtains. . . . The light fell as if on old oil paintings. . . . The light fell on my grandmother's hands as she sat rocking, saying her rosary.

In these evocations of her closeness to Antoinette, Di Prima recalls the hypnotic style of James Joyce's romantic story from *Dubliners*, "Araby," in which a similar pattern of light imagery is employed in Joyce's descriptions of the loved girl: "The light from the lamp opposite our door caught the white curve of her neck, lit up her hair that rested there and, falling, lit up the hand upon the railing." In narrating the relationship between her atheist grandfather Domenico and Antoinette who was a devout Catholic, Di Prima turns to the *I Ching* to describe how her grandfather reacted to his wife's religiosity: "As for him, he never seemed to inquire. Though those clear blue eyes saw everywhere. The *I Ching* has the phrase: 'He let many things pass without being duped.'" An allusion to *Hexagram 36*, "Ming I/Darkening of the Light," Di Prima has quite intentionally selected this passage for it contains imagery which also counterpoints light with darkness, ending with the phrase Di Prima cited:

> In a time of darkness it is essential to be cautious and reserved. One should not needlessly awaken overwhelming enmity by inconsiderate behavior. In such times one ought not to fall in with the practices of others; neither should one drag them censoriously into the light. In social intercourse one should not try to be all-knowing. One should let many things pass, without being duped.

One is struck by Di Prima's deep familiarity with the *I Ching*, with which as we have seen, she first became acquainted in the early 1950s. She thus by the time of composing *Recollections* had established a familiarity with the text of close to a half-century. It is clear that she knew the *I Ching* intimately enough to be able to effortlessly invoke passages from the text in relationship to aspects of her personal life which she wished to emphasize.

Di Prima breaks up the flow of her chronological narrative to record dreams she has experienced in the present. For example, she recounts a dream from autumn, 1987, in which she finds herself in an ancient Sicilian church which reminds her of a mosque, a stone structure replete with vivid golden, green, and red satin and brocaded cloths. The vision recounts the death of her Uncle Joe and she hears melismatic Arabic funeral music which makes her curious concerning her own possible roots in Arab culture. This passage is revelatory since at various moments throughout her work, Di Prima drops hints about the possibility of Arab ancestry in her family: indeed Arabs invaded Sicily in 827 CE and conquered Palermo in 831 CE which they made their capital. As we shall see, Di Prima would soon compose a poem entitled "Awkward Song on the Eve of War" about the US invasion of Iraq in which she identifies with the sufferings of Arabic people, announcing "The center of my heart is Arab song./It is woven around my heartstrings." Di Prima has commented that "it's in the culture, and I think it's very close in Sicily to Middle Eastern song. To melody lines in Middle Eastern music. It's influenced me a lot." Di Prima also purposely kept the structure of *Recollections of My Life as a Woman* faithful to the process of remembering events as they occurred to her in the act of composition, switching between her earlier life in New York and later move to California:

> I trust where my mind goes, so that if I'm writing about 1937 and my grandparents, and then I remember my mother when she came out here in 1983 and what she said to me at the conservatory, that's where it goes, because there is a shape that the mind has already woven of all this material, and part of what I was trying to do in the book was lay out the actual process of remembering.[14]

For example, in the final chapter she also moves from her narrative of events in August of 1965 to an italicized passage regarding events three decades later: "*Now it is August, 1995, and we are moving again. I am sorting out things for the bookstores, things for storage. Things for the Poetry Archive, maybe, at SF State. Things for the free box, for the Mother Teresa nuns. For the Community Thrift Shop, the Friends of the Library. The Street. My friend Laura's attic. Butterfield's auction block.*"[15] This gives the book the feel of a contemporary document telling of prior events, but not privileging the past.

This passage also illustrates the deft way Di Prima juxtaposes the quotidian with broader political—here donating to the poor and to "the Mother Teresa nuns"—and philosophical questions. For example, in a central passage in Chapter Nineteen she again strives to elucidate several countercultural themes. Her approach is to understand the "mythic" or "archetypal" meaning of these historical phases and she also expounds another version of the metaphysics of light, for she tells us that she conceptualized her spiritual quest as involving immanent supernatural forces "dancing with light" which shape human lives.[16] The *I Ching*, the study of magic, the awesome mystery of the universe which cannot be controlled or "rationally understood" but only experienced—were defining aspects or her generation's conception of reality. There is a sense of surrender here, but not fatalism. Like the Yoruba people of Africa whose supreme deity was *Orisha* or the concept of the

Yidam—the manifestation of Buddhahood or enlightened mind in Tantric Vajrayana—the postwar generation who wanted to find a greater meaning to life and "had replaced religion, family, society, ethics with Beauty" were in a sense the playthings of historical forces greater than themselves. Perhaps this is the significance of the "dawning of the Age of Aquarius": the historical cycle which W. B. Yeats's described in "The Second Coming" was coming to an end—"And what rough beast, its hour come round at last, /Slouches towards Bethlehem to be born?"—and a new era beginning. This imaginative quest for love and beauty also echoes a famous saying of John Keats—from a letter to Benjamin Bailey, November 22, 1817—which Di Prima frequently quoted: "I am certain of nothing but the holiness of the Heart's affections and the truth of the imagination." This unyielding dedication to the artistic and spiritual life would lead to the "downfall," to employ Di Prima's term, of some of her compatriots—Freddie Herko for example—and it is evident that one function of *Recollections of My Life as A Woman* is an attempt to fathom the cosmic forces underlying the post–Second World War American counterculture.

Several figures in the artistic and literary worlds with whom Di Prima had been friends passed on during this period. The collagist and correspondence artist Ray Johnson whose work appeared on the cover of *The Floating Bear* #36 and whose career has recently been undergoing a critical reevaluation committed suicide at the age of sixty-seven and was memorialized in Di Prima's poem "To Ray Johnson." One of Di Prima's closest friends over four decades—Allen Ginsberg—died in May 1997. As we have seen, she had rendered him homage in *Memoirs of a Beatnik* where she praised the central importance of *Howl* in awakening her to the existence of fellow seekers in a nascent American counterculture and in *Loba* she included a few verses clearly inspired by Ginsberg. The lines are intended as affectionate, humorous parody both of the subject matter and style of *Howl*, featuring Di Prima's clever imitation of Ginsberg's anaphora in his repetition of "who": "who walked across America behind gaunt violent yogis/& died o-d'ing in methadone jail/scarfing the evidence . . . who left tapestries, evidence, baby bottle behind in Vancouver/& hitched to Seattle for the mushroom season/trailing welfare checks & stolen money orders/Chicago gangster in earrings who minded the baby." In her memorial essay, she recalled their initial meeting in 1957, as well as a later encounter in the early 1960s after Ginsberg had returned from India wearing a new beard

> and many tales of his encounters with gurus. I was then presiding over a domain that included a husband and three children, a theater and innumerable writing projects. Allen was frequently in and out of my house in those days, asking forthright questions as I chased a baby down the hall (How was my sex life?) or settling in for the evening to lead us all in a *satsang*. It was a time when we, all of us, cared about mantras.

Satsang is a gathering together of spiritual students with their guru, and Di Prima affectionately recalls both her friendship with Ginsberg and his immersion in Eastern wisdom. She also spent time with her friend Philip Whalen, dining with him as well as Michael McClure regularly at a favorite Japanese restaurant in San Francisco. As Whalen's health declined, Di Prima began meeting him at the Hartford Zen Center: when he died in 2002, Di Prima felt she had lost a dear compatriot. She also took time in several poems composed during this period to pay her respects to friends lost to the AIDS epidemic including "A Farewell Rite" to former lover Peter Hartman: "you can put down your drugs now/put down/your fierce lust/only the Light Body travels/east wind/blowing you west toward the dark/put down your fine wines/your cymbals from Sikkim/Light Body rises like mist/from your swollen corpse."[17] In Dzogchen, this is the *jalus* or "rainbow body": at the time of death the adept's physical body dissolves into light. She worked on a manuscript entitled *Death Poems for All Seasons* which developed from a workshop—"The Poetics of Loss"—she had conducted across the country. Di Prima declared she "started it because of the AIDS epidemic. I'm doing it because I feel that people need to be able to talk about not only death but loss in general. This is a country of vast denial. You've probably noticed. And we're good out here compared to New York. In New York if you even talk about the past—not even about death, just the past—they'll say why are you being so morbid. And LA's like that too."[18] If American culture denied Life, it has also denied Death: our society has attempted to make antiseptic and sterile the great ritual transitions of the life cycle and in so doing has removed us from our connection to Nature: in denying death, we deny life. Di Prima seeks to restore this unity of life and death by honoring loss as deeply as she celebrates expansive cosmic energies. It is precisely this American "denial of death" which led the counterculture to classic texts such as *The Tibetan Book of the Dead* in order to spiritualize and ritualize the soul's preparing of what D. H. Lawrence called—in one of his great poems—"the ship of death" for its journey into the afterlife.

Di Prima continued to lecture widely and to teach. On April 27, 2000, she read from her work and delivered a lecture on "Poetry as a Spiritual Practice" at Columbia College in Chicago and taught creative writing seminars in San Francisco in 2002, "Theory and Study of Poetics." In one iteration of the course, she required students to read the essays of Robert Creeley concerning line breaks and syncopation as well as *The Third Mind* by William S. Burroughs and Brion Gysin regarding random techniques of composition. She took time to celebrate the fiftieth anniversary of City Lights, giving a reading at San Francisco's celebrated book shop in 2003 and in 2004 exhibited a series of collages created from materials she kept in her appointment books at Bird and Beckett Books and Records under the title "The Moon Will Claim Me." In her "Artist's Statement" for the show, she revealed: "I have always loved the work of the Dadaists and Surrealists, and these little collages are an *homage* to those men and women." She also continued to add poems to *Revolutionary Letters* as she had with her other work-in-progress, *Loba*. "Revolutionary Letter Number Ninety-Three: Memorial Day, 2003" begins with an epigraph: "*Today is Memorial Day. Take time to remember those brave souls who gave their lives for freedom.—Dear Abby.*" Then as if in answer to "Dear Abby"—the well-known newspaper advice columnist—Di Prima begins a two-page catalogue in the spirit of her *Revolutionary Letters* naming heroes and heroines she believes *should* be honored on Memorial Day: "Remember Sacco & Vanzetti/Remember Haymarket/Remember John Brown/Remember the slave revolts/Remember Malcolm/Remember Paracelsus." In the second stanza, she becomes more hip and casual: "Hey, do you remember Hypatia?/Socrates?/Giordano Bruno?/Remember my buddy, Esclarmonde de Foix/Remember Seton the Cosmopolite/Remember Edward Kelly, alchemist murdered in prison." Hypatia (ca. 350–415), the brilliant female Alexandrian mathematician and astronomer killed by Christian zealots; de Foix (1151–1215) was a Cathar/Gnostic lady responsible for rebuilding the fortress of "heretics" at Montsegur; Alexander Seton was a Scottish alchemist, while Edward Kelley helped John Dee in his communications with angels. Di Prima thus takes over an American holiday honoring the war dead, turning it into an exhortation to live one's life fully and honor great spiritual heroes:

> Remember to take yr life back into yr hands
> It's Memorial Day, remember
> what you love
> & do it—don't wait.

So too, Di Prima wants people on Memorial Day to remember they must fight against the forces of regimentation and claim their own authentic, existential truths: rather than be *subjected*, they must through force of will transform themselves into individual *subjects*. As William Blake declared, "I must create a system, or be enslaved by another man's." Di Prima also asserts that Wounded Knee—where indigenous people met their deaths at the hands of the American invaders—and Kent State—where students were slain by bullets fired by the National Guard—should be honored on this "memorial day" and that we must rescue our lives from conformity and death-in-life by remembering "where you stand:/in the midst of empire, & the Huns/are coming/Remember Vercingetorix, Max Jacob, Apollinaire & Suhrawardi, remember/that all you need to remember is what you love/Remember to Marry the World."[19] As we have seen previously, Suhrawardi—or Sohrawardi (1154–91)—is the Persian mystic whose most eminent modern interpreter was esotericist Henry Corbin (1903–78), author of *Les motifs zoroastriens dans la philosophie de Sohrawardi* (1946), and admired by both Robert Duncan and Charles Olson. Thus Di Prima again reimagines American life in the shape of her own robust and hopeful imagination, conceives it as a place where we honor the right heroes and live our lives in such a way that we at last "marry the world."

Following September 11, 2001, and the World Trade Center attacks, the United States invaded Iraq and Afghanistan, initiating a new decade of perpetual warfare. Di Prima responded with "Revolutionary Letter Number Eighty-Eight: Notes Toward a Poem of Revolution," composed in November, two months after two planes crashed into the Twin Towers in November. The poem was published as *Towers Down/Notes Toward a Poem of Revolution* (2002) with a poem of Clive Matson by Eidolon Editions. It also appeared in the anthology *An Eye for an Eye Makes the Whole World Blind: Poets on 9/11* (2002) along with poems by Lawrence Ferlinghetti, Robert Pinsky, Daniel Berrigan, and Robert Creeley. She asks: "What did we in all honesty expect?/That fascist architecture flaunting/@ the sky/converted now to fluid/toxic/smoke, ASH/the long finger of impermanence/touches us all & nobody/can hog all the marbles & expect/the others to play." Although Americans grieve the death of more than three thousand people in the Twin Towers, she questions "how many/starve/thanks to our greed/our unappeasable/hunger." She tells of the "quivering" voice of her daughter as she watches the towers fall. In the building were not only middle-class and upper-class financiers, but also "janitors," "sandwich makers" and "toilet cleaners" who perished, and Di Prima wonders if they too will be eligible for "that/two-million-per-victim/in aid?" The struggle for freedom is an ongoing battle: she lists as historical examples the Gnostic stronghold of Montsegur, Prague, and the Haymarket uprising in Chicago on May 4, 1886, when anarchists rallied in support of labor seeking an eight-hour working day. America's aggressions have come home to roost, and we must understand the "terrorist" attack on our "homeland"—as George W. Bush might have phrased it—as representing a kind of karmic recompense or payback for our own prior transgressions. Di Prima certainly expressed the minority view in this poem: the impulse of many Americans was to swiftly inflict retributive violence.

While billions of dollars were spent on the military to "avenge" the attack on the "homeland," Hurricane Katrina from August 23 to August 31, 2005, battered New Orleans and the Louisiana coast, killing at least 1,245 people. This tragedy formed the background of *TimeBomb* (2006) bearing a dedication "for the bayou" and published in a small run of 100 copies by Di Prima's Eidolon Editions. As with the genesis of many of her poems, an insistent voice began speaking to her unconscious. She describes the creative process as if she is possessed by an external force—the Muse—who demands fealty. According to Di Prima, "TimeBomb was written on the night of September 12–13, between 2:00 and 3:30 a.m. When the poems began, I wrote them down as best I could—as if I was taking dictation. Many of them came in as tiny snapshots in that state between dreaming and waking." There is an essentially passive aspect to this experience: in her description it is noteworthy that she employs the phrase "dictation" and "when *the poems begin*," rather than "when *I begin* writing the poems."[20] Katrina devastated the African American community of New Orleans, and Di Prima's poem documents the destruction wreaked not only by this natural disaster, but by the American federal and state governments which were slow to arrive with help.

TimeBomb opens with a haunting sense of cosmic disaster as the "moon had fallen down." Each page contains brief lyric verses, some as few as two lines. In the initial pages occurs a reference to Jacob and the angel in *Gen.* 32:66: "I will not let thee go/except thou bless me" which alludes to "And he said, Let me go, for the day breaketh. And he said, I will not let the go, except thou bless me." This suggests that like Jacob, the speaker is wrestling with her angel, confronting an apocalypse which is visiting the poor and oppressed of America. Iona Cosma in *Angels In-Between: The Poetics of Excess and the Crisis of Representation* (2009) asserted that for many contemporary poets "the proper archetype seems to be Jacob's struggle with the angel and in all these instances the angel appears as the double, the guide, man's, or artist's alter ego." A variety of creatures are then invoked: white loon, ducks, spiders, crocodiles, dragonflies, ants, alligators, nutria—the large, rat-like animals which live in the swamps of Louisiana—as well as orris and mandrake, the former associated in alchemy with Mars and the latter with the Moon. One passage describes "swamp/Indians/arcadians/pirates/ slaves/a soup," indicating the mix of historical cultures of New Orleans. *TimeBomb* also alludes to Tibetan spirituality: "at that pt/in Vajrasattva/ all the world/becomes white/it takes/a lot of/klesas/to bring back color." *Vajrasattva* is a practice in which one repeats a hundred thousand times the mantra of Vajrasattva to confess and purify oneself, while *klesas* in Sanskrit are "afflictions" which disturb the mind.[21] The phrase "becomes white" derives from the fact that "Vajrasattva is a sambhogakaya manifestation; he unifies all the five Buddha-families within himself in the same way that the white color of his body (in iconography) unifies all the five colors."[22]

The disaster's actual physical horrors—bodies floating in water, omnipresent death and horror—are indelibly depicted: "chrome fender/like an elbow/with neither/hand nor mouth/zipper/burst round a belly/with no jeans/no legs attached"; "baby alligator/followed the boats/for meat on a string"; "she was hanging/onto a chimney/in the wind"; "boats turned back/ not enuf/life jackets"; "long hair/on the thick arm/sloshes back and forth/ the body/caught/in the reeds"; "bracelets/hooked/on a chain link fence/ blue hand/it strangled/raised in a mudra." A *mudra* is a spiritual gesture employing the hands and fingers in Hinduism and Buddhism. Gary Snyder in his "Smokey the Bear Sutra" depicts the iconic symbol of preventing forest fires with his paw raised in a friendly gesture of compassion and kindness, but here we have the pathos of a dead body with a hand raised in Buddhist salute. The poem voices Di Prima's outrage at the injustices visited upon America's poor—when a natural disaster strikes a wealthy, white neighborhood, aid often appears on the scene immediately. And again she deploys her knowledge of spiritual traditions to place her political opposition within the context of the hidden religions.

Hurricane Katrina demonstrated just how deeply America was still divided along class lines between rich and poor, educated and uneducated, whites and "minorities." Di Prima's politics had from the beginning been aimed at healing this fragmentation, and the countercultural turn to communal living demonstrated the hunger for forms of authentic fellowship. Indeed, the desire for a *sangha*—a group of fellow Buddhists—would motivate Di Prima as well as poets like Gary Snyder and Philip Whalen toward creating such a community. In December 2008, Di Prima delivered an "Acceptance Speech" upon receiving the Reginald Lockett Award at the PEN Oakland ceremony in which she reviewed her life as a continual quest for affirming the "power of COMMUNITY." She recalled that when she first left her family's home and then returned to New York from Swarthmore, she found herself living with invited roommates as well as runaway youths from New Jersey who arrived at her door. Later, during the time of *Dinners and Nightmares* and other early works, her household consisted of writers, painters, and dancers. When she established the New York Poets Theater with Amiri Baraka, James McDowell, Alan Marlowe, and James Waring, it involved "taking in the stage-manager, her baby, the drop-out before his time from Canada who became our electrician and trouble-shooter, and half the cast when necessary."[23] As we have seen, she would live in Timothy Leary's Millbrook community for six months, in Rammurti Mishra's ashram, and in 1970 resided in the commune at Black Bear Ranch. Thus in this speech before the PEN club, Di Prima reaffirmed the role of creating a life in common with others as part of her spiritual and political commitment to a more just world: she followed the advice of her anarchist grandfather who as we have seen counseled her to share her bread when she had it with others who were in need.

In addition to the AIDS crisis and Hurricane Katrina disaster, Di Prima continued to speak out against war and composed a luminous poem— "Awkward Song on the Eve of War" which became "Revolutionary Letter Number Seventy-Seven"—in response to the destruction of al-Mutanabbi Street, the historical center of bookselling in Baghdad: it appears in the anthology *Al-Mutanabbi Street Starts Here: Poets and Writers Respond to the March 5, 2007, Bombing of Baghdad's "Street of the Booksellers"* (2012). Charles Olson in his play *Apollonius of Tyana: A Dance, with Some Words, for Two Actors*, lauded Baghdad as "the intellectual center, the old intellectual center, and much more in touch with the nerve ends of the old path than Alexandria ever was, or than the newest Alexandria, your Manhattan is, today, any clue to the path, the path which doesn't die, the path which is no more than yourself, if you can find it." Di Prima brings together several of the themes we have hitherto considered, now specifically in relation to destruction visited upon Iraq: "The center of my heart is Arab song./It is woven around my heartstrings/I cannot uproot it./It is the song of the Beloved as Other/The Other as God, it is all about Light/and we never stop singing it." The mystical theme of the loved one as Other/Divine is a theme Di Prima traced back to the troubadours as well as Sufis and which she elaborated in *Loba*. She goes on to invoke the Tree of Life from the Kabbalah and "the perfumes of Lebanon, lapis of Persia/The mountains, ziggurats, ladders of ascent/The hut in the field we entered as Her body," a geographical survey of world spiritual traditions, from ancient Persia, Mesopotamia, and the rich history of the Middle East. The most moving verses of the poem follow:

> The fabric of our seeing is dark & light
> Ahriman/Ahura the two lobes
> of the brain. Or yin and yang.
> The paintings of Turkestan echo in caves
> of North China. The Manichee's eyes are carved
> in Bone Oracles.
> I cannot cut the light from my eyes
> or the woven shadow from the curves of my brain.

> The dance of the I Ching is the dance of the star tide
> Mathematics of the Zend Avesta
> Geometries of life
> There is only one Sun and it is just rising.[24]

Ahriman and Ahura are the opposing principles of dark and light in Persian Zoroastrianism, the *Zend-Avesta* its sacred text, while *yin* and *yang* are the complementary opposites in Taoism. The ancient Chinese oracle bones were pieces of animal bone employed for divination, and there is also a tradition of Manichaeism practiced in China. This passage echoes material from Denis de Rougemont's (1906–85) classic *Love in the Western World* concerning the "beloved object . . . as symbol of a longing for the divine" and Suhrawardi—a trope to which Di Prima repeatedly returns. De Rougemont observes: "Suhrawardi, who died in 1191, supposed Plato—whom he knew at second hand from Plotinus, Proclus, and the Athenian school—to be a successor of Zoroaster. Indeed, his Neo-Platonism displays marked Persian mythical features. In particular, the doctrines about an antithetical relation of the World of Light and the World of Darkness which he borrowed from the Zend-Avesta were those that had inspired Manes and that became the root of the Catharist faith. These doctrines—exactly as happened later with those of the Cathars—were transmuted into a chivalrous love rhetoric." Thus Di Prima asserts a doctrine of mystical love while also affirming the unity of the world's spiritual traditions as she declares: "My eyes stare from ten thousand Arab faces/A deer sniffs at the stiffening corpse of her yearling./There is only one Sun and it is rising/It is much too strong in the desert of our minds./Shield us from the desert of greed/The desert of hate/ Shield us from the desert of chauvinism/*Le désert désespéré.*" There is an ironic pun here in the repetition of "desert" and "shield" on "Operation Desert Shield": President George H. W. Bush's August 7, 1990, order to commit American troops to the Middle East in response to Iraq's invasion of Kuwait. Finally, Di Prima responds to this man-made tragedy of war and greed by invoking the unity of mankind and the power of art and poetry to redeem: "*Let us read each other's maps at the foot of the Tree/Where the stream of Song moves out in all directions.*"[25]

As she arrived at the milestone of her sixty-fifth birthday, Di Prima was included in *The Beats: A Graphic History* which featured illustrations of her life and work by Mary Fleener and text by Harvey Pekar. She was also honored as Poet Laureate of San Francisco in 2009. She delivered a lecture recalling her first visit to San Francisco in 1961, "a magical place—a city of bright air and beveled glass, of jazz and poets—stained glass windows tucked above the front door in even the poorest neighborhoods, and vistas of bay and hills and sailboats that took my breath away while I waited for a bus."[26] New York by the 1960s had grown "too harsh"—she remembered the time of Joseph McCarthy's communist witch hunts, the death of Wilhelm Reich, the Rosenbergs—and she came to California to "work in new ways for change: the grace of possibility that had opened on this coast."[27] After reading several poems from various points in her career, she concluded with "First Draft: Poet Laureate Oath of Office," dedicated to "all poets everywhere" which is at once an ode to San Francisco and poetry's magnificence: "It is the poem I serve/ luminous, through time/that celebration/of human breath, of *melos*/it is and always has been/the muse androgynous and ruthless/as any angel scattering words that need no/radio frequency no broadband." Again Di Prima brings together light—*luminous*—with the angel who like the poet is a messenger bringing into being a new creative vision. Light returns in the third stanza:

it is the light on the ocean here and
the sky in all its moods
luminous fog that wakes me up
to write, and something I call the
"Imp of the Short poem"

it is the people of San Francisco
in their beauty
Bright luminous eyes looking out
from homeless faces[28]

Luminous returns, now to describe the people of San Francisco, the poor and homeless who walk the streets and sleep on the sidewalks on pieces of cardboard unheeded. William Saroyan (1908–81)—the Armenian American

FIGURE 6.2 *Di Prima Reading at Olson Festival, October 10, 2010. Photo by Dan Wilcox.*

story writer and playwright who preceded the Beats in San Francisco by two decades and was a major influence on Jack Kerouac—wrote a tender play entitled *The People with the Light Coming Out of Them* (1941) affirming the "common men and women" of America of all ethnicities, and it is this same spirit of human love and sympathy which Di Prima urges in her "Inaugural Address." One also recalls the hopeful, innocent, and generous mood of Scott McKenzie's hit song "If You're Going to San Francisco" (1967) celebrating the new generation of "flower children" in which young people are urged to wear flowers in their hair when they come to the city.

In October 2010, Di Prima journeyed to Gloucester, Massachusetts, to give a reading in celebration of the 100th anniversary of Charles Olson's birth, and also to New York where she reconnected with an old friend, the theater director Judith Malina.[29] In 2010, an issue of the *Paterson Literary Review* included a special section devoted to Di Prima containing sixteen new poems and the autobiographical essay "The Evolution of Landscape." One poem—"Alchemical Signals"—returns to the idea of the concept of microcosm/macrocosm which is central in hermetic thought and the ability to interpret "signs":

> for instance, the aurora borealis
> lightning, a beached whale
> the dream you didn't have or
> a slip of the tongue
>
> these are *signs*
> (everyone else is telling stories)

signs can't be told
tho you can learn
to read them—

if you're lucky enough to
catch one going by

keep it to yourself[30]

One notes in Di Prima's late style a masterful technical economy in which
she transmits an implied message with the utmost skill. Like a Zen *koan*,
there is a riddling aspect to this poem, yet the impact is felt powerfully as its
hidden significance slowly sinks in. Di Prima's entire life's work in a sense
has been the spiritual quest for the secret messages the world presents us:
it is the function of the art of poetry to give us hints of these camouflaged
meanings, but without explicitly *telling* us—that is what a "story" does—
how each of us individually should interpret them and what they might
signify for our own lives is up to us.

"The Evolution of Landscape," although billed in the *Paterson Literary
Review* as a "short story," is actually a narrative essay describing Di Prima's
time teaching in Wyoming's schools in Wyoming during the early 1970s,
which as we have seen inspired both *Loba* and *Wyoming Series*. This was
a turbulent period in her personal life. She had divorced Alan Marlowe in
1969, gave birth to her fifth child Rudi in 1970, began living at Tomales Bay,
and would marry Grant Fisher in 1972: the marriage would end in 1975.
"The Evolution of Landscape" shifts back and forth between San Francisco
and the Wyoming landscape, where Di Prima witnesses the fractured lives
of both Native Americans and those attempting to help them in their plight.
Di Prima describes her excitement in going to this "mythical land" and in
preparation she rereads Ralph K. Andrist's *The Long Death: The Last Days
of the Plains Indians* where she likely read about the Sand Creek Massacre.
In a poem composed during this period—"Brief Wyoming Meditation"—Di
Prima recalls this bloodbath in Colorado when on November 29, 1864, the
Colorado US Volunteer Cavalry slaughtered and mutilated more than 100
Cheyenne and Arapaho: "White Antelope's scrotum/became tobacco pouch/
for Colorado Volunteer." She goes on to reflect that "at least two-thirds" of
the inhabitants of Wyoming "voted for madman Nixon/were glad to bomb
the 'gooks' in their steamy jungle." Di Prima finds it increasingly difficult
to find common ground with her fellow Americans as she seeks "the place
where your nature meets mine, the place where we touch."

Upon arriving in Wyoming, she is horrified encountering the squalor and
terror of Native Americans' lives marked by "anger, alcohol and violence."
She meets "a little girl whose hands had been permanently maimed by being
held in the fire by her mother as a punishment for stealing food in her own
house for her baby sitter who was crying from hunger."[31] She then leaves

Caspar to go to Sheridan and the Wyoming Girls' School, admiring during
her journey the Bighorn and Powder River. Her pupils in Sheridan astonish
with "drawings, poems, stories tumbled from bursting bodies barely held
in check. Agony of reprisal against the living dead. Who had imprisoned
them."[32] Di Prima now leaves Wyoming to return to San Francisco, coming
back a year later during a ten-week tour to give workshops across the United
States. She goes to Worland to work in the reformatory for men, and during
the journey again admires the Wind River Canyon, sharing with her fellow
teachers Helen and Rick the blues of Bessie Smith. When Helen visits her
then takes her leave, Di Prima reflects: "The pale blue of the sky. Desolate,
desolate, emptied and folded back. I went that night for a walk under the
moon in the eternal wind. Prayed, nothing else left to do in this nadir."[33]
Thus the landscape represents in Di Prima's imagination the despairing
lives of those who live there and the American government's continuing
oppression of Native American peoples.

In 2011, Melanie La Rosa produced a brief, twenty-seven-minute
"impressionstic documentary" entitled "The Poetry Deal: A Film with Diane di
Prima" which depicts the poet reading several poems as well as commentary by
Michael McClure. Now approaching her eightieth birthday, Di Prima gave a
reading and lectured on "How I Write" at Stanford University on November 6,
2013, and also began teaching a course at the Bay Area Public School at 2141
Broadway in Oakland on November 3, 17, and December 1, 2013, entitled "The
Dream of Pre-History." According to her course description, "All versions of prehistory, whether scholarly or not, are inevitably somebody's dream of the past."
This indeed might be said to be Di Prima's attitude toward all written history,
a claim which echoes that of Hayden White who in *Metahistory* explored the
ways historical narratives are a literary genre structured employing the same
forms as fiction. History is a story told, and as such shares characteristics with
fiction to the degree that certain elements are highlighted to underline their
importance, events are structured as plots leading to a climax and resolution,
there are "good guys" and "bad guys." Indeed, the typical structuring of the
liberal arts curriculum has been to emphasize the achievements of men and
ignore those of women. Di Prima states that the "class explores the beginnings
of what we call 'human'—the fall of Neanderthal and the rise of Cro-Magnon
culture—the beginnings, dominance, and eclipse of matriarchy—the double
invasions of patriarchy and oligarchy—and the persistent dream of a non-
hierarchical society." Her reading list includes Rachel Levy's *The Gate of Horn*,
Hamlet's Mill, *The White Goddess* as well as Margaret Murray's *The God
of the Witches* (1931). Adrienne Rich has declared that women require an
awareness of their own history, but

the university curriculum, the high-school curriculum, do not provide
this kind of knowledge for women, the knowledge of Womankind, whose
experience has been so profoundly different from that of Mankind . . . the

content of education itself validates men even as it invalidates women. Its very message is that men have been the shapers and thinkers of the world, and that this is only natural. The bias of higher education, including the so-called sciences, is white and male, racist and sexist; and this bias is expressed in both subtle and blatant ways.

It is clear that Di Prima in her role as educator has sought to address this glaring inequality in the teaching of the history of women.

And just as she has cast a retrospective eye on the books and ideas which have preoccupied her in her recent teaching, Di Prima's two most recent literary works—*The Poetry Deal* (2014) and *Out-Takes* (2016)—are at once memory books and necrologies, honoring the deaths of those she has known and admired. "November 2, 1972 (for Ezra Pound)" recalls her visit to the poet at St. Elizabeth's: Pound made a gift of food, telling her that "poets have to eat." "Audre Lorde" commemorates her friend in a brief, haiku-like five verses: "before you died you went to Mt. Pelee/for the solar eclipse/you told me/you had an appointment/with the goddess." The volcanic Mt. Pelee near the northern coast of Martinique erupted in 1902, killing 30,000 people: thus witnessing a solar eclipse on the top of this mountain would indeed be an appropriate locus for an encounter with the goddess. "Three Dharma Poems" honor Chogyam Trungpa Rinpoche and Di Prima also fondly remembers the marriage of Amy Evans and Michael McClure—"*love is the immortality/we carry with us.*"

FIGURE 6.3 *Diane di Prima and Michael McClure, City Lights Bookstore, San Francisco, 2003.* © *2003 Larry Keenan.*

She honors Kirby Doyle (1932–2003) in an eponymous poem which carries an American Indian prayer as epigraph: "*we live in true relation to the people/we live in true relation to the earth*." Doyle—author of the underground classic *Happiness Bastard* (1968), composed like Kerouac's *On the Road* on a long scroll, as well as *Sapphobones* (1966) published by Di Prima's Poets Press—lived long periods in the woods so thus she honors Doyle's love of Nature and recalls him as the person "at whose house/Freddie Herko/&/George Herms/wd play." Philip Whalen is remembered in "Deaths: Philip Whalen, June 26, 2002": "Large man/great light/mind/as a beacon/ across the city/across/the nation."[34] Di Prima had not only collaborated with Whalen in publishing his work, but the two poets shared a deep engagement with Hindu and Buddhist thought which they incorporated both into their works and lives: they also shared a frequently impish sense of humor.

In addition to these homages to important friends and artists in her life, *The Poetry Deal* also demonstrates that she had lost none of her sense of humor, as in the poem "Where Are You?" which skewers a modern world held hostage by omnipresent technology: "friends know where other friends live/not their emails or cell phone numbers/not something called their 'contact information.'" Di Prima goes on to bemoan the further impediments to human touch: "she doesn't say 'stay in touch' and mean Facebook/or LinkedIn/stay in touch means you touch each other, lovers or/ not." She incisively satirizes our brave new sterile technological world: "stay in touch doesn't mean a touch screen or even an /iPhone/it means she'll drive you to look at the ocean/or say goodbye to your ex/he'll do your shopping or pick up a prescription." Di Prima concludes with the exhortation: "Have you ever tried to email chicken soup? make love for the last time on Skype? Or give that one more hug before the train leaves/by reaching all the way out through cyberspace?"[35] Our modern world—while claiming to make our lives "faster" and "easier"—paradoxically through the proliferation of shiny gadgets has created more barriers to authentic connection.

Out-Takes (2016) contains tributes to Amira Baraka, William Burroughs, Allen Ginsberg, Philip Whalen, John Wieners, and Ezra Pound. In "For Bill Burroughs," Di Prima observes that when Burroughs died, obituaries duly noted his drug addictions, his life in "The Bunker"—his underground, windowless, and Spartan residence in the Bowery—and of course his shooting of wife Joan but neglected to mention the hidden, tender side of Burroughs: "I remember the love w/which you spoke of the lemurs/at Duke you wanted to adopt one/*but the responsibility*, you told me, *was too much/* at yr age—who wd care for it/when you died?" She also admires Burroughs's relentless quest for life's secret meanings: "You combed Egypt for clues/You ransacked Tibet/turned nothing down." And following Burroughs's death, Di Prima conducts for him a ceremony: "I did *P'howa* for you sending you reluctant/to the Pure Land." In Vajrayana Buddhism, *P'howa* is a method by which one's consciousness is mentally transferred to a pure realm at the moment of death. Di Prima and Sheppard Powell spent several months reading aloud Burroughs's collected works whom they referred to as their "invisible roommate" since they became so absorbed in his life and writings. Di Prima recalled that Burroughs

> was a thousand people, but there were two that I saw all the time. The cynical tough-talking guy, and the other who showed me the machine he used to heal his cats. . . . The machine was based on the 19th century theory of pulling energy out of the air. You need an attenna, a clamp and the picture of what you want to heal. He said it's much easier to heal cats than heal people—because cats don't put up any resistance.

"Sestina: The Tent at Pisa, for Ezra Pound," is an impressive demonstration of virtuosity and *Out-Takes* illustrates Di Prima's lifelong study of a variety of poetic forms for she includes both a *pantoum* and a *ghazal* in the book. The sestina form—thought to have been invented by troubadour Arnaut Daniel—is composed of six stanzas of six lines each, closing with a three-line *envoi*. The words at the end of the first stanza are employed as line endings in each of the following stanzas, rotated in a set pattern and Pound himself composed a great poem in this form, "Sestina: Altaforte" (1909) which as we have seen earlier Di Prima echoed in her "Canticle to St. Joan." Di Prima describes the time when Pound was kept as a political prisoner by American troops in Pisa, Italy:

> under the fruit trees, between the furrows the eyes of lynxes
> edging the mountain top a nimbus of flame
> how near they approach the fire, that keen edge
> where night is divided, sickly under the vines
> and the whisper of insects is thick, is terrible
> among the flowers and scrub oaks that wait on sunrise

Di Prima's inspiration here is Pound's *Canto LXXIX*: "O Lynx keep watch on my fire. . . . Cythera, here are lynxes/Will the scrub-oak burst into flower?/There is a rose vine in this underbrush/Red? White? No, but a color between them/When the pomegranate is open and the light falls/half thru it." Di Prima renders homage to the great poet she had met in 1956 who inspired her as she began her own career as poet, imitating with admiring fidelity Pound's precise imagistic virtuosic, light-bringing magic. In addition to the sestina, Di Prima also composed a "Pantoum for Sheppard" thus illustrating her desire to experiment in a variety of poetic forms.

However, for all her astounding productivity, Di Prima in her later years has voiced a sense of frustration that there are several unfinished projects which she would like to complete. She had the advantage of being a true bibliophile, and thus has had access to her own private texts, noting earlier in her career that she preferred not to check out books from the library because she would typically annotate them heavily. In *Recollections*, she describes a large collection of some four thousand volumes, declaring that "to this day, I have trouble spending money on myself for clothes, or to fix my teeth, but no guilt at all in spending hundreds of dollars on books: the only permitted escape"[36] One project she hoped to realize was to gather and write up material from her "The Literature of the Hidden Religions of Europe" courses and also to develop another seminar on "theories of the imagination in the Western world from Heraclitus to the present."[37] Di Prima also by her own reckoning has at least fourteen volumes of unpublished work. For example, as we have seen, a work which exists only in manuscript—*Not Quite Buffalo Stew*—is an entertaining, surreal comic novella involving life in San Francisco. Other manuscripts in progress are a study of the ways Percy Bysshe Shelley employed traditional Western magic in his life and work, tentatively titled variously *Shelley: A Personal View* and *One Too Like Thee*; a poem cycle *Alchemical Fragments*; and a project involving her reimagining of the verse of Sappho (ca. 630–570 BCE): Di Prima has "promised Aphrodite that I would renew her worship in this age." As Di Prima has pointed out,

> I have more books unpublished than I have out in the world, by far. I'd like to get my work in some kind of order, my papers in some kind of order, so that people can make some sense of things. I tend to have a habit of writing a poem wherever I am on whatever I've got, like in the back of whatever book I'm reading . . . . If I had my druthers in this world right now, I would be doing nothing except writing, typing up the writing I've got, painting, and meditating.

However she also notes

> there's a certain part of me that knows that if I didn't publish anything else for the rest of my life, at some point somebody would dig up those notebooks, and publish stuff. So the priority becomes more to get the goodies and to get them written down. To *travel*—I don't mean on Earth—to travel and get the goodies.[38]

Diane di Prima has been a compelling force in American poetry and prose. Now an octogenarian, she has had significant health issues which have limited her mobility; however, she has continued to dedicate herself to "the visions of the new forms of consciousness" which will speak to a new generation of readers:

> I think the poet is the last person who is still speaking the truth when no one else dares to. I think the poet is the first person to begin the shaping and visioning of the new forms and the new consciousness when no one

else has begun to sense it, so that there's both of those happening all the time. . . . And we see very dramatically in our time how without even reaching that high plane, like Dante or Shakespeare, the work of Allen and Kerouac in the 50s and so on has informed the 70s. And in the same sense I think that the job for us it to get the vision clear and transmit it in its purity . . . the visions of the new forms of consciousness are the visions of the artists. Poetry is not a place where you can bluff. So that you speak direct to the hearts of people. People are hungry for that directness. It's like the days of dying in the desert yearning for a glass of water, for any speech that's speech of the heart. And there's way too much speech of the brain, and there's way too much information about what's going on and not anything of the gut and not anything of the heart happening. So whatever else we do, the first thing is to reactivate the feeling, we reactivate the possibility of living a life of emotion and of the flesh, as well as the life of the brain. . . . Because without the livingness of the words, there's no living of mind consciousness. . . . And right now we are fighting an incredible dead weight of newspaper, television, magazines, movies, and so on.[39]

Yet Di Prima remains hopeful and contrasted life during the 1950s with the present:

When the time came for me, I went out on the streets and said what I had to say. Before that, we holed up and just talked about it among ourselves. Remember, in the late Fifties there were maybe hundreds of us that could network across the nation; that's all, hundreds. Yet, we could make things happen and it changed the world. With the internet, with all the new technologies that younger people have at their disposal, the opportunities for networking and sharing information and ideas there's so much more that can happen now. So we've got to be hopeful, I'm optimistic.[40]

As we have seen throughout this book, Di Prima saw the role of the poet in modern times to be the creation of a visionary poetics rooted in the hidden spiritual traditions which might rejuvenate and bring humans to a higher state of love, joy, community, and awareness. The life and work of Diane di Prima consistently affirmed the values of her great hero John Keats: the truths of the imagination, the holiness of the heart's affections, and the speech of the heart.

NOTES

Introduction

1 Anthony Lioi, "Real Presence: The *Numina* in Italian American Poetry," *MELUS*, 34, no. 2 (Summer 2009), 148; on Di Prima's inclusion in anthologies, see Alan Golding, *From Outlaw to Classic: Canons in American Poetry* (Madison: The University of Wisconsin Press, 1995), 31; on canon formation, see John Guillory, *Cultural Capital: The Problem of Literary Canon Formation* (Chicago: University of Chicago Press, 1993); Paul Lauter, *Canons and Contexts* (New York: Oxford University Press, 1991).

2 Diane di Prima, *Recollections of My Life as a Woman* (New York: Viking, 2001), 351. Coincidentally, the son of Carlo Tresca—Peter D. Martin— was one of the founders, along with Lawrence Ferlinghetti, of City Lights Bookstore which would publish Di Prima's work. See Lawrence Ferlinghetti and Nancy J. Peters, *Literary San Francisco: A Pictorial History from Its Beginnings to the Present Day* (City Lights Books and Harper and Row, 1980), 163.

3 William Marling, *Gatekeepers: The Emergence of World Literature and the 1960s* (New York: Oxford University Press, 2016), 73.

4 http://magmapoetry.com/archive/magma-11-poetry-from-san-francisco/articles/the-movement-of-the-mind/

5 "A Visit to Diane di Prima" "RE/Search Visits Diane di Prima," 2015; V. Vale and John Sulak, *Modern Pagans: An Investigation of Contemporary Pagan Practices: Interviews* (San Francisco: RE/Search Publications, 2001), 38.

6 Diane di Prima, "Keep the Beat," in *The Poetry Deal* (San Francisco: City Lights, 2014), 80–83.

7 Anne Waldman, "Interview with Diane di Prima," *Rocky Ledge*, Vol. 7, February–March 1981, 41.

8 Diane di Prima, *The Mysteries of Vision: Some Notes on H.D.* (Santa Barbara, CA: Am Here Books, 1988), 6–7.

9 John Milton, "Il Penseroso," lines 85–92 in *The Oxford Authors: John Milton*, eds. Stephen Orgel and Jonathan Goldberg (Oxford: Oxford University Press, 1990), 27–28; Sir Isaac Newton, "The Key: The Commentary on the Emerald Tablet," in *The Alchemy Reader: From Hermes Trismegistus to Isaac Newton*, ed. Stanton J. Linden (Cambridge: Cambridge University Press, 2003), 243–47; David Kubrin, "Newton's Inside Out!: Magic, Class Struggle, and the Rise

of Mechanism in the West," in *The Analytic Spirit: Essays in the History of Science in Honor of Henry Guerlac*, ed. Harry Woolf (Ithaca and London: Cornell University Press, 1981), 112; Brian P. Copenhaver, *Hermetica: The Greek Corpus Hermeticum and the Latin Asclepius* (Cambridge: Cambridge University Press, 1996), xxii–xxiii; John G. Burke, "Hermetism as Renaissance World View," in *The Darker Vision of the Renaissance: Beyond the Fields of Reason* (Berkeley: University of California Press, 1974), 95–117; Richard Kieckhefer, *Magic in the Middle Ages* (Cambridge: Cambridge University Press, 1990), 26; Simon During, *Modern Enchantments: The Cultural Power of Secular Magic* (Cambridge, MA: Harvard University Press, 2002), 11–12; Diane di Prima, *R.D.'s H.D., Lost and Found: The CUNY Poetics Document Initiative*, Series 2, Number 3 (Spring 2011), 2.

10   Eric Haralson, ed., *Encyclopedia of American Poetry: The Twentieth Century* (New York: Routledge, 2012), 179; Diane di Prima, *Recollections of My Life as a Woman* (New York: Viking Press, 2001), 224.

11   Gloria Anzaldua, *Borderlands/La Frontera* (San Francisco: Aunt Lute Books, 1999), 60; Kenneth Starr, *Golden Dreams: California in an Age of Abundance, 1950-1963*, 328. See also Lawrence Ferlinghetti and Nancy J. Peters, *Literary San Francisco: A Pictorial History from the Beginnings to the Present Day* (San Francisco: City Lights and Harper & Row, 1980), 160–61; Andrew Schelling, *Tracks Along the Left Coast: Jaime de Angulo and Pacific Coast Culture* (Berkeley: Counterpoint, 2017); Christopher Wagstaff, ed., *A Poet's Mind: Collected Interviews with Robert Duncan, 1960-1985* (Berkeley: North Atlantic Books, 2012), 232, 230; also see Ekbert Faas, *Young Robert Duncan: Portrait of the Artist as Homosexual in Society* (Santa Barbara: Black Sparrow Press, 1983), 88–89; 282–85; on transvestite shamans, see Piers Vitebsky, *Shamanism* (Norman: University of Oklahoma Press, 1995), 93; T. S. Eliot, *The Wasteland* in *Collected Poems: 1909-1935* (New York: Harcourt, Brace and Company, 1936), 80; Robert M. Baum, "Homosexuality and the Traditional Religions of the Americas and Africa," in *Homosexuality and World Religions*, ed. Arlene Swidler (Valley Forge: Trinity Press International, 1993).

12   Jay Murphy and Mary Jane Ryals, "Red Bass Interview: Allen Ginsberg," *Red Bass* 7 (1984), 30; Charles Y. Glock and Robert N. Bellah, eds, *The New Religious Consciousness* (Berkeley: University of California Press, 1976), 340; Georges Bataille, *Inner Experience*, trans. Stuart Kendall (Albany: State University of New York, 2014).

13   Thomas J. Ferraro, "Catholic Ethnicity and Modern American Arts," in *The Italian American Heritage: A Companion to Literature and the Arts*, ed. Pellegrino A. D'Acierno (New York: Garland, 1999), 331–52.

Chapter 1

1   Diane di Prima, *Recollections of My Life as a Woman*, 11, 12; Stephan Thernstrom, ed., *Harvard Encyclopedia of American Ethnic Groups* (Cambridge, MA: Harvard University Press, 1981), 545; *The Voices We*

Carry: Recent Italian American Women's Fiction, ed. Mary Jo Bona (Toronto: Guernica, 2007), 25; Thomas Sowell, *Ethnic America: A History* (New York: Basic Books, 1981), 100; Phyllis Stowell, "My Work Is My Life: An Interview with Diane di Prima," *City Miner*, 4, no. 2 (1979), 19; Di Prima, "Backyard," in *Pieces of a Song* (San Francisco: City Lights, 1990), 114.

2   Steven Clay and Rodney Phillips, *A Secret Location on the Lower East Side: Adventures in Writing, 1960-1980* (New York: The New York Public Library, 1998), 89; Antoine Faivre, "Renaissance Hermetism," in *The Cambridge Handbook of Western Mysticism and Esotericism*, ed. Bryan Alexander Magee (New York: Cambridge University Press, 2016), 139–40. On Carlo Tresca, see Nunzio Pernicone, "War among the Italian Anarchists: The Galleanisti's Campaign against Carlo Tresca," in *The Lost World of Italian-American Radicalism: Politics, Labor, and Culture*, eds. Philip V. Cannistraro and Gerald Meyer (Westport, CT: Praeger, 2003), 77–97.

3   Franklin Rosemont, "Surrealist, Anarchist, Afrocentrist: Philip Lamantia Before and After the 'Beat Generation,'" in *Are Italians White?: How Race is Made in America*, eds. Jennifer Guglielmo and Salvatore Salerno (New York and London: Routledge, 2003), 129–30; Dana Gioia, "What Is Italian American Poetry?," in *Beyond the Godfather: Italian American Writers on the Real Italian American Experience*, eds. A. Kenneth Ciongoli and Jay Parini (Hanover and London: University Press of New England, 1997), 170; Di Prima, "Diane di Prima's Acceptance Speech at PEN Oakland Awards, December 2008" http://sisterezili.blogspot.com/2009/04/diane-diprimas-acceptance-speech-at-pen.html;Di Prima, *Recollections*, 10.

4   *Pseudo-Dionysius: The Complete Works*, trans. Colm Luibheid (New York: Paulist Press, 1987), 135.

5   *Recollections*, 15; V.Vale, *RE/Search Visits Diane di Prima* (San Francisco: RE/Search Publications, 2015), 5.

6   *Recollections*, 7, 15.

7   Larissa Bendel, *The Requirements of Our Life is the Form of Our Art: Autobiographik von Frauen der Beat Generation* (Frankfurt: Peter Lang, 2005), 192, translation mine; Di Prima, *Recollections*, 1; Di Prima, *Calculus of Variation* (San Francisco: Eidolon, 1972), n.p.

8   *Recollections*, 3; Lawrence Ferlinghetti, "The Old Italians Dying" (San Francisco: City Lights, 1976).

9   *Recollections*, 10; *Selected Poems: 1956-1975* (Berkeley: North Atlantic Books, 1975), 254. In a sequel entitled "To My Father—2," Di Prima returned to her father's grief and fear and her own trauma: "How many nights w/a pillow over my face/did I struggle w/rage/or desire/exhaustion." She vows to reject her father's death-in-life: "I will know/the tower inside & out, the goddess/in the lingam." Thus she invokes Tarot—"the tower"—and Hinduism—"lingam," symbol of Shiva and male sexual complement to Shakti, the *yoni*—as her ways toward affirming her independent power in the form of the "goddess." She also alludes in the poem to the Egyptian goddess Bes, worshipped as protector of households. Thus the poem illustrates the ways Di Prima strives to understand her own experience in relation to her developing

spirituality and to develop a symbolic mode of transcending and transmuting her psychological struggles through a learned poetics which alludes constantly to an archetypal mythological tradition. See Di Prima, "To My Father—2," in *Pieces of a Song: Selected Poems*, 149.

10   *Recollections*, 34, 37–38. Estibaliz Encarnacion-Pinedo views Di Prima's struggle with the trauma of her childhood expressed in *Recollections of My Life as a Woman* in terms of the need to reassert the autonomy and strength of her physical body: "Throughout the rest of the memoir she initiates the healing and feminist process of reclaiming the body, recognizing it as a collective necessity shared by other oppressed individuals. As she puts it: 'I seek now, like how many others?, to reclaim the body.'" See "Memoir as the Reconstruction of History: Women of the Beat Generation," in *Out of the Shadows; Beat Women Are Not Beaten Women*, eds. Frida Forsgren and Michael J. Prince (Kristiansand: Portal Books, 2015), 159.

11   Di Prima, *The Mysteries of Vision: Some Notes on H.D.* (Santa Barbara: Am Here Books, 1988), 22–23.

12   Di Prima, *Recollections*, 18; Di Prima, "Whose Day Is It Anyway? The Poet Mulls Over Some of the Choices," in *Avanti Popolo: Italian-American Writers Sail Beyond Columbus*, ed. The Italian American Political Solidarity Club (San Francisco: Manic D Press, 2008), 13–16; Di Prima, "Dream Poem," in *Pieces of a Song*, 148.

13   *Recollections*, 28.

14   See Fred Gardaphe, "The Double Burden of Italian American Women Writers," in *Breaking Open: Reflections on Italian American Women's Writing*, eds. Mary Ann Vigilante Mannino and Justin Vitiello (West Lafayette, IN: Purdue University Press, 2003), 265–77; also see Anthony Julian Tamburri, "Umbertina: The Italian/American Woman's Experience," in *From the Margin: Writings in Italian Americana*, eds. Anthony Julian Tamburri, Paolo A. Giordano, and Fred L. Gardaphe (West Lafayette, IN: Purdue University Press, 1991), 357–73; *Recollections*, 54; "Backyard," in *Pieces of a Song: Selected Poems* (City Lights; San Francisco, 1990), 114.

15   *Recollections*, 70; "Spring and Autumn Annals: A Celebration of the Seasons for Freddie," in *The Outsider*, 2, no. 4/5 (Winter, 1968–69), 47.

16   *Recollections*, 77, 6, 78. Also see Di Prima's "Ode to Keats" in *Pieces of a Song*, 57–59; on Keats's influence on Di Prima, see Polina Mackay, "Narratives of Emergence: Diane di Prima's Vision of John Keats," in *Out of the Shadows: Beat Women Are Not Beaten Women* (Kristiansand: Portal, 2015), 89–107.

17   Audre Lorde, *Zami*, quoted in Julia Watson, "Unspeakable Differences: The Politics of Gender in Lesbian and Heterosexual Women's Autobiographies," in Sidonie Smith and Julia Watson, eds., *De/Colonizing the Subject: The Politics of Gender in Women's Autobiography* (Minneapolis: University of Minnesota Press, 1992), 152; Robert Reid-Pharr, "African American and African-Diasporic Writing, Post-1930," in *The Cambridge History of Gay and Lesbian Literature*, eds. E. L. McCallum and Mikko Tuhkanen (New York: Cambridge University Press, 2014), 582; Zora Neale Hurston, "How It Feels to Be

Colored Me," in *I Love Myself When I Am Laughing . . . and Then Again When I Am Looking Mean and Impressive*, ed. Alice Walker (New York: The Feminist Press of the City University of New York, 1979), 155; bell hooks, "Contemplation and Transformation," in *Buddhist Women on the Edge: Contemporary Perspectives from the Western Frontier* (Berkeley: North Atlantic Books, 1996), 287; Alexis De Veaux, *Warrior Poet: A Biography of Audre Lorde* (New York: W. W. Norton, 2004), 26; Vale, *Modern Pagans*, 36.

18   Ann Braude, *Radical Spirits: Spiritualism and Women's Rights in Nineteenth-Century America*, second edition (Bloomington and Indianapolis: Indiana University Press, 2001); "The Gnosis Interview: Diane di Prima on Magic, Healing, and the Western Esoteric Tradition," *Gnosis: A Journal of the Western Inner Traditions*, no. 2 (Spring/Summer 1986), 12.

19   Jackson Ellis, "Diane di Prima's Liberation News Service: An Interview," *Beat Scene*, no. 72 (Spring 2014), 9; Di Prima, "'Don't Solidify the Adversary!': A Response to Rudolph Vecoli," in *Through the Looking Glass: Italian and Italian /American Images in the Media—Selected Essays from the 27th Annual Conference of the American Italian Historical Association*, eds. Mary Jo Bona and Anthony Julian Tamburri (Staten Island, NY: American Italian Historical Association, 1996), 26; D. H. Lawrence, letter to Ernest Collings, January 17, 1913 in *The Selected Letters of D.H. Lawrence*, ed. James T. Boulton (Cambridge: Cambridge University Press, 1997), 53.

20   *Recollections*, 150.

21   Ibid., 151, 156.

22   Ibid., 156.

23   Ibid., 79, 83.

24   Ibid., 83.

25   Steven Watson, *The Birth of the Beat Generation: Visionaries, Rebels, and Hipsters, 1944-1960* (New York: Pantheon Books, 1995), 270; William S. Burroughs, "On Coincidence," in *The Adding Machine: Selected Essays* (New York: Arcade Publishing, 1993), 101; on the influence of Crowley on Burroughs, see Ron Roberts, "The High Priest and the Great Beast at *The Place of Dead Roads*, in *Retaking the Universe: William S. Burroughs in the Age of Globalization*, eds. Davis Schneiderman and Philip Walsh (London: Pluto Press, 2004), 225–40; *Recollections*, 94; Di Prima, "'Don't Solidify the Adversary!'": A Response to Rudolf Vecoli," 26.

26   Di Prima, *Dinners and Nightmares* (San Francisco: Last Gasp, 1998), 30.

27   *Recollections*, 92.

28   Di Prima, *Diary*, May 11, 1953, University of Kansas, Kenneth Spencer Research library.

29   Tony Moffeit, "Diane di Prima Interview: Boulder, Colorad, July 29, 1990," 15–16. Diane di Prima papers, University of Louisvlle Librart, Box 8, Folder 2.

30   Raul Sebazco, "Interview with Diane di Prima," *New Blood*, 6 (April 1982), 104.

31   *Recollections*, 104.

Chapter 2

1 *Diary of Diane di Prima, 1953-1961*, 1, University of Kansas, Kenneth
   Spencer Research Library, MS 71:1.

2 Di Prima *Recollections*, 103, 105.

3 Moffeit, "Diane di Prima Interview," 16.

4 Di Prima has created a prodigious number of notebooks throughout her
   career. Striking examples are the *San Francisco Notebook 5* (November 22–
   March 31, 1973) which is a mixed-media journal bound in hand-decorated,
   paper covered boards and a mixed-media journal bound in hand-decorated
   cloth binding. This notebook contains a page with a drawing of a Tarot card
   with a notation concerning Kirby Doyle, the description of a dream and a
   reproduction from one of the triptychs of Hieronymus Bosch's "The Garden of
   Earthly Delights." The *West Coast Notebook 13* (November 23, 1975—March
   20, 1976) has a page containing a newspaper clipping from the February 21,
   1976, issue of the *San Francisco Chronicle* concerning the death of Wallace
   Berman, a page of Hebrew letters as well as a Kabbalistic drawing. See *Semina
   Culture: Wallace Berman and His Circle*, 123. The notebooks are in the Diane
   di Prima Collection, Rare Book Collection, Wilson Library, University of
   North Carolina at Chapel Hill; *Recollections*, 180; *Diary of Diane di Prima,
   1953-1961*, University of Kansas, Kenneth Spencer Research Library, MS 71:1;
   http://articles.chicagotribune.com/2000-04-19/features/0004190043_1_beat-
   generation-jack-kerouac-di-prima*Recollections*, 104; "RE/Search Di Prima
   Visits Diane di Prima," 18.

5 John Elderfield, *de Kooning: A Retrospective* (New York: The Museum of
   Modern Art, 2011), 83; RoseLee Goldberg, *Performance Art; From Futurism
   to the Present* (London: Thames and Hudson, 2011), 141; Di Prima, *The
   Calculus of Variation*, n.p.

6 Larissa Harris and Media Farzin, eds., *Thirteen Most Wanted Men: Andy
   Warhol and the 1964 World's Fair* (Queens, NY: Queens Museum of Art,
   2014), 131, 132; Di Prima, *Recollections*, 151; Di Prima, *Diary*, 11.

7 Diane di Prima, "Movement and Tableau in the Dance," *Carolina Quarterly*,
   8, no. 1 (1955), 20.

8 See Ezra Pound, Chapter 4 of *ABC of Reading* (New York: New Directions,
   1960), 37ff; Di Prima, "Movement and Tableau," 22, 24.

9 Samantha Baskind, *Raphael Soyer and the Search for Modern Jewish Art*
   (Chapel Hill: University of North Carolina Press, 2004), 131, and for
   "Village East Street Scene," 132; Maurice Tuchman, *The Spiritual in Art:
   Abstract Painting, 1890-1985* (New York: Abbeville Press, 1986), 118, 96;
   Catherine Spretnak, *The Spiritual Dynamic in Modern Art: Art History
   Reconsidered, 1800 to the Present* (New York: Palgrave Macmillan, 2014);
   Di Prima, "Magick in Theory & Practice," in *Pieces of a Song*, 75; Di Prima,
   "The House," *Selected Poems, 1956-1975*, 77. On Jim Dine, see RoseLee
   Goldberg, *Performance Art: From Futurism to the Present* (London: Thames
   and Hudson, 2011), 127, 131, and Nicolas Calas and Elena Calas, *Icons*

and Images of the Sixties (New York: E. P. Dutton, 1971), 91–97; Di Prima, "Folly Beach," in *Pieces of a Song*, 133; on Ted Joans, see *Black, Brown, and Beige: Surrealist Writing from Africa and the Diaspora*, ed. Franklin Rosemont and Robin D. G. Kelley (Austin: University of Texas Press, 2009), 228, 230; Sally Banes, *Greenwich Village 1963: Avant-Garde Performance and the Effervescent Body* (Durham and London: Duke University Press, 1993), 22; Mario Maffi, *Gateway to the Promised Land: Ethnic Cultures on New York's Lower East Side* (New York and London: New York University Press, 1995), 38.

10 W. J. Rorabaugh, *American Hippies* (New York: Cambridge University Press, 2015), 29; Diane di Prima, *The Poetry Deal*, 39. On meeting with Pound, also see A. David Moody, *Ezra Pound Poet, Volume III: The Tragic Years 1937-1972* (New York: Oxford University Press, 2015), 311; on Pound's stay at St. Elizabeth's, see Daniel Swift, *The Bughouse: The Poetry, Politics and Madness of Ezra Pound* (New York: Farrar, Straus and Giroux, 2017).

11 Richard Ardinger, ed., *What Thou Lovest Well Remains: 100 Years of Ezra Pound* (Boise, ID: Limberlost Press, 1986); on Yeats, Theosophy and Mathers, see Austin Warren, "William Butler Yeats: The Religion of a Poet," in *Religion and Modern Literature: Essays in Theory and Criticism*, eds. G. B. Tennyson and Edward E. Ericson, Jr. (Grand Rapids, MI: William B. Eerdmans Publishing Company, 1975), 272–73; Ezra Pound, *Guide to Kulchur* (New York: New Directions, 1970), 144–45.

12 Robert Duncan, "The Lasting Contribution of Ezra Pound," in *Collected Essays and Other Prose* (Berkeley: University of California Press, 2014), 100; "A Retrospect," in T. S. Eliot, ed., *Literary Essays of Ezra Pound* (New York: New Directions, 1968), 4; Phyllis Stowell, "My Work Is My Life: An Interview with Diane di Prima," *City Miner*, 4, no. 2 (1979), 21; Di Prima, "Apparauit," in *Pieces of a Song*, 189.

13 *Recollections*, 100, 103, 148; Di Prima, *Memoirs of a Beatnik* (New York: Penguin, 1998), 176, 177; Allen Ginsberg, *Howl: Original Draft Facsimile*, ed. Barry Miles (New York: HarperCollins, 1995), 126.

14 *Recollections*, 150.

15 http://articles.chicagotribune.com/2000-04-19/features/0004190043_1_beat-generation-jack-kerouac-di-prima; *Recollections*, 101.

16 Moffiet, "Diane di Prima Interview," 10–11.

17 Kent Johnson and Craig Paulenich, eds, *Beneath a Single Moon: Buddhism in Contemporary American Poetry* (Boston: Shambhala, 1993), 56.

18 J. J. Clarke, *Oriental Enlightenment: The Encounter between Asian and Western Thought* (London: Routledge, 1997), 103; Blossom S. Kirschenbaum, "Diane di Prima: Extending *La Famiglia*," *MELUS*, 14, nos. 3–4 (Fall–Winter 1987), 64; *Recollections*, 108, 182, 183–84. 186, 188; http://magmapoetry.com/archive/magma-11-poetry-from-san-francisco/articles/the-movement-of-the-mind/; *A Secret Location on the Lower East Side*, 91. For a good anthology on "cool," see *The Cool School: Writing from America's Hip Underground*, ed. Glenn O'Brien (New York: The Library of America, 2013).

19 Lawrence Ferlinghetti, "Introduction," *This Kind of Bird Flies Backward* (New York: Paper Book Gallery, 1963), n.p.; Di Prima, "Hymn," in *Selected Poems*, 162; Amiri Baraka, *The Autobiography of LeRoi Jones*, 176; Di Prima, "Notes on *The Art of Memory*," in *Pieces of a Song*, 147.

20 Morris Dickstein, *Leopards in the Temple: The Transformation of American Fiction, 1945-1970* (Cambridge, MA: Harvard University Press, 2002), 87; *This Kind of Bird Flies Backward*, 2, 10, 42.

21 Steven Belletto, "Five Ways of Being Beat, Circa 1958-59," in *The Cambridge Companion to The Beats* (New York: Cambridge University Press, 2017), 104; *This Kind of Bird*, 9, 19.

22 Di Prima, *Earthsong: Poems 1957-1959* (New York: Poets Press, 1968), n.p.

23 Ibid; Ezra Pound, "Canto I," in *Selected Poems of Ezra Pound* (New York: New Directions, 1957), 96; on Beats and the classics, see *Hip Sublime: Beat Writers and the Classical Tradition*, eds. Sheila Murnagham and Ralph M. Rosen (Columbus, OH: 2018); Philip Whalen, "Sourdough Mountain Lookout," in *The Collected Poems of Philip Whalen*, ed. Michael Rothenberg (Middletown, CT: Wesleyan University Press, 2007), 45; Di Prima, "The Practice of Magical Evocation," *Selected Poems, 1956-1975*, 39; Michael Davidson, *The San Francisco Renaissance: Poetics and Community at Mid-Century* (New York: Cambridge University Press, 1989), 178.

24 Ibid., "Track."

25 Ibid., "After Cavalcanti"; Walter Burkert, *Ancient Mystery Cults* (Cambridge, MA: Harvard University Press, 1987), 4–5.

26 "Diane di Prima in Conversation with Margarita Meklina and Andrew Meklin," *Ars Interpres 7: An International Journal of Poetry, Translation and Art*"; Ezra Pound, "Credo" in *Selected Prose: 1909-1965* (New York: New Directions, 1973), 53; John North, *Cosmos: An Illustrated History of Astronomy and Cosmology* (Chicago: University of Chicago Press, 2008), 252; Miriam Nichols, ed., *The Astonishment Tapes: Talks on Poetry and Autobiography with Robin Blaser and Friends* (Tuscaloosa, AL: University of Alabama Press, 2015); Carroll F. Terrell, "A Commentary on Grosseteste with an English Version of De Luce," *Paideuma*, 2, no. 3 (Winter 1973), 450–51; Peter Liebregts, *Ezra Pound and Neoplatonism* (Madison, NJ: Farleigh Dickinson University Press, 2004), 108; Ezra Pound, *Guide to Kulchur* (New York: New Directions, 1970), 77; David C. Lindberg, *The Beginnings of Western Science: The European Scientific Tradition in Philosophical, Religious, and Institutional Context, Prehistory to A.D. 1450*, Second Edition (Chicago: The University of Chicago Press, 2007), 234, 255. On Grosseteste, also see Wilhelm Schmidt-Biggemann, *Philosophia Perennis: Historical Outlines of Western Spirituality in Ancient, Medieval and Early Modern Thought* (Dordrecht: Springer, 2004), 283–87; Dante Alighieri, *Paradiso* XXXIII, ll. 85–90.

27 Di Prima, *Diary*; on the metaphysics of light, see James McEvoy, *Robert Grosseteste* (New York: Oxford University Press, 2000), 87ff.

28 Di Prima, *Diary, 1953-1961,* University of Kansas Libraries, Kenneth Spencer Research Library.

29 Diane di Prima and LeRoi Jones, *The Floating Bear: A Newsletter, Numbers 1-37, 1961-1969* (La Jolla, CA: Laurence McGilvery, 1973); for Robert Grosseteste, "On Light, or The Beginning of Forms," see Issue #29, 1964, 347–54.

30 *Recollections*, 204.

31 Di Prima, "Early Pot Notes," *The Beat Book Volume 4*, eds. Arthur & Glee Knight (California, PA, 1974), Michael McClure, "Peyote Poem," in *The Portable Beat Reader*, ed. Ann Charters; on Dionysus, see James George Frazer, *The Golden Bough: A Study in Magic and Religion* (London: Oxford University Press, 1994), 396–404; Luhrmann, *Persuasions of the Witch's Craft*, 95–96; Caitlin and John Matthews, *The Western Way, A Practical Guide to the Western Mystery Tradition: Volume II, The Hermetic Tradition* (London: Arkana, 1986), 24; Raymond H. Prince, "Cocoon Work: An Interpretation of the Concern of Contemporary Youth with the Mystical," in *Religious Movements in Contemporary America*, eds. Irving I. Zaretsky, and Mark P. Leone (Princeton: Princeton University Press, 1975), 255; also see R.K. Mishra, "The Twentieth Century American Mysticism: Transcendental Immanence," in *Studies in Contemporary Literature: Multiple Contexts and Insights*, eds. Sheobhushan Shukla and Anu Shukla (New Delhi: Sarup and Sons, 2003), 71–77; Barbara Tedlock, *The Woman in the Shaman's Body: Reclaiming the Feminine in Religion and Medicine* (New York: Bantam Books, 2006); on Di Prima and her experiments with entheogens, see *Shaman Woman, Mainline Lady: Women's Writings on the Drug Experience*, ed. Cynthia Palmer and Michale Horowitz (New York: Quill, 1982); Gregory Corso, *An Accidental Autobiography*, 213, 215; *The Collected Poems of Philip Lamantia*, ed. Garrett Caples (Berkeley: University of California Press, 2013), xliii; Corso, "Greece" in *Long Live Man* (New York: New Directions, 1962), 25, 26.

32 Bonnie Bremser, *Troia: Mexican Memoirs* (Champaign, IL: Dalkey Archive Press, 2007), 136; Kay Johnson, "The White Room," *The Outsider* (Spring 1963), 13; Carolyn Cassady, "Foreword" to *Grace Beats Karma* in *Beat Down to Your Soul: What Was the Beat Generation?*, ed. Ann Charters (New York: Penguin, 2001), 81–82; Maria Damon, "Revelations of Companionate Love; or, The Hurts of Women: Janine Pommy Vega's 'Poems to Fernando," in *Girls Who Wore Black: Women Writing the Beat Generation*, eds. Ronna C. Johnson and Nancy M. Grace (New Brunswick, NJ: Rutgers University Press, 2002), 205–26; Stuart D. Hobbs, *The End of the American Avant-Garde* (New York and London: New York University Press, 1997), 105; *Recollections*, 202–03; 370; "Chronology" in *Pieces of Song*, 198; Martin Duberman, *Black Mountain: An Exploration in Community* (New York: E. P. Dutton, 1972), 350; Kay Larson, *Where the Heart Beats: John Cage, Zen Buddhism, and the Inner Life of Artists* (New York: Penguin Books, 2013), 253–54; *13 Most Wanted Men: Andy Warhol and the 1964 World's Fair*, 13; Sally Banes, *Greenwich Village 1963: Avant-Garde Performance and the Effervescent Body* (Durham: Duke University Press, 1993), 26; Rosa Lee Goldberg, *Performance Art: From Futurism to the Present*.

33   "Diane di Prima: Memoirs of a Beatnik," *Research* #2 (1981), 9; Di Prima,
     "Murder Cake" in *Kulchur 9*, Volume 3 (Spring 1963), 50, 53; Nancy Grace,
     "Diane di Prima as Playwright: The Early Years," in *Beat Drama: Playwrights
     and Performances of the "Howl" Generation*, ed. Deborah R. Geis (London:
     Bloomsbury 2016), 171.

34   Stephen J. Bottoms, *Playing Underground: A Critical History of the 1960s
     Off-Off-Broadway Movement* (Ann Arbor: The University of Michigan Press,
     2007), 63–64; Di Prima, *Diary*; Di Prima, *The Discovery of America* in *Res
     Gestae*, Vol 1. No, 4; Hayden White, *Metahistory: The Historical Imagination
     Nineteenth-Century Europe* (Bathmore: Johns Hopkins University Press, 1973).

35   "Research Interview," 9; Andrew Epstein, *Beautiful Enemies: Friendship and
     Postwar American Poetry* (New York: Oxford University Press, 2006), 200;
     LeRoi Jones, "Black Dada Nihilismus," in *The Dead Lecturer* (New York:
     Grove Press, 1964), 62; Werner Sollors has observed that "the vehicle for
     Baraka's critique of reason is alchemy, the 'black art' taken from the Egyptian
     god Thoth, whose Greek name, Hermes Trismegistos, is invoked in the poem.
     His name suggests the Egyptian theme in Baraka's poetry and summons up
     the memory of 'pre-Western' Hermetic cults; in this tradition, Baraka writes
     'hermetic' poetry." See Sollors, *Amiri Baraka/LeRoi Jones: The Quest for a
     "Populist Modernism"* (New York: Columbia University Press, 1978), 91;
     Conversations with Amiri Baraka, ed. Charlie Reilly (Jackson: University
     Press of Mississippi, 1994), 57–58; Di Prima, "Brass Furnace Going Out:
     Song, after an Abortion," in *Selected Poems*, 92,93,94, 95; William Blake,
     "The Tyger"; on Ginsberg's vision of Blake, see David Stephen Calonne, *The
     Spiritual Imagination of the Beats* (New York: Cambridge University Press,
     2017), 85–89; and Alicia Ostriker, "Blake, Ginsberg, Madness, and the Prophet
     as Shaman," in *William Blake and the Moderns*, eds. Robert J. Bertholf and
     Annette S. Levitt (Albany: State University of New York Press, 1982), 111–31;
     Lyndy Abraham, *A Dictionary of Alchemical Imagery* (New York: Cambridge
     University Press, 1998), 2, 82; Mircea Eliade, *The Forge and the Crucible: The
     Origins and Structures of Alchemy* (Chicago: The University of Chicago Press,
     1978), 57; on Blake and the counterculture, see Stephen F. Eisenman and Mark
     Crosby, *William Blake and the Age of Aquarius* (Princeton: Princeton University
     Press, 2017); Amy L. Friedman, "'I SAY MY NEW NAME': Women Writers of the
     Beat Generation," in *The Beat Generation Writers*, ed. A. Robert Lee (East
     Haven, CT: Pluto Press, 1996), 206; *Recollections*, 272; Robert Duncan,
     "Taking Away from God His Sound," *The Nation*, 200, no. 22 (May 31, 1965),
     596–97; Bent Sorensen, "Tarot and the Poets," online. For a sociological study
     which concentrates on the use of Tarot among American "occult" communities,
     see Danny L. Jorgensen and Lin Jorgensen, "Social Meanings of the Occult,"
     The Sociological Quarterly 23 (Summer 1982), 373–89.

36   Brad Gooch, *City Poet: The Life and Times of Frank O'Hara* (New York:
     Harper, 2014), 368, 369; *Recollections*, 239; on O'Hara, also see David
     Bergman, "The Queer Writer in New York," in *The Cambridge Companion to
     Gay and Lesbian Writing*, ed. Hugh Stevens (New York: Cambridge University
     Press, 2011), 225, 226, 229; Terence Diggory, *Encyclopedia of New York
     School Poets* (New York: Facts on File, 2009).

37   Di Prima, "Introduction," *The Floating Bear: A Newsletter, Numbers 1-37, 1961-1969* (La Jolla, CA: Laurence McGilvery, 1973), viii–ix; Richard Howard, *Alone with America: Essays on the Art of Poetry in the United States Since 1950* (New York: Atheneum, 1980), 479; Gregory Corso, *Writings from Unmuzzled Ox Magazine* (New York: Unmuzzled Ox Foundation, Ltd., 1981), 156; Ann Charters, *The Portable Beat Reader*, 399; Gooch, *City Poet: The Life and Times of Frank O'Hara*, 369–70.

38   David Lehman, *The Last Avant-Garde: The Making of the New York School of Poets* (New York: Doubleday, 1998), 337; Diane di Prima, "For Frank O'Hara, An Elegy," in *Selected Poems*, 163.

39   Ibid.; Paul Deussen, *The Philosophy of the Upanishads* (New York: Dover Publications, 1966), 101.

40   Norman Mailer, "The White Negro," in *The Portable Beat Reader*, ed. Ann Charters (New York: Penguin Books, 1992), 597; on yoga and the counterculture, see Stefanie Syman, *The Subtle Body: The Story of Yoga in America* (New York: Farrar, Straus and Giroux, 2012), 198–232; Di Prima, *Various Fables from Various Places* (New York: G. P. Putnam's Sons, 1960), 182; C. G. *The Red Book, Liber Novus,* ed. Sonu Shamdasani (New York and London: W. W. Norton & Company, 2009), 154.

41   See Steven M. Wasserstrom, *Religion after Religion: Gershom Scholem, Mircea Eliade and Henry Corbin at Eranos* (Princeton: Princeton University Press, 1999); Johanna Drucker, qtd. in Linda A. Kinnahan, *Lyric Interventions: Feminism, Experimental Poetry, and Contemporary Discourse* (Iowa City: University of Iowa Press, 2004), 34–35; http://jacketmagazine.com/18/diprima-iv.html; on Donald Allen's role in disseminating Beat writers, see Loren Glass, *Counterculture Colophon: Grove Press, the Evergreen Review, and the Incorporation of the Avant-Garde* (Stanford: Stanford University Press, 2013), 22–24; Di Prima, *Big Table*, no. 4 (Spring 1960); *The Postmoderns: The New American Poetry Revised* Don Allen, ed. The history of *Big Table* recapitulates the many censorship battles of the 1950s and 1960s. Sections of Burroughs's *Naked Lunch* were published in the *Chicago Review* in 1958 which offended the administration of the University of Chicago. Editor Irving Rosenthal then established *Big Table* in order to print the censured Burroughs material. See Glass, *Counterculture Colophon*, 117.

Chapter 3

1   On James Frazer, see *Recollections*, 370; Ludwig Wittgenstein, *Remarks on Frazer's Golden Bough* (Atlantic Highland, NJ: Humanities Press, 1979); Tom Clark, *Charles Olson: The Allegory of a Poet's Life* (Berkeley: North Atlantic Books, 2000), 198; Vale, *Modern Pagans*, 36; Martin P. Nilsson, *Primitive Time-Reckoning: A Study in the Origins and First Development of the Art of Counting Time Among the Primitive and Early Culture Peoples* (Lund: C. W. K. Gleerup, 1920), see especially Chapters IX: "Calendar Regulation.1. The Intercalation," 240–66; Chapter X: "Calendar Regulation.

2. Beginning of the Year," 267–81; Chapter XII: "Solstices and Equinoxes. Aids to the Determination of Time," 311–23; Chapter XIII: "Artificial Periods of Time. Feasts," 324–46; Chapter XIV: "The Calendar-Makers," 347–54; on Brion Gysin and Winter Solstice celebrations, see *Recollections*, 371; Di Prima, "Revolutionary Letter #59," in *Revolutionary Letters* (San Francisco: Last Gasp, 2007), 76; "Diane di Prima: Memoirs of a Beatnik," *RE/Search 2*, 1981,"Wednesday Night 1962-3-4," 8; Di Prima, *Diary of Diane di Prima, 1953-1961*, University of Kansas, Kenneth Spencer Library, MS 71:1, Letter to Peter, February 21, 1961; *Spring and Autumn Annals: A Celebration of the Seasons for Freddie*, MS, n.p.; on witchcraft and its origins, see Mircea Eliade, *Occultism, Witchcraft, and Cultural Fashions* (Chicago: University of Chicago Press, 1976), 57–58; 69–93; also see David Waldron, *The Sign of the Witch: Modernity and the Pagan Revival* (Durham, NC: Carolina Academic Press, 2008); "Self-Reliance," in *Ralph Waldo Emerson: The Oxford Authors*, ed. Richard Poirier (Oxford: Oxford University Press, 1990), 149; V. Vale, "RE/Search Visits Diane di Prima," 2015, 40; Di Prima, "Notes on the Solstice," *Alcheringa*, 1, no. 2 (1975), 82–88; T. M. Luhrmann, *Persuasions of the Witch's Craft: Ritual Magic in Contemporary England* (Cambridge, MA: Harvard University Press, 1989), 1989, 47; Robert Graves, *The White Goddess* (New York: Farrar, Straus and Giroux, 2013); on goddess worship, also see Mary Jo Neitz, "In Goddess We Trust," in *In Gods We Trust: New Patterns of Religious Pluralism*, ed. Thomas Robbins and Dick Anthony (New Brunswick, NJ: Transaction Publishers, 1990), 352–72; Jeffrey B. Russell and Brooks Alexander, *A New History of Witchcraft: Sorcerers, Heretics and Pagans* (London: Thames and Hudson, 2015); for a good anthology on paganism, see *The Paganism Reader*, eds. Chas. S. Clifton and Graham Harvey (New York and London: Routledge, 2004); Diane di Prima, *Dinners and Nightmares* (San Francisco: Last Gasp, 1998), 17.

2 *Dinners and Nightmares,* 19, 98.

3 Ibid., 22.

4 Ibid., 23, 32; Nancy M. Grace, "The Beat Fairy Tale and Transnational Spectacle Culture: Diane di Prima and William S. Burroughs," in *The Transnational Beat Generation*, ed. Nancy M. Grace and Jennie Skerl (New York: Palgrave Macmillan, 2012), 84.

5 Ibid., 26.

6 Ibid., 33, 34.

7 Ibid., 37; Ezra Pound, "For a New Paiedeuma," in *Selected Prose, 1909-1965* (New York: New Directions, 1975), 284.

8 Diane di Prima, in *Campfires of the Resistance: Poetry from the Movement*, ed. Todd Gitlin (Indianapolis: Bobbs-Merrill, 1971), 102; Wini Breines, "The 'Other' Fifties: Beats and Bad Girls," in Joanne Meyerowitz, *Not June Cleaver: Women and Gender in Postwar America, 1945-1960* (Philadelphia: Temple University Press, 1994), 402; *Dinners and Nightmares,* 74; "Memories of Childhood," in Paul Goodman, ed., *Seeds of Liberation* (New York: George Braziller, 1964), 523–25.

9   On persecution of homosexuals, see Gayle Rubin, "Thinking Sex: Notes for
    a Radical Theory of the Politics of Sexuality," in *The Norton Anthology of
    Theory and Criticism*, Second Edition, ed. Vincent B. Leitch (New York: W. W.
    Norton, 2010), 2379–80; *Dinners and Nightmares.*, 93–94.

10 *13 Most Wanted Men: Andy Warhol and the 1964 World's Fair*, 132; Jerry
    Gafio Watts, *Amiri Baraka: The Politics and Art of a Black Intellectual*
    (New York and London: New York University Press, 2001), 46; Steven Clay
    and Rodney Phillips, *A Secret Location on the Lower East Side: Adventures in
    Writing, 1960-1980* (New York: The New York Public Library and Granary
    Books, 1998), 75; *Recollections*, 244; *The Autobiography of LeRoi Jones/
    Amiri Baraka* (New York: Freundlich Books, 1984), 251; Bill Morgan, *The
    Typewriter is Holy: The Complete, Uncensored History of the Beat Generation*
    (New York: Free Press, 2010), 155.

11 Ron Loewinsohn, "After the (mimeograph) Revolution," *Triquarterly* 18
    (Spring 1970), 222.

12 *Black Mountain College: An Experiment in Art*, ed. Vincent Katz (Cambridge,
    MA: The MIT Press, 2003), 183; Charles Olson, *Mayan Letters*, ed. Robert
    Creeley (London: Jonathan Cape, 1968), 6; Charles Olson, "Human Universe,"
    in *Selected Writings*, ed. Robert Creeley (New York: New Directions, 1966),
    57; on Olson and Mexico, also see Daniel Hoffman, ed., *The Harvard Guide
    to Contemporary American Writing* (Cambridge, MA: Harvard University
    Press, 1979), 528; Charles Olson, *The Special View of History*, ed. Ann
    Charters (Berkeley: Oyez, 1970), 11, 20; Jack Foley, *Visions and Affiliations,
    A California Literary Time Line: 1940-2005, Part Two, 1980-2005* (Oakland,
    CA: 2011), 232; *The Floating Bear: A Newsletter, Numbers 1-37, 1961-1969*,
    eds. Diane di Prima and LeRoi Jones (La Jolla, CA: Laurence McGilvery,
    1973), x; *A Secret Location on the Lower East Side*, 29.

13 Diane di Prima, "Old Father. Old Artificer: Charles Olson Memorial
    Lecture," *Lost and Found: The CUNY Poetics Document Initiative*, Series
    3, No 4 (Fall 2012), 6; *Recollections*, 354; Mary Zeppa, "Interview with
    Diane di Prima," *Poet News: Sacramento's Literary Calendar and Review*,
    May 1985, 6; for Di Prima's account of the arrest, see *The Floating Bear:
    A Newsletter, Numbers 1-37, 1961-1969*, xiii–xv; *13 Most Wanted Men:
    Andy Warhol and the 1964 World's Fair*, 134; Ted Morgan, *Literary Outlaw:
    The Life and Times of William S. Burroughs* (New York: W. W. Norton,
    2012), 351, 352; Barry Miles, *Call Me Burroughs: A Life* (New York:
    Twelve, 2013), 437, 438; "Diane di Prima: Memoirs of a Beatnik," *RE/
    Search 2*, 1981, 8; Di Prima, "Revolutionary Letter Number Forty-Five," in
    Revolutionary Letters, 58;

14 *A Secret Location*, 89.

15 *Recollections*, 256.

16 *The East Side Scene: American Poetry, 1960-1965*, ed. Allen De Loach
    (Garden City, NY: Anchor Books, 1972), 13; Stephen J. Bottoms, *Playing
    Underground: A Critical History of the 1960s Off-Off-Broadway Movement*
    (Ann Arbor: The University of Michigan Press, 2004), 63, 65; Anne Waldman,
    "Interview with Diane di Prima," *Rocky Ledge* (1981), 40; Di Prima,

Recollections, 382; Jimmy Fazzino, *World Beats: Beat Generation Writing and the Worlding of U.S. Literature* (Hanover, NH: Dartmouth College Press, 2016), 79; "To Have Done With the Judgment of God, A Radio Play," in *Antonin Artaud: Selected Writings*, ed. Susan Sontag (New York: Farrar, Straus and Giroux, 1976), 555–71; Artaud would also influence Charles Bukowski, who reviewed Jack Hirschman's *Artaud Anthology*. See Charles Bukowski, *Portions from a Wine-Stained Notebook, Uncollected Stories and Essays 1944-1990*, ed. David Stephen Calonne (City Lights: San Francisco, 2008), 49–53; Ed Sanders, *Fug You: An Informal History of the Peace Eye Bookstore* (Boston: Da Capo Press, 2011), 134; *13 Most Wanted Men: Andy Warhol and the 1964 World's Fair*, 134.

17 Ingmar Bergman, *The Magic Lantern: An Autobiography* (London: Hamish Hamilton, 1988), 73; on the "cinephilia" which possessed the young filmgoers of the 1950s, 1960s, and 1970s, see Susan Sontag, "A Century of Cinema," in *Where the Stress Falls: Essays* (New York: Picador, 2001), 117–22; Bill Morgan, *The Beat Generation in San Francisco* (San Francisco: City Lights, 2003), 155; *Recollections*, 261, 263, 264, 266, 267; David Meltzer, ed., *San Francisco Beat: Talking with the Poets* (San Francisco: City Lights, 2001), 17; *The Calculus of Variation*, n.p.

18 Di Prima, *The Calculation of Variation*; Robert Duncan, *The H.D. Book*, eds. Michael Boughn and Victor Coleman (Berkeley: University of California Press, 2011), 126, 128–29.

19 Dore Ashton, *The New York School: A Cultural Reckoning* (New York: The Viking Press, 1973), 227; on the premiere of *Howl*, also see David Stephen Calonne, *The Spiritual Imagination of the Beats* (New York: Cambridge University Press, 2017), 29; Denis Johnston, *Precipitations: Contemporary American Poetry as Occult Practice* (Middletown, CT: Wesleyan University Press, 2002), 12; on Blake and California artists, see Elizabeth Ferrell, "William Blake on the West Coast," in *William Blake and the Age of Aquarius*, ed. Stephen F. Eisenman (Princeton: Princeton University Press, 2017), 101–39; Richard Candida Smith, *The Modern Moves West: California Artists and Democratic Culture in the Twentieth Century* (Philadelphia: University of Pennsylvania Press, 2009), 79, 95; on nexus between Beats, spirituality, and California art, see Ilene Susan Fort, "Altered State(s): California Art and the Inner World," and John P. Bowles, "Shocking 'Beat' Art Displayed: California Artists and the Beat Image," in *Reading California: Art, Image, and Identity, 1900-2000* (Berkeley: University of California Press, 2000), 30–48, 221–46; Rebecca Peabody, ed., *Pacific Standard Time: Los Angeles Art, 1945-1980* (Los Angeles: The Getty Research Institute, 2011), 89; *Semina Culture*, 104; William Hjortsberg, *Jubilee Hitchhiker: The Life and Times of Richard Brautigan* (Berkeley: Counterpoint, 2012), 160; *Recollections*, 305–06, 266; Rebecca Solnit, *Secret Exhibition: Six California Artists of the Cold War Era* (San Francisco: City Lights, 1990), 87; on assemblage, also see Stephen Fredman, *Contextual Practice: Assemblage and the Erotic in Postwar Poetry and Art* (Stanford: Stanford University Press, 2010); *Loba*, 152; on Cameron, see Richard Candida Smith, *Utopia and Dissent: Art, Poetry, and Politics in*

California (Berkeley: University of California Press, 1995), 227, 257–58; also see William Hackman, *Out of Sight: The Los Angeles Art Scene of the Sixties* (New York: Other Press, 2015), 56–58; *Beneath a Single Moon*, 56–57; Mary Kerr, "Out of the Shadows: Women in the California Cultural Underground—1950s/60s," in *Out of the Shadows: Beat Women Are Not Beaten Women*, eds. Frida Forsgren and Michael J. Prince (Kristiansand: Portal, 2015), 260; Michael Duncan and Kristine McKenna, *Semina Culture: Wallace Berman & His Circle* (New York: D.A.P./Distributed Art Publishers, Inc., 2005), 108,109.

20   Rick Fields, *How the Swans Came to the Lake: A Narrative History of Buddhism in America* (Boston: Shambhala, 1992), 168–70; On Suzuki, see Donald S. Lopez Jr., ed., *A Modern Buddhist Bible: Essential Readings from East and West* (Boston: Beacon Press, 2002), 127–37; also see *Asian Religions in America: A Documentary History*, eds. Thomas A. Tweed and Stephen Prothero (New York: Oxford University Press, 1999), 261–64; *Recollections*, 319. On the *guru*, see Heinrich Zimmer, *Philosophies of India*, ed. Joseph Campbell (Princeton: Princeton University Press, 1974), 16–17, 21–22, 44; Di Prima, "Statement on Poetry and Buddhism," in *America Zen: A Gathering of Poets*, eds. Ray McNiece and Larry Smith (Huron, OH: Bottom Dog Press, 2004), 46, 47.

21   *Recollections*, 311, 315, 316; *San Francisco Beat*, 15.

22   *Recollections*, 352–53; Robert A. Wilson, *Seeing Shelley Plain: Memories of New York's Legendary Phoenix Book Shop* (New Castle, DE: Oak Knoll Press, 2001), 101; *Beneath A Single Moon*, 57; *The Princeton Dictionary of Buddhism*, ed. Robert E. Buswell Jr. and Donald S. Lopez Jr. (Princeton: Princeton University Press, 2014), 541; *The Shambhala Dictionary of Buddhism and Zen*, trans. Michael H. Kohn (Boston: Shambhala, 1991), 144; Di Prima, "For the Dead Lecturer," in *Selected Poems*, 137; *Recollections*,318, 387.

23   *San Francisco Beat*, 15–16.

24   *Recollections*, 340, 222.

25   *Recollections*, 227, 228; see Zimmer, *Philosophies of India*, 174–74.

26   Di Prima, "Vector" in *The New Handbook of Heaven* (San Francisco: The Auerhahn Press, 1963), n.p.

27   Ibid., "The Jungle," "Blue Nirvana," "archive," n.p.

28   Ibid., "The Beach," "Lord Jim," n.p.

29   *Recollections*, 370; Rob Haskins, *John Cage* (London: Reaktion Books, 2012), 62; Peter Rowley, *New Gods in America: An Informal Investigation into the New Religions of American Youth Today* (New York: David McKay Company, Inc., 1972), 187–98.

30   Jorge Luis Borges, "For A Version of *I Ching*," in *The Sonnets*, ed. Stephen Kessler (New York: London, 2010); A. C. Graham, "Rationalism and Anti-Rationalism in Pre-Buddhist China," in *Rationality in Question: On Eastern and Western Views of Rationality*, ed. Shlomo Biderman and Ben-Ami Scharfstein (Leiden: E. J. Brill, 1989), 160.

31 Di Prima, "Paracelsus: An Appreciation," in *The Alchemical Tradition in the Late Twentieth Century: Io 31*, ed. Richard Grossinger (Berkeley: North Atlantic Books, 1983), 28; William S. Burroughs, "On Coincidence," in *The Adding Machine*, 103; Richard J. Smith, *The I Ching: A Biography* (Princeton and Oxford: Princeton University Press, 2012); also see C. G. Jung, "Foreword to the *I Ching*" in *Psychology and Religion: West and East* (Princeton: Princeton University Press, 1973), 589–608. For a recent exploration of Jung's fascination with the *I Ching*, the concept of synchronicity and his friendship with the physicist Wolfgang Pauli, see Arthur I. Miller, *Deciphering The Cosmic Number: The Strange Friendship of Wolfgang Pauli and Carl Jung* (New York: W. W. Norton, 2009), 181–207.

32 *Poet's Vaudeville*, 7.

33 *The I Ching or Book of Changes: The Richard Wilhelm Translation* (Princeton: Princeton University Press, 1971), 86.

34 Di Prima, "I Ching" in *Pieces of Song*, 42.

35 Di Prima, "Revolutionary Letter #18" in *Revolutionary Letters* (San Francisco: City Lights, 1971), 29.

36 Di Prima, "Revolutionary Letter #45" in *Revolutionary Letters*, 58.

37 *Bob Dylan: The Essential Interviews*, ed. Jonathan Cott (New York: Wenner Books, 2006), 58–59.

38 Neville Drury, *Dictionary of Mysticism and the Occult* (New York: Harper and Row, 1985), 116.

39 Nancy M. Grace and Ronna C. Johnson, *Breaking the Rule of Cool: Interviewing and Reading Women Beat Writers* (Jackson: University Press of Mississippi, 2004), 99.

40 Reva Wolf, *Andy Warhol: Poetry, and Gossip in the 1960s* (Chicago: University of Chicago Press, 1997), 44; Di Prima, *The Calculus of Variation*, n.p.

41 Ibid. Further references in the text are to this edition, which is unpaginated.

42 Christine Brooke-Rose, *A ZBC of Ezra Pound* (Berkeley: University of California Press, 1971), 94; Henry Corbin, "Preface," David L. Miller, *The New Polytheism : Rebirth of the Gods and Goddesses* (Dallas: Spring Publications, Inc., 1981), 2; E. M. Cioran, *The New Gods*, trans. Richard Howard (New York: Quadrangle/The New York Times Book Co., 1974), 22, 24; Di Prima, *Recollections*, 412. On Huncke, see *The Herbert Huncke Reader*, ed. Benjamin G. Schafer (New York: Morrow and Co., 1997); Hilary Holladay, *Herbert Huncke: The Times Square Hustler Who Inspired Jack Kerouac and the Beat Generation* (Tucson, AZ: Schaffner Press, 2015).

43 Naomi R. Goldenberg, *Changing of the Gods: Feminism and the End of Traditional Religions* (Boston: Beacon Press, 1979), 104; Daniel Kane, *All Poets Welcome: The Lower East Side Poetry Scene in the 1960s* (Berkeley: University of California Press, 2003), 39; Joe Brainard, *I Remember* (New York: Granary Books, 2001), 69; *A Secret Location on the Lower East Side*, 89; David Allyn, *Make Love Not War: The Sexual Revolution, An*

Unfettered History (Boston: Little Brown, 2000), 44, 46; Di Prima, "Theatre Poem #1," in *The East Side Poetry Scene: American Poetry, 1960-1965*, ed. Allen De Loach (Garden City, NY: Anchor Books, 1972), 71; Di Prima, "Fuzz's Progress," *The Nation*, May 4, 1964; Gretchen Lemke-Santangelo, *Daughters of Aquarius: Women of the Sixties Counterculture* (Lawrence, KS: University Press of Kansas, 2009), 64; Di Prima, "I Get My Period, September 1964," in *Selected Poems: 1956-1975*, 136; Ron Whitehead, Sharon Gibson, and Kent Fielding, "Diane di Prima: Memoirs of a Beatnik," interview in *Beat Scene*, No. 27, 16–17; Bill Morgan, *Beat Atlas: A State by State Guide to the Beat Generation in America* (San Francisco: City Lights, 2011), 219; on Di Prima and Stan Brakhage, see Daniel Kane, *We Saw the Light: Conversations Between the New American Cinema and Poetry* (Iowa City: University of Iowa Press, 2009), 24; Wolf, *Andy Warhol: Poetry, and Gossip in the 1960s*, 43–44; See also *13 Most Wanted Men: Andy Warhol and the 1964 World's Fair*, 132.

44   *13 Most Wanted Men: Andy Warhol and the 1964 World's Fair*, 133; Steven Watson, *Factory Made: Warhol and the Sixties* (New York: Pantheon Books, 2003), 100; P. Adams Sitney, *Visionary Film: The American Avant-Garde, 1943-2000* (New York: Oxford University Press, 2002), 337; on Jack Smith's "anarchism,' see Sheldon Renan, *An Introduction to the American Underground Film* (New York: E. P. Dutton, 1967), 181.

45   Jack Sargent, *Naked Lens: An Illustrated History of Beat Cinema* (London: Creation Books, 1997), 107, 110; on Burroughs and film, see Barry Miles, *Call Me Burroughs*.

46   Jennifer Doyle, "Between Friends," in *A Companion to Lesbian, Gay, Bisexual, Transgender, and Queer Studies*, eds. George E. Haggerty and Molly McGarry (Malden, MA: Blackwell Publishing, 2007), 325, 326.

47   Steven Watson, *Factory Made*, 57.

48   John Strausbaugh, *The Village: Four Hundred Years of Bohemians, Radicals and Rogues, a History of Greenwich Village* (New York: Ecco, 2013), 370; Callie Angell, *Andy Warhol Screen Tests: The Films of Andy Warhol Catalogue Raisonne, Volume 1* (New York: Harry N. Abrams, 2006), 93. On Herko, see Tim Teeman's article in *The Guardian*: https://www.theguardian.com/stage/2014/oct/23/fred-herko-life-and-dramatic-death-avant-garde-hero

49   *Recollections*, 403, 405; *13 Most Wanted Men: Andy Warhol and the 1964 World's Fair*, ed. Larissa Harris and Media Farzin (Queens, NY: Queens Museum of Art, 2014), 131.

50   Sarah M. Pike, *New Age and Neopagan Religions in America* (New York: Columbia University Press, 2004), 21; also see Sabina Magliocco, *Neo-Pagan Sacred Art and Altars: Making Things Whole* (Jackson: University Press of Mississippi, 2001); "Spring and Autumn Annals: A Celebration of the Seasons for Freddie," *The Outsider*, Vol. 2, no 4/5, Winter 1968–69, 50. On Di Prima's contributions to the Webbs's underground magazine, see Jeff Weddle, *Bohemian New Orleans: The Story of the* Outsider *and Lujon Press* (Jackson: University Press of Mississipppi, 2007), 60, 143, 171, 178.

51 Di Prima, *Freddie Poems* (Point Reyes, CA: Eidolon, 1974), n.p.

52 Steven Watson, *Factory Made*, 140.

53 Jose Esteban Munoz, *Cruising Utopia: The Then and There of Queer Futurity* (New York: New York University Press, 2009), 165.

54 RoseLee Goldberg, *Performance Art: From Futurism to the Present* (London: Thames and Hudson, 2011), 140; *The Floating Bear, A Newsletter: Numbers 1-37, 1961-1969*, eds. Diane di Prima and LeRoi Jones (La Jolla, CA: 1973), 239; Goldberg, *Performance Art*, 141; S. J. Tambiah, "The Magical Power of Words," *Man, New Series*, 3, no. 2 (June 1968), 175–208; T. M Luhrmann, *Persuasions of the Witch's Craft*, 51; Donald S. Lopez, Jr., *The Tibetan Book of the Dead: A Biography* (Princeton: Princeton University Press, 2011), 2; Andy Warhol and Pat Hackett, *POPism: The Warhol Sixties* (New York: Harcourt Brace Jovanovich, 1990), 85.

55 I. P. Couliano, *Out of this World: Otherworldly Journeys from Gilgamesh to Albert Einstein* (Boston and London: Shambhala, 1991), 93; Giuseppe Tucci, *The Religions of Tibet* (Berkeley: University of California Press, 1980), 64; *Recollections*, 397; Paul Feyerabend, *Knowledge without Foundations: Two Lectures Delivered on the Nellie Heldt Lecture Fund* (Oberlin: Oberlin College, 1962), 19, 23. The essay is reprinted in John Preston, ed., Paul Feyerabend, *Knowledge, Science and Relativism: Philosophical Papers, Volume III* (Cambridge: Cambridge University Press, 1999), 50–77; Di Prima, "Revolutionary Letter Number Sixty-Three."

56 Isaiah Berlin, *The Roots of Romanticism* (Princeton: Princeton University Press, 1999), 50; also on Blake, see Berlin, "The Counter-Enlightenment," in *The Proper Study of Mankind: An Anthology of Essays* (New York: Farrar, Straus and Giroux, 1997), 259–60; Di Prima, "Revolutionary Letter Number Ten"; Wade Clark Roof, *A Generation of Seekers: The Spiritual Journeys of the Baby Boom Generation* (San Francisco: Harper San Francisco, 1994),117; on the spiritual movements of the 1960s, also see Beth Bailey, "Religion," in David Farber and Beth Bailey, *The Columbia Guide to America in the 1960s* (New York: Columbia University Press, 2001), 296–304; Frances A. Yates, *The Occult Philosophy in the Elizabethan Age* (London and New York: Routledge and Kegan Paul, 1999), 90; Di Prima, "Paracelsus" in *Pieces of a Song*, 156; Di Prima's "Introduction" to Paracelsus is reprinted in "Paracelsus: An Appreciation," in *The Alchemical Tradition in the Late Twentieth Century: Io 31*, ed. Richard Grossinger (Berkeley: North Atlantic Books, 1983); Duncan, "Rites of Participation," *The H.D. Book*, 153; *Recollections*, 423; Jean Seznec, *The Survival of the Pagan Gods: The Mythological Tradition and Its Place in Renaissance Humanism and Art* (New York: Pantheon, 1953), 59; http://magmapoetry.com/archive/magma-11-poetry-from-sanfranchise/articles/the-movement-of-the-mind.

57 William R. Newman, *Promethean Ambitions: Alchemy and the Quest for a Perfect Nature* (Chicago: University of Chicago Press, 2004), 2–5; Paul Feyerabend, *Philosophy of Nature*, eds. Helmut Heit and Eric Oberheim (Cambridge: Polity Press, 2016), 180–81; Di Prima, "Prophetissa" in *Pieces of a Song*, 141–43; on Maria Prophetissima, see M. E. Warlick, "Moon Sisters:

Women and Alchemical Imagery," in *The Golden Egg: Alchemy in Art and Literature*, eds. Alexandra Lembert and Elmar Schenkel (Berlin: Glada+Wilch Verlag, 2002), 188–89; Raphael Patai, *The Jewish Alchemists: A History and Sourcebook* (Princeton: Princeton University Press, 1995); Theodore Ziolkowski, *The Alchemist in Literature: From Dante to the Present* (Oxford: Oxford University Press, 2015), 119–20; Jane Nelson, *Form and Image in the Fiction of Henry Miller* (Detroit: Wayne State University Press, 1970), 86; from Jung, *Mysterium Coniunctionis*, Introduction, xvii; Jung, *Aion*, 169.

58   http://magmapoetry.com/archive/magma-11-poetry-from-san-francisco/articles/ the-movement-of-the-mind; Di Prima, "Techniques and Structures of Magic," 18–19.

59   *Intersection Newsletter,* 10, no. 2 (Spring 1980), 6; on *bhakti*, see R. C. Zaehner, *Hinduism* (New York: Oxford University Press, 1971), 126; Di Prima, "Hymn to Lord Shiva," "Hymn" in *Selected Poems*, 230, 162. On Hinduism in the counterculture, see Andrea Grace Diem and James R. Lewis, "Imagining India: The Influence of Hinduism on the New Age Movement" in *Perspectives on the New Age*, eds. James R. Lewis and J. Gordon Melton (Albany: State University of New York, 1992), 48–58.

60   Jeffrey J. Kripal, *Mutants and Mystics: Science Fiction, Superhero Comics, and the Paranormal* (Chicago: The University of Chicago Press, 2011), 170; *"Old Father, Old Artificer": Charles Olson Memorial Lecture* (2012), 7–13.

61   Di Prima, "Jacob's Ladder" in *Selected Poems: 1956-1975,* 297; Sarah M. Pike, *New Age and Neopagan Religions in America* (New York: Columbia University Press, 2004), 33–34; Timothy Gray, *Urban Pastoral: Natural Currents in the New York School* (Iowa City: University of Iowa Press, 2010), 155; "Trajectory," 1970 broadside, published by Ken and Ann Mikolowski's Alternative Press, Detroit, Michigan; *The Princeton Dictionary of Buddhism*, 676; *San Francisco Beat*, 13; *A Secret Location on the Lower East Side*, 89. While at Millbrook, continuing her Yoga practice sometimes was challenging. According to Stefanie Syman, "Psychedelics tended to displace a sustained yoga practice. At Millbrook, Di Prima, for one, found it difficult to make time for yoga with much regularity, and her favorite yoga teacher had left for California by the late fall of 1966." Di Prima's Hatha Yoga classes were taught by an instructor by the name of Yarek and she noted in her *Millbrook Journal, 1966-67* that "he taught with 'great intuitive tact and understanding' and his class was quite long and 'a little more complete than the others.'" See Stefanie Syman, *The Subtle Body: The Story of Yoga in America* (New York: Farrar, Straus and Giroux, 2010), 225, 344. On Timothy Leary, see Don Lattin, *The Harvard Psychedelic Club: How Timothy Leary, Ram Dass, Huston Smith and Andrew Weil Killed the Fifties and Ushered in a New Age for America* (New York: HarperCollins, 2010), and more recently, Bill Minutaglio and Steven L. Davis, *The Most Dangerous Man in America: Timothy Leary, Richard Nixon and the Hunt for the Fugitive King of LSD* (New York; Twelve, 2018).

62   "The Gnosis Interview: Diane di Prima on Magic, Healing, and the Western Esoteric Tradition," 17–18; Di Prima, "The Holidays at Millbrook—1966," in

Shaman Woman, Mainline Lady: Women's Writings on the Drug Experience, eds. Cynthia Palmer and Michael Horowitz (New York: Quill, 1982), 226–27, 228. Also see Robert Greenfield, *Timothy Leary: A Biography* (New York: Harcourt, Inc, 2006), 291–95.

63   http://jacketmagazine.com/18/diprima-iv.html; David Schneider, *Crowded by Beauty: The Life and Zen of Poet Philip Whalen*, 214.

64   For reproductions of Herms's illustrations and Di Prima's haikus, see George Herms, *The River Book, Volume 2* (Venice, CA: Hamilton Press, 2014), 166–71; Di Prima, *The Poetry Deal*, 1.

65   *Recollections*, 272; Joan Wylie Hall, ed., *Conversations with Audre Lorde* (Jackson: University Press of Mississippi, 2004), 11; Di Prima, "Introduction" to *First Cities* (New York: Poets Press, 1968); Alexis De Veaux, *Warrior Poet: A Biography of Audre Lorde* (New York: W. W. Norton, 2004), 105. Also see, https://blogs.lib.unc.edu/rbc/index.php/2013/06/25/sisters-outsider-diane-di-prima-and-audre-lorde/.

66   Di Prima, *Hotel Albert* (New York: Kriya Press/Poets Press, 1968), n.p.

67   See Helen Farley, "Tarot" in *The Occult World*, 571; Jean-Pierre Laurant, "Tarot" in *Dictionary of Western Gnosis and Western Esotericism*, 1110, 1111; Virginia Moore, *The Unicorn: William Butler Yeats' Search for Reality* (New York: The Macmillan Company, 1954), 59, 60. For a study of the symbolism of the Tarot and the spiritual and political history of the 1960s, see William Cook Haigwood, *Journeying the Sixties: A Counterculture Tarot* (CreateSpace, 2013).

68   Paul Waldo-Schwartz, *Art and the Occult* (New York: George Braziller, 1975), 10–21; Ronald Decker, Thierry Depaulis, Michael Dummett, *A Wicked Pack of Cards: The Origins of the Occult Tarot* (New York: Saint Martin's Press, 1996); Donald Decker and Michael Dummett, *A History of the Occult Tarot: 1870-1970* (London: Duckworth, 2002). On Frye, see Robert D. Denham, *Northrop Frye: Religious Visionary and Architect of the Spiritual World* (Charlottesville: University of Virginia Press, 2004), 236–40.

69   Tom Clark, *Charles Olson: The Allegory of a Poet's Life* (Berkeley: North Atlantic Books, 2000), 114.

70   Jack Spicer, "A Plan for a Book on Tarot," *boundary 2*, 6.1 (1977), 26, 27; Ibid.

71   Di Prima, "Rant, from a Cool Place," *Revolutionary Letters*, 148, 149; Jack Kerouac, *The Dharma Bums*; Andrew Epstein, *Beautiful Enemies: Friendship and Postwar American Poetry* (New York: Oxford University Press, 2006), 230.

72   *Pieces of a Song*, "Diane di Prima Chronology," 199; Bill Morgan, *The Beat Generation in San Francisco: A Literary Tour* (San Francisco: City Lights, 2003),162; W. J. Rorabaugh, *American Hippies* (New York: Cambridge University Press, 2015), 63; http://exhibits.library.ucsc.edu/exhibits/show/love-on-haight/writing; *San Francisco Beat*, 19.

73   Diane di Prima, "Preface" to *Collected Poems of Lenore Kandel* (Berkeley: North Atlantic Books, 2012), xiii.

Chapter 4

1 See W. J. Rorabaugh, *American Hippies* (New York: Cambridge University Press, 2015); Timothy S. Miller, *The Hippies and American Values* (Knoxville: University of Tennessee Press, 2011); Arthur Marwick, *The Sixties*; "The Gnosis Interview: Diane di Prima on Magic, Healing, and the Western Esoteric Tradition," 19–20.

2 *Rocky Ledge*, 1981, 33; Trevor Carolan, "Grounded in Humanity: Gary Snyder on *Back on the Fire*," *Bloomsbury Review* (July/August 2007), 24.

3 Gretchen Lemke-Santangelo, *Daughters of Aquarius: Women of the Sixties Counterculture* (Lawrence, KS: University Press of Kansas, 2009), 47; Jack Foley, *O Powerful Western Star: Poetry & Art in California* (Oakland, CA: Pantograph Press, 2000), 187; *The Poetry Deal*, 1; Di Prima, "Memories of Moe," in *On the Finest Shore: Poems and Reminiscences of Moe* (Berkeley: Moe's Books, 1997), n.p.; Bill Morgan, *The Beat Generation in San Francisco: A Literary Tour* (San Francisco: City Lights Books, 2003), 162; Mark Hamilton Lytle, *America's Uncivil Wars: The Sixties Era from Elvis to the Fall of Richard Nixon* (New York: Oxford University Press, 2006), 212, 213; Robert P. Sutton, *Modern American Communes: A Dictionary* (Westport, CT: Greenwood Press, 2005), 42; also see Timothy Miller, *The 60s Communes: Hippies and Beyond* (Syracuse, NY: Syracuse University Press, 1999), 43–44; Timothy Miller, *The Hippies and American Values* (Knoxville: The University of Tennessee Press, 1991), 105, 106; Laurence Veysey, *The Communal Experience: Anarchist and Mystical Communities in Twentieth-Century America* (Chicago: The University of Chicago Press, 1978).

4 *The Poetry Deal*, 7–8.

5 Ralph A. Cook and Lori Cook, *City Lights Books: A Descriptive Bibliography* (Metuchen, NJ: Scarecrow Press, 1992), 94–95; James D. Sullivan, *On the Walls and in the Streets: American Poetry Broadsides from the 1960s* (Urbana and Chicago: University of Illinois Press, 1997), 61.

6 http://www.poetrymagazines.org.uk/magazine/record.asp?id=3401; Thomas Albright, "Visuals: How the Beats Begat the Freaks," in *The Rolling Stone Book of the Beats: The Beat Generation and American Culture*, ed. Holly George-Warren (New York: Hyperion, 1999), 354; Jesse Cohn, *Underground Passages: Anarchist Resistance Culture, 1848-2011* (Oakland, CA: AK Press, 2014), 86.

7 Di Prima, "Number Twenty-Eight," *Revolutionary Letters*; "Hymn to Maitreya in America" in *Collected Poems of Lenore Kandel, with a preface by Diane di Prima* (Berkeley: North Atlantic Books, 2012), 167–69; *The Princeton Dictionary of Buddhism*, 517.

8 M. H. Abrams, *Natural Supernaturalism: Tradition and Revolution in Romantic Literature* (New York: W. W. Norton, 1973), 170; Frances M. Boldereff, *Hermes to His Son Thoth: Being Joyce's Use of Giordano Bruno in Finnegans Wake* (Woodward, PA: Classic Non-Fiction Library, 1968); James Joyce, "The Bruno Philosophy," review of J. Lewis McIntyre's *Giordano Bruno*

in *The Critical Writings of James Joyce*, eds. Ellsworth Mason and Richard Ellmann (New York: The Viking Press, 1972), 134.

9 Walt Whitman, epigraph in Daniel G. Brinton, Thomas Davidson, *Giordano Bruno: Philosopher and Martyr, Two Addresses* (Philadelphia: David McCkay, 1890); Christoph Delius, et al. *The Story of Philosophy from Antiquity to the Present* (H.F. Ullman: Potsdam, 2005/7), 30; Ted Honderich, ed., *The Oxford Companion to Philosophy* (New York: Oxford University Press, 1995), 106; Arthur O. Lovejoy, *The Great Chain of Being: A Study of the History of an Idea* (Cambridge, MA: Harvard University Press, 1964), 118; Mircea Eliade, "The Occult and the Modern World," in *Occultism, Witchcraft, and Cultural Fashions: Essays in Comparative Religions* (Chicago: University of Chicago Press, 1976), 57; Frances A. Yates, *Giordano Bruno and the Hermetic Tradition* (Chicago: University of Chicago Press, 1991), 238; Lyndy Abraham, *A Dictionary of Alchemical Imagery* (Cambridge: Cambridge University Press, 1998), 124. On Bruno, also see Wouter J. Hanegraaff, *Dictionary of Gnosis and Western Esotericism*, Vol. 1 (Leiden: Brill, 2005), 206–13; Brian Copenhaver, *The Book of Magic: From Antiquity to the Enlightenment* (St. Ives: Penguin, 2015), 435–41.

10 *Revolutionary Letters*, 76.

11 Warren J. Belasco, *Appetite for Change: How the Counterculture Took on the Food Industry* (Ithaca and London: Cornell University Press, 2007), 30–31, 47–48; also see more recently, Jonathan Kauffman, *Hippie Food: How Back-to-the-Landers, Longhairs, and Revolutionaries Changed the Way We Eat* (New York: William Morrow, 2018); Yates, *Giordano Bruno and the Hermetic Tradition*, 312; Yates comments further on the "Giordanisti": "Bruno was said to have founded a sect in Germany called the 'Giordanisti,' suggesting that this might have something to do with the Rosicrucians, the mysterious brotherhood of the Rosy Coss announced by manifestos in the early seventeenth century in Germany, about which so little is known that some scholars argue that it never existed . . . . Bruno, at any rate, propagated his views in both England and Germany, so his movements might conceivably be a common source for both Rosicrucianism and Freemasonry." See Frances A. Yates, *The Art of Memory* (Chicago: The University of Chicago Press, 1974), 303; on Yates, see Marjorie C. Jones, *Frances Yates and the Hermetic Tradition* (Lake Worth, FL: Ibis Press, 2008).

12 *Pieces of a Song: Selected Poems*, 104.

13 Brian P. Copenhaver, *Magic in Western Culture: From Antiquity to the Enlightenment* (New York: Cambridge University Press, 2015), 315; Michael D. Bailey, *Magic and Superstition in Europe: A Concise History from Antiquity to the Present* (Lanham, MD: Rowman and Littlefield, 2007), 190; Yates, *Giordano Bruno and the Hermetic Tradition*, 367ff; Northrop Frye, *Fearful Symmetry: A Study of William Blake* (Boston: Beacon Press, 1967), 153. Also see Robert D. Denham, *Northrop Frye: Religious Visionary and Architect of the Spiritual World* (Charlottesville: University of Virginia Press, 2004), 193–203; Milton O. Percival, *William Blake's Circle of Destiny* (New York: Columbia University Press, 1938), 197–215; Peter F. Fisher, *The Valley of*

Vision: Blake as Prophet and Revolutionary, ed. Northrop Frye (Toronto: University of Toronto Press, 1961), 172–75.

14 Amiri Baraka, "In Memory of Radio" in *The Portable Beat Reader*, ed. Ann Charters (New York: Penguin, 1992), 341; Ed Park, "A Word-Magus Gets His Due," www.latimes.com/style/la-bkw-park7oct07-story-html; W. Y. Evans-Wentz, ed., *The Tibetan Book of the Dead: or The after-Death Experiences on the Bardo Plane, according to Lama Kazi Dawa-Samdup's English Rendering* (New York: Oxford University Press, 1980), "May it come that all the Radiances will be known as one's own radiances," 202.

15 "Revolutionary Letter #68: Life Chant," 89.

16 "Revolutionary Letter #49," 62–64.

17 Ibid.; https://www.moma.org/documents/moma_press-release_326692.pdf; Susan Rosenbaum, "The 'do it yourself' Avant-Garde: American Women Poets and Experiment," in *A History of Twentieth-Century American Women's Poetry*, ed. Linda A. Kinnahan (New York: Cambridge University Press, 2016), 333; *Rising Tides: 20th Century American Women Poets*, eds. Laura Chester and Sharon Barba (New York: Washington Square Press, 1973); *No More Masks: An Anthology of Poems by Women*, eds. Florence Howe and Ellen Bass (Garden City, NY: Anchor Books, 1973); on anthologies of poetry by women, see Marsha Bryant, "The WP Network: Anthologies and Affiliations in Contemporary American Women's Poetry," in *A History of Twentieth-Century American Women's Poetry*, 186–201; on separatist movement within the gay community, see David Allyn, *Make Love, Not War, The Sexual Revolution: An Unfettered History* (Boston: Little, Brown and Company, 2000), 159–60; Eric Keenaghan, "Queer Poetry in the Long Twentieth Century," in *The Cambridge History of Gay and Lesbian Literature*, eds. E. L. McCallum and Mikko Tuhkanen (New York: Cambridge University Press, 2014), 599; "Revolutionary Letter #11," 21.

18 Kirby Doyle, "An Unfinished Letter: To Diane di Prima," in *The Collected Poems of Kirby Doyle* (North Beach, San Francisco: Greenlight Press, 1983), 116; "R.D.'s H.D.," 21–22. On the underground press, see Chapter 8: "Sex, Drugs, Rock 'n' Roll and Politics: The Influence of the American Underground," in *Merz to Émigré and Beyond: Avant-Garde Magazine Design of the Twentieth Century*, ed. Steven Heller (London: Phaidon, 2003), 182–205.

19 James D. Sullivan, *On the Walls and in the Streets: American Poetry Broadsides from the 1960s*, 24, 76, 77.

20 Di Prima, "Canticle of St. Joan," in *Selected Poems*, 223–26; Di Prima, "A Counterspell for Millbrook: First Day of Winter," *Intrepid* #8, June 1967, n.p.; Ezra Pound, "Sestina: Altaforte," in *Selected Poems of Ezra Pound* (New York: New Directions, 1957), 7; Jeffrey B. Russell and Brooks Alexander, *A New History of Witchcraft: Sorcerers, Heretics and Pagans* (London: Thames and Hudson, 2015), 78; Margaret Murry, *The Gods of the Witches* (London: Sampson Low, Marston and Co, 1933), 175, 176, 179; Ron Whitehead, Sharon Gibson and Kent Fielding, "Diane di Prima: Memoirs of a Beatnik," interview in *Beat Scene* No. 27, 11; Norman Cohn, *The Pursuit of the Millennium: Revolutionary Millenarians and Mystical Anarchists of the*

Middle Ages (New York: Oxford University Press, 1970), 233, 234; Di Prima, *Spring and Autumn Annals,* np; Lyndy Abraham, *A Dictionary of Alchemical Imagery,* 135; Di Prima, "To the Unnamed Buddhist Nun," Diane di Prima, ed., *War Poems* (New York: Poets Press, 1968), 5; the poem is reprinted in Di Prima, *Selected Poems: 1956-1975,* 160.

21 John Strausbaugh, *The Village: 400 Years of Beats and Bohemians, Radicals and Rogues, A History of Greenwich Village* (New York: Ecco, 2013), 350; Di Prima, *Monuments,* in Steve Susoyev, *Return to the Caffe Cino: A Collection of Plays and Memoirs,* 15, 354–61; *The Princeton Dictionary of Buddhism,* 657; Di Prima, "Afterword—Writing Memoirs," *Memoirs of a Beatnik,* 189; Wendell C. Stone, *Caffe Cino: The Birthplace of Off-Off-Broadway* (Carbondale: Southern Illinois University Press, 2005), 165.

22 "Phoenix Memories" in Robert Wilson, *The Phoenix Book Shop: A Nest of Memories* (Candia, NH: John LeBow, 1997), 33.

23 Diane di Prima, *L.A. Odyssey* (New York: Poets Press, 1969), n.p.

24 Ibid., "Rooftop, Hollywood."

25 *Recollections of My Life As A Woman,* 342; Di Prima, "Phosphoros" in *Pieces of a Song,* 162; "The Absence of the Hero" in Charles Bukowski, *Absence of the Hero,* ed. David Stephen Calonne (San Francisco: City Lights, 2010), 65; on Miller's *The Air-Conditioned Nightmare,* see David Stephen Calonne, *Henry Miller: Critical Lives* (London: Reaktion Books, 2014), 79–83.

26 *De Kooning: A Retrospective,* ed. John Elderfield (New York: Museum of Modern Art, 2011), 307, 325; Mark Stevens and Annalyn Swan, *de Kooning: An American Master* (New York: Alfred A. Knopf, 2004), 570; "Diane di Prima in Conversation with Margarita Meklina and Andrew Meklin," *Ars Interpres: An International Journal of Poetry, Translation and Art,* No. 7; Dore Ashton, *The New York School: A Cultural Reckoning* (New York: Penguin, 1979), 227; also see David Lehman, *The Last Avant-Garde: The Making of the New York School of Poets* (New York: Doubleday, 1998); David Shapiro, *Poets & Painters: Denver Art Museum, November 21, 1979—January 13, 1980* (Denver: Denver Art Museum, 1979); *Poets on Painters: Essays on the Art of Painting by Twentieth-Century Poets,* ed. J. D. McClatchy (Berkeley: University of California Press, 1988); on Beats and Art, see Donald Friedman, *The Writer's Brush: Paintings, Drawings, and Sculptures by Writers* (Minneapolis: Mid-List Press, 2007); on Ferlinghetti, see William T. Lawlor, "When He Looks at Pictures: Lawrence Ferlinghetti and the Literary Tradition of Ekphrasis," in *Beat Culture: The 1950s and Beyond,* eds. Cornelis A. van Minnen, Jaap van der Bent, Mel van Elteren (Amsterdam: VU University Press, 1999), 195–208; http://www.arsint.com/2006/d_d_7.html; Martin Duberman, *Black Mountain: An Exploration in Community* (New York: E. P. Dutton, 1972), 281; John Strausbaugh, *The Village,* 246.

27 *Recollections,* 199; Di Prima, "So Fine" and "On the First Day of Spring I Visit the Museum," in *Selected Poems,* 248, 43.

28 Di Prima, *L.A. Odyssey* (New York: Poets Press, 1969), n.p. Further references are to this edition; Harry F. Gaugh, *De Kooning* (New York: Abbeville Press, 1983), 22, 36; Di Prima, "Prayer to the Ancestors," *Pieces of a Song,* 96.

29 *Buddhist Texts Through the Ages*, trans. and ed. Edward Conze (Oxford: Oneworld, 1995), 200; Hugh B. Urban, *Tantra: Sex, Secrecy, Politics, and Power in the Study of Religion* (Berkeley: University of California Press, 2003), 225; Di Prima, "Afterword," *Memoirs of a Beatnik;* John De St Jorre, *Venus Bound: The Erotic Voyage of the Olympia Press and Its Writers* (New York: Random House, 1994), 275–76; Nancy M. Grace, "Snapshots, Sand Paintings and Celluloid: Formal Considerations in the Life Writing of Women Writers from the Beat Generation," in *Girls Who Wore Black: Women Writing the Beat Generation*, eds. Ronna C. Johnson and Nancy M. Grace (Rutgers, NJ: Rutgers University Press, 2002), 161; Fred L. Gardaphe, in *The Italian American Experience: An Encyclopedia* (New York: Routledge, 1999), 49.

30 Christopher Gair, *The Beat Generation: A Beginner's Guide* (Oxford: Oneworld, 2008), 133; Di Prima, *Memoirs of a Beatnik* (New York: Penguin, 1998), 3.

31 Ibid., 14.

32 Ibid., 133.

33 Donald S. Lopez, Jr., *The Princeton Dictionary of Buddhism*, 662.

34 *Memoirs of a Beatnik*, 176, 177.

35 Ibid., 185.

36 *The Princeton Dictionary of Buddhism*, 1018.

37 Maria Farland, "'Total System, Total Solution, Total Apocalypse': Sex Oppression, Systems of Property, and the 1970s Women's Liberation Front," *The Yale Journal of Criticism*, 18, no. 2 (2005), 381, 382; Mary Zeppa, "Interview with Diane di Prima," *Poet News*, 1985, 8; "The Gnosis Interview: Diane di Prima on Magic, Healing, and the Western Esoteric Tradition," 14; Di Prima, "'Old Father, Old Artificer': Charles Olson Memorial Lecture," *Lost and Found: The CUNY Poetics Document Initiative*, Series 3, Number 4, Fall 2012, 34; on Black Bear Ranch, see Sutton, *Modern American Communes: A Dictionary*, 16–17; Miller, *The 60s Communes: Hippies and Beyond*, 72–74; Jeroen W. Boekhoven, *Genealogies of Shamanism: Struggles for Power, Charisma and Authority* (Barkhuis, 2011), 200; Victor Turner, *The Ritual Process: Structure and Anti-Structure* (New York: Aldine de Gruyter, 1995), 112–13.

38 Richard Hughes Seager, *Buddhism in America* (New York: Columbia University Press, 2012), 49–50; Di Prima, "Tassajara," in *The Wisdom Anthology of North American Buddhist Poetry*, ed. Andrew Schelling (Boston: Wisdom Publications, 2005), 56; Di Prima, "Tassajara, 1969," in *Pieces of a Song*, 86.

39 Ibid., 59.

40 Ingrid Fischer-Schreiber, Franz-Karl Ehrhard, Michael S. Diener, *The Shambhala Dictionary of Buddhism and Zen* (Boston: Shambhala, 1991), 61, 62. Philip Whalen composed a poem in 1966, "The War Poem for Diane di Prima," which in Section II also lists in capital letters all Twelve Nidanas. See Philp Whalen, *Overtime: Selected Poems* (New York: Penguin Books, 1999), 151–52.

41 Di Prima, *San Francisco Notebook 2*, August 30, 1971 to March 1972, University of North Carolina at Chapel Hill, Folder 570; Phyllis Stowell, "My Work Is My Life: An Interview with Diane di Prima," *City Miner*, 4, no. 2 (1979), 19; Ron Whitehead, Sharon Gibson and Kent Fielding, "Diane di Prima: Memoirs of a Beatnik," interview, *Beat Scene*, No. 27, 14; H.D., *Tribute to Freud*, 41; Robert Duncan, in *The H.D. Book*, cites the same passage, 251.

42 Di Prima, "The Mysteries of Vision: Some Notes on H.D.," 20.

43 Morgan, *The Beat Generation in San Francisco*, 91; Barry Silesky, *Ferlinghetti: The Artist in His Time* (New York: Warner Books, 1990), 181; "Chronology," in *Pieces of a Song*, 199.

44 Judith Bolinger and Jim Hartz, "Diane di Prima: An Interview," *Intersection Newsletter*, 10, no. 2 (Spring 1980), 2.

45 Ibid., 8, 9–10, 12.

46 Di Prima, University of North Carolina, Folder 1076, Diane di Prima Papers, 1955–2008; Joy Harjo, "They Had Some Horses," in *Nothing But the Truth: An Anthology of Native American Literature*, ed. John L. Purdy and James Ruppert (Upper Saddle River, NJ: Prentice Hall, 2001), 474; *American Indian Art: Form and Tradition* (New York: E. P. Dutton, 1972); on the relationship between the counterculture and the Native Americans, see Sherry L. Smith, *Hippies, Indians, and the Fight for Red Power* (New York: Oxford University Press, 2012); "Chronology," 199.

47 http://www.verbicidemagazine.com/2010/07/29/interview-diane-di-prima/;*Writing as Enlightenment: Buddhist American Literature into the Twenty-First Century*, eds. John Whalen-Bridge and Gary Storhoff (Albany: State University of New York Press, 2011), 12; Fabrice Midal, *Chogyam Trungpa: His Life and Vision* (Boston: Shambhala, 2004), 257; for an account of the literature and writing program at Naropa, see Whalen-Bridge's essay in *Writing as Enlightenment*, "Poetry and Practice at Naropa University," 157–84. Constanzo Allione's *Fried Shoes, Cooked Diamonds: The Beats at Naropa Institute* (1978) is a documentary featuring Allen Ginsberg, Timothy Leary, Anne Waldman, Gregory Corso, Chogyam Trungpa, Peter Orlovsky, and Di Prima who reads her "Birthday Poem for Grandpa" from *Revolutionary Letters*. See https://www.youtube.com/watch?v=jEWvJ0jpPpw

48 Vale, *Modern Pagans*, 39; on Burroughs and the occult, see Matthew Levi Stevens, *The Magical Universe of William S. Burroughs* (Oxford: Mandrake, 2014); and Arthur Versluis, *American Gurus: From American Transcendentalism to New Age Religion* (New York: Oxford University Press, 2014), 95–108; Jennifer W. Wunder, *Keats, Hermeticism, and the Secret Societies* (Aldershot: Ashgate, 2008); Di Prima, "Light/and Keats," *Talking Poetics from Naropa Institute*, eds. Anne Waldman and Marilyn Webb, Volume 1 (Boulder and London: Shambhala, 1978), 19, 20, 21, 25.

49 Di Prima, "Light/and Keats," 13.

50 Christopher Marlowe, *Faust*; on Agrippa, see Catherine Albanese, *A Republic of Mind and Spirit: A Cultural History of American Metaphysical Religion* (New Haven and London: Yale University Press, 2007), 34–35.

51 Di Prima, "Light/and Keats," 14.

52 Ibid., 32, 33. On Henry Corbin, see Wouter J. Hanegraaff, *Esotericism and the Academy: Rejected Knowledge in Western Culture* (New York: Cambridge University Press, 2012), 301.

53 Northrop Frye, *The Critical Path: An Essay on the Social Context of Literary Criticism* (Bloomington and London: Indiana University Press, 1973), 145; Gregory Corso, "Nevermore Baltimore," in *Mindfield: New and Selected Poems* (New York: Thunder's Mouth Press, 1989), 183–84; on Dylan, see Simon Warner, "Chains of Flashing Memories: Bob Dylan and the Beats, 1959-1975," Chapter 2 of *Texts and Drugs and Rock 'N' Roll: The Beats and Rock Culture* (New York: Bloomsbury, 2014), 107–33; Frances A. Yates, *The Occult Philosophy in the Renaissance* (London and New York: Routledge, 2001), 2–3; George Quasha and Charles Stein, "Publisher's Foreword," in *The Secret Garden: An Anthology in the Kabbalah*, ed. David Meltzer (Barrytown, NY: Station Hill Openings, 1998), n.p.; *San Francisco Beat*, 16.

54 Theodore Ziolkowski, *Lure of the Arcane: The Literature of Cult and Conspiracy* (Baltimore: The Johns Hopkins University Press, 2013), 47–48; also see Andrew Weeks, *German Mysticism, from Hildegard of Bingen to Ludwig Wittgenstein: A Literary and Intellectual History* (Albany: State University of New York Press, 1993); Harold Bloom, *Kabbalah and Criticism* (New York: The Seabury Press, 1975), 16; Joseph Leon Blau, *The Christian Interpretation of the Cabala in the Renaissance* (New York: Columbia University Press, 1944); Vale, *Modern Pagans: An Investigation of Contemporary Pagan Practices* (San Francisco: RE/Search Publications, 2001), 37; Johanna Drucker, *The Alphabetic Labyrinth: The Letters in History and Imagination* (New York: Thames and Hudson, 1995), 137.

55 Kathleen Raine, "Yeats, the Tarot and the Golden Dawn," in *Yeats the Initiate: Essays on Certain Themes in the Work of W.B. Yeats* (Mountrath: The Dolmen Press, 1986), 186; Alex Owen, *The Place of Enchantment: British Occultism and the Culture of the Modern* (Chicago: The University of Chicago Press, 2004), 56, 73–74; Egil Asprem, "The Golden Dawn and the O.T.O.," in *The Cambridge Handbook of Western Mysticism and Esotericism*, ed. Glenn Alexander Magee (New York: Cambridge University Press, 2016), 279; Joseph Leon Blau, *The Christian Interpretation of the Cabala in the Renaissance* (New York: Columbia University Press, 1944), 2, 9.

56 Di Prima, "Revolutionary Letter Number Fifty-Seven" in *Revolutionary Letters*, 73; "Number Seventy-Seven," 109.

57 Joseph Dan, ed., *The Christian Kabbalah: Jewish Mystical Books and Their Christian Interpreters* (Cambridge, MA: Harvard College Library, 1997), 211.

58 Jorge Luis Borges, "The Kabbalah," in *Seven Nights* (New York: New Directions, 1984), 106; John North, *Cosmos: An Illustrated History of Astronomy and Cosmology* (Chicago: University of Chicago Press, 2008), 256; Peter Marshall, *The Magic Circle of Rudolf II: Alchemy and Astrology in Renaissance Prague* (New York: Walker and Company, 2006); Lewis Spence, *An Encyclopedia of Occultism* (New York: Carol Publishing Group, 1996), 115; Brian P. Copenhaver, *Magic in Western Culture: From*

Antiquity to the Enlightenment (New York: Cambridge University Press, 2015), 287; Gyorgy E. Szonyi, "John Dee," in *Dictionary of Gnosis and Western Esotericism, Vol. 1*, ed. Wouter J. Hanegraaff (Leiden: Brill, 2005), 302, 303; Barry Miles, *The Beat Hotel: Ginsberg, Burroughs, and Corso in Paris, 1958-1963* (New York: Grove Press, 2000), 162, 193; Matthieu Poirier, "Hyper-optical and Kinetic Stimulation, 'Happenings' and Films in France," in *Summer of Love: Psychedelic Art, Social Crisis and Counterculture in the 1960s*, eds. Christoph Grunenberg and Jonathan Harris (Liverpool: Liverpool University Press, 2005), 288; Lenore Kandel, "First They Slaughtered the Angels," in *Collected Poems of Lenore Kandel, with a Preface by Diane di Prima* (Berkeley: North Atlantic Books, 2012), 28, 31; Peter J. French, *John Dee: The World of an Elizabethan Magus* (London: Routledge and Kegan Paul, 1972), 76–77, 80–81; John Dee, *The Hieroglyphic Monad* (York Beach, ME: 2000), 18; *John Dee on Astronomy: Propaedeumata Aphoristica (1558 and 1568), Latin and English*, ed. and trans. Wayne Shumaker (Berkeley: University of California Press, 1978), 204; Roob, *The Hermetic Museum*, 480; Frances A. Yates, *The Rosicrucian Enlightenment* (London and New York: Routledge, 2002), 64; also see Yates, *The Art of Memory*, 263; Di Prima, "Preface," John Dee, *The Hieroglyphic Monad* (New York: Samuel Weiser, Inc., 1975), iii. On Dee's Hermeticism, see Betty Jo Teeter Dobbs, *The Foundations of Newton's Alchemy, or "The Hunting of the Greene Lyon"* (Cambridge: Cambridge University Press, 1975), 54–55.

59 Di Prima, "John Dee," in *Pieces of a Song*, 158; Lyndy Abraham, *A Dictionary of Alchemical Symbolism* (Cambridge: Cambridge University Press), 140.

60 Di Prima, "John Dee," 158; Kenneth K. Knoespel, "The Narrative Matter of Mathematics: John Dee's Preface to the *Elements* of Euclid of Megara (1570)," *Philological Quarterly* 66 (1987), 37, 38–39.

61 Di Prima, "R.D.'s H.D.," 15–16.

62 Judith Bolinger and Jim Hartz, "Diane di Prima: An Interview," *Intersection*, 10, no.2 (Spring 1980), 10, 13.

63 "Chronology," *Pieces of a Song*, 199; Diane di Prima, "Ted Joans in Paris, 1976," in *Poet Painter/Former Villager Now/World Traveller: Ted Joans Part I, Lost and Found: The CUNY Poetics Document Initiative*, Series 6, No. 4, Part I (Spring 2016), 14–15.

64 James D. Sullivan in *On the Walls and in the Streets: American Poetry Broadsides from the 1960s*, 24; Di Prima, "The Belltower," in *Selected Poems: 1956-1975*, 306.

65 Di Prima, "Darkness Invocation"; J. B. Allen, "Marsilio Ficino," in *Dictionary of Gnosis and Western Esotericism*, 363. On Ficino, also see *Marsilio Ficino: Western Esoteric Masters Series*, ed. Angela Voss (Berkeley: North Atlantic Books, 2006).

66 Vale, *Modern Pagans*, 38.

67 See Lyndy Abraham, *A Dictionary of Alchemical Imagery* (Cambridge: Cambridge University Press, 2001), 26, 135–36.

68 For video of the reading, see https://www.pastemagazine.com/articles/2011/01/
the-band-get-yer-cut-throat-off-my-knife-revolutionary-letter-4-diane-diprima.
html. According to Lisa Jarnot, the Duncan and Di Prima performances were
left out of the final Scorsese film; *Robert Duncan, The Ambassador from
Venus: A Biography,* 345, 490; Di Prima, "The Fire Guardian," in *Selected
Poems,* 338; Di Prima, "Kenneth Patchen and the Early 1950s," *Tribute to
Kenneth Patchen* (London: Enitharmon Press, 1977), 38.

69 "Chronology," *Pieces of a Song,* 199.

70 Luhrmann, *Persuasions of the Witch's Craft,* 191; *Recollections,* 351; Di
Prima, "Narrow Path into the Back Country," in *Pieces of a Song,* 111.

71 For a review of the 1978 edition, see Susan Mernit, "Praying to the Loba,"
in *New Women's Times Feminist Review,* no. 15 (April/May 1981), 1, 3; Di
Prima, "Light/and Keats," 35.

72 Ezra Pound, "Piere Vidal Old"; Di Prima, "For E.P.," in *Selected Poems,* 267;
Alicia Suskin Ostriker, *Stealing the Language: The Emergence of Women's
Poetry in America* (Boston: Beacon Press, 1986), 215; George Steiner,
Grammars of Creation (New Haven and London: Yale University Press, 2001),
239; Di Prima, "Light/and Keats," 36; Robert Creeley, *Selected Letters,* eds.
Rod Smith, Peter Baker and Kaplan Harris (Berkeley: University of California
Press, 2014), 327; Leon Surette, *The Birth of Modernism: Ezra Pound, T.S.
Eliot, W.B. Yeats, and the Occult* (Montreal and Kingston: McGill-Queen's
University Press, 1993), 142, 143; Lynn Keller, *Forms of Expansion: Recent
Long Poems by Women* (Chicago: The University of Chicago Press, 1997), 5.

73 Di Prima, *Loba,* 43.

74 Whitman, *Leaves of Grass; Breaking the Rule of Cool,* 94; Di Prima, *Loba,*
3, 5, 6.

75 Di Prima, *Loba, 57;* Hans Jonas, *The Gnostic Religion: The Message of the
Alien God and the Beginnings of Christianity* (Boston: Beacon Press, 1970),
60; Di Prima, *Loba,* 69; Jonas, *The Gnostic Religion,* 60; E. R Dodds, *Pagan
and Christian in an Age of Anxiety: Some Aspects of Religious Experience
from Marcus Aurelius to Constantine* (New York: Cambridge University Press,
1990), 72.

76 *Loba,* "Hymn: The Other Face," 149; Di Prima, "The Mysteries of Vision," 22.

77 Di Prima, "Light/and Keats," *Talking Poetics from Naropa Institute,* 29, 30;
"Reprise," *Loba,* 150. On Montsegur, see Yuri Stoyanov, *The Other God:
Dualist Religions from Antiquity to The Cathar Heresy* (New Haven: Yale
University Press, 2000), 212–15; Zoe Oldenbourg, *Massacre at Montsegur: A
History of the Albigensian Crusade,* trans. Peter Green (New York: Pantheon,
1961).

78 Akiko Miyake, *Ezra Pound and the Mysteries of Love: A Plan for the Cantos*
(Durham: Duke University Press, 1991), 9; Di Prima, *Loba,* 15, 28; on wolf
symbolism in *Loba,* also see S. K. Robisch, *Wolves and the Wolf Myth in
American Literature* (Reno: University of Nevada Press, 2009), 354–57.

79 Paula Gunn Allen, "Deer Woman" in *Nothing But the Truth: An Anthology
of Native American Literature,* ed. John L. Purdy and James Ruppert (Upper

Saddle River, NJ: Prentice Hall, 2001), 255–62; Jeffrey B. Russell, *A New History of Witchcraft: Sorcerers, Heretics and Pagans*, 28.

80 Barry Silesky, *Ferlinghetti: The Artist in His Time* (New York: Warner Books, 1990), 219; Lawrence Ferlinghetti and Nancy J. Peters, *Literary San Francisco: A Pictorial History from Its Beginnings to the Present Day* (San Francisco: City Lights Books and Harper and Row, 1980). "The Legacy of Henry Corbin: Corbin and American Poetry Part 12," http://henrycorbinproject. blogspot.com/2009/12/ralph-maud-suggests-that-move-into.html'; Ralph Maud, *Charles Olson at the Harbor* (Vancouver, BC: Talonbooks, 2008), 211. Maud, *Charles Olson's Reading: A Biography* (Carbondale: Southern Illinois University Press, 1996), 8, 160, 171, 176, 199, 202, 205; also see Tom Clark, *Charles Olson: The Allegory of a Poet's Life* (Berkeley: North Atlantic Books, 2000), 282–83.

81 Robert Duncan, *The H.D. Book*, eds. Michael Boughn and Victor Coleman (Berkeley: University of California Press, 2011), 128, 519–21; Harold Bloom, *Omens of Millennium: The Gnosis of Angels, Dreams, and Resurrection* (New York: Riverhead Books, 1996); Henry Corbin, *Swedenborg and Esoteric Islam* (West Chester, PA: Swedenborg Foundation, 1995), 1, 9.

82 Henry Corbin, *Creative Imagination in the Sufism of Ibn 'Arabi* (Princeton: Princeton University Press, 1969), 11; Diane di Prima, "Notes for a Lecture on Angels Given at Minneapolis Jung Institute Sept 1979," University of North Carolina Special Collections.

83 Di Prima, *Notebook 50*, June 18–September 2, 1983, University of North Carolina, Folder 618; Di Prima quotes from Henry Corbin, *Avicenna and the Visionary Recital*, 18, 19; Tom Cheetham in *After Prophecy: Imagination, Incarnation, and the Unity of the Prophetic Tradition* (New Orleans: Spring Journal, 2007), 22.

84 Corbin, *Creative Imagination*, 22.

85 Mary Boyce, *Zoroastrianism: Its Antiquity and Constant Vigour* (Costa Mesa, CA: Mazda Publishers, 1992), 93; Henry Corbin, *Avicenna and the Visionary Recital*, 15; elsewhere, Corbin describes the encounter with the Angel in equally lyrical terms: "Israel was able to serve only 'its' God, and could proclaim the unity of only 'its' God (which theophanically is the sixth Sephiroth according to the Kabbalists). Each of us, as well, has to recognize 'his' God, the one to which he [is able to] respond. I believe our researches open the way, of necessity, to angelology (that of a Proclus, that of the Kabbala) which will be reborn with increasing potency. The Angel is the Face that our God takes for us, and each of us finds his God only when he recognizes that Face. The service which we can render others is to help them encounter that Face about which they will be able to say: *Talem eum vidi qualem capere potui* ('I am able to grasp such as I have seen')." Henry Corbin, "Preface" to David L. Miller, *The New Polytheism*, 4; Jerome Rousse-Lacordaire, "Henry Corbin" in *Dictionary of Gnosis and Western Esotericism*, ed. Wouter J. Hanegraaff (Leiden: Brill, 2005), 271.

Chapter 5

1   On Di Prima's Kerouac lecture, see Regina Weinrich's essay in *Cambridge Companion to the Beats*, 54–55; Ammiel Alcalay, "Afterword," Diane di Prima, "R.D.'s H.D.," *Lost and Found; The CUNY Poetics Document Initiative*, Series 2, Number 3 (Spring 2011), 20.

2   *http://www.brooklynrail.org/2015/02/criticspage/the-enamord-mage-magic-alchemy-and-esoteric-thought-in-works-by-robert-duncan-and-jess*

3   Meltzer, *San Francisco Beat*, 17–18.

4   Di Prima, "Books Used in 'Hidden Religions' course at New College Poetics Program," University of Louisville, "Teaching Materials, Box 15, Folder 13; Christopher Lehrich, *The Occult Mind: Magic in Theory and Practice* (Ithaca and London: Cornell University Press, 2007), 3; Adrienne Rich, "Prepatriarchal Female/Goddess Images," in *The Politics of Women's Spirituality: Essays on the Rise of Spiritual Power Within the Feminist Movement*, ed. Charlene Spretnak (New York: Anchor Press, 1982), 33; "The Gnosis Interview: Diane di Prima on Magic, Healing, and the Western Esoteric Tradition," 12; Paul Feyerabend, *Philosophy of Nature* (Cambridge: Polity Press, 2016), 42; David Kubrin, "How Sir Isaac Newton Helped Restore Law 'n' Order to the West," *Liberation*, 16, no. 10 (March 1972), 32, 41; also see David Kubrin, "Newton and the Cyclical Cosmos: Providence and the Mechanical Philosophy," in *Newton: A Norton Critical Edition*, ed. I. Bernard Cohen and Richard S. Westfall (New York: W. W. Norton, 1995), 281–96.

5   Guy Davenport, "Olson," in *The Geography of Imagination: Forty Essays* (New York and San Francisco: Pantheon Books, 1981), 88; Mary Zeppa, "Interview with Diane di Prima," *Poet News* (1985), 8; Linden, *The Alchemy Reader: From Hermes Trismegistus to Isaac Newton* (Cambridge: Cambridge University Press, 2003), 243–47; Gilles Quispel, "Gnosis and Alchemy: The Tabula Smaragdina," in *From Poimandres to Jacob Boehme: Gnosis, Hermetism and the Christian Tradition*, ed. Roelof van den Broek and Cis van Heertum, 304; John Maynard Keynes, "Newton, the Man," in *Newton: A Norton Critical Edition*, eds. I. Bernard Cohen and Richard S. Westfall (New York: W. W. Norton, 1995), 314; Brian P. Copenhaver, *Magic in Western Culture: From Antiquity to the Enlightenment* (New York: Cambridge University Press, 2015), 417. Also see Richard S. Westfall, "Newton and Alchemy," in *Occult and Scientific Mentalities in the Renaissance*, ed. Brian Vickers (Cambridge: Cambridge University Press, 1984); Betty Jo Teeter Dobbs, *The Janus Face of Genius: The Role of Alchemy in Newton's Thought* (New York: Cambridge University Press, 1991).

6   Hinda Lanser, "Allen Ginsberg: Blowin' in the Breeze," *Six-Thirteen*, no. 1 (February 1976), 66.

7   Vale, *Modern Pagans*, 39, 37. A pupil at one of Di Prima's visualization sessions reported that the students "did a whole weekend called 'going to level' (a technique she picked up from the Diggers, who appropriated it from Silva Mind Control, which corporations were using to boost performance and sales).

She talked us through various visioning scenarios through which we'd find our temple and spirit guide." See *Tripping: An Anthology of True-Life Psychedelic Adventures*, ed. Charles Hayes (New York: Penguin, 2000), 359; Sarah M. Pike, *New Age and Neopagan Religions in America* (New York: Columbia University Press, 2004), 21; Di Prima, "Structures of Magic and Techniques of Visioning," 34, 17, 19, University of North Carolina at Chapel Hill.

8 Di Prima, "Foreword," Angelina Hekking, *Seeds of Light: Images of Healing* (San Francisco: Angel Publishing, 1990), n.p.

9 Di Prima, "Role of the Hermetic in poetry," *Straits: Newsletter of the Detroit River Press*, 1, no. 2 (September 1982), n.p.; Cleanth Brooks and William Wimsatt, Jr., *Literary Criticism: A Short History*, 128; Frances A. Yates, *Giordano Bruno and the Hermetic Tradition*, 281; *Dictionary of Gnosis and Western Esotericism*, 360, 361; *De Amore*, trans. Sears Jayne; "Studies in Light," in *Pieces of a Song*, 144; Umberto Eco, *Art and Beauty in the Middle Ages*, 46; Grosseteste, *De Luce*, 13; Vale, *Modern Pagans*, 39.

10 *Beneath the Buddhist Moon*, 57–58.

11 *Modern Pagans*, 39; also see Chogyam Trungpa, "Padmasambhava and the Energy of Tantra," in *Crazy Wisdom* (Boston: Shambhala, 1991), 75–94.

12 "Tsogyal," in *Loba*, 302–03.

13 *Princeton Dictionary of Buddhism*, 1026.

14 Anne Carolyn Klein, *Meeting the Great Bliss Queen: Buddhists, Feminists, and the Art of the Self* (Boston: Beacon Press, 1995), 17.

15 *Princeton Dictionary of Buddhism*, 120, 560.

16 Keith Dowman, *Sky Dancer: The Secret Life and Songs of the Lady Yeshe Tsogyel* (Ithaca: Snow Lion Publications, 1996), 230; Mircea Eliade, *Yoga: Immortality and Freedom* (Princeton: Princeton University Press, 1990), 206; Mircea Eliade, *The Sacred and the Profane: The Nature of Religion* (New York: Harcourt, Brace and World, 1959), 172; Giuseppe Tucci, *The Theory and Practice of the Mandala* (Mineola, NY: Dover Publications, 2001), 78.

17 Barbara Tedlock, *The Woman in the Shaman's Body: Reclaiming the Feminine in Religion and Medicine* (New York: Random House, 2005).

18 *Poet News*, 6.

19 Nancy M. Grace and Tony Trigilio, "Troubling Classical and Buddhist Traditions in Diane di Prima's *Loba*," in *Hip Sublime: Beat Writers and the Classical Tradition*, eds. Sheila Murnaghan and Ralph M. Rosen (Columbus: The Ohio State University Press, 2018), 238; Di Prima, "Prayer to the Mothers" in *Pieces of a Song*, 91; H.D., *End to Torment*, 22–23; also see Matte Robinson, *The Astral H.D.: Occult and Religious Sources and Contexts for H.D.'s Poetry and Prose* (London: Bloomsbury, 2016); Diane di Prima, "For H.D.," in *Selected Poems, 1956-1975* (Plainsfield, VT: 1975), 341; Jo Gill, "Reading H.D.: Influence and Legacy," in *The Cambridge Companion to H.D.*, eds. Nephie J. Christodoulides and Polina Mackay (Cambridge: Cambridge University Press, 2012), 80; Di Prima, "The Mysteries of Vision: Some Notes on H.D.," *Lost and Found: The CUNY Poetics Document*

Initiative, Series 2, Number 2 (Spring 2011), 1, 3. This essay also appeared in an earlier edition in 1988, published by Am Here Books in Santa Barbara.

20 Roger Gilbert, "Awash with Angels: The Religious Turn in Nineties Poetry," *Contemporary Literature, Special Issue: American Poetry of the 1990s*, 42, no. 2 (Summer 2001), 247; H.D., "Tribute to Angels," *Collected Poems*, 547–48; Peter Gardella, *American Angels: Useful Spirits in the Material World* (Lawrence, KS: University Press of Kansas, 2007), 68; Di Prima, "To a Student," in *The Poetry Deal* (San Francisco: City Lights, 2014), 53; Di Prima, "For Rilke" in *Kerhonkson Journal*, n.p., reprinted in *Selected Poems, 1956-1975*, 166; Walter Benjamin, "Theses on the Philosophy of History," in *Illuminations* (New York: Schocken, 1973), 257–58; Robert Alter, *Necessary Angels: Tradition and Modernity in Kafka, Benjamin, and Scholem* (Cambridge, MA: Harvard University Press, 1991), 115–16; Giorgio Agamben, "Walter Benjamin and the Demonic: Happiness and Historical Redemption," in *Potentialities: Collected Essays in Philosophy* (Stanford: Stanford University Press, 2000), 145, 146. On the proliferation of angels in the 1990s, also see Brian McHale, *The Cambridge Introduction to Postmodernism* (New York: Cambridge University Press, 2015), 157–70.

21 Di Prima, "The Mysteries of Vision," 6–7.

22 Ibid., 5.

23 Ibid., 11.

24 Di Prima, "A Dharmadhatu Service," *Poetry Flash: The Bay Area's Poetry Review & Literary Calendar*, no. 180 (March 1988), 3; Di Prima, entry for December 3, 1989, in *Notebook 82*, November 17, 1989–February 9, 1990, *Diane di Prima Papers, 1955-2008*, University of North Carolina, Chapel Hill, Folder 650; "R.D.'s H.D.," 9.

25 Ibid., 10.

26 Suzanne Hobson, "A New Angelology: Mapping the Angel through Twentieth-Century Literature," *Literature Compass*, 4, no. 2 (2007), 500; Di Prima, "H.D.'s Angel Magic," manuscript, University of Michigan, Special Collections.

27 Harkness, *John Dee's Conversations with Angels*, 86–87; Umberto Eco, *The Search for the Perfect Language* (Oxford: Blackwell, 1995), 126–27.

28 Drucker, *The Alphabetic Labyrinth*, 172.

29 *Dictionary of Gnosis*, "Trithemius," 1138.

30 Di Prima, "H.D.'s Angel Magic," manuscript, University of Michigan, Special Collections.

31 "The Gnosis Interview: Diane di Prima on Magic, Healing, and the Western Esoteric Tradition," *Gnosis: A Journal of the Western Inner Traditions*, no. 2 (Spring/Summer 1986), 20; Yeats writes: "One remembers the six wings of Daniel's angels, the Pythagorean numbers, a venerated book of the Cabala where the beard of God winds in and out among the stars, its hairs all numbered, those complicated mathematical tables that Kelly saw in Dr. Dee's black scrying-stone." See W. B. Yeats, *A Vision* (New York: Collier Books,

1966), 23; Sean Pryor, *W. B. Yeats, Ezra Pound and the Poetry of Paradise* (Farnham: Ashgate, 2011), 60; Tim Armstrong, *Modernism: A Cultural History* (Cambridge: Polity, 2005), 123; Austin Warren, "William Butler Yeats: The Religion of a Poet," in *Religion and Modern Literature: Essays in Theory and Criticism*, eds. G. B. Tennyson and Edward E. Ericson, Jr. (Grand Rapids, MI: William B. Eerdmans Publishing Company, 1975), 273; Barry Miles, *Call Me Burroughs: A Life* (New York: Twelve, 2013), 595; Robert Siegel, "Writing Downtown," in *The Downtown Book: The New York Art Scene 1974-1984* (Princeton: Princeton University Press, 2006), 136; Nancy J. Peters, "The Beat Generation and San Francisco's Culture of Dissent," in *Reclaiming San Francisco: History, Politics, Culture*, eds. James Brook, Chris Carlsson, and Nancy J. Peters (San Francisco: City Lights, 1998), 214.

32   Di Prima, *Wyoming Series* (San Francisco: Eidolon editions, 1988), n.p.; Roger Gilbert, "Awash with Angels: The Religious Turn in Nineties Poetry," *Contemporary Literature*, XLII (Summer 2001), 243; Linda V. Bamber, "Reading as a Buddhist," in *Buddha Mind in Contemporary Art*, eds. Jacquelynn Baas and Mary Jane Jacob (Berkeley: University of California Press, 2004), 23; Di Prima, *Notebook 82*, November 17, 1989–February 9, 1990, *Diane di Prima Papers, 1955-2008*, University of North Carolina, Chapel Hill, Folder 650; Robert Creeley, "Foreword: For Diane," Di Prima, *Pieces of a Song* (San Francisco: City Lights, 1990), vii; Chogyam Trungpa, *Crazy Wisdom* (Boston: Shambhala, 1991), 9–10.

33   V. Vale, *Modern Pagans: An Investigation of Modern Pagan Practices* (San Francisco: RE/Search Publications, 2001), 36–37.

34   Di Prima, *Seminary Poems* (Point Reyes Station: Floating Island Publications, 1991), n.p.; Di Prima, *Notebooks*, August 23, 1988–October 1988, University of North Carolina at Chapel Hill, Folder 645.

35   Di Prima, *The Ones I Used to Laugh With: A Haibun Journal* (San Francisco: Habenicht Press, 2003).

36   Ibid., 1.

37   Ibid., 2.

38   *Princeton Dictionary of Buddhism*, 126.

39   Giuseppe Tucci, *The Religions of Tibet* (Berkeley: University of California Press, 1988), 23; Ibid.

40   Gerhard Herm, *The Celts* (New York: St. Martin's Press, 1976), 159; T. G. E. Powell, *The Celts* (London: Thames and Hudson, 1991), 149; *The Ones I Used to Laugh With*, 5.

41   Ibid., 8; *Loba*, "Point of Ripening: Lughnasa," 307.

42   Ibid., 7.

43   Ibid., 9.

44   Ibid., 10.

45   Ibid., 11.

46   Ibid., 12.

Chapter 6

1 Diane di Prima, *Not Quite Buffalo Stew*, unpublished manuscript archived at The University of North Carolina, Special Collections Library, 1, 6, 23, 26, 14, 44, 45; Jack Foley, *Visions and Affiliations, A California Literary Time Line: Poets and Poetry 1940-2009*, 268; Maria Bruno, "Italian-American Writing," in *The Oxford Companion to Women's Writing in the United States*, eds. Cathy N. Davidson and Linda Wagner-Martin (New York: Oxford University Press, 1995), 425–26; "Diane di Prima in Conversation with Margarita Melina and Andrew Melkin," *Ars Interpres 7: An Internatinal Journal of Poetry, Translation and Art*; , http://www.arsint.com/2006/d_d_7.html; http://www.metroactive.com/papers/metro/04.12.01/diprima-0115.html

2 Thorkild Jacobsen, *The Treasures of Darkness: A History of Mesopotamian Religion* (New Haven: Yale University Press, 1976), 135, 136; Di Prima, *Loba* (New York: Penguin, 1998), 269.

3 Judith Ochshorn, *The Female Experience of the Divine* (Bloomington: University of Indiana Press, 1981), 46–47; Luhrmann, *Persuasions of the Witch*, 94–96; also see Samuel Noah Kramer, *Sumerian Mythology: A Study of Spiritual and Literary Achievement in the Third Millenium B.C.* (New York: Harper and Row, 1961), 86–87; Sylvia Brinton Perera, *Descent to the Goddess: A Way of Initiation for Women* (Toronto: Inner City Books, 1981); on goddess worship, also see Camille Paglia, "Erich Neumann: Theorist of the Great Mother," *Arion*, 13 no. 3 (Winter 2006), 8; Neumann groups together "the mother figure of Demeter, goddess of the Eleusinian mysteries . . . the Greek and non-Greek Artemis as well as Egyptian Isis, Babylonian Ishtar, Buddhist Kwan-yin, and innumerable other goddesses of all ages and nations." See Erich Neumann, *The Great Mother: An Analysis of the Archetype* (Princeton: Princeton University Press, 1970), 80; Betty de Shong Meador, *Inanna, Lady of Largest Heart: Poems of the Sumerian High Priestess* (Austin: The University of Texas Press, 2001), xvii; *Dictionary of Gnosis*, 651;

4 Di Prima, *Recollections of My Life as a Woman*, 2, 167, 169, 170, 171; Di Prima, *Loba*, 107; Di Prima, "The Loba Dances," *Loba*, 19.

5 Di Prima, "Kali-Ma," *Loba*, 284; Di Prima, "Poem to a Statue of Shiva in the Garments of Kali," in *Selected Poems*, 157; *The Beat Generation*, 226; Also see *Encountering Kali: In the Margins, at the Center, in the West*, eds. Jeffrey J. Kripal and Rachel Fell McDermott (Berkeley: University of California Press, 2003); Philip Whalen, "Souffle," in *The Collected Poems of Philip Whalen*, ed. Michael Rothenberg (Middletown, CT: Wesleyan University Press, 2007), 72; David Kinsley, *Hindu Goddesses: Visions of the Divine Feminine in the Hindu Religious Tradition* (Berkeley: University of California Press, 1986), 95.

6 Moffeit, "Diane di Prima Interview," 22.

7 Di Prima, *Loba*, "Tahuti Poems" 173.

8 Ibid., 178.

9 Ibid., 173.

10   Estella Lauter, *Women as Mythmakers: Poetry and Visual Art by Twentieth-Century Women* (Bloomington: Indiana University Press, 1984), 198, 200.

11   http://www.metroactive.com/papers/metro/04.12.01/diprima-0115.html

12   http://www.poetrymagazines.org.uk/magazine/record.asp?id=3401

13   Di Prima, "Afterword," to Maria Mazziotti Gillan, *Where I Come From: Selected and New Poems* (Toronto and New York: Guernica, 1995), 117; Di Prima, "Introduction" to Giuseppe Conte, *The Seasons*, trans. Laura Stortoni-Hager (Annali D'Italanistica, Inc, 2001).

14   Di Prima, "'Don't Solidify the Adversary!': A Response to Rudolph Vecoli," in *Through the Looking Glass: Italian and Italian/American Images in the Media*, 27–29; Di Prima, *Recollections of My Life as a Woman*, "Acknowledgments," 1; *The I Ching, or Book of Changes*, trans. Richard Wilhelm (Princeton: Princeton University Press, 1971), 140; *Recollections*, 15–16; Tommaso Astarita, *Between Salt and Holy Water: A History of Southern Italy* (New York: W. W. Norton and Co., 2005), 18; Di Prima, "Revolutionary Letter #77: Awkward Song on the Eve of War," *Revolutionary Letters*, 109; "Diane di Prima in Conversation with Margarita Meklin and Andrew Meklin," *Ars Interpres 7: An International Journal of Poetry, Translation and Art*, http://www.arsint.com/2006/d_d_7.html http://jacketmagazine.com/18/diprima-iv.html

15   Di Prima, *Recollections of My Life as a Woman*, 419.

16   Ibid., 368–69.

17   Di Prima, "The Loba Recovers the Memory of a Mare," in *Loba*, 125; Di Prima, "Lust for Life," *Los Angeles Times*, May 18, 1997; Di Prima, "A Farewell Rite" in *The Poetry Deal*, 97.

18   *Princeton Dictionary of Buddhism*, 377; http://www.poetrymagazines.org.uk/magazine/record.asp?id=3401

19   "Diane di Prima in Conversation with Margarita Meklina and Andrew Meklin," *Ars Interpres 7: An International Journal of Poetry, Translation and Art*; Charles Bukowski, "The Laughing Heart"; Di Prima, "Memorial Day, 2003," in *The Poetry Deal*, 63–64.

20   Di Prima, "Revolutionary Letter Number Eighty-Eight: Notes Toward a Poem of Revolution," *Revolutionary Letters*, 132–37; Di Prima, *TimeBomb* (San Francisco: Eidolon Editions, 2006), n.p. On inspiration, see Penelope Murray, "Poetic Genius and Its Classical Origins," in *Genius: The History of an Idea* (New York: Basil Blackwell, 1989), 9–31.

21   Iona Cosma, *Angels In-Between: The Poetics of Excess and the Crisis of Representation*, University of Toronto Dissertation, 2009, 19; *Princeton Dictionary of Buddhism*, 956, 438.

22   *Shambhala Dictionary of Buddhism and Zen*, 241.

23   http://sisterezili.blogspot.com/2009/04/diane-diprimas-acceptance-speech-at-pen.html

24   Charles Olson, *Apollonius of Tyana: A Dance, with Some Words, for Two Actors* in *Selected Writings*, ed. Robert Creeley (New York: New Directions,

1967), 140; Di Prima, "Revolutionary Letter #77: Awkward Song on the Eve of War," *Revolutionary Letters*, 109.

25 Denis de Rougemont, *Love in the Western World* (Princeton: Princeton University Press, 1983), 102–03; Ibid., 109–10, 111.

26 *The Beats: A Graphic History*, ed. Paul Buhle (New York: Hill and Wang, 2009), 150–53; Di Prima, "Inaugural Address," *The Poetry Deal*, 1.

27 Ibid., 2, 3.

28 Ibid., 17.

29 https://www.giveforward.com/fundraiser/dz11

30 Di Prima, "Alchemical Signals," *Paterson Literary Review* 2010–11, Issue 38, ed. Maria Mazziotti Gillan, 26.

31 Ibid., 45, 46, 47; Di Prima, "Brief Wyoming Meditation" in *Selected Poems: 1956–1975*, 296.

32 Ibid., 47, 48.

33 Ibid., 51, 52.

34 http://allenginsberg.org/2014/08/diane-di-primas-80th-birthday/; https://sudoroom.org/events/diane-di-prima-the-dream-of-prehistory-3/; Adrienne Rich, "Taking Women Students Seriously," in *On Lies, Secrets and Silence: Selected Prose, 1966-1978*; Di Prima, *The Poetry Deal*, 39, 87, 93, 43, 49, 32. On Kirby Doyle, see Rod Phillips, *"Forest Beatniks" and "Urban Thoreaus": Gary Snyder, Jack Kerouac, Lew Welch, and Michael McClure* (New York: Peter Lang, 2000), 131–32.

35 Ibid., 101–02.

36 Di Prima, *Out-Takes* (San Francisco: Omerta Publications, 2016), 3,4, 16; https://www.washingtonpost.com/graphics/2017/lifestyle/the-beat-generation/?utm_term=.30f6631550a6; *Recollections*, 41.

37 "The Gnosis Interview: Diane di Prima on Magic, Healing, and the Western Esoteric Tradition," 20.

38 Ibid.; https://www.washingtonpost.com/graphics/2017/lifestyle/the-beat-generation/?utm_term=.92d4e476960d]; http://www.verbicidemagazine.com/2010/07/29/interview-diane-di-prima/

39 *Rocky Ledge*, 1981, 47–48.

40 http://www.prrb.ca/articles/issue07-di_prima.htm

UNIVERSITY LIBRARY COLLECTIONS OF DIANE DI PRIMA'S WORK

The published and unpublished works of Diane di Prima are archived at a number of institutions. The unpublished material includes—among other items—letters, diaries, the novella *Not Quite Buffalo Stew*, notes or lectures, poems, interviews, and stories.

University of California at Berkeley, Bancroft Library

University of Connecticut, Thomas J. Dodd Research Center

University of Delaware, Morris Library, Department of Special Collections

Indiana University Bloomington, Lilly Library

University of Kansas Libraries; Kenneth Spencer Research Library

University of Louisville

University of Michigan, Ann Arbor

University of North Carolina at Chapel Hill, Wilson Library

Southern Illinois University

Syracuse University

BIBLIOGRAPHY

Works by Diane di Prima

Di Prima, Diane. "Movement and Tableau in the Dance." *Carolina Quarterly*, 8, no. 1 (1955), 20–25.

Di Prima, Diane. *This Kind of Bird Flies Backward*. New York: Totem Press, 1958.

Di Prima, Diane, ed. *Various Fables from Various Places*. New York: G. P. Putnam's Sons, 1960.

Di Prima, Diane. *Dinners and Nightmares*. New York: Corinth Books, 1961.

Di Prima, Diane. *The New Handbook of Heaven*. San Francisco: The Auerhahn Press, 1963.

Di Prima, Diane, trans. *Seven Love Poems from the Middle Latin*. New York: The Poets Press, 1965.

Di Prima, Diane. "Paracelsus: An Appreciation." In A. E. Waite, ed., *The Hermetic and Alchemical Writings of Paracelsus the Great in Two Volumes*. New York: University Books, Inc., 1967.

Di Prima, Diane. *Earthsong: Poems, 1957-1959*. New York: Poets Press, 1968.

Di Prima, Diane. *Hotel Albert: Poems*. New York: Poets Press, 1968.

Di Prima, Diane, ed. *War Poems*. New York: The Poets Press, 1968.

Di Prima, Diane. *L.A. Odyssey*. New York: Poets Press, 1969.

Di Prima, Diane. *Memoirs of a Beatnik*. New York: Traveller's Companion Series, 1969.

Di Prima, Diane. *Kerhonkson Journal*. Berkeley: Oyez, 1971.

Di Prima, Diane and LeRoi Jones, eds. *The Floating Bear: A Newsletter, Numbers 1-37, 1961-1969*. La Jolla, CA: Laurence McGilvery, 1973.

Di Prima, Diane. *The Freddie Poems*. Point Reyes: Eidolon Editions, 1974.

Di Prima, Diane. *The Calculus of Variation*. San Francisco: Privately Printed, 1972.

Di Prima, Diane. *Selected Poems; 1956-1975*. Berkeley: North Atlantic Books, 1975.

Di Prima, Diane. *Loba: Parts I-VIII*. Berkeley: Wingbow Press, 1978.

Di Prima, Diane. *Wyoming Series*. San Francisco: Eidolon Editions, 1988.

Di Prima, Diane. *Pieces of a Song: Selected Poems*. City Lights: San Francisco, 1990.

Di Prima, Diane. *Seminary Poems*. Point Reyes: Floating Island Publications, 1991.

Di Prima, Diane. *Loba*. New York: Penguin, 1998.

Di Prima, Diane. "Preface" to John Dee, *The Hieroglyphic Monad*. Boston: Weiser Books, 2000.

Di Prima, Diane. *Introduction to Giuseppe Conte, The Seasons*, ed., and trans. Laura Stortoni-Hager. Chapel Hill, NC: Annali d'Italianistica, Inc., 2001.

Di Prima, Diane. *The Ones I Used to Laugh With: A Haibun Journal*. San Francisco: Habenicht Press, 2003.

Di Prima, Diane. *TimeBomb*. San Francisco: Eidolon Editions, 2006.

Di Prima, Diane. *Revolutionary Letters*. San Francisco: Last Gasp, 2007.

Di Prima, Diane. *R.D.'s H.D.*, ed. Ammiel Alcalay. *Lost and Found: The CUNY Poetics Documents Initiative*, Series 2, Number 3, Spring 2011.

Di Prima, Diane. *The Poetry Deal: San Francisco Poet Laureate Series No. 5*. San Francisco: City Lights Foundation, 2014.

Di Prima, Diane. *Out-takes*. San Francisco: Omerta Publications, 2016.

Work by Diane di Prima in Anthologies

Allen, Donald and George F. Butterick. *The Postmoderns: The New American Poetry Revised*. New York: Grove Press, 1982.

Axel, Brett, ed. *Will Work for Peace: New Political Poems*. Trenton, NJ: Zeropanik Press, 2000.

Barolini, Helen, ed. *The Dream Book: An Anthology of Writing by Italian American Women*. New York: Schocken Books, 1985.

Berlandt, Herman and Neeli Cherkovsi, eds. *Peace or Perish: A Crisis Anthology*. San Francisco: Fort Mason Center, 1983.

Breyne, de Mathis, ed. *Baby Beat Generation: An Anthology*. La Souterraine: La Main Courante, 2005.

Brinkmann, R. D. and R. R. Rygula. *Neue Amerikanische Szene*. Darmstadt: Marz Verlag, 1969.

Chester, Laura and Sharon Barba, eds. *Rising Tides; Twentieth Century American Women Poets*. New York: Washington Square Press, 1973.

Cohen, Alan and Clive Matson, eds. *An Eye for an Eye Makes the Whole World Blind: Poets on 9/11*. Oakland, CA: Regent Press, 2002.

Corso, Gregory and Walter Hollerer, eds. *Junge Amerikanische Lyrik*. Munchen: Carl Hanser Verlag, 1961.

De Loach, Allen, ed. *The East Side Scene: American Poetry, 1960-1965*. New York: Anchor Books, 1972.

Durand, Christopher, ed. *The Yes! Press Anthology*. Santa Barbara: Christopher's Books, 1972.

Eastoak, Sandy, ed. *Dharma Family Treasures; Sharing Mindfulness with Children*. Berkeley: North Atlantic Books, 1994.

Fisher, Stanley, ed. *Beat Coast: An Anthology of Rebellion*. New York: Excelsior Press, 1960.

Gach, Gary, ed. *What Book!? Buddha Poems from Beat to Hiphop*. Berkeley: Parallax Press, 1998.

Gilbert, Sandra M. and Susan Gubar. *The Norton Anthology of Literature by Women*, Third Edition. New York: W. W. Norton, 2007.

Gillan, Maria Mazziotti and Jennifer Gillan, eds. *Unsettling America: An Anthology of Contemporary Multicultural Poetry*. New York: Penguin Books, 1994.

Ginsberg, Allen, ed. *Poems for the Nation: A Collection of Contemporary Political Poems*. New York: Seven Stories Press, 2000.

Gitlin, Todd, ed. *Campfires of the Resistance: Poetry from the Movement.* Indianapolis: Bobbs-Merrill, 1971.

Goodman, Paul, ed. *Seeds of Liberation.* New York: George Braziller, 1964.

Hoover, Paul, ed. *Postmodern American Poetry: A Norton Anthology.* New York: W. W. Norton, 1994.

Howe, Florence, ed. *No More Masks! An Anthology of Twentieth-Century American Women Poets,* revised and expanded ed. New York: Harper Perennial, 1993.

Howe, Florence and Ellen Bass, eds. *No More Masks! An Anthology of Poems by Women.* Garden City, NY: Anchor, 1973.

Italian-American Political Solidarity Club, ed. *Avanti Popolo: Italian-American Writers Sail Beyond Columbus.* San Francisco: Manic D Press, 2008.

Johnson, Kent and Craig Paulenich. *Beneath a Single Moon: Buddhism in Contemporary American Poetry.* Boston: Shambhala, 1991.

Jones, Hettie, ed. *Poems Now.* New York: Kulchur Press, 1966.

Kaufman, Alan. *The Outlaw Bible of American Poetry.* New York: Basic Books, 1999.

Kherdian, David, ed. *Beat Voices: An Anthology of Beat Poetry.* New York: Henry Holt, 1995.

Knight, Brenda. *Women of the Beat Generation.* New York: MJF Books, 2000.

Kowit, Steve, ed. *The Maverick Poets: An Anthology.* Portrero, CA: Gorilla Press, 1988.

Marler, Regina, ed. *Queer Beats: How the Beats Turned America On to Sex.* San Francisco: Cleis Press, 2004.

Mayo, Michael, ed. *Practising Angels: A Contemporary Anthology of San Francisco Bay Area Poetry.* Eugene, OR: Seismographic Publications, 1986.

Muten, Burleigh. *Her Words: An Anthology of Poetry about the Great Goddess.* Boston: Shambhala, 1999.

O'Brien, Glenn, ed. *The Cool School: Writing from America's Hip Underground.* New York: The Library of America, 2013.

Piercy, Marge. *Early Ripening: American Women's Poetry Now.* London: Pandora, 1987.

Quasha, George, ed. *An Active Anthology.* Fremont, MI: The Sumac Press, 1974.

Randall, Margaret, ed. *Women Brave in the Face of Danger: Photographs of and Writings by Latin and North American Women.* Trumansburg, NY: The Crossing Press, 1985.

Reed, Ishmael. *From Totems to Hip-Hop: A Multicultural Anthology of Poetry Across the Americas.* New York: Thunder's Mouth Press, 2003.

Reilly, J.N. and Ira Cohen, eds. *Shamanic Warriors Now Poets.* Glasgow: R and R Publishing, 2003.

Rothenberg, Jerome and Diane Rothenberg, eds. *Symposium of the Whole: A Range of Discourse Toward an Ethnopoetics.* Berkeley: University of California Press, 1983.

Schelling, Andrew, ed. *The Wisdom Anthology of North American Buddhist Poetry.* Boston: Wisdom Publications, 2005.

Susoyev, Steve and George Birimisa, eds. *Return to the Caffe Cino.* San Francisco: Moving Finger Press, 2007.

Tamburri, Anthony Julian, Paolo A. Giordano, and Fred L. Gardaphe, eds.
    From the Margin: Writings in Italian Americana. West Lafayette, IN: Purdue
    University Press, 2000.
Tea, Michelle, ed. *Without a Net: The Female Experience of Growing up Working
    Class*. Berkeley: Seal Press, 2003.
Tonkinson, Carol. *Big Sky Mind: Buddhism and the Beat Generation*. New York:
    Riverhead Books, 1995.
Waldman, Anne, ed. *The Beat Book: Poems and Fiction of the Beat Generation*.
    Boston: Shambhala, 1996.
Wong, Matthew. *On the Finest Shore: Poems and Reminiscences of Moe*. Berkeley:
    Moe's Books, 1997.

Secondary Sources

Abrams, M. H. *Natural Supernaturalism: Tradition and Revolution in Romantic
    Literature*. New York: W. W. Norton and Company, 1973.
Adams, P. Sitney. *Visionary Film: The American Avant-Garde, 1943-2000*.
    New York: Oxford University Press, 2002.
Adler, Margot. *Drawing Down the Moon: Witches, Druids, Goddess-Worshippers
    and Other Pagans in America*. New York: Penguin, 2006.
Agamben, Giorgio. *Potentialities: Collected Essays in the Philosophy of History*
    1999.
Agamben, Giorgio. *Profanations*. New York: Zone Books, 2007.
Agrippa, Heinrich Cornelius, ed. Willis F. Whitehead. *Agrippa's Occult Philosophy:
    Natural Magic*. Mineola, NY: Dover Publications, 2006.
Albanese, Catherine L. *A Republic of Mind and Spirit: A Cultural History of
    American Metaphysical Religion*. New Haven: Yale University Press, 2007.
Albright, Thomas. *Art in the San Francisco Bay Area, 1945-1980: An Illustrated
    History*. Berkeley: University of California Press, 1985.
Alexander, Michael. *The Poetic Achievement of Ezra Pound*. Berkeley: University of
    California Press, 1981.
Alfonsi, Ferdinando P. *Dictionary of Italian-American Poets*. New York: Peter
    Lang, 1989.
Allyn, David. *Make Love Not War: The Sexual Revolution: An Unfettered History*.
    Boston: Little, Brown and Company, 2000.
Alter, Robert. *The Necessary Angel: Tradition and Modernity in Kafka, Benjamin
    and Scholem*. Cambridge: Harvard University Press, 1991.
Amram, David. *Offbeat: Collaborating with Kerouac*. New York: Thunder's Mouth
    Press, 2002.
Anfam, David. *Abstract Expressionism*. New York: Thames and Hudson, 1990.
Angell, Callie. *Andy Warhol Screen Tests: The Films of Andy Warhol Catalogue
    Raisonne, Volume 1*. New York: Harry N. Abrams, 2006.
Anzaldua, Gloria. *Borderlands/La Frontera*. San Francisco: Aunt Lute Books,
    1999.
Ashton, Jennifer. *The Cambridge Companion to American Poetry Since 1945*.
    New York: Cambridge University Press, 2013.

Astarita, Tommaso. *Between Salt and Holy Water: A History of Southern Italy.* New York: W. W. Norton, 2005.

Baas, Jacquelynn, and Mary Jane Jacob. *Buddha Mind in Contemporary Art.* Berkeley: University of California Press, 2004.

Baker, David. "Probable Reason, Possible Joy." *Kenyon Review*, 14, no. 1 (Winter 1992), 146–157 [Review of Di Prima's *Pieces of a Song*].

Banes, Sally. *Democracy's Body: Judson Dance Theater 1962-1964.* Ann Arbor, MI: UMI Research Press, 1980.

Banes, Sally. *Greenwich Village 1963: Avant-Garde Performance and the Effervescent Body.* Durham: Duke University Press, 1993.

Banes, Sally, ed. *Reinventing Dance in the 1960s.* Madison: University of Wisconsin Press, 2003.

Barron, Stephanie, Sheri Bernstein, and Ilene Susan Fort, eds. *Reading California: Art, Image, and Identity, 1900-2000.* Berkeley: University of California Press, 2000.

Bartlett, Lee, ed. *The Beats: Essays in Criticism.* Jefferson, NC: McFarland, 1981.

Battersby, Christine. *Gender and Genius: Towards a Feminist Aesthetics.* London: The Women's Press, 1989.

Battistini, Matilde. *Astrology, Magic, and Alchemy in Art.* Los Angeles: The J. Paul Getty Museum, 2004.

Beausoleil, Beau and Deema K. Shehabi. *Al-Mutanabbi Street Starts Here.* Oakland, CA: PM Press, 2012.

Belasco, Warren James. *Appetite for Change: How the Counterculture Took on the Food Industry.* Ithaca: Cornell University Press, 2007.

Belgrad, Daniel. *The Culture of Spontaneity: Improvisation and the Arts in Postwar America.* Chicago: The University of Chicago Press, 1998.

Bell, Catherine. *Ritual: Perspectives and Dimensions.* New York: Oxford University Press, 1997.

Belletto, Steven, ed. *The Cambridge Companion to The Beats.* New York: Cambridge University Press, 2017.

Benjamin, Walter. "Theses on the Philosophy of History." In Hannah Arendt, ed., *Illuminations.* New York: Schocken, 1973.

Bendel, Larissa. *The Requirements of Our Life Is the Form of Our Art: Autobiographik von Frauen der Beat Generation.* Frankfurt: Peter Lang, 2005.

Bercovitch, Sacvan, ed. *The Cambridge History of American Literature: Prose Writing, 1940-1990. Vol. 7.* New York: Cambridge University Press, 1999.

Berlin, Isaiah. *The Roots of Romanticism.* Princeton: Princeton University Press, 1999.

Bertholf, Robert J., and Annette S. Levitt, ed., *William Blake and the Moderns.* Albany: State University of New York Press.

Beyer, Stephen. *The Cult of Tara: Magic and Ritual in Tibet.* Berkeley: University of California Press, 1973.

Biderman, Shlomo and Ben-Ami Scharfstein, ed. *Rationality in Question: On Eastern and Western Views of Rationality.* Leiden: E. J. Brill, 1989.

Bizot, Jean-Francois. *200 Trips from the Counterculture: Graphics and Stories from the Underground Press Syndicate.* London: Thames and Hudson, 2006.

Bjorklund, Diane. *Interpreting the Self: Two Hundred Years of American Autobiography.* Chicago: University of Chicago Press, 1998.

Blain, Virginia, Isobel Grundy, and Patricia Clements. *The Feminist Companion to Literature in English: Women Writers from the Middle Ages to the Present*. New Haven and London: Yale University Press, 1990.

Blau, Joseph Leon. *The Christian Interpretation of the Cabala in the Renaissance*. New York: Columbia University Press, 1944.

Bloom, Harold. *Kabbalah and Criticism*. New York: The Seabury Press, 1975.

Bloom, Harold. *Omens of the Millennium: The Gnosis of Angels, Dreams, and Resurrection*. New York: Riverhead Books, 1996.

Bloom, Harold. *Fallen Angels*. New Haven: Yale University Press, 2007.

Bona, Mary Jo. *Claiming a Tradition: Italian American Women Writers*. Carbondale: Southern Illnois University Press, 1999.

Bona, Mary Jo. *The Voices We Carry: Recent Italian American Women's Fiction*. Toronto: Guernica, 2007.

Bona, Mary Jo and Anthony Julian Tamburri, eds. *Through the Looking Glass: Italian and Italian/American Images in the Media. Selected Essays from the 27th Annual Conference of the American Italian Historical Association*. New York: American Italian Historical Association, 1996.

Boon, Marcus. *The Road of Excess: A History of Writers on Drugs*. Cambridge, MA: Harvard University Press, 2002.

Borges, Jorge Luis. *Seven Nights*. New York: New Directions, 1984.

Bottoms, Stephen J. *Playing Underground: A Critical History of the 1960's Off-Off Broadway Movement*. Ann Arbor: The University of Michigan Press, 2007.

Boyce, Mary. *Zoroastrianism: Its Antiquity and Constant Vigour*. Costa Mesa, CA: Mazda Publishers, 1992.

Brainard, Joe. *I Remember*. New York: Granary Books, 2001.

Brann, Noel L. *Trithemius and Magical Theology: A Chapter in the Controversy Over Occult Studies in Early Modern Europe*. Albany: State University of New York Press, 1999.

Braude, Ann. *Women and American Religion*. New York: Oxford University Press, 2001.

Braude, Ann. *Radical Spirits: Spiritualism and Women's Rights in Nineteenth-Century America*. Bloomington, IN: Indiana University Press, 2011.

Bromell, Nicholas K. *Tomorrow Never Knows: Rock and Psychedelics in the 1960s*. Chicago: University of Chicago Press, 2000.

Brook, James, Chris Carlsson, and Nancy J. Peters. *Reclaiming San Francisco: History, Politics, Culture*. San Francisco: City Lights, 1998.

Buck, Claire, ed. *The Bloomsbury Guide to Women's Literature*. New York: Prentice Hall General Reference, 1992.

Bucke, Richard M. *Cosmic Consciousness: A Study in the Evolution of the Human Mind*. New York: E. P. Dutton, 1969.

Butler, E. M. *The Myth of the Magus*. Cambridge: Cambridge University Press, 1948.

Butler, E. M. *Ritual Magic*. Cambridge: Cambridge University Press, 1949.

Cacciari, Massimo. *The Necessary Angel*. Albany: State University of New York Press, 1994.

Cage, John. *For the Birds: John Cage in Conversation with Daniel Charles*. London: Marion Boyars, 1980.

Calas, Nicolas and Elena Calas. *Icons and Images of the Sixties*. New York: E. P. Dutton, 1971.

Calonne, David Stephen. *William Saroyan: My Real Work Is Being*. Chapel Hill and London: The University of North Carolina Press, 1983.

Calonne, David Stephen. *Henry Miller*. London: Reaktion Books, 2014.

Calonne, David Stephen. *The Spiritual Imagination of the Beats*. New York: Cambridge University Press, 2017.

Cannistraro, Philip, and Gerald Meyer, eds. *The Lost World of Italian-American Radicalism: Politics, Labor and Culture*. Westport, CT: Praeger, 2003.

Carden, Mary Paniccia. *Women Writers of the Beat Era: Autobiography and Intertextuality*. Charlottesville: University of Virginia Press, 2018.

Carolan, Trevor. *New World Dharma: Interviews and Encounters with Buddhist Teachers, Writers, and Leaders*. Albany: State University of New York Press, 2016.

Carson, Kay. *Where the Heart Beats: John Cage, Buddhism, and the Inner Life of Artists*. New York: Penguin, 2012.

Castelao-Gomez, Isabel. "Beat Women Poets and Writers: Countercultural Urban Geographies and Feminist Avant-Garde Poetics." *Journal of English Studies*, 14 (2016), 47–72.

Chadwick, David. *Crooked Cucumber: The Life and Zen Teaching of Shunryu Suzuki*. New York: Broadway Books, 1999.

Charters, Ann, ed. *The Beats: Literary Bohemians in Postwar America*. Detroit: Gale Research Company, 1983.

Charters, Ann. "Diane di Prima and the Loba Poems: Poetic Archetype as Spirit Double." In Rudi Horemans, ed., *Beat Indeed!*, 107–115. Antwerp: EXA, 1985.

Choucha, Nadia. *Surrealism and the Occult: Shamanism, Magic, Alchemy, and the Birth of an Artistic Movement*. Rochester, VT: Destiny Books, 1992.

Christodoulides, Nephie J and Polina Mackay, eds. *The Cambridge Companion to H.D.* Cambridge: Cambridge University Press, 2012.

Churton, Tobias. *Gnostic Philosophy: From Ancient Persia to Modern Times*. Rochester, VT: Inner Traditions, 2005.

Ciongli, A. Kenneth and Jay Parini, eds. *Beyond the Godfather: Italian American Writers on the Real Italian American Experience*. Hanover, NH: University Press of New England, 1997.

Clay, Steven, and Rodney Phillips. *A Secret Location on the Lower East Side: Adventures in Writing, 1960-1980*. New York: The New York Public Library and Granary Books, 1998.

Cohen, Alan. *The San Francisco Oracle: Facsimile Edition*. Berkeley: Regent Press, 1991.

Cohn, Jesse. *Underground Passages: Anarchist Resistance Culture, 1848-2011*. Oakland, CA: AK Press, 2014.

Clark, Steve, Tristanne Connolly, and Jason Whittaker. *Blake 2.0: William Blake in Twentieth-Century Art, Music and Culture*. New York: Palgrave Macmillan, 2012.

Clark, Stuart. *Thinking with Demons: The Idea of Witchcraft in Early Modern Europe*. New York: Oxford University Press, 1999.

Clarke, J. J. *Oriental Enlightenment: The Encounter between Asian and Western Thought*. London: Routledge, 1997.

Clay, Steven, and Rodney Phillips. *A Secret Location on the Lower East Side: Adventures in Writing, 1960-1980*. New York: The New York Public Library, 1998.

Cook, Ralph T. *City Lights Books: A Descriptive Bibliography*. Metuchen, NJ: The Scarecrow Press, Inc, 1992.

Copenhaver, Brian P. *Magic in Western Culture: From Antiquity to the Enlightenment*. New York: Cambridge University Press, 2015.

Corbin, Henry. *Avicenna and the Visionary Recital*. New York: Pantheon, 1960.

Cosma, Iona. *Angels In-Between: The Poetics of Excess and the Crisis of Representation*. Dissertation, University of Toronto, 2009.

Couliano, Ioan. *Eros and Magic in the Renaissance*. Chicago: University of Chicago Press, 1987.

Couliano, Ioan. *Out of this World: Otherworldly Journeys from Gilgamesh to Albert Einstein*. Boston and London: Shambhala, 1991.

Creeley, Robert. *Selected Letters*, eds. Rod Smith, Peter Baker, and Kaplan Harris. Berkeley: University of California Press, 2014.

Cunningham, Andrew and Rosemary Jardine, eds. *Romanticism and the Sciences*. Cambridge: Cambridge University Press, 1990.

Curtis, David. *Experimental Cinema*. New York; Delacorte, 1971.

Dan, Joseph. *Jewish Mystical Books and Their Christian Interpreters*. Cambridge, MA: Harvard College Library, 1997.

Davidson, Cathy N, and Linda Wagner-Martin, eds. *The Oxford Companion to Women's Writing in the United States*. New York: Oxford University Press, 1995.

Davidson, Gustav. *A Dictionary of Angels*. New York: The Free Press, 1971.

Davidson, Michael. *The San Francisco Renaissance: Poetics and Community at Mid-Century*. Cambridge: Cambridge University Press, 1989.

De Santillana, Giorgio. *Hamlet's Mill: An Essay on Myth and the Frame of Time*. Boston: Gambit, Incorporated, 1969.

Deussen, Paul. *The Philosophy of the Upanishads*. New York: Dover Publications, 1966.

De Veaux, Alexis. *Warrior Poet: A Biography of Audre Lorde*. New York: W. W. Norton & Company, 2004.

Dickstein, Morris. *Leopards in the Temple: The Transformation of American Fiction, 1945-1970*. Cambridge: Harvard University Press, 2002.

Dodds, E. R. *Pagan and Christian in an Age of Anxiety: Some Aspects of Religious Experience from Marcus Aurelius to Constantine*. New York: Cambridge University Press, 1990.

Dolittle, Hilda [HD]. *Helen in Egypt*. New York: New Directions, 1974.

Dolittle, Hilda [HD]. *Notes on Vision*. San Francisco: City Lights, 2001.

Dowman, Keith. *Sky Dancer: The Secret Life and Songs of the Lady Yeshe Tsogyel*. London: Routledge and Kegan Paul, 1984.

Dresser, Marianne, ed. *Buddhist Women on the Edge; Contemporary Perspectives from the Western Frontier*. Berkeley: North Atlantic Books, 1996.

Duberman, Martin. *Black Mountain: An Exploration in Community*. New York: E. P. Dutton, 1972.

Dumoulin, Heinrich. *A History of Zen Buddhism*. London: Faber, 1963.

Duncan, Michael and Kristine McKenna. *Semina Culture: Wallace Berman and His Circle*. New York: D.A.P./Distributed Art Publishers, Inc, 2005.

Duncan, Robert. *The H.D. Book*. Berkeley: University of California Press, 2011.

During, Simon. *Modern Enchantments: The Cultural Power of Secular Magic*. Cambridge: Harvard University Press, 2002.

Eagleton, Mary, ed. *Feminist Literary Theory: A Reader*. Oxford: Basil Blackwell, 1986.

Ebeling, Florian. *The Secret History of Hermes Trismegistus: Hermeticism from Ancient to Modern Times*. Ithaca: Cornell University Press, 2007.

Eco, Umberto. *Art and Beauty in the Middle Ages*. New Haven: Yale University Press, 1986.

Eco, Umberto. *The Search for the Perfect Language*. Oxford: Blackwell, 1995.

Ehrenreich, Barbara. *The Hearts of Men: American Dreams and the Flight from Commitment*. Garden City, NY: Anchor Press, 1983.

Elderfield, John. *De Kooning: A Retrospective*. New York: The Museum of Modern Art, 2011.

Eliade, Mircea. *Occultism, Witchcraft, and Cultural Fashions: Essays in Comparative Religions*. Chicago: University of Chicago Press, 1976.

Eliade, Mircea. *The Forge and the Crucible: The Origins and Structure of Alchemy*. Chicago: University of Chicago Press, 1978.

Elkholy, Sharin N. *The Philosophy of the Beats*. Louisville, KY: The University Press of Kentucky, 2012.

Engelbach, Barbara, Friederike Wappler, Hans Winkler, and Kasper Konig, eds. *Looking for Mushrooms: Beat Poets, Hippies, Funk, Minimal Art: San Francisco, 1955-68*. Koln: Museum Ludwig Verlag der Buchandlung Walter Konig, 2008.

Epstein, Andrew. *Beautiful Enemies: Friendship and Postwar American Poetry*. New York: Oxford University Press, 2006.

Faas, Ekbert, ed. *Towards a New American Poetics: Essays & Interviews*. Santa Barbara: Black Sparrow Press, 1978.

Faivre, Antoine. *The Eternal Hermes: From Greek God to Alchemical Magus*. Grand Rapids, MI: Phanes Press, 1995.

Faivre, Antoine and Jacob Needleman, eds. *Modern Esoteric Spirituality*. New York: SCM Ltd., 1992.

Fanger, Clare, ed. *Invoking Angels: Theurgic Ideas and Practices, Thirteenth to Sixteenth Centuries*. University Park, PA: The Pennsylvania State University Press, 2012.

Farber, David and Beth Bailey. *The Columbia Guide to America in the 1960s*. New York: Columbia University Press, 2001.

Farland, Maria. "'Total System, Total Solution, Total Apocalypse': Sex Oppression, Systems of Property, and 1970s Women's Liberation Fiction." *The Yale Journal of Criticism*, 18, no. 2 (Fall 2005), 381–407.

Farley, Helen. *A Cultural History of Tarot: From Entertainment to Esotericism*. London: I. B. Tauris, 2009.

Farrell, James J. *Spirit of the Sixties: The Making of Postwar Radicalism*. New York: Routledge, 1997.

Feder, Lillian. *Ancient Myth in Modern Poetry*. Princeton: Princeton University Press, 1971.

Ferraro, Thomas J. "Catholic Ethnicity and Modern American Arts." In Pellegrino A. D'Acierno, ed., *The Italian American Heritage: A Companion to Literature and the Arts*, 331–52. New York: Routledge, 1998.

Flaherty, Alice W. *The Midnight Disease: The Drive to Write, Writer's Block, and the Creative Brain*. Boston: Houghton Mifflin, 2004.

Flood, Gavin. *An Introduction to Hinduism*. Cambridge: Cambridge University Press, 1996.

Foley, Jack. *O Powerful Western Star: Poetry & Art in California*. Oakland, CA: Pantograph Press, 2000.

Ford, Phil. *Dig: Sound and Music in Hip Culture*. New York: Oxford, 2013.

Forsgren, Frida, and Michael J. Prince. *Out of the Shadows: Beat Women Are Not Beaten Women*. Kristiansand: Portal Books, 2015.

Fredman, Stephen. *Contextual Practice: Assemblage and the Erotic in Postwar Poetry and Art*. Stanford: Stanford University Press, 2010.

Friedman, Donald. *The Writer's Brush: Paintings, Drawings, and Sculpture by Writers*. Minneapolis: Mid-List Press, 2007.

Friedman, Susan Stanford, and Rachel Blau DuPless, eds. *Signets: Reading H.D.* Madison: The University of Wisconsin Press, 1990.

Gair, Christopher. *The Beat Generation: A Beginner's Guide*. Oxford: Oneworld, 2008.

Gardaphe, Fred L. *Italian Signs, American Streets: The Evolution of Italian American Narrative*. Durham, NC: Duke University Press, 1996.

Gardella, Peter. *American Angels: Useful Spirits in the Material World*. Lawrence, KS: University Press of Kansas, 2007.

Gatti, Hillary. *Essays on Giordano Bruno*. Princeton: Princeton University Press, 2011.

Gaugh, Harry F. *Willem De Kooning*. New York: Abbeville Press, 1983.

Gilbert, Roger. "Awash with Angels: The Religious Turn in Nineties Poetry." *Contemporary Literature* XLII, no. 2 (Summer 2011), 238–69.

Gilbert, Sandra M. and Susan Gubar. *Feminist Literary Theory and Criticism: A Norton Reader*. New York: W. W. Norton, 2007.

Ginsberg, Allen. *Deliberate Prose: Selected Essays 1952–1995*. New York: Harper, 2001.

Glass, Loren. *Counterculture Colophon: Grove Press, the Evergreen Review, and the Incorporation of the Avant-Garde*. Stanford: Stanford University Press, 2013.

Goldberg, RoseLee. *Performance Art: From Futurism to the Present*. London: Thames and Hudson, 2011.

Goldenberg, Naomi R. *Changing of the Gods: Feminism and the End of Traditional Religions*. Boston: Beacon Press, 1979.

Gooch, Brad. *City Poet: The Life and Times of Frank O'Hara*. New York: Harper Perennial, 2014.

Grace, Nancy M. "Diane di Prima as Playwright: The Early Years 1959-1964." In Deborah R. Geis, ed., *Beat Drama: Playwrights and Performances of the "Howl" Generation*. London: Bloomsbury, 2016.

Grace, Nancy M. and Jennie Skerl, ed. *The Transnational Beat Generation*. New York: Palgrave Macmillan, 2012.

Graves, Robert. *King Jesus*. New York: Farrar, Straus and Giroux, 1981.

Graves, Robert. *The White Goddess*. New York: Farrar, Straus and Giroux, 2013.

Gray, Timothy. *Urban Pastoral: Natural Currents in the New York School*. Iowa City: University of Iowa Press, 2010.

Grazia, Edward de. *Girls Lean Back Everywhere: The Law of Obscenity and the Assault on Genius*. New York: Vintage, 1992.

Greenfield, Robert. *Timothy Leary: A Biography*. New York: Harcourt, Inc., 2006.

Grunenberg, Christoph, ed. *Summer of Love: Art of the Psychedelic Era*. London: Tate Publishing, 2005.

Grunenberg, Christoph and Jonathan Harris, eds. *Summer of Love: Psychedelic Art, Social Crisis and Counterculture in the 1960s*. Liverpool: Liverpool University Press, 2005.

Guglielmo, Jennifer and Salvatore Salerno, ed. *Are Italians White?: How Race is Made in America*. New York and London: Routledge, 2003.

Hackman, William. *Out of Sight: The Los Angeles Art Scene of the Sixties*. New York: Other Press, 2015.

Haggerty, George E., and Molly McGarry, eds. *A Companion to Lesbian, Gay, Bisexual, and Queer Studies*. Oxford: Blackwell, 2007.

Hanegraaff, Wouter J. *Esotericism and the Academy: Rejected Knowledge in Western Culture*. New York: Cambridge University Press, 2013.

Hanegraaff, Wouter J., ed. *Dictionary of Gnosis and Western Esotericism*. Leiden: Brill, 2006.

Harkness, Deborah E. *John Dee's Conversations with Angels: Cabala, Alchemy, and the End of Nature*. New York: Cambridge University Press, 1999.

Harris, Larissa and Media Farzin, eds. *Thirteen Most Wanted Men: Andy Warhol and the 1964 World's Fair*. New York: Queens Museum, 2014.

Harvey, Peter. *An Introduction to Buddhism: Teachings, History and Practices*. New York: Cambridge University Press, 2013.

Haskins, Rob. *John Cage*. London: Reaktion Books, 2012.

Hayes, Charles, ed. *Tripping: An Anthology of True-Life Psychedelic Adventures*. New York: Penguin, 2000.

Heller, Steven. *Merz to Émigré: Avant-Garde Magazine Design of the Twentieth Century*. London: Phaidon Press, 2003

Herms, George. *The River Book: Volume One*. Venice, CA: Hamilton Press, 2014.

Hicks, John. *An Interpretation of Religion: Human Responses to the Transcendent*. New Haven: Yale University Press, 1989.

Hobbs, Stuart D. *The End of the American Avant Garde*. New York and London: New York University Press, 1997.

Hobson, Suzanne. "A New Angelology: Mapping the Angel through Twentieth-Century Literature." *Literature Compass*, 4, no. 2 (2007), 494–507.

Hoffman, Daniel. *Harvard Guide to Contemporary American Writing*. Cambridge, MA: Harvard University Press, 1979.

Horemans, Rudi, ed. *Beat Indeed!* Antwerp, Belgium: EXA, 1985.

Jacobsen, Thorkild. *The Treasures of Darkness: A History of Mesopotamian Religion*. New Haven: Yale University Press, 1976.

Jarnot, Lisa. *Robert Duncan: The Ambassador from Venus, A Biography*. Berkeley: University of California Press, 2012.

Johnson, Kent and Craig Paulenich. *Beneath a Single Moon: Buddhism in Contemporary American Poetry*. Boston and London: Shambhala, 1991.

Johnson, Ronna C. and Nancy M. Grace. *Girls Who Wore Black: Women Writing the Beat Generation*. New Brunswick, NJ: Rutgers University Press, 2002.

Johnston, Devin. *Precipitations: Contemporary American Poetry as Occult Practice*. Middletown, CT: Wesleyan University Press, 2002.

Jonas, Hans. *The Gnostic Religion: The Message of the Alien God and the Beginnings of Christianity*. Boston: Beacon Press, 1963.

Jones, Marjorie. *Frances Yates and the Hermetic Tradition*. Lake Worth, FL: Ibis Press, 2008.

Jorgensen, Danny L. and Lin Jorgensen. "Social Meanings of the Occult." *The Sociological Quarterly*, 23 (Summer 1982), 373–89.

Josten, C. H., ed. and trans. "A Translation of John Dee's 'Monas Hieroglyphica' (Antwerp, 1564), with an introduction and Annotations." *Ambix*, 12 (1964): 84–221.

Jung, Carl Gustav. *The Red Book*, ed. Sonu Shamdasani. New York: W. W. Norton, 2009.

Kalaidjian, Walter, ed. *The Cambridge Companion to Modern American Poetry*. New York: Cambridge University Press, 2015.

Kandel, Lenore. *Collected Poems of Lenore Kandel with a Preface by Diane di Prima*. Berkeley: North Atlantic Books, 2012.

Kane, Daniel. *All Poets Welcome: The Lower East Side Poetry Scene in the 1960s*. Berkeley: University of California Press, 2003.

Kane, Daniel. *We Saw the Light: Conversations Between the New American Cinema and Poetry*. Iowa City: University of Iowa Press, 2009.

Kapleau, Philip. *The Three Pillars of Zen: Teaching, Practice, and Enlightenment*. New York: Anchor Books, 2000.

Kapstein, Matthew T. *Tibetan Buddhism: A Very Short Introduction*. Oxford: Oxford University Press, 2014.

Katz, Steven T., ed. *Mysticism and Religious Traditions*. New York: Oxford University Press, 1983.

Katz, Vincent, ed. *Black Mountain College: Experiment in Art*. Cambridge, MA: The MIT Press, 2002.

Keller, Lynn. *Forms of Expansion: Recent Long Poems by Women*. Chicago: The University of Chicago Press, 1997.

Kieckhefer, Richard. *Magic in the Middle Ages*. Cambridge: Cambridge University Press, 1990.

Kilcher, Andreas, ed. *Die Enzyklopaedik der Esoterik*. Paderborn: Wilhelm Fink, 2010.

Kinnahan, Linda A. *Lyric Interventions: Feminism, Experimental Poetry, and Contemporary Discourse*. Iowa City: University of Iowa Press, 2004.

Kinnahan, Linda A., ed. *A History of Twentieth-Century American Poetry*. New York: Duquesne, 2016.

Kinsley, David. *Hindu Goddesses: Visions of the Divine Feminine in Hindu Religious Tradition*. Berkeley: University of California Press, 1986.

Kinsman, Robert S. *The Darker Vision of the Renaissance: Beyond the Fields of Reason*. Berkeley: University of California Press, 1974.

Kirschenbaum, Blossom S. "Diane di Prima: Extending La Famiglia." *Melus*, 14, nos. 3-4 (Fall–Winter 1987).

Kitagawa, Joseph M. and Mark D. Cummings, eds. *Buddhism and Asian History*. New York: Macmillan Publishing Company.

Klein, Anne Carolyn. *Meeting the Great Bliss Queen: Buddhists, Feminists, and the Art of the Self*. Boston: Beacon Press, 1995.

Knellwolf, Christa and Christopher Norris, eds. *The Cambridge History of Literary Criticism, Volume Nine: Twentieth-Century Historical, Philosophical and Psychological Perspectives*. Cambridge: Cambridge University Press, 2001.

Knight, Brenda. *Women of the Beat Generation: The Writers, Artists and Muses at the Heart of a Revolution*. New York: MJF Books, 2000.

Kramer, Samuel Noah. *Sumerian Mythology: A Study of Spiritual and Literary Achievement in the Third Millennium B.C.* New York: Harper and Row, 1961.

Kripal, Jeffrey, J. *Mutants and Mystics: Science Fiction, Superhero Comics, and the Paranormal*. Chicago: The University of Chicago Press, 2011.

Kristeller, Paul Oskar. *Eight Philosophers of the Italian Renaissance*. Stanford: Stanford University Press, 1964.

Kubrin, David. "Newton's Inside Out! Magic, Class Struggle, and the Rise of Mechanism in the West." In Harry Woolf, ed., *The Analytic Spirit: Essays in the History of Science in Honor of Henry Guerlac*, 96–121. Ithaca and London: Cornell University Press, 1981.

Kubrin, David. "How Sir Isaac Newton Helped Restore Law 'n' Order to the West." *Liberation*, 16, no. 10 (March 1972), 32–41.

Lambert, Alexandra and Elmar Schenkel, ed. *The Golden Egg: Alchemy in Art and Literature*. Berlin: Galda+Wilch Verlag, 2002.

Lardas, John. *The Bop Apocalypse: The Religious Visions of Kerouac, Ginsberg and Burroughs*. Urbana: University of Illinois Press, 2001.

Larson, Kay. *Where the Heart Beats: John Cage, Zen Buddhism, and the Inner Life of Artists*. New York: Penguin Books, 2013.

Lattin, Don. *The Harvard Psychedelic Club: How Timothy Leary, Ram Dass, Huston Smith, and Andrew Weil Killed the Fifties and Ushered in a New Age for America*. New York: HarperCollins, 2011.

Lauter, Estella. *Women as Mythmakers: Poetry and Visual Art by Twentieth-Century Women*. Bloomington: Indiana University Press, 1984.

Leavitt, June. *Esoteric Symbols: The Tarot in Yeats, Eliot, and Kafka*. Lanham, MD: University Press of America, 2007.

Lee, A. Robert, ed. *The Beat Generation Writers*. London: Pluto Press, 1996.

Lee, A. Robert. *Modern American Counter Writing: Beats, Outsiders, Ethnics*. London: Routledge, 2010.

Lehman, David. *The Last Avant-Garde: The Making of the New York School of Poets*. New York: Doubleday, 1998.

Lehrich, Christopher I. *The Occult Mind: Magic in Theory and Practice*. Ithaca and London: Cornell University Press, 2007.

Leland, John. *Hip: The History*. New York: Ecco, 2004.

Lemke-Santangelo. *Daughters of Aquarius: Women of the Sixties Counterculture*. Lawrence: University Press of Kansas, 2009.

Lepetit, Patrick. *The Esoteric Secrets of Surrealism: Origins, Magic, and Secret Societies*. Rochester, VT: Inner Traditions, 2012.

Lepper, Gary M. *A Bibliographical Introduction to Seventy-Five Modern American Authors*. Berkeley: Serendipity Books, 1976.

Lewis, I. M. *Ecstatic Religion: A Study of Shamanism and Spirit Possession*. London and New York: Routledge, 2003.

Lewis, James R., ed. *Magical Religion and Modern Witchcraft*. Albany: State University of New York, 1996.

Lewis, James R. and J. Gordon Melton, eds. *Perspectives on the New Age*. Albany: State University of New York Press, 1992.

Lindberg, David C., *The Beginnings of Western Science: The European Scientific Tradition in Philosophical, Religious*, and *Institutional Context, Prehistory to A.D. 1450*, Second Edition. Chicago: The University of Chicago Press, 2007.

Linden, Stanton J. *The Alchemy Reader: From Hermes Trismegistus to Isaac Newton*. Cambridge: Cambridge University Press, 2003.

Loewinsohn, Ron. "Reviews: After the (Mimeograph) Revolution." *Triquarterly*, 18 (Spring 1970): 221–36.

Longenbach, James. *Stone Cottage: Pound, Yeats, and Modernism*. New York: Oxford University Press, 1988.

Lopez, Donald S., Jr., ed. *A Modern Buddhist Bible: Essential Readings from East and West*. Boston: Beacon Press, 2002.

Lopez, Donald S., Jr. *The Tibetan Book of the Dead: A Biography*. Princeton and Oxford: Princeton University Press, 2011.

Loriggio, Francesco, ed. *Social Pluralism and Literary History: The Literature of the Italian Emigration*. Toronto: Guernica, 1996.

Lorde, Audre. *The First Cities*. New York: Poets Press, 1968.

Lorde, Audre. *Zami: A New Spelling of My Name*. New York: Crossing Press, 1982.

Loriggio, Francesco, ed. *Social Pluralism and Literary History: The Literature of the Italian Emigration*. Toronto: Guernica, 1996.

Lovejoy, A. O. *The Great Chain of Being: A Study of the History of an Idea*. Cambridge, MA: Harvard University Press, 1964.

Luhrmann, T. M., *Persuasions of the Witch's Craft: Ritual Magic in Contemporary England*. Cambridge, MA: Harvard University Press, 1989.

Luscombe, David. *A History of Western Philosophy: II Medieval Thought*. Oxford: Oxford University Press, 1997.

Lytle, Mark Hamilton. *America's Uncivil Wars: The Sixties Era from Elvis to the Fall of Richard Nixon*. New York: Oxford University Press, 2006.

Magee, Glenn Alexander, ed. *The Cambridge Handbook of Western Mysticism and Esotericism*. New York: Cambridge University Press, 2016.

Mannino, Mary Ann Vigilante and Justin Vitiello, eds. *Breaking Open: Reflections on Italian American Women's Writing*. West Layfayette, IN: Purdue University Press, 2003.

Marenbon, John. *The Oxford Handbook of Medieval Philosophy*. New York: Oxford University Press, 2012.

Marling, William. *Gatekeepers: The Emergence of World Literature and the 1960s*. New York: Oxford University Press, 2016.

Marshall, Peter. *The Magic Circle of Rudolf II: Alchemy and Astrology in Renaissance Prague*. New York: Walker and Company, 2006.

Marwick, Arthur. *The Sixties: Cultural Revolution in Britain, France, Italy, and the United States, c. 1958-c. 1974*. New York: Oxford University Press, 1998.

Materer, Timothy. *Modernist Alchemy: Poetry and the Occult*. Ithaca and London: Cornell University Press, 1995.

Maynard, John Arthur. *Venice West: The Beat Generation in Southern California*. New Brunswick: Rutgers University Press, 1991.

McCallum, E. L. and Mikko Tuhkanen, eds. *The Cambridge History of Gay and Lesbian Literature*. New York: Cambridge University Press, 2014.

McClure, Michael. *Scratching the Beat Surface*. New York: Penguin, 1994.

McDonagh, Don. *The Rise and Fall of Modern Dance*. New York: Outerbridge and Diensffrey, 1970.

McEvoy, James. *Robert Grosseteste*. New York: Oxford University Press, 2000.

McHale, Brian. *The Cambridge Introduction to Postmodernism*. New York: Cambridge University Press, 2015.

McIntosh, Christopher. *Eliphas Levi and the French Occult Revival*. London: Rider, 1972.

McIntosh, Christopher. *The Rosicrucians: The History, Mythology and Rituals of an Occult Order*. Northhamptonshire: Crucible, 1987.

McLeod, Hugh. *The Religious Crisis of the 1960s*. Oxford: Oxford University Press, 2007.

McMillian, John. *Smoking Typewriters: The Sixties Underground Press and the Rise of Alternative Media in America*. New York: Oxford University Press, 2011.

McNeice, Ray and Larry Smith, eds. *America Zen: A Gathering of Poets*. Huron, OH: Bottom Dog Press, 2004.

Mebane, John S. *Renaissance Magic and the Return of the Golden Age: The Occult Tradition and Marlowe, Jonson, and Shakespeare*. Lincoln: University of Nebraska Press, 1989.

Meador, Betty de Shong. *Inanna, Lady of Largest Heart: Pomes of the Sumerian High Priestess*. Austin: University of Texas Press, 2001.

Mellors, Anthony. *Late Modernist Poetics: From Pound to Prynne*. Manchester and New York: Manchester University Press, 2005.

Meltzer, David, ed. *The Secret Garden: An Anthology in the Kabbalah*. Barrytown, NY: Station Hill Openings, 1998.

Meltzer, David. *San Francisco Beat: Talking with the Poets*. San Francisco: City Lights, 2001.

Melville, Keith. *Communes in the Counterculture: Origins, Theories, Styles of Life*. New York: William Morrow and Company, 1972.

Meyerowitz, Joanne. *Not June Cleaver: Women and Gender in Postwar America, 1945-1960*. Philadelphia: Temple University Press, 1994.

Midal, Fabrice. *Chogyam Trungpa: His Life and Vision*. Boston: Shambhala, 2004. Philadelphia: Temple University Press, 1994.

Miles, Barry. *The Beat Hotel: Ginsberg, Burroughs, and Corso in Paris, 1958-1963*. New York: Grove Press, 2000.

Miles, Barry. *Hippie*. New York: Sterling Publishing Co., Inc., 2003.

Miles, Barry. *Call Me Burroughs*: New York: Twelve, 2013.

Miller, Lisa J., ed. *The Oxford Handbook of Psychology and Spirituality*. New York: Oxford University Press, 2012.

Miller, Timothy. *The Hippies and American Values*. Knoxville: The University of Tennessee Press, 1991.

Miller, Timothy and Harold Coward, eds. *America's Alternative Religions*. Albany: State University of New York Press, 1995.

Minnen, Cornelius A. van, Jaap van der Bent, and Mel van Elteren, eds. *Beat Culture: The 1950s and Beyond*. Amsterdam: VU University Press, 1999.

Mishra, R. K. "The Twentieth Century American Mysticism: Transcendental Immanence." In Sheobhushan Shukla and Anu Shukla, eds., *Studies in Contemporary Literature: Multiple Contexts and Insights*, 71–77. New Delhi: Sarup and Sons, 2003.

Miyake, Akiko. *Ezra Pound and the Mysteries of Love*. Durham; Duke University Press, 1991.

Mlakar, Heike. *Merely Being There Is Not Enough: Women's Roles in Autobiographical Texts by Female Beat Writers*. Boca Raton, FL: Dissertation. com, 2007.

Moody, A. David. *Ezra Pound: Poet: Volume III, The Tragic Years 1939-1972*. New York: Oxford University Press, 2015.

Moore, Virginia. *The Unicorn: William Butler Yeats' Search for Reality*. New York: The Macmillan Company, 1954.

Moran, Bruce. *Distilling Knowledge: Alchemy, Chemistry and the Scientific Revolution*. Cambridge: Harvard University Press, 2005.

Morgan, Bill. *The Beat Generation in San Francisco: A Literary Tour*. San Francisco: City Lights, 2003.

Morgan, Bill. *I Celebrate Myself: The Somewhat Private Life of Allen Ginsberg*. New York: Viking, 2006.

Morgan, Bill. *The Typewriter Is Holy: The Complete, Uncensored History of the Beat Generation*. New York: Free Press, 2010.

Morgan, Bill. *Beat Atlas: A State by State Guide to the Beat Generation in America*. San Francisco: City Lights, 2011.

Morgan, Ted. *Literary Outlaw: The Life and Times of William S. Burroughs*. New York: W. W. Norton, 2012.

Munoz, Jose Esteban. *Cruising Utopia: The Then and There of Queer Futurity*. New York: New York University Press, 2009.

Munroe, Gretchen H. "Diane di Prima." In *Dictionary of Literary Biography: Volume 5: American Poets Since World War II, Part I: A-K*. Detroit: Gale Research Company, 1980.

Murnaghan, Sheila, and Ralph M. Rosen, eds. *Hip Sublime: Beat Writers and the Classical Tradition*. Columbus, OH: Ohio State University Press, 2018.

Murray, Margaret A. *The God of the Witches*. London: Sampson Low, Marston and Co, 1933.

Murray, Penelope, ed., *Genius: The History of an Idea*. New York: Basil Blackwell, 1989.

Natsoulas, John. *The Beat Generation Galleries and Beyond*. Davis, CA: John Natsoulas Press, 1996.

Neumann, Erich. *The Great Mother: An Analysis of the Archetype*. Princeton: Princeton University Press, 1970.

Nicholls, David, ed. *The Cambridge Companion to John Cage*. New York: Cambridge University Press, 2002.

North, John. *Cosmos: An Illustrated History of Astronomy and Cosmology*. Chicago: University of Chicago Press, 2008.

Nuttall, A. D. *The Alternative Trinity: Gnostic Heresy in Marlowe, Milton and Blake*. New York: Oxford University Press, 1998.

O'Brien, Glenn, ed. *The Cool School: Writing from America's Hip Underground*. New York: Library of America, 2013.

Ochshorn, Judith. *The Female Experience of the Divine*. Bloomington: Indiana University Press, 1981.

Ogawa, Satoko. "A Female Beat, Diane di Prima: The Practice of Magical Evocation." *Paterson Literary Review*, no. 39 (2011).

Olby, R. C. ed. et al., *Companion to the History of Modern Science*. London: Routledge, 1996.

Oldmeadow, Harry. *Journeys East: 20th Century Western Encounters with Eastern Religious Traditions*. Bloomington, IN: World Wisdom, 2004.

Olney, James, ed. *Studies in Autobiography*. New York: Oxford University Press, 1988.

Orsini, Maximillian J. *The Buddhist Beat Poetics of Diane di Prima and Lenore Kandel*, Dissertation, Drew University, 2016.

Ostriker, Alicia Suskin. *Stealing the Language: The Emergence of Women's Poetry in America* Boston: Beacon Press, 1986.

Pagels, Elaine. *The Gnostic Gospels*. New York: Vintage, 1989.

Paglia, Camille. "Erich Neumann: Theorist of the Great Mother." *Arion*, 13, no. 3 (Winter 2006).

Park, Katharine, ed. *The Cambridge History of Science, Volume Three: Early Modern Science*. New York: Cambridge University Press, 2006.

Parry, Glynn. *The Arch-Conjuror of England: John Dee*. New Haven: Yale University Press, 2011.

Parsons, William B., ed. *Teaching Mysticism*. New York: Oxford University Press, 2011.

Partridge, Christopher, ed. *The Occult World*. New York: Routledge, 2015.

Peabody, Rebecca, ed. et al. *Pacific Standard Time: Los Angeles Art 1945-1980*. Los Angeles: Getty Research Institute, 2011.

Pearlman, Ellen. *Nothing and Everything: The Influence of Buddhism on the American Avant-Garde, 1942-1962*. Berkeley: Evolver Editions, 2012.

Peck, Abe. *Uncovering the Sixties: The Life and Times of the Underground Press*. New York: Pantheon Books, 1985.

Perloff, Marjorie. *Frank O'Hara: Poet among Painters*. Austin and London: University of Texas Press, 1977.

Perry, Charles. *The Haight-Ashbury: A History*. New York: Random House, 1984.

Perry, Helen S. *The Human Be-In*. New York: Basic Books, 1970.

Petrich, Tatum. *The Girl Gang: Women Writers of the New York Beat Community*. Dissertation, Temple University, 2012.

Philips, Lisa, ed. *Beat Culture and the New America: 1950-1965*. New York: Whitney Museum of American Art, 1995.

Pike, Sarah M. *Earthly Bodies, Heavenly Selves: Contemporary Pagans and the Search for Community*. Berkeley: University of California Press, 2001.

Pike, Sarah M. *New Age and Neopagan Religions*. New York: Columbia University Press, 2004.

Pound, Ezra. *The Literary Essays of Ezra Pound*, ed. T. S. Eliot. New York: New Directions, 1968.

Pound, Ezra. *The ABC of Reading Guide to Kulchur*. New York: New Directions, 1970.

Pradittatsanee, Darin. *In Search of Liberation: Buddhism and the Beat Writers*. Bangkok: Chulalongkorn University, 2008.

Prothero, Stephen. "On the Holy Road: The Beat Movement as Spiritual Protest."
    The Harvard Theological Review, 84, no. 2 (1991), 205–22.
Raine, Kathleen. *Yeats the Initiate: Essays on Certain Themes in the Work of W.B.
    Yeats.* Mountrath: The Dolmen Press, 1986.
Renan, Sheldon. *An Introduction to American Underground Film.* New York:
    Dutton, 1967.
Riedl, Clare C. *Robert Grosseteste: On Light (De Luce).* Milwaukee: Marquette
    University Press, 1978.
Robbins, Thomas and Dick Antony, eds. *In Gods We Trust: New Patterns of
    Religious Pluralism.* New Brunswick, NJ: Transaction Publishers, 1990.
Robinson, Matte. *The Astral H.D.: Occult and Religious Sources and Contexts for
    H.D.'s Poetry and Prose* London: Bloomsbury, 2016.
Robisch, S. K. *Wolves and the Wolf Myth in American Literature.* Reno: University
    of Nevada Press, 2009.
Roof, Wade Clark. *A Generation of Seekers: The Spiritual Journeys of the Baby
    Boom Generation.* New York: HarperSanFrancisco, 1993.
Rorabaugh, W. J. *American Hippies.* New York: Cambridge University Press, 2015.
Rose, Barbara, ed. *Readings in American Art, 1900-1975.* New York: Holt,
    Rinehart and Winston, 1975.
Rosemont, Franklin and Robin D. G. Kelley. *Black, Brown, and Beige:
    Surrealist Writing from Africa and the Diaspora.* Austin: University of Texas
    Press, 2009.
Ross, Nancy Wilson, ed. *The World of Zen: An East-West Anthology.* New York:
    Vintage Books, 1960.
Roszak, Theodore. *The Making of a Counter Culture: Reflections on the
    Technocratic Society and Its Youthful Opposition.* New York: Doubleday, 1969.
Rothenberg, Jerome and Diane Rothenberg, eds. *Symposium of the Whole: A
    Range of Discourse Toward an Ethnopoetics.* Berkeley: University of California
    Press, 1983.
Rougemont, Denis de. *Love in the Western World.* Princeton: Princeton University
    Press, 1983.
Rowley, Peter. *New Gods in America: An Informal Investigation into the New
    Religions of American Youth Today.* New York: David McKay Company, Inc.,
    1972.
Rudolf, Kurt. *Gnosis: The Nature and History of Gnosticism.* New York: Harper
    San Francisco, 1987.
Russell, Jeffrey B. and Brooks Alexander. *A New History of Witchcraft: Sorcerers,
    Healers and Pagans.* London: Thames and Hudson, 2015.
Salomonsen, Jone. *Enchanted Feminism: Ritual, Gender and Divinity among
    the Reclaiming Witches of San Francisco.* London and New York; Routledge,
    2002.
Sanders, Ed. *Fug You: An Informal History of the Peace Eye Bookstore, the Fuck
    You Press, The Fugs, and Counterculture in the Lower East Side.* Boston: Da
    Capo Press, 2011.
Schelling, Andrew, ed. *The Wisdom Anthology of North American Buddhist Poetry.*
    Boston: Wisdom Publications, 2005.
Schelling, Andrew, ed. *Tracks Along the West Coast: Jaime de Angulo and Pacific
    Coast Culture.* Berkeley: Counterpoint, 2017.

Schmidt-Biggemann, Wilhelm. *Philosophia Perennis: Historical Outlines of Western Spirituality in Ancient, Medieval and Early Modern Thought*. Dordrecht, The Netherlands: Springer, 2004.

Schneider, David. *Crowded by Beauty: The Life and Zen of Philip Whalen*. Berkeley: University of California Press, 2015.

Scholem, Gershom. *Kabbalah*. New York: Meridian, 1974.

Seager, Richard Hughes. *Buddhism in America*. New York: Columbia University Press, 2012.

Seligmann, Kurt. *Magic, Supernaturalism and Religion*. New York: Pantheon Books, 1971.

Seznec, Jean. *The Survival of the Pagan Gods: The Mythological Tradition and Its Place in Renaissance Humanism and Art*. New York: Pantheon, 1953.

Shipley, Morgan. *Psychedelic Mysticism: Transforming Consciousness, Religious Experiences, and Voluntary Peasants in Postwar America*. Lanham, MD: Lexington Books, 2015.

Shumaker, Wayne. *Renaissance Curiosa: John Dee's Conversations with Angels, Girolamo Cardano's Horoscope of Christ, Johannes Trithemius and Cryptography, George Dalgarno's Universal Language*. Binghamton: Center for Medieval and Early Renaissance Studies, 1982.

Silesky, Barry. *Ferlinghetti: The Artist in His Time*. New York: Warner Books, 1990.

Singleton, Charles S., ed. *Art, Science, and History in the Renaissance*. Baltimore; The Johns Hopkins Press, 1967.

Sitney, P. Adams. *Visionary Film: The American Avant-Garde 1943-2000*. New York: Oxford University Press, 2002.

Smith, Richard Candida. *Utopia and Dissent: Art, Poetry, and Politics in California*. Berkeley: University of California Press, 1995.

Smith, Richard Candida. *The Modern Moves West: California Artists and Democratic Culture in the Twentieth Century*. Philadelphia: University of Pennsylvania Press, 2009.

Smith, Sherry L. *Hippies, Indians, and the Fight for Red Power*. New York: Oxford University Press, 2012.

Smith, Sidonie and Julia Watson, eds. *De/Colonizing the Subject; The Politics of Gender in Women's Autobiography*. Minneapolis: University of Minnesota Press, 1992.

Sollors, Werner. *Amiri Baraka/LeRoi Jones: The Quest for a "Populist Modernism."* New York: Columbia University Press, 1978.

Solnit, Rebecca. *Secret Exhibition: Six California Artists of the Cold War Era*. San Francisco: City Lights Books, 1990.

Spretnak, Charlene, ed. *The Politics of Women's Spirituality*. New York: Anchor Press, 1982.

Spretnak, Charlene. *The Spiritual Dynamic in Modern Art: Art History Reconsidered, 1800 to the Present*. New York: Palgrave Macmillan, 2014.

St Jorre, John de. *Venus Bound: The Erotic Voyage of the Olympia Press and Its Writers*. New York: Random House, 1994.

Stein, R. A. *Tibetan Civilization*. London: Faber and Faber, 1972.

Stephenson, Gregory. *The Daybreak Boys: Essays on the Literature of the Beat Generation*. Carbondale and Edwardsville: Southern Illinois University Press, 1990.

Stevens, Hugh, ed. *The Cambridge Companion to Gay and Lesbian Writing.* New York: Cambridge University Press, 2011.

Stevens, Matthew Levi. *The Magical Universe of William S. Burroughs.* Oxford: Mandrake, 2014.

Stewart, Katie Jennifer. *"A Kind of Singing in Me": A Critical Account of Women Writers of the Beat Generation.* Dissertation, University of Glasgow, June 2007.

Stone, Wendell C. *Caffe Cino: The Birthplace of Off-Off-Broadway.* Carbondale: Southern Illinois University Press, 2005.

Strausbaugh, John. *The Village: 400 Years of Beats and Bohemians, Radicals and Rogues, A History of Greenwich Village.* New York: Ecco, 2013.

Stryker, Susan. *Transgender History: The Roots of Today's Revolution.* New York: Seal Press, 2017.

Styers, Randall. *Making Magic: Religion, Magic, and Science in the Modern World.* New York: Oxford University Press, 2004.

Sukenick, Ronald. *Down and In: Life in the Underground.* New York: Collier Books, 1987.

Sullivan, James D. *On the Walls and in the Streets: American Poetry Broadsides from the 1960s.* Urbana: University of Illinois Press, 1997.

Surette, Leon. *A Light from Eleusis: A Study of Ezra Pound's Cantos.* Oxford: Clarendon Press, 1979.

Surette, Leon. *The Birth of Modernism: Ezra Pound, T.S. Eliot, W.B. Yeats and the Occult.* Montreal and Kingston: McGill-Queen's University Press, 1993.

Surette, Leon and Demetres Tryphonopoulos, eds. *Literary Modernism and the Occult Tradition.* Orono: The National Poetry Foundation, 1996.

Suster, Gerald. *John Dee: Essential Readings.* Berkeley: North Atlantic Books, 2003.

Sutton, Robert P. *Modern American Communes: A Dictionary.* Westport, CT: Greenwood Press, 2005.

Suzuki, D. T. and Edward Conze, ed. *On Indian Mahayana Buddhism.* New York: Harper and Row, 1968.

Suzuki, Shunryu. *Zen Mind, Beginner's Mind: Informal Talks on Zen Meditation and Practice.* Boston: Shambhala, 2011.

Syman, Stefane. *The Subtle Body: The Story of Yoga in America.* New York: Farrar, Straus and Giroux, 2010.

Taylor, Marvin J., ed. *The Downtown Book: The New York Art Scene 1974-1984.* Princeton: Princeton University Press, 2006.

Tennyson, G.B. and Edward E. Ericson, Jr., eds. *Religion and Modern Literature: Essays in Theory and Criticism.* Grand Rapids, MI: William B. Eerdmans Publishing Company, 1975.

Thernstrom, Stephan, ed. *Harvard Encyclopedia of American Ethnic Groups.* Cambridge, MA: Harvard University Press, 1981.

Trawick, Leonard M., ed. *World, Self, Poem; Essays on Contemporary Poetry from the "Jubilation of Poets."* Kent, OH: The Kent State University Press, 1990.

Trungpa, Chogyam. *Cutting Through Spiritual Materialism.* Boston and London: Shambhala, 1973.

Trungpa, Chogyam. *Crazy Wisdom.* Boston and London: Shambhala, 1991.

Tucci, Giuseppe. *The Religions of Tibet.* Berkeley: University of California Press, 1980.

Tucci, Giuseppe. *The Theory and Practice of the Mandala*. Mineola, NY: Dover Publications, 2001.

Tuchman, Maurice. *The Spiritual in Art: Abstract Painting 1890-1985*. New York: Abbeville Press, 1986.

Tryphonopoulos, Demetres P. *The Celestial Tradition: A Study of Ezra Pound's The Cantos*. Waterloo, ON: Wilfrid Laurier University Press, 1992.

Tryphonopoulos, Demetres P. and Stephen J. Adams. *The Ezra Pound Encyclopedia*. Westport, CT: Greenwood Press, 2005.

Turner, Victor. *The Ritual Process; Structure and Anti-Structure*. New York: Aldine de Gruyter, 1995.

Tweed, Thomas and Stephen Prothero. *Asian Religions in America: A Documentary History*. New York: Oxford University Press, 1999.

Urban, Hugh B. *Tantra: Sex, Secrecy, Politics, and Power in the Study of Religion*. Berkeley: University of California Press, 2003.

Versluis, Arthur. *American Gurus: From American Transcendentalism to New Age Religion*. New York: Oxford University Press, 2014.

Veysey, Laurence. *The Communal Experience: Anarchist and Mystical Communities in Twentieth-Century America*. Chicago: The University of Chicago Press, 1978.

Waldman, Anne and Waldo-Schwartz, Paul. *Art and the Occult*. New York: George Braziller, 1975.

Waldron, David. *The Sign of the Witch: Modernity and the Pagan Revival*. Durham, NC: Carolina Academic Press, 2008.

Walker, D. P. *Spiritual and Demonic Magic: From Ficino to Campanella*. University Park, PA: Pennsylvania State University Press, 2003.

Wallraven, Miriam. *Women Writers and the Occult in Literature and Culture: Female Lucifers, Priestesses, and Witches*. New York and London: Routledge, 2015.

Warhol, Andy and Pat Hackett. *POPism: The Warhol '60's*. San Diego: Harcourt, Brace, Jovanovich, 1990.

Warner, Simon. *Text and Drugs and Rock 'N' Roll: The Beats and Rock Culture*. New York: Bloomsbury, 2014.

Wasserstrom, Steven. *Religion after Religion: Gershom Scholem, Mircea Eliade and Henry Corbin at Eranos*. Princeton: Princeton University Press, 1999.

Watanangura, Pornsan and Heinrich Detering, eds. *Buddhism and Buddhist Philosophy in World Literature*. Bangkok: Chulalongkorn University Press, 2011.

Watson, Steven. *The Birth of the Beat Generation: Visionaries, Rebels, and Hipsters 1944-1960*. New York: Pantheon Books, 1995.

Watson, Steven. *Factory Made: Warhol and The Sixties*. New York: Pantheon Books, 2003.

Watts, Jerry Gafio. *Amiri Baraka: The Politics and Art of a Black Intellectual*. New York and London: New York University Press, 2001.

Webster, Charles. *Paracelsus: Medicine, Magic and Mission at the End of Time*. New Haven: Yale University Press, 2008.

Whalen, Philip. *The Collected Poems of Philip Whalen*, ed. Michael Rothenberg. Middletown, CT: Wesleyan University Press, 2007.

Whalen-Bridge, John and Gary Storhoff, eds. *The Emergence of Buddhist American Literature*. Albany: State University of New York Press, 2009.

Whalen-Bridge, John and Gary Storhoff, eds. *Writing as Enlightenment: Buddhist American Literature into the Twenty-First Century*. Albany: State University of New York, 2011.

Wilson, Bob, Kenneth Koubrava, and John LeBow, eds. *The Phoenix Book Shop: A Nest of Memories*. Candia, NH: John LeBow, 1997.

Wilson, Robert A. *Seeing Shelley Plain*. New Castle, DE: Oak Knoll Press, 2001.

Wind, Edgar. *Pagan Mysteries in the Renaissance*. Harmondsworth: Penguin Books, 1967.

Wolf, Leonard, ed. *Voices from the Love Generation*. Boston: Little, Brown and Company, 1968.

Wuthnow, Robert. *Experimentation in American Religion*. Berkeley: University of California Press, 1978.

Wuthnow, Robert. *After Heaven: Spirituality in America Since the 1950s*. Berkeley: University of California Press, 1998.

Yates, Frances A. *The Rosicrucian Enlightenment*. London and New York: Routledge, 1972.

Yates, Frances A. *Giordano Bruno and the Hermetic Tradition*. Chicago: The University of Chicago Press, 1991.

Young, Serinity. *Courtesans and Tantric Consorts: Sexualities in Buddhist Narrative, Iconography, and Ritual*. New York and London: Routledge, 2004.

Yu-Lan, Fung. *A Short History of Chinese Philosophy*. New York: The Free Press, 1966.

Zaehner, R. C. *Hinduism*. New York: Oxford University Press, 1971.

Zaretsky, Irving I. and Mark P. Leone, eds. *Religious Movements in Contemporary America*. Princeton: Princeton University Press, 1975.

Ziolkowski, Theodore. *Lure of the Arcane: The Literature of Cult and Conspiracy*. Baltimore, MD: The John Hopkins University Press, 2013.

Ziolkowski, Theodore. *The Alchemist in Literature: From Dante to the Present*. Oxford: Oxford University Press, 2015.

INDEX

CPSIA information can be obtained
at www.ICGtesting.com
Printed in the USA
LVHW052326091120
671192LV00015B/196

9 781501 366574